A Parting of Ways

GOVERNMENT AND
THE EDUCATED PUBLIC
IN RUSSIA
1801–1855

A Parting of Ways

GOVERNMENT AND THE EDUCATED PUBLIC IN RUSSIA 1801–1855

NICHOLAS V. RIASANOVSKY

OXFORD
AT THE CLARENDON PRESS
1976

Oxford University Press, Walton Street, Oxford, OX2 6DP

OXFORD LONDON GLASGOW NEW YORK
TORONTO MELBOURNE WELLINGTON CAPE TOWN
IBADAN NAIROBI DAR ES SALAAM LUSAKA ADDIS ABABA
KUALA LUMPUR SINGAPORE JAKARTA HONG KONG TOKYO
DELHI BOMBAY CALCUTTA MADRAS KARACHI

ISBN 0 19 822533 4

Printed in Great Britain
at the University Press, Oxford
by Vivian Ridler
Printer to the University

TO
JOHN, NICHOLAS
AND MARIA

PREFACE

FOR more than thirty years I have been concerned with the government and the educated public in Russia in the first half of the nineteenth century. Indeed, my undergraduate honours thesis was devoted to the Decembrists. My first book analysed perhaps the most interesting and controversial group of Russian intellectuals of that age, the Slavophiles. My second focused on the government: on Nicholas I and the doctrine of Official Nationality. Shorter pieces dealt with such topics as the Petrashevtsy, Khomiakov's concept of *sobornost*, or Pogodin's and Shevyrev's position in Russian intellectual history.[1] For over two decades I have conducted seminars and directed dissertations within the inclusive heading of state and society in imperial Russia. Yet at the end of a long process of study I can claim no real mastery of the subject, let alone a full knowledge of the material or a complete solution of the problems involved. The limitations are both my own and those produced by the general state of scholarship in the field. Most damaging is the lack of a detailed and reliable social history of the time. Without it, the crucial concept of the educated public itself—central to post-Petrine Russian history—remains in large part vague and even impressionistic. Other deficiencies range from the absence of consensus on the economic development of Russia in the period under consideration to the lack of data on specific writers and publications. My present effort, then, is an attempt to do what can be done under the circumstances rather than a bid to say the final word on the subject.

Because this book follows naturally from my earlier work, my gratitude must extend to those who made that earlier work possible, too numerous to be mentioned here by name. The present project profited from a Guggenheim Fellowship and, especially, from two IREX grants to the Soviet Union, for a brief visit in 1965 and a more extended stay in 1969. I was marvellously well received by my Soviet colleagues, many of

---

[1] For Russian words and names throughout this book I use a modified version of the Library of Congress system of transliteration.

them leading scholars in my field of interest, who did their best to make my research in their country fruitful and pleasant. Needless to say, neither they nor others who helped me elsewhere can be held responsible for the final product. I want to thank particularly the authorities at TsGAOR and at the manuscript division of the Lenin Library for the use of archival materials. Almost as valuable for me was the use of the Lenin Library itself as well as of the convenient library of the Institute of Russian History of the Academy of Sciences of the U.S.S.R. I am similarly indebted to libraries and librarians in Western Europe and in the United States, particularly to those at my own university in Berkeley.

A number of my friends read this study in manuscript and made useful corrections and suggestions. They included Professors Hugh McLean, Martin Malia, Henry May, Wolfgang Sauer, Frederick Wakeman, and Reginald Zelnik, all of the University of California, Berkeley, and Professor Terence Emmons of Stanford University; Professor Gerald Cavanaugh of George Mason University read and criticized the first two chapters. I especially appreciate the privilege of discussing matters that interest me with them. The Institute of International Studies of the University of California, Berkeley, contributed to my sabbatical support, provided research assistantships, and arranged for the typing of the manuscript. Mr. Gary Marker and Mr. Michael Von Herzen, my research assistants in succession, did much to improve this study. Arlene, my wife, without succession, deserves much more credit than can be given in this note.

NICHOLAS V. RIASANOVSKY

University of California
Berkeley

CONTENTS

PART I

Government and the Educated Public in Russia in the Enlightenment

'Russia is a European State.'
Catherine the Great, *The Nakaz* of 1767.

1

Introduction: The Eighteenth Century

'What imperishable glory!
What resounding praise!
The rule of Catherine
And her wise actions
Whom and where did they fail to astonish?'

Derzhavin[1]

MODERN Russian history was inaugurated by Peter the Great's reign and reforms. To be sure, Russian interest in the West had antedated by many generations the activities of the first emperor, with Westernization developing into a strong and accelerating current in seventeenth-century Russia. To be sure, too, the iconoclastic ruler himself, as well as the great majority of his assistants, came out of Muscovite society and reflected its limitations, aspirations, and needs. An emphasis on continuity is quite as legitimate as an emphasis on change. Yet even those who argue that Peter the Great merely speeded up the already established, logical course of Russian history, or that he simply added the elements of drive and compulsion to what had been a less harried and self-conscious process, generally recognize the profound historical significance of the reformer's

[1]   Kakaia nezabvenna slava!
    Kakaia zvuchnaia khvala!
    Ekaterinina derzhava
    I mudrye ee dela
    Kogo i gde ne udivili?

From G. R. Derzhavin, 'Na priobretenie Kryma' ('On the Acquisition of the Crimea'), *Sochineniia Derzhavina s obiasnitelnymi primechaniiami*, St. Petersburg, 1895, i. 58.

actions. Although many of Peter the Great's innovations and changes failed to take root, others became basic to the Russian state and society until 1917 and even beyond that date, while the total impact of his reign on Russia proved to be both momentous and irreversible.

The perennial debate concerning Peter the Great's historical role has been nourished in part by the vast differences in the reformer's influence on various aspects of Russian life. The evolution of Russian society experienced no turning-point around the years 1700 or 1725. Also in the field of economics the reign of the first emperor marked no startling new departure, although the monarch's frantic activity added considerable energy to the economic development of the country—in particular to manufacturing—and bequeathed some valuable beginnings to the future. By contrast, Peter the Great changed wholesale the government institutions and the entire administrative apparatus of Muscovite Russia, including the location of the capital. Efforts to delimit clearly the authority of every agency, to separate powers and functions, to standardize procedure, and to spell out each detail could well be considered revolutionary from the old Muscovite point of view. On the surface at least, the new system seemed to bear a greater resemblance to Sweden and the German states than to the realm of the reformer's father, the good Tsar Alexis. Content, however, did not necessarily agree with form. Many scholars have argued that while statutes, prescriptions, and precise regulations looked good on paper, in actuality in the main cities and especially in the enormous expanses of provincial Russia, everything depended as of old on the initiative, ability, and behaviour of officials, on their personal and arbitrary rule. Peter the Great's foreign policy and its results presented yet another pattern for analysis. Quite traditional in its orientation and aims, this policy became epoch-making through sheer success. If fighting the Turks and the Swedes and being involved with Poland represented nothing new in Russian history, the decisive victory in the Great Northern War propelled Russia to the dominant position in northern Europe and into the ranks of major powers. But it was in the sphere of culture and the intellect that Peter the Great initiated or helped to initiate the most decisive, if not immediate, changes.

The forceful and forced turning towards Western civilization meant the coming of a new age of thought and artistic expression to Russia: before long the cultural products of the St. Petersburg period of Russian history bore little resemblance to those of Muscovy.

Not that Russian culture represented a *tabula rasa* when Peter the Great ascended the throne. Based on Christianity and the Byzantine heritage in general, as well as on the artistic creativity of the East Slavs, it resembled broadly the medieval civilization of western and central Europe, to which it was related by religion, language, customary law, and much else. Moreover, the Russians had managed to maintain some connections with their western neighbours even during the worst years of isolation and foreign yoke, and, after the set-back caused by the Time of Troubles, these connections rapidly multiplied. The seventeenth century witnessed manifold Western influences taking root and flourishing in Russia, in literature and in art as much as in mining and gunnery. It also witnessed the last creative period of the great tradition of icon painting after which icon painting declined into a craft, as well as other evidence that medieval Russian culture had run its course. Still, all the links fruitfully established by specialists between Russian thought and culture in the seventeenth century and the eighteenth should not obscure the fundamental gap. Muscovite civilization resembled that of medieval Europe, not the Europe of the Enlightenment. It was in particular the secular nature of the modern world that ran counter to the most basic Muscovite assumptions and beliefs. Whereas Archpriest Avvakum stands out as the most brilliant and significant writer in seventeenth-century Russia, in the eighteenth that place of honour belonged either to the poet Derzhavin or the playwright Fonvizin. Reading through the writings of the three throws much light on the road covered by Russia and Russian culture in the intervening century. Similarly, one might compare with profit the *Weltanschauung* of Tsar Alexis to that of Empress Catherine the Great.

As a vast borderland of Christendom, Russia was historically subject to the usual fate of borderlands: invasions from the outside, relative isolation, and retardation. Peter the Great's reforms represented the most determined Russian effort to catch up with the West, or at least the most determined Russian effort until Stalin's Five-Year Plans. As Von Laue and other writers on modernization have emphasized, the ultimate sanction for that phenomenon is survival itself. In the Russian case, repeated defeats at the hands of small Polish detachments during the Time of Troubles and after, the unresolved issue of the southern frontier, and even the difficulty of keeping order at home revealed repeatedly the dangerous backwardness of the Russian military and state apparatus. Indeed, the Petrine reforms themselves were ignited by the raging fires of the crucial Great Northern War fought against the much more modern Sweden.

Dire need and all kinds of immediate, practical considerations largely determined the nature and course of the measures undertaken by the first emperor, all the more so because one step led naturally to another. Miliukov, who made a brilliant analysis of the Petrine fiscal structure and economy, and other scholars have shown how military considerations repeatedly led to financial measures, and in turn to edicts aiming to stimulate Russian commerce and industry, to changes in the administrative system to implement those edicts, to attempts to foster the education necessary for a modern administration to function, and on and on.[1] The twin curses of war and bankruptcy, in conditions of a relatively backward agrarian society, drove the reformer, his assistants, and his subjects to heroic efforts.

The Petrine Westernization of Russia thus provides, or can be made to provide, an attractive model for many historians, ranging from the older proponents of the *Primat der Aussenpolitik* and the Marxist champions of the concepts of the base and the superstructure in dialectical change to the contemporary ideologues of modernization. Historical inevitability and brutal, pragmatic realism have staked huge claims in the emergence of modern Russia. Yet, without necessarily denying the validity of any of the above approaches, students of Russian history might find it helpful to pay more attention to the intellectual world of the time and in particular to the Western intellectual world which Russia was in the process of joining.

[1] See especially P. Miliukov, *Gosudarstvennoe khoziastvo Rossii v pervoi chetverti XVIII stoletiia i reforma Petra Velikogo*, 2nd edn., St. Petersburg, 1905. For the best summary of the reign in English see B. H. Sumner, *Peter the Great and the Emergence of Russia*, London, 1950. See also L. Jay Oliva, *Russia in the Era of Peter the Great*, Englewood Cliffs, N.J., 1969.

Whether merely a part of the superstructure or otherwise derivative and secondary, ideas are quite important for people who hold them. They are needed not only to rationalize or manipulate the world but, in the first place, to see it and make sense of it.

When Peter the Great began reforming Russia, he turned to a variety of European models and examples. Many writers have emphasized the emperor's special liking for Sweden and for the northern German states, but he also tried in many ways to learn from and to emulate Holland, England, France, and still other countries. On the basis of what he found in the West, and in the course of some twenty-five years devoted primarily to war, he not only created a navy and transformed an army, but also reformed the central and local government in Russia as well as Church administration and finance, and at the same time he effected important changes in Russian society, economy, and culture.

Ideas and ideologies came with the reforms. In a sense, as already indicated, Peter the Great was fascinated with the entire Western experience, and he paid particular attention to relatively well-organized and effective monarchies. While the first emperor borrowed many of his legal and administrative formulations from Sweden, his able apologist, Archbishop Theophanes, or Feofan, Prokopovich justified his authority and rule on the basis of 'the works of theoreticians of monarchism of the extreme Right, Thomas Hobbes, Hugo Grotius and Samuel Pufendorf'.[1] Similarly, German cameralism proved useful to the Russian government from the early part of the century to 1762, when the accession of Catherine the Great led to the publication of a number of cameralist works in Russia, and even to 1843, when a special cameralist section was established in the school of law of the University of St. Petersburg, and beyond. An American historian reminded us recently of the importance for Russia of the German *Aufklärung* with its emphases on natural law, Neostoicism, and Pietism, all directed towards eliciting obedience, and indeed dedicated performance,

---

[1] N. I. Pavlenko, 'Idei absoliutizma v zakonodatelstve XVIII v.', in *Absoliutizm v Rossii (XVII–XVIII vv.)*, ed. by N. M. Druzhinin, N. I. Pavlenko, and L. V. Cherepnin, Moscow, 1964, p. 391. One can accept Pavlenko's general exposition and argument without accepting his classification of Grotius or Pufendorf as 'the extreme Right'.

from the subject to the state and the ruler.[1] As the century advanced and their own country became more Westernized, these and other intellectual currents culminated for educated Russians, whether in or out of the government, in the full impact of the European Enlightenment.

Some objections notwithstanding,[2] both 'Enlightenment' and 'Age of Reason', the two terms most commonly applied to the period, denote its thought surprisingly well. It was the optimistic belief in reason, in the possibility and feasibility of reasonable solutions to human problems that constituted the leading inspiration of the age. The problems ranged from technical matters of administration, economics, or finance to the broader issues of the nature of a genuine education, or of an ideal society and polity. Indeed, reason refused to recognize any bounds and expanded to include ethics and religion itself: for many advanced eighteenth-century intellectuals deism represented admirably the principle of reason as applied to the Supreme Being and the workings of the universe. And it was the same concept of reason which, by providing the common measure and link for all men and all human societies, was largely responsible for the magnificent cosmopolitanism of the Enlightenment.

Together with the stress on reason—some would say ahead of it—went an emphasis on criticism. A number of the leading students of the Enlightenment have persuasively presented the thought of their period as above all a critique of the existing order of things in the world. If reason constituted the standard of judgement, the beliefs, institutions, and affairs of men left very much to be desired. Most importantly, the *philosophes* assailed Church and traditional religion, thus continuing and greatly accentuating the process of the secularization of European thought and culture which had been going on from the time of

---

[1] Raeff, *Imperial Russia, 1682–1825: The Coming of Age of Modern Russia*, New York, 1871, pp. 140–3.

[2] Among them are those of the latest major American author on the Enlightenment, Professor Peter Gay, who emphasizes the *philosophes*' critique of all-embracing rationalist systems, as well as their rich allowance for passions, and, therefore, challenges 'reason' as the denominator of the age. Yet his own exposition illustrates admirably the crucial role of reason in the thought of the period, provided reason is given its usual and broad meaning rather than that of a kind of rationalist metaphysics. See Gay, *The Enlightenment: An Interpretation*, vol. ii, *The Science of Freedom*, New York, 1969.

the Renaissance. But for Voltaire and his fellow thinkers the hated *infâme* extended beyond the ecclesiastical establishment to encompass all the prejudice, all the unreason, of humanity as well as the ignorance which made that prejudice possible.

The answer lay, of course, in education, knowledge, *les lumières*, Enlightenment itself. The Age of Reason readily became one of the most didactic periods in the history of human thought. Assisted by Lockean psychology, the field of education proper came to occupy the centre of attention and hope. Moreover, implicit and very frequently explicit didacticism permeated all literature, from fugitive poems to authentic or spurious tales of travel, from fable to drama. Most of the '400,000 volumes' denounced by Charles Fourier as designed to mislead mankind were published in France in the eighteenth century. Whereas Hebrew prophets, Greek philosophers, or Byzantine theologians stood out as the essential spokesmen of their ages, the Enlightenment found its authentic expression in the combination of pragmatic reason, the critical approach, and ceaseless teaching characteristic of the *philosophe*.

For post-Petrine Russia the thought of the Age of Reason was new, highly appropriate, and very important. If an application of reason held promise for the England of George III or the France of Louis XVI, it could be easily considered the only and at the same time the most profoundly inspiring hope in the much more backward Russian condition. If reason called for a break with the past even in advanced European countries, Russia had in a sense already accomplished the break, and, to emphasize the point, the gulf between the new, reformed Russia and the ignorant masses increased throughout the century. In no other state had custom and tradition been challenged so directly and so bluntly in the name of reason and progress as they were challenged by Peter the Great in Muscovy. As for criticism, while the Russians did not have to worry about scholastic theology nor, after the establishment of the Holy Synod, about an excessive power of the Church in relation to state and society, the reforming emperor himself, his assistants, and his successors found the essentially secular Western outlook most congenial. Moreover, the critical approach of the Age of Reason broadly conceived could scarcely desire a better field of application than Russia. In a country where for decades literate people could not be found for immediate state needs, an attack on ignorance required no justification. Criticizing the old was directly helpful to the new in Russia. Didacticism too acquired an enlarged scope in the land of the tsars. If the *philosophes* wanted to reform early modern European societies along certain lines, in Russia such a society had to be formed in the first place. Throughout the century much of the educational effort of the government went simply into teaching its subjects European manners and usages. On the whole, from gunnery to the Academy of Sciences, from vaccination to periodicals, both Peter the Great and Catherine the Great, in their very different ways, spent more time and effort teaching than any contemporary monarchs. In this respect, as in so many others, the two sovereigns did much to set the tone for the Russian culture of the Enlightenment. In other ways too the thought of the Age of Reason corresponded to Russian aspirations and needs. Cosmopolitanism, and certain proselytizing tendencies for that matter, proved extremely welcome to a country that wanted to join the European society of states. Even such more specific concepts as that of the emerging religious tolerance received ready application in the increasingly multireligious and multicultural empire of the Romanovs. Indeed, Catherine II has been called the most tolerant in religion of all the rulers of the age.[1]

Russian autocracy itself received rich support from the thought and practice of the Age of Reason. Although some specialists have questioned the usefulness of the concept of enlightened despotism as needlessly confusing ideas and politics, or as trying artificially to bring together disparate phenomena in different lands, most scholars have found it relevant to their exposition and analysis of the period. A belief in the enlightened ruler as the source of progress permeated deeply the thought of the Enlightenment. Moreover, it has been argued, this belief was intrinsic to that thought. In other words, if a society was sunk in ignorance and prejudice and was to be pulled out of its stupor, it required a lever, an outside force to do the pulling. The enlightened despot was to be such a force, and his

---

[1] On the last point see, e.g., K. A. Papmehl, 'The Problem of Civil Liberties in the Records of the "Great Commission" ', *The Slavonic and East European Review*, vol. xli, No. 99 (Dec. 1963), p. 277.

presence became more imperative as that of God grew more/ distant.[1]

Peter the Great was a true enlightened despot. That he has not generally been so called is to be explained by the facts that that appellation has been usually reserved for the second half of the eighteenth century, that the Russian history of the period has not been sufficiently studied in the European context, and that the crudity and cruelty of the reformer, as well as the barbarism of his surroundings, have stood in the way of a full recognition of his place among the elect of the age.[2] Yet, if Enlightenment meant bringing light, as understood at the time, into darkness, no other ruler of the period could compete in the scope, decisiveness, and irreversibility of his actions with the Russian emperor. Peter the Great not only performed impressively as an enlightened despot, but also bequeathed enlightened despotism to his successors. They knew whence the legacy came: 'To Peter I, Catherine II'.[3]

When Peter the Great was attracted by the West, he turned to it with a remarkably open, broad, and searching mind. While it is possible to argue that 'objectively' Russia undertook modernization to defend its society and values against superior or potentially superior rivals on the European continent, there is no doubt where the reformer's subjective preferences lay. Negative impressions of palace torpor and intrigue, an unusual boyhood spent in large part in the foreign suburb of Moscow and in independent self-discovery, and an insatiable curiosity to learn and do novel things were some of the factors which

[1] A recent affirmation of this view, with particular reference to more backward countries, can be found in Lucien Goldmann, 'La Pensée des "Lumières" ', *Annales: économies, sociétés, civilisations*, Year 22, No. 4 (July–Aug. 1967), pp. 768–9.

[2] For one of the better Soviet discussions of enlightened despotism in Russia see N. M. Druzhinin, 'Prosveshchennyi absoliutizm v Rossii', *Absoliutizm v Rossii* (*XVII–XVIII vv.*), pp. 428–59. Druzhinin skilfully presents Catherine the Great's rule as part and parcel of European enlightened despotism. He is unwilling, however, to extend this concept to the reign of Peter the Great, although he is fully aware of the many enlightened ideas and measures of the reformer, essentially because, in his opinion, the Russian economy was not ready for it until the second half of the century. Druzhinin also excludes the rule of Alexander I from enlightened despotism on the ground that it went beyond it in its constitutional appeal before finally turning to reaction. I am using the conventional English 'enlightened despotism' where Druzhinin, writing in Russian, refers to 'enlightened absolutism'.

[3] The inscription on the monument, the celebrated Bronze Horseman, erected by Catherine the Great in St. Petersburg to Peter the Great.

combined to make Tsar Alexis's son violently reject the old and enthusiastically grasp the new. The absolute ruler was never happier than when building a ship or learning another trade, and his favoured companions were foreign specialists of all sorts. Indeed, the informal and unrestrained atmosphere of the foreign suburb, with its smoking, drinking, love-making, rough good humour, conglomerate of tongues, and especially its profusion and variety of technical experts, became an enduring part of the emperor's life. As to Peter the Great's frightful hatreds, characteristically they were directed against the *streltsy* or against the clique surrounding the heir apparent Alexis, not against foreigners in or out of Russia, not even against the Swedes. At times they seemed to extend to all opponents of change. The spirit of Petrine reform was violent and intolerant, shared by its promoters with their relentless leader.

Much has been written about the practical abilities and orientation of Peter the Great, and for good reason. The emperor became proficient in some twenty crafts, and he studied the callings of soldier and sailor from the bottom up, serving first in the ranks and learning the use of each weapon before promoting himself to his first post as an officer. The monarch attained the grade of full general after the victory of Poltava and of full admiral after the successful conclusion of the Great Northern War. His mind proved on the whole active and practical, able quickly to seize problems and devise solutions, if not to construct theories. Yet it is also true that with time Peter the Great became more interested in general issues and broader patterns. Besides, while the reformer was no theoretician, he had the makings of a visionary. With grandeur and optimism, themselves typical of the Age of Reason, he saw ahead the image of a modern, powerful, prosperous, and educated country and it was to the realization of that image that he dedicated his life.

Whatever the rationale of Muscovite tsardom might have been, the reformed Petrine state cherished the principles and spoke the words of the Enlightenment. The concept of the common good, *obshchee blago*, was first advanced in 1702, in a ukase concerned with inviting foreign specialists into Russian service, and it became the stock-in-trade of the Russian imperial government.[1] Peter the Great himself spoke constantly of

---

[1] Pavlenko, op. cit., pp. 398–401.

service to the state. On one occasion, when reorganizing the army, he crossed out 'the interests of His Tsarist Majesty' as the object of military devotion and substituted 'the interests of the state'.[1] The common good to be promoted by the state certainly included the arts and the sciences, education, enlightenment itself. 'For learning is good and fundamental, and as it were the root, the seed, and first principle of all that is good and useful in church and state.'[2]

It is usual to indicate that relaxation and reaction followed in Russia the death of Peter the Great. Some of the schools established by the tireless reformer could find no students, while intrigue and corruption ran rampant in government and administration. More important still, without Peter the Great, it quickly became impossible to exact a full measure of service from the gentry, to propound the principle of position and reward strictly according to merit. So-called gentry emancipation developed into a major trend of the century. But there was no essential change in terms of intellectual orientation and ideology. Peter the Great's chief assistant, Prince Alexander Menshikov, or the princes Dolgorukiis and Golitsyns for that matter, not to mention the insignificant rulers themselves with their numerous favourites and hangers-on, frequently of foreign origin, had nothing to offer in lieu of the first emperor's direction and vision. In Russia the only truly alternative view of the world resided among the dark masses, Old Believers and Orthodox, and among the unreconstructed monks, priests, and nuns. But these had no voice in the councils or destiny of their country. The authorities, on the other hand, proceeded to invoke loudly, in and out of turn, the name and the example of Peter the Great. Empress Elizabeth, Peter's daughter, who reigned from 1741 to 1761 (or 1762, depending on the calendar used), emphasized especially her utter devotion to her father, his policies, and his legacy. With august sponsorship, from the early efforts of such contemporaries of the reformer as Feofan Prokopovich through the mid-eighteenth-century writings of

---

[1] Sumner, op. cit., pp. 59–60.

[2] Peter the Great as translated in Sumner, op. cit., p. 149. Huge biographical materials on Peter the Great have been compiled by Russian historians ranging from I. I. Golikov, who worked in the second half of the eighteenth century, to N. G. Ustrialov, who published in the middle of the nineteenth, to M. M. Bogoslovskii, who died in 1929.

Michael Lomonosov, a fully fledged cult of Peter the Great came to dominate Russian political and historical thought.

Catherine II, also known as the Great, ruled Russia for almost the entire last third of the century, from 1762 to 1796. As already indicated, she too glorified Peter the Great and considered herself his direct successor. But beyond that, she was determined to surpass him and win her own immortal place in history. If Peter the Great had the good sense to turn out of Muscovite darkness towards Western light, Catherine believed herself to be in a position to guide the intellectual development of the Age of Reason. If Peter began to force his barbarian subjects to learn Western ways, Catherine was going to provide them with the most advanced laws, the best schools, and the most enlightened government. Dedicated like Peter to military glory and success in foreign policy, she aimed to attain fame also as a writer, a preceptor, a *philosophe*. Or, to change the perspective somewhat, if Peter the Great was in practice the most effective enlightened despot, Catherine the Great made the most striking bid for that honour in theory and propaganda.

The character and attitude of the famous empress have both impressed and puzzled historians, notably including those particularly concerned with her relationship to the Enlightenment. A woman quite out of the ordinary, Catherine possessed high intelligence, a natural ability to administer and govern, a remarkable practical sense, energy to spare, and an iron will. Along with her determination went courage and optimism: the empress believed that she could prevail over all obstacles, and more often than not events proved her right. Self-control, skill in discussion and propaganda, and a clever handling of men and circumstances to serve her ends were additional assets of that unusual monarch. Catherine herself asserted that it was ambition that sustained her, and the historians can well agree, provided that ambition is understood broadly—that is, as a constant, urgent drive to excel in everything and bring everything under one's control. Yet these formidable virtues had their dark side. Determination easily became ruthlessness, ambition fed vanity just as vanity fed ambition, skill in propaganda would not stop short of asserting lies. Above all, the empress was a supreme egoist. As with most true egoists, she had few beliefs or standards of value outside of herself and her own overpowering wishes. Even Catherine's admirers sometimes noticed that she lacked something, call it charity, mercy, or human sympathy, and incidentally, that she looked her best in masculine attire. It was also observed that the sovereign took up every issue with the same unflagging drive and earnestness, be it the suppression of Pugachev's rebellion or correspondence with Voltaire, the partitions of Poland or her latest article for a periodical. Restless ambition, to repeat, served as the only common denominator in her many activities, and was, apparently, the only thing that mattered. Thus, in spite of Catherine's enormous display of enlightened views and sentiments and of her adherence to the principles of the Age of Reason, it remains extremely difficult to tell what the empress actually believed, or whether she believed anything.

But no amount of deviousness or hypocrisy on her part can dissociate the remarkable Russian empress from the Enlightenment. For one thing, it can well be argued that Catherine's scepticism and cynicism, which many scholars have found so disturbing, were not necessarily inappropriate in a high priestess of the Age of Reason. More importantly, Catherine the Great belonged entirely to the intellectual world of the West. The question raised in connection with Peter the Great as to how a traditional Muscovite milieu could produce such an iconoclast does not occur in the case of his famous successor, for Catherine II had no Muscovite background, no Russian background of any kind for that matter. Brought up in the modest but cultured surroundings of a princely house in a petty German principality, the future Russian autocrat learned French as a child and proceeded to read avidly in French belles-lettres and later in the *philosophes*. The German and the French enlightenments always remained her intellectual ambience. As to Russia, where she arrived at the age of fifteen, Catherine did her best to become well acquainted with the country and to learn and use its language, but, as Soviet scholars delight in pointing out, she could never write Russian idiomatically. If Catherine the Great did not hesitate to manipulate skilfully her avowed 'prayer book', Montesquieu's *Spirit of the Laws*, the fact remains that in a very real sense she had no other.

The Russian empress, of course, subscribed fully to the concept of enlightened despotism. She strove to give it a broad and rich meaning, and at times even went beyond the bounds of the concept. Thus in her correspondence with Grimm she liked to refer to herself not only as a great libertarian, but even as a republican, and she included 'republican sentiments' in the epitaph which she composed for herself. On the whole, however, Catherine the Great kept emphasizing the necessity and the virtues of absolute monarchical rule, at least in Russia. As she put the matter in strikingly Age of Reason terms in her celebrated *Instruction to the Legislative Commission*, the *Nakaz*:

9. The Sovereign is absolute; for there is no other Authority but that which centers in his single Person, that can act with a Vigour proportionate to the Extent of such a vast Dominion.

10. The Extent of the Dominion requires an absolute Power to be vested in that Person who rules over it. It is expedient so to be, that the quick Dispatch of Affairs, sent from distant Parts, might make ample Amends for the Delay occasioned by the great Distance of the Places.

11. Every other Form of Government whatsoever would not only have been prejudicial to Russia, but would even have proved its entire Ruin.

12. Another Reason is; That it is better to be subject to the Laws under one Master, than to be subservient to many.

13. What is the true End of Monarchy? Not to deprive People of their natural Liberty; but to correct their Actions, in order to attain the *supreme Good*.

14. The Form of Government therefore, which best attains this End, and at the same Time sets less Bounds than others to natural Liberty, is that which coincides with the Views and Purposes of rational Creatures, and answers the End, upon which we ought to fix a stedfast Eye in the Regulation of civil Polity.[1]

The supreme good, or the common good, embraced 'the Glory of the Citizens, of the State, and of the Sovereign',[2] but it was also frequently defined in a more humane manner. In the words chosen by Catherine the Great for her own tombstone: 'When she had ascended the throne of Russia, she wished to do good, and tried to bring happiness, freedom and prosperity to her subjects.'[3] Such goals, including the

---

[1] Reddaway, ed., op. cit., pp. 216–17. Numbers denote articles in the *Nakaz*. Italics here and throughout the book are original.

[2] Ibid.   [3] Ibid., p. xxvi.

incongruous one of liberty, kept occurring in the thought, and correspondence, of the empress throughout her life. The autocrat presented herself to Voltaire and others as the protector of freedom in Russia, and deplored its decline in Sweden and France. Russian freedom would rest on just and rational laws which Catherine the Great promised to introduce in her empire. 'The Equality of the Citizens consists in this; that they should all be subject to the same laws.'[1] Moreover: 'Nothing ought to be forbidden by the Laws, but what may be prejudicial, either to every Individual in particular, or to the whole Community in general.'[2] The autocrat concluded forcefully:

> 520. All this will never please those Flatterers, who are daily instilling this pernicious Maxim into all the Sovereigns on Earth, *That their People are created for them only*. But *We* think, and esteem it *Our* Glory to declare, 'That *We* are created for *Our* People;' and, for this Reason, *We* are obliged to Speak of Things just as they ought to be. For God forbid! that, after this Legislation is finished, any Nation on Earth should be more just; and, consequently should flourish more than Russia; otherwise the Intention of *Our* Laws would be totally frustrated; an Unhappiness *which I do not wish to survive*.[3]

Yet, while the empress was preoccupied with the importance of rational law and correct legal procedure, and while she followed Beccaria to promise the most enlightened criminal code for Russia, she remained equally concerned with the economic well-being of her subjects, the substantive, so to speak, as much as the formal, elements of happiness. The *Nakaz* itself dwelt on such topics as the importance of agriculture for the prosperity of the country. It contained even the following remarkable article: '346. An Alms bestowed on a Beggar in the Street, can never acquit a State of the Obligation it lies under, of affording all its Citizens a certain Support during Life; such as wholesome Food, proper Cloathing, and a Way of Life not prejudicial to Health in general.'[4] In her correspondence with the *philosophes* Catherine II liked to stress, frequently incorrectly, that she was waging her wars and embellishing her court without raising new taxes, and that in general her foremost thought was not to burden her subjects. If perfect laws belonged to the

---

[1] Ibid., p. 219.   [2] Ibid., p. 220.
[3] Ibid., p. 293.   [4] Ibid., p. 271.

future, economic prosperity had, apparently, already been achieved, or so the empress wrote, shamelessly, to Voltaire: 'Besides, our taxes are so modest that there is not a peasant in Russia who does not eat a chicken when he wants to; recently there have appeared provinces where turkeys are preferred to chickens.'[1]

The vision of the Russian peasant choosing at will between chicken and turkey illustrates well the chasm between fancy and fact in eighteenth-century Russia and might put into question the very notion of Enlightenment as applied to the government and society of that country. Still, fairness requires a closer look.[2] Policies of church control and secularization, as practised by Russian rulers, certainly correspond to the injunctions of the Age of Reason, while their benefits extended, according to Soviet historians, even to the peasants. 'The only major measures which helped the peasantry in the period of 'enlightened despotism' was the secularization of church estates.'[3] Inaugurated wholesale by Peter the Great, administrative reforms continued throughout the century and included the introduction of a new system of local government by Catherine the Great in 1775. Although the Legislative Commission failed to produce a code of laws, Russian legislation experienced some influence of the climate of the Enlightenment, as in the case of Empress Elizabeth's celebrated abolition of capital punishment. The government repealed internal tariffs in 1753, built new canals following the example of Peter the Great, and promoted commerce in various other ways. In fact, the Russian government consistently played a greater role in the economic development of the country than did governments elsewhere. Once again, the concept of enlightened despotism seemed to fit especially well the realm of the tsars. Even the cruel social policy of the Russian rulers which had led, or at least contributed, by the end of the century both to the so-called emancipation of the gentry and to the climax, in nature and

---

[1] Reddaway, ed., op. cit., p. 30.

[2] For a summary account of eighteenth-century Russian history, see e.g. my *History of Russia*, 2nd edn., New York, 1969, pp. 235–332. The best accounts in English include: Raeff, op. cit.; M. Florinsky, *Russia: A History and an Interpretation*, New York, 1953, i. 305–628; and P. Miliukov, C. Seignobos, L. Eisenman, *et al.*, *History of Russia*, New York, 1968, i. 212–334, vol. ii. 3–169.

[3] Druzhinin, op. cit., p. 444.

extent, of the institution of serfdom, possessed—or so it has been claimed—its positive side. Peter III's abolition of compulsory gentry service to the state in 1762 and Catherine the Great's Charter to the Gentry in 1785 created, it has been argued, the first essentially independent class in modern Russian history, that necessary initial step on the road of liberalism and progress.

Government efforts in the field of education and culture were especially striking as well as consonant with the ideas of the Age of Reason. The Academy of Sciences, planned by Peter the Great, opened its doors immediately following his death. In 1755 Russia acquired its first university, the University of Moscow. Although ordinary Russian schools remained few and far between until the end of the century, and indeed long after, Catherine the Great pioneered the education of women, establishing notably the famous Smolny Institute, and she tried to apply the most advanced pedagogical theories of the Enlightenment to the upbringing of her subjects. Russian rulers proved to be remarkable builders. Founded in 1703 by Peter the Great as the capital of the new age of Russian history, St. Petersburg was, by the end of Catherine the Great's reign, well on the way to becoming one of the most magnificent cities in the world. Its glittering court could rival any other. Architects and artists of all sorts, Russian and foreign, profited from imperial patronage. The Theatre, the opera, and the ballet were among its greatest beneficiaries. Writers of different kinds also had their share. From Peter the Great's reform of the alphabet and his creation of the first Russian newspaper to Catherine the Great's sponsorship of periodicals, Russian monarchs worked hard to bring literacy and literature to their subjects.

The imperial Russian government was brilliantly successful in the eighteenth century in another field, or fields, this time unrelated and perhaps even inimical to the spirit of the Enlightenment: international relations, war, and expansion. From the defeat at Narva at the hands of Charles XII of Sweden in 1700 until the time of Napoleon, Russian troops suffered no major military disaster, and they scored many notable victories. Military achievements, together with effective diplomacy, led to the capture of all of southern Russia from Turkey, and to the astounding, if tragic and in a sense self-defeating, partitioning

of Poland. While enormous lands fell under the sceptre of the
Romanovs, Russian soldiers occupied Berlin in the course of the
Seven Years' War and Russian seamen sailed the Mediter-
ranean in their campaigns against the Sultan. The once isolated
Muscovy had clearly become a major European power deeply
involved in the affairs of the Continent. Enlightened or not, the
Russian monarchy could certainly claim respect according to
the older and more generally accepted criteria of power and
success.

And Russia obtained respect. Returning to the theme of the
Enlightenment, however, it is worth stressing that this new
appreciation of Russia arose not only among rulers, statesmen,
and generals, but also and especially among the *philosophes*.
Voltaire, who first studied and presented Peter the Great as a
historically decisive enlightened despot and later fell under the
spell of Catherine the Great, led the way. The correspondence
between him and the Russian empress is a remarkable literary,
psychological, and intellectual document, where the most
famous writer of the century heaps endless and boundless praise
upon the autocrat and her works. Catherine the Great was both
'la première personne de l'univers, sans contredit'[1] and Voltaire's own 'passion dominante'.[2] She was a model to the world
and a benefactress of mankind. Her legislative work would surpass that of Justinian. It was her destiny to recover Constantinople and restore Greece. Voltaire, on his part, intended 'venir
achever ma vie',[3] and actually to die on a pilgrimage[4] to 'the
North star', 'Notre-Dame de Pétersbourg'.[5] '*Te Deum . . . Te
Deam!*'[6] Diderot's description of the empress, whom he did get
to visit in 1773, had a more strictly classical ring: Catherine the
Great possessed 'the spirit of Brutus in the body of Cleopatra,
the courage of the one, and the charms of the other'.[7] D'Alembert joined his colleagues of the *Encyclopédie* in unmeasured
praise of the autocrat. As Voltaire explained the matter: 'We

---

[1] Reddaway, ed., op. cit., p. 119.
[2] Ibid., p. 67.   [3] Ibid., p. 15.
[4] The tombstone would declare: 'Here lies an admirer of august Catherine, who
had the honor of dying as he went to present his profound respect to her' (ibid.,
p. 34).
[5] Ibid., p. 165.   [6] Ibid., p. 37, and elsewhere.
[7] Quoted from G. Makogonenko, *Nikolai Novikov i russkoe prosveshchenie XVIII
veka*, Moscow–Leningrad, 1951, p. 114.

are three, Diderot, d'Alembert, and I who are setting up altars to you.'[1] Three such priests should have proved sufficient for any cult, but in fact many others joined them in the course of the Enlightenment.

There was an opposition, to be sure. The celebrated names of Catherine II's fawning admirers were contradicted by other illustrious names—Rousseau, Mably, Raynal, or Condillac. To be sure, too, the admirers themselves were not always faithful. Diderot's journey to Russia proved to be a disappointment, and he became much more critical of that state and its ruler. Even Voltaire could express himself in a different manner when he wrote about Catherine the Great rather than to her. There were, of course, extraneous reasons for paying homage to the Russian monarch. In Voltaire's case, they ran the gamut from a burning desire to expel barbarous Turkey from Europe and restore glorious Greece to a need to sell watches produced by his Swiss tenants. Also, much must be allowed for the style, manner, and amenities of the period. Thus the image of old Voltaire, on his knees, kissing the hands, or feet, of the imperial goddess—while persistently criticizing the Russian habit of kissing the hands of priests—can be largely written off as an epistolary flourish.

And yet, in the last analysis, the admiration of many *philosophes* for Russia was both serious and revealing. As a French scholar recently put it:

With Voltaire Europe saw that this immense land, peopled by ignorant and brutish muzhiks, 'had given birth to Peter the Great, tsar legislator and reformer', that next it placed as its head a 'new Semiramis', Catherine, whose writings and codes were admired by all; the *philosophes* wept as they read these laws, laws so beautiful that it was the duty of all the sovereigns of the world to take them as their example. Within a few decades Russia steps out of its historical and intellectual 'non-being', provides for itself 'rational, harmonious' laws and becomes for western intellectuals a kind of model state, which attracts the eyes of all the theoreticians in politics and philosophy. The 'Muscovy' of 1700 has transformed itself into an 'enlightened' empire, into a country of 'Light', into an example.[2]

Diderot and others suggested what was to be repeated so often

[1] Reddaway, ed., op. cit., p. 13.
[2] F. de Labriolle, 'Le *prosveščenie* russe et les lumières en France (1760–1798)', *Revue des études slaves*, vol. 45 (1966), pp. 75–91; quoted from p. 75.

in later times—namely, that it was the very newness of Russian participation in history and culture that augured so well for the progress and success of that country. Imprisoned by its own past, the Age of Reason looked with hope at the unencumbered giant who was validating and would continue to validate its most cherished beliefs. No wonder that there occurred what its closest student called 'the Russian mirage in France in the eighteenth century'.[1]

To repeat, the evolution of Russia fitted well, and especially seemed to fit well, the views of the Enlightenment, and the land of the tsars was in many ways fortunate to join the European society of nations in that particular age.

What was the attitude of the Russian educated public when Catherine the Great was bidding for the position of the foremost enlightened despot in the world and when Voltaire, Diderot, and d'Alembert were singing her praises? More broadly, what was the role of the educated public in the evolution of Russia in the eighteenth century as well as its own perception of that evolution and that role?

The modern Russian educated public was created by the reforms of Peter the Great and his successors. Its very *raison d'être* was the turning of the country towards the West and Western Light. In Russian conditions, the government completely dominated that process. In contrast to Western states, Russia in the eighteenth century lacked an independent caste of lawyers, advanced private education, and a powerful church balancing the state or competing for the minds of men in the modern world. More fundamentally still, the development of Muscovy based on the service gentry and serfdom deprived the country of a middle class of any prominence, of precisely that Third Estate which was crucial to the Western Age of Reason. Russian Enlightenment remains the despair of those who must

---

[1] A. Lortholary, *Le Mirage russe en France au XVIIIe siècle*, Paris, n.d. Incidentally, the victims of the mirage proved adulatory enough to satisfy the most exacting Soviet taste. To quote from one of the worst Soviet journals during the last harrowing years of Stalin's life: 'Voltaire, together with a group of *philosophes* who joined him on "the Russian question", knew how to play an exceptional role in spreading just, unbiased judgements about Russia, the Russian people, its culture and science in France and in all of Europe.' V. I. Chuchmarev, 'Frantsuzskie entsiklopedisty XVIII veka ob uspekhakh razvitiia russkoi kultury' ('French Encyclopedists of the XVIII Century on the Successes in the Development of Russian Culture'), *Voprosy Filosofii (Problems of Philosophy)*, No. 6 (1951), p. 179.

link that phenomenon to a new stage in the development of a market economy, to a victorious rise of the bourgeoisie, or to a diffusion of literature and learning among broad layers of population. In Russia the educated public, especially at first but to a large extent even later in the century, remained a small, thin, sectarian layer, conscious at all times of its break with the past and its separation from the masses. Its dependence on the government was almost total; indeed one might argue that, rather than merely offering alliance to it, it fully identified itself with the government and its Westernizing policies.

Nor were this identification and the general role of the Russian educated public in the eighteenth century essentially demeaning, unless one insists on the primacy of class struggle, the transcendent superiority of the democratic ideal, or some other inappropriately extraneous standard. Russian government and society shared the herculean task of learning from the West and of implanting the new knowledge in their own country. The obstacles were enormous, and the best efforts of innovators must have often seemed no more than a ripple on the surface of deep waters. Yet, educated Russians, like their rulers, found profound encouragement and support in the philosophy of the Enlightenment. After all, they were performing the fundamental work of creating a new, rational world on the debris of the old. If change proved slow, no informed person could mistake its direction. 'Man's labor and reason, what is there in the world that they do not overcome!'[1]

On the whole, educated Russians accomplished much. The development of the Russian language is one critical example of their achievement. On the eve of Peter the Great's reforms Russian linguistic usage was in a state of transition as everyday Russian began to assert itself in literature at the expense of the archaic, bookish, Slavonicized forms. This basic process continued in the eighteenth century, but it was complicated further by a mass instrusion of foreign words and expressions which came with Westernization. The language used by Peter the Great and his associates was in a chaotic state, and at one time

---

[1] The assertion belongs to S. E. Desnitskii, professor of law at the University of Moscow and one of the leading figures of the Russian Enlightenment. Quoted from S. A. Pokrovskii, *Politicheskie i pravovye vzgliady S. E. Desnitskogo*, Moscow, 1955, p. 42.

apparently the first emperor wanted to solve the problem by having educated Russians adopt Dutch as their tongue! However, in the course of the century the basic linguistic issues were resolved, and modern literary Russian emerged. The battle of styles, although not entirely over by 1800, resulted in a definitive victory for the contemporary Russian over the Slavonicized, for the fluent over the formal, for the practical and the natural over the stilted and the artificial. As to foreign words and expressions, they were either rejected or gradually absorbed into the Russian language, leading to a great increase in its vocabulary. The Russian language of 1800 could handle many series of terms and concepts unheard of in Muscovy. That the Russian linguistic evolution of the eighteenth century was remarkably successful can best be seen from the fact that the golden age of Russian literature, still the standard of linguistic and literary excellence in modern Russian, followed shortly after. Indeed, Pushkin was born in the last year of the eighteenth century.

The linguistic evolution was linked to a conscious preoccupation with language, to the first Russian grammars, dictionaries, and philological and literary treatises. These efforts, which were of course, an aspect of Westernization, contributed to the establishment of modern Russian literary culture. Lomonosov deserves special recognition for the first effective Russian grammar, published in 1755, which proved highly influential. A rich dictionary prepared by some fifty authors, including almost every writer of note, appeared in six volumes in 1789–94. Theoretical discussion and experimentation by Basil Trediakovskii, Lomonosov, and others led to the creation of the now established system of modern Russian versification.

Similarly, it became the pressing task of educated eighteenth-century Russians to introduce and develop in their homeland such other major forms of Western literary expression as the drama and the novel. The emergence of an original and highly creative Russian literature took time, and the century had to be primarily imitative and in a sense experimental, with only the last decades considerably richer in creative talent. Still, the pioneer work of eighteenth-century writers made an important contribution to the establishment and development of modern Russian literature.

Of the early innovators, Antioch Kantemir, 1709–44, a Moldavian prince educated in Russia and employed in the Russian diplomatic service, has been called the originator of modern Russian belles-lettres. He produced original works as well as translations, poetry and prose, satires, songs, lyrical pieces, fables, and essays. Michael Lomonosov, 1711–65, a central figure in the culture of the entire age, is best remembered in literature for his odes, some of which are still considered classics of their kind, in particular when they touch upon the vastness and glory of the universe. Alexander Sumarokov, 1718–77, a prolific and influential writer, has been honoured as the father of Russian drama. In addition to creating tragedies and comedies as well as satires and poetry and publishing a periodical, Sumarokov was the first director of a permanent Russian theatre. With Sumarokov, the pseudo-classical drama of the Age of Reason found a Russian audience.

The reign of Catherine the Great witnessed both a considerable improvement in the quality of Russian literature and a remarkable increase in its quantity. The place of honour belonged to the writer of comedies, Denis Fonvizin, 1745–92, and the poet Gabriel Derzhavin, 1743–1816, but they attracted an always increasing number of talented and not so talented followers. Catherine the Great's effort to stimulate journalism in her state produced a ready response—a response, indeed, which, the Soviet commentators insist, went beyond the intentions of the empress and made her retreat. In any case, in 1769–74 Russia suddenly acquired a remarkable series of satirical journals. And if these particular periodicals generally did not last, journalism as a whole became firmly established in Russia. From love-lyric to classical tragedy to feuilleton, Russians came to participate in the European literary development.

Other educated Russians, and occasionally the same ones, devoted themselves to Western science and scholarship and to acclimatizing their new knowledge in their native land. Lomonosov, who represented the Russian counterpart of the great encyclopedic scholars of the West, appeared quite early on the scene, and, as it turned out, he was not to be matched in the annals of Russian science for the rest of the century and beyond. But if Russia could not produce another Lomonosov, lesser specialists increased in numbers. Science and scholarship in Russia had a firm foundation because of the invitation of foreigners, sometimes of the highest distinction, to the Academy of Sciences in St. Petersburg and later to the university in Moscow. With the passage of time, Russians began to supplement and even replace foreigners. Thus when the University of Moscow opened its doors in 1755, the teaching was done mostly by foreigners and in Latin; by the end of the century it was done mostly by natives and in Russian. Even in the conservative Academy the relative weight of the Russians rose steadily at the expense of the entrenched German element.

The arts joined literature and the sciences. Russians learned, sometimes with conspicuous success, portrait painting, sculpture, and modern music. In 1757 the art section of the Academy of Sciences became an independent Academy of Arts. As already indicated, architecture flourished in eighteenth-century Russia, with the neoclassical style gradually replacing the earlier baroque. In the reign of Catherine the Great its leading practitioners came to include, in addition to distinguished foreigners, such outstanding Russians as Basil Bazhenov and Matthew Kazakov. Although the first native Russian theatre became established only in the 1750s, by the end of the century Russia possessed several public theatres, a theatrical school, and a periodical, *The Russian Theatre*. Moreover, great landlords began to organize their own private theatres, some fifteen of them in Moscow alone.

Immersion in the literary, scientific, or artistic culture of the West meant, of course, participation in the intellectual world of the Age of Reason. And indeed almost all specialists refer, at least for the reign of Catherine the Great, to a Russian Enlightenment, although there is little agreement on its exact nature and significance. To be sure, the celebrated French *philosophes* loomed largest in Russia as elsewhere. Catherine II's special admiration for Voltaire, whom she considered to be, among his other accomplishments, the best writer in world literature, was shared by many of her educated subjects. Voltairianism has frequently been mentioned as a leading orientation of educated Russians of the Age of Reason. Although Catherine the Great's offer to transfer the publication of the *Encyclopédie* to her empire when it met with difficulties in France produced no results, the subjects of the enlightened empress read avidly the writings of Diderot, d'Alembert, and their associates, as well as those of other *philosophes*.[1] Translations multiplied and appeared more and more promptly. 'It can be said that in the second half of the century and more especially in the last third all the texts published in France are almost immediately known in Russia, where some enlightened spirits make it their duty to spread them. . . . From that time on Russia has made up her "delay".'[2]

Moreover, many Russians did not need translations to read the *philosophes*. From the reign of Empress Elizabeth in mid-century, French became the favourite language of the Russian aristocracy and the Russian educated public in general. While in preferring French the Russians merely followed the common European taste of the period, their devotion to it proved particularly strong and lasting, as readers of Tolstoy well know. A few figures of the Russian Enlightenment wrote everything, even poetry, only in French, while for generations some Russian aristocrats and intellectuals were more at home writing the language of Voltaire than their own tongue. With the rise of national consciousness, persistent attacks on Gallomania paid unwilling tribute to this Russian devotion to French language and culture. But perhaps even more instructive than Fonvizin's resounding sallies in *Brigadier* are such bits as the following passage in Prince P. A. Viazemskii's notebooks: 'What is Mikhail Aleksandrovich Saltykov doing in Moscow?—Still sighing over the change in the French language.'[3]

Yet, in several ways Germany was even more important for the Russian Enlightenment than France. If Russian literary culture tended to follow the French example, science and scholarship in Russia were dominated, long and heavily, by Germans. Leibniz, from the time of his early contacts with Peter the Great, Christian Wolff, and other Germans rivalled French *philosophes* in their impact on the intellectual emergence

---

[1] As P. N. Berkov emphasizes, in the eighteenth century neither the entire *Encyclopédie* nor any of its volumes had been completely translated into Russian. Nevertheless, there appeared between 1767 and 1804 in Russian translation 500 different articles and notices taken from the *Encyclopédie* and twenty-four separate volumes of such selections. P. N. Berkov, 'Histoire de l'Encyclopédie dans la Russie du XVIIIᵉ siècle', *Revue des études slaves*, vol. 44 (1965), pp. 51–2.

[2] De Labriolle, op. cit., p. 76.

[3] P. A. Viazemskii, *Zapisnye knizhki (1813–1848)*, Moscow, 1963, p. 221.

and development of modern Russia. Although the matter has
not been studied closely, it is probable that in the eighteenth
century more Russians attended German universities than all
other foreign universities combined. Lomonosov's years at the
University of Marburg, or Alexander Radishchev's at the
University of Leipzig,[1] are representative of similar seminal
periods in the lives of numerous other figures of the Russian
Enlightenment. German was second only to French as the
language of education and culture in Russia. Moreover, after
the Treaty of Nystadt the empire of the Romanovs acquired
Baltic provinces with their German upper classes of landlords
and townsmen. Other Germans lived in Russia proper, not only
as colonists on the Volga, but, more importantly, as artisans and
professionals in St. Petersburg, where they had their own
churches, theatre, and other institutions. Dynastic and court
foreign connections were also overwhelmingly German. In fact,
Catherine the Great herself may be considered as a gift of
German Enlightenment to Russia.[2]

Great Britain too played an important role in the Russian
Age of Reason. Peter the Great's leading assistants included the
Scots, Patrick Gordon and James Bruce, and the first emperor
himself visited England, where he attempted to learn more than
merely naval matters. 'The originator of modern Russian belles-
lettres', Antioch Kantemir, spent six or seven creative years of
his short life as a Russian diplomat in London, and the influence
of English literature on him is only now receiving the attention
it deserves.[3] In the course of the century young Russians went
to British, as well as other Western, universities. Thus two
future University of Moscow professors, I. A. Tretiakov and
the already mentioned S. E. Desnitskii, in the course of their
several years of studies at the University of Glasgow in the
1760s, attended the lectures of Adam Smith. Tretiakov appa-

[1] It is possible to argue, however, that in Leipzig Radishchev was especially
influenced by the works of French radical thinkers. For a readable account in
English see D. M. Lang, *The First Russian Radical: Alexander Radishchev, 1749–1802*,
London, 1959, esp. pp. 29–58.

[2] As well as Marc Raeff's book mentioned in p. 8 n. 1, see his article, 'Les
Slaves, les Allemands et les "Lumières"', *Canadian Slavic Studies*, vol. i, No. 4
(winter 1967), pp. 521–51. Much valuable work on the German–Russian relations
in the Age of Reason has been done in the last decades by Professor Eduard Winter
of East Berlin and his associates.

[3] I have in mind especially the work in progress of Professor Valentin Boss.

rently later passed them on, almost verbatim, to his own students.[1]
But it must be emphasized that on the whole Great Britain was
much more culturally remote from educated Russians than
France or Germany. In spite of such early Anglophiles as the
remarkable Vorontsov family,[2] most educated Russians read
English writings in French translation, and it was also primarily
through the French medium that the fundamental British
contributions to the Age of Reason made their impact on Russia.

Italy attracted Russians of the period especially because of
its art and music, although occasionally they attended such
universities as that of Padua, and read, their enlightened empress at their head, such significant authors as Beccaria. Still
other countries contributed in a variety of ways to the intellectual and cultural development of former Muscovy. They ranged
from Sweden and Holland, so important for Peter the Great, to
the North American colonies, later the United States of America,
which affected Russian radical thought from Radishchev to the
Decembrists and beyond. On the whole, Russia gathered a rich
heritage. Its varied nature and provenance should not obscure
the fact that the Enlightenment was an outspokenly cosmopolitan age with an essentially common ideology.

Not only were the educated Russians of the Age of Reason
influenced by many Western sources, but frequently a single
Western thinker or writer, especially a major figure, exercised
a variety of influences in Russia. As a striking illustration of this
phenomenon—and nothing more than an illustration is possible
within the scope of this chapter—one might refer to Professor
Iu. M. Lotman's excellent analysis of 'Rousseau and the
Russian Culture of the Eighteenth Century'.[3]

After a brief discussion of Rousseau's views, Lotman turns
to a listing of the eighteenth-century translations of Rousseau
into Russian, but he does so with an important caveat:

However, one should not forget that the composition of such a list

[1] To the embarrassment of Soviet scholarship. See N. Taylor, 'Adam Smith's
First Russian Disciple', *The Slavonic and East European Review*, vol. xlv, No. 105
(July 1967), pp. 425–38.
[2] A recent contribution on the Vorontsovs is Gleb Struve, 'An Anglo-Russian
Medley: Woronzows, Pembrokes, Nicolaÿs, and Others: Unpublished Letters and
Historical Notes', *California Slavic Studies*, vol. v (1970), pp. 93–135 and six remarkable plates.
[3] Iu. M. Lotman, 'Russo i russkaia kultura XVIII veka', *Epokha prosveshcheniia. Iz
istorii mezhdunarodnykh sviazei russkoi literatury*, Leningrad, 1967, pp. 208–81.

would not give us even remotely the picture of the acquaintance with the works of Rousseau in eighteenth-century Russia. If for English literature in those years translation (Russian, French) represented the basic connecting link to the Russian reader, the main acquaintance with French sources took place directly. Therefore if the absence of a translation cannot be considered as evidence of a lack of acquaintance of the Russian reader with this or that work, its presence is an act of a certain recognition, an affirmation of the value of the text in the eyes of Russian society. It is all the more interesting, then, to note that almost all the basic works of Rousseau were translated in the eighteenth century into the Russian language.[1]

The first stage in the Russian reception of Rousseau, represented especially effectively by Sumarokov, consisted in a reaction against the Genevan *philosophe's* attack on the arts and the sciences. Sumarokov argued further, citing Locke, that the assumption of the natural goodness of man was a delusion, that the political element was necessary in human society, and that Rousseau's injunctions would lead to the extinction of humanity. Russian strictures constituted, of course, part of the general campaign of the main body of the champions of the Age of Reason against the dangerous heretic.

The Social Contract and related views of Rousseau led to a more complicated response. While Catherine the Great condemned the author, who in addition to his dangerous theories had had the temerity to interpret the Petrine reforms as a betrayal of the national character, and banned *Émile*, Rousseau remained popular in the Russian court circles and among the educated public. Indeed in 1766 the empress's favourite, Count Gregory Orlov, invited Rousseau to Russia, offering the *philosophe* his estates and palaces 'in gratitude for what I found in your books'.[2] Rousseau's influence was present, if usually indirectly and implicitly, in Catherine's celebrated *Instructions* and in the work of the Legislative Commission, for instance, when the empress made a sustained effort to separate the views of Beccaria from those of Rousseau, or when Prince Michael Shcherbatov borrowed some of Rousseau's arguments to defend the interests of the landlords.

Educated Russians also read avidly Rousseau's letters to Voltaire, which appeared early in a Russian translation, and

---

[1] Iu. M. Lotman, op. cit., p. 215.
[2] Ibid., p. 230.

again their reactions varied. 'If Catherine II in her struggle against Rousseau's democratism tended to rely on the authority of Voltaire, there existed at the same time a tendency to counterpose "good" and believing Rousseau to "evil", sarcastic sceptic Voltaire.'[1] A special emphasis on Rousseau, and in the democratic sense, can be found in the works of an important Russian intellectual, Ia. P. Kozelskii, who in 1768 published his *Philosophical Propositions* and praised Rousseau as the greatest thinker of the Enlightenment.

Rousseau's death in 1778 led to a renewed interest in him in Russia, especially as a writer, and to a new prominence of his *Confession*. Many Russians became interested in the personality of Rousseau, in his passions, in the unity of his creative genius. More important, however, was the ideological involvement with Rousseau's thought, which from the 1780s on had to be taken into account, in one way or another, by Russian ideologists of different persuasions:

One testimony to the great stature which Rousseau acquired for Russian culture of those years is the emergence—together with the problem of the reception—of a definite need of overcoming the ideas of 'Rousseauism'. And this overcoming will be as complex as the reception. In some systems it will be an overcoming of Rousseau's democratism, in others of his basis for dictatorship; some systems will 'lift' Rousseau's dialectic, others will blame him for the straightforward nature of his Robinsonlike views.[2]

Thus Nicholas Novikov and his fellow Freemasons fundamentally opposed Rousseau's view of human nature, but nevertheless published and republished his works, and were strongly attracted by certain Utopian elements in his teaching. Denis Fonvizin, an admirer of Montesquieu and Voltaire, followed Sumarokov in assailing Rousseau's attack on civilization, and in general the basic outlook of the Russian writer could not be reconciled with that of the unorthodox *philosophe*. Still, Fonvizin adopted and adapted arguments from *The Social Contract* to champion an aristocratic political position against both despotic autocracy and democracy. Moreover, when in the last stage of his life Fonvizin came to be preoccupied with moral problems, he reconsidered Rousseau and developed a very high appreciation of *The Confession*. It was *The Confession*, both as model and as

[1] Ibid., p. 239.   [2] Ibid., p. 235.

antagonist, that dominated Fonvizin's *Sincere Confession of My Actions and Thoughts*.[1] Alexander Radishchev, the greatest Russian radical of the age, from his youth felt Rousseau's influence, but he combined it with other influences to create a personal synthesis sharply distinct from, yet frequently related to, the ideology of the seminal Genevan thinker.

The French Revolution heightened Russian interest in Rousseau, and even made him into something of a prophet. It also tended to polarize Russian opinion of the disturbing *philosophe* along political lines, for Rousseau's connection with the events in France could not be denied. Yet the complicated Russian struggle both for and against Rousseau continued, finding its most remarkable expression at this stage in the writings of a leading literary figure of the period, Nicholas Karamzin. Karamzin had been greatly influenced by Rousseau, but, in contrast to Radishchev, not Rousseau the political thinker, but Rousseau the psychologist and the sociologist, the enemy of destitution, riches, and plutocracy. As late as 1793 Karamzin tried to save the positive aspects of Rousseau, and the Enlightenment, while denouncing the mistakes. Moving further to the Right, he assailed next the Genevan's *Confession* and *Émile*. But while Karamzin's *My Confession* can be considered as a kind of 'anti-*Émile*', the unfinished *Knight of Our Time* is more complex:

A polemic against Rousseau was here combined with a continuation of his tradition and with direct correspondence of episodes. An attempt at the same time to argue against Rousseau in *My Confession* and to continue him in the *Knight of Our Time* is characteristic of the position of Karamzin in those years, and also of the problems of Russian literature—in other words, in the formulation of the problem which will become central for the new stage of Russian literature —from Lermontov to Tolstoi.[2]

And indeed it was Rousseau's writings that 'set in the consciousness of the Russian reader the antithesis of unnatural reality

---

[1] Lotman emphasizes that in Rousseau's celebrated statement, 'Je veux montrer à mes semblables un homme dans toute la vérité de la nature; et cet homme, ce sera moi', Fonvizin translated into Russian, a language without articles, 'un homme' as 'man' rather than 'one man', thus generalizing the statement. Later Karamzin was to stress the particularistic aspect of Rousseau's approach. Iu. M. Lotman, op. cit., pp. 255–6.

[2] Ibid., p. 277.

and man's "natural" essence',[1] leading to such literary heroes as children, 'Robinsons', virtuous peasants or highwaymen, even animals. It was Rousseau who influenced the characteristically 'philosophic' prose of the eighteenth century in Russia, more especially when it took the form of a novel. It was Rousseau's impact that continued to affect 'the three main ideological-artistic directions in the Russia of the nineteenth century'[2]— those taken by Chernyshevskii, Tolstoi, and Dostoevskii. 'The ideological-artistic heritage of Rousseau has been organically woven into the development of Russian culture. Herzen had reason to state: "We lived through Rousseau in the same manner . . . as the French." '[3]

Even a cursory glance at Lotman's analysis of Rousseau's influence on eighteenth-century Russia suggests a certain richness and variety of the Russian Age of Reason, and this richness and variety should not be underestimated. Still, on the whole and in the European context, the thought and culture of the Russian Enlightenment were both stark and thin. They were stark because, as already indicated, they represented, to begin with, the effort of a small group of men, and they never obtained the social and historical foundation and background characteristic of the West. To repeat, the simple Russian model of bringing reason and light to a dark world possessed in a sense a greater authenticity, in terms of the ideology of the time, than the more complicated patterns in other European countries. But this purity of line had its dangers; in fact, the perfect model could easily become a caricature of itself.

To put it a little differently, the thought and culture of the Russian Enlightenment were stark because they were so pristine, representing the first stage in the evolution of modern Russia. For the same reason they were thin. The thinness resulted not so much from an insufficient Russian borrowing of the advanced ideas of the Age of Reason: as we have already seen, Russians borrowed effectively and rapidly, although clearly not everything could be transposed immediately into the realm of the tsars. Rather, it was again a product of a lack of historical background, of the absence of the intellectual development which preceded for centuries and also surrounded the thought of the *philosophes*. While the Age of Reason can be said to represent

---

[1] Ibid., p. 278.   [2] Ibid., p. 281.   [3] Ibid.

a new wave of modern European interest in the classical world, following naturally upon the Renaissance and its aftermath, classical themes in the Russian Enlightenment were merely a feeble ripple in the wake of that wave. Only very occasionally, as in Derzhavin's imitation of Horace's eternal monument, did individual genius make the Russian efforts memorable. Whereas the religious argument was central to Western intellectual life of the period and constituted, especially in Great Britain, an extremely complex, differentiated, and nuanced body of thought, Russians simply borrowed scepticism from Voltaire, or comfortable deism, again from Voltaire or from another *philosophe*, with only some clerical denunciations of free-thinking to provide a semblance of a debate. Kliuchevskii and numerous other students of the epoch criticized Russians for the superficiality of their contacts with the West, as in the case of the tourist who paced St. Peter's to establish its dimensions and other tourists who engaged in still less edifying pursuits. Probably valid, although not unusual, in their own right, these criticisms might point to a more irreducible superficiality characteristic of a new-comer to an established society of nations. The thought and culture of the Russian Enlightenment simply did not possess the rich texture found in other European countries, or in the United States for that matter.[1]

Several themes dominated the thought and literature of the Russian Enlightenment. As in the West, criticism poured forth. The first modern Russian writer, Antioch Kantemir, proved to be most successful as a satirist, and his nine satires written between 1729 and 1739 were to be highly characteristic of the entire age. Beginning with the first and most important one, entitled *To One's Reason or against Those Who Deprecate Education*, Kantemir assailed such crucial Russian evils as the superstitiousness, ignorance, and drunkenness of the common people, the poor state of the clergy, the dishonesty of merchants,

---

[1] The richness of the American Enlightenment resulted primarily from its close following of the British religious and secular thought—indeed, it was in a very real sense part of that thought—although it also experienced other major influences, mainly French. On the American Enlightenment, I am especially indebted to a forthcoming study by my Berkeley colleague, Professor Henry F. May. Of course, a thorough and many-sided religious debate, in the British or American style, was impossible in the conditions of Russian censorship. The point is, however, that the elements for such a debate were not present in Russia.

the uselessness and the vices of the gentry, and the venality of officials. Kantemir's translations, it might be added, included Montesquieu's *Persian Letters* and, in an effort to combat superstition and ignorance, Bernard de Fontenelle's *Plurality of Worlds*.

Following Kantemir, satire remained a favourite genre among Russian writers of the eighteenth century, ranging from the brilliant comedies of Fonvizin to the pedestrian efforts of Catherine the Great herself and numerous other aspiring authors. Fables, fed in large part by the same critical and satirical approach to reality, constituted another popular literary form in eighteenth-century Russia to culminate in Ivan Krylov's immortal creations in the nineteenth. Krylov, born in 1768, became a prominent writer and journalist in the reign of Catherine the Great, although he did not really hit his stride until later. But if Basil the Cat, the liar, the quartet, Demian's fish soup, and other items forever connected with Krylov are strictly speaking outside the scope of this chapter, it is remarkable how many eighteenth-century authors are remembered best for their critical and satirical efforts. And these authors range in quality and contribution. Whereas Fonvizin's greatest gift to his contemporaries and to posterity remains his magnificent satirical comedy, *The Minor*, which depicts the penetration of the newly necessary education into the milieu of the provincial Russian gentry, the once popular poet and dramatist, Basil Kapnist, is remembered best for a mere four or five lines from his savage satirical play about bribery and corruption, *Chicane*, produced in 1798.[1]

The same satire, the same social criticism inspired journalism; in fact, no clear line divided journalism from literature. Both during the remarkable outburst of 1769–74 and in general throughout the century, Russian writers and publicists inveighed against the backwardness, boorishness, and corruption of their countrymen, without neglecting such newer sins as Gallomania and a craving for luxury. The critical spirit spread

---

[1] Beri, bolshoi tut net nauki;   Take, it does not require much learning;
Beri, chto tolko mozhno vziat.   Take, whatever can be taken.
Na chto-zh privesheny nam ruki   What for are arms attached to us,
Kak ne na to chtob brat?   If not to take?
Brat, brat, brat?   [All repeat] Take, take, take?

V. V. Kapnist, *Sochineniia*, St. Petersburg, 1849, p. 101.

everywhere. When in 1789 a periodical, *Conversing Citizen* (*Beseduiushchii Grazhdanin*), decided to translate foreign terms into Russian, it chose as the equivalent of 'criticism', *kritika*, the words *zdravoe suzhdenie* 'sensible judgment'.[1]

Naturally, there was criticism and criticism. One can well appreciate the attempts of Soviet scholars to arrange it meaningfully according to its content and significance, and even their preference for the more over the less concrete. Much Russian eighteenth-century satire and denunciation aimed at general human vices and weaknesses, virtually a critique out of time and place, so to speak. These sallies, however, acquired a much sharper edge when occasionally directed against particular human beings and their specific sins. The propriety of attacking individuals in print was much debated during the period, while some modern specialists have achieved a high expertise in deciphering hints and allusions. Next to the question of the human condition, and intrinsically linked to it, stood the problem of an enormous backward country steeped in superstition and ignorance, against which the Russian writers battled indefatigably, in the best Enlightenment tradition, throughout the century. The deepest belief and inspiration of the Age of Reason found expression in their mighty effort.

Yet this sweeping, essentially cultural, general critique failed on the whole to assert itself specifically in the political and the social realms. In politics, as already indicated and as we shall see in more detail later, the Russia of the Age of Reason remained almost entirely under the sign of enlightened despotism. In social matters serfdom formed the main obstacle to progressive Russian thought and action. That institution, while the very opposite of enlightened, was both so well accepted and so fundamental to Russian life that few in the eighteenth century dared challenge it. The period was, after all, the age of the Russian gentry. Catherine the Great herself, after some vague preliminary wavering, came out entirely on the side of the gentry and its power over the peasants. The fact that the newly created Free Economic Society, patronized by the empress, awarded its first prize to a work advocating the even-

---

[1] P. N. Berkov, *Istoriia russkoi zhurnalistiki XVIII veka*, Moscow–Leningrad, 1952, p. 377. Berkov's valuable account of the Russian periodicals of the eighteenth century is even excessively sensitive to their critical content.

tual abolition of serfdom remained an isolated incident. Numerous writers proceeded to criticize certain individual excesses of serfdom, such as the cruelty of one master or the wastefulness of another, but they did not assail the system itself. Moreover, painful references to the transgressions of 'bad' landlords were usually balanced by appropriate depictions of 'good' ones, lifeless though these pictures commonly were. Nicholas Novikov and a very few others went further: their image of serf relations could not be ascribed to individual aberrations, and it cried for reform. Still, it remained to Alexander Radishchev to make the condemnation of serfdom total and unmistakably clear. His attack on serfdom, in particular in his *Journey from Petersburg to Moscow* published in 1790, marked the high point of the social critique of the Russian Age of Reason and in a sense the culmination of that entire trend.

Education was, of course, the pendant to criticism and the antidote to prejudice and ignorance, and it too constituted a dominant theme in the Russian, as well as the general European, Enlightenment. One could write an entire intellectual and literary history of the period in Russia focusing it simply on the issue of education, almost as effectively as if one were to focus it on criticism. Kantemir not only entitled his first satire *Against Those Who Deprecate Education*, devoted another satire to education, and kept bringing the subject up on still other occasions, but, in a broader sense, dedicated himself to enlightening Russia. 'Kantemir's love of learning had a utilitarian character in the spirit of Peter the Great: he valued both learning itself and his own literary activity only to the extent to which they could advance Russia towards well-being, and the Russian people towards happiness. This determines, in the main, the importance of Kantemir as a public figure and a writer.'[1] Kantemir's mentality and pattern of literary activity were basic to the age, in Russia as elsewhere. Major and minor figures of the Russian Enlightenment differed in talent and accomplishment, but usually not in orientation or inspiration.

One thinks of Novikov, 1744–1818, both as a representative

[1] R. Sementkovskii, 'Kantemir (kn. Antiokh Dmitrievich)', *Entsiklopedicheskii Slovar* (Brockhaus–Efron), vol. xlv, Book 27, p. 315. For a discussion of Kantemir's views on education, in the context of European Enlightenment, see M. Ehrhard, 'La Satire "De l'éducation" de A. D. Kantemir', *Revue des études slaves*, vol. 38 (1961), pp. 73–9.

intellectual of the period and the outstanding Russian counter-part of the great Western *philosophes*, those indefatigable teachers of humanity. Thinker, writer, translator, and a uniquely important pioneer publicist and publisher, Novikov made better use than any other individual of the opportunities pro-vided by Catherine the Great to spread enlightenment, only to fall victim to the reaction at the end of her reign. 'Novikov's place in the Russian enlightenment is defined by the fact that he created a love and a trust of books, and a passion for reading them, that he sowed widely and generously, acting not alone but together, knowing how to unite hundreds of people around his educational activities.'[1]

If Novikov stood for the breadth of the Russian Enlighten-ment, some others expressed even better than he the depth of its educational message. It was surely a testimony to the centrality of the problem of education in the Age of Reason that it inspired some of its best literature. To take a notable Russian example, the entire work of perhaps the greatest Russian creative literary genius of the age, Fonvizin, can be and has been interpreted as a treatment of the crucial issue of education in the particular setting of his native land:

Fonvizin's dramatic output is not large: he wrote only two plays, *The Brigadier* (1769) and *The Minor* (1782), and he left three sketches, one of them composed before *The Brigadier* and known as *The First Minor (Rannii Nedorosl)'* The other two date from the end of his life, *The Good Teacher (Dobryi nastavnik)* around 1784 and *The Choice of a Tutor (Vybor guvernera)* around 1790 or 1792.

But this output possesses the interesting characteristic of being entirely devoted to the same problem, essential in the eyes of 'the civilizers', the problem of education. Well, the permanence of a theme across the entire output makes it easier to follow at the same time the evolution of this theme—at least to the extent that the author does not repeat himself, which Fonvizin does not do—and the evolution of its form of expression. The aim of this study is to demonstrate that ceaseless reflection on the same problem led our author to approach it in different, always richer, ways, that this enrichment of his thought caused a profound transformation of his dramatic conception, and, finally, that this aesthetic discovery of

[1] Makogonenko, op. cit., p. 538. For a similar opinion by a contemporary, cf. N., 'O knizhnoi torgovle i liubvi ko chteniiu v Rossii', *Vestnik Evropy*, No. 9 (May 1802), pp. 57–8.

Fonvizin exercised such an influence on the Russian drama that one can see in it one of the deep reasons for the turning of that drama towards realism.[1] . . . His essential preoccupation did not change; he dedicated his life to demonstrating to the Russian public the importance of education in a modern state.[2]

Criticism and concern with education permeated the entire Age of Reason everywhere, although they experienced local modifications. Also central to the thought of the Age of Reason was the concept of enlightened despotism. Again, this was developed best by the Western *philosophes,* but in the West it had to compete with other theoretical alternatives and practical possibilities. For example, it had no relevance for Geneva and little for Great Britain. By contrast, it was entirely relevant for the empire of the Romanovs, and it became fully dominant there.

Russian historians, beginning with Basil Tatishchev, 1686–1750, interpreted the development of their country largely in terms of enlightened despotism. Russian playwrights, such as the prolific Sumarokov, glorified powerful and benevolent rulers. But the most resounding affirmation of enlightened despotism came from poets, and their characteristic vehicle was the ode, just as satire served the critics especially well. 'The ode in Elizabeth's and Catherine's Russia was an important institution. There was a constant demand for odes at court, and ode writing brought more tangible results in the form of pensions and honours than any other kind of literary exercise. The average level of ode writing was naturally low.'[3] Yet the ode writers included the always impressive Lomonosov, whose extravagant praise of Peter the Great rang true and who largely set the style for the genre, and Derzhavin, the bard of Catherine the Great and one of the authentic creative geniuses of the age. While Fonvizin expressed best both the spirit of criticism and the urgent need of education in Russia, Derzhavin remains associated for ever with enlightened despotism. The two were the greatest Russian writers of the period.

Much has been written about the composers of Russian odes

---

[1] F. de Labriolle, 'La Dramaturgie de Fonvizin', *Revue des études slaves,* vol. 46 (1967), pp. 65–80; quoted from pp. 65–6.

[2] Ibid., p. 79.

[3] D. S. Mirsky, *A History of Russian Literature,* New York, 1949, p. 47.

and their enthusiastic support of the rulers, but perhaps the
most judicious appraisal was made long ago by Plekhanov:

Our ode writers flattered beyond all measure. This, unfortunately,
cannot be denied. But, in the first place, flattery in an ode was
demanded by the custom of the time. It was a disgusting custom,
but the contemporary readers and listeners knew that the exaggerated plaudits, contained in odes, had to be accepted *cum grano salis*.
And the most important thing—precisely what I want to point out
to the reader—the ode writers were adorers of autocratic power not
only from fear but also out of conviction. From it, and from it only,
they expected the impulse for progressive development in Russia.
How then could they fail to glorify it and sing it in their odes?[1]

Plekhanov went on to indicate that, in addition, ode writers
frequently mixed advice with their praise and indeed introduced
a whole series of projects to promote enlightenment under the
guise of eulogizing the wisdom of the ruler.

The ideology of enlightened despotism faithfully reflected the
historical position of a vast country driven into modernization
by an autocracy supported by a small and sectarian educated
class, separated from the masses. The period was one of an
essentially monolithic unity between state and 'society' linked
by the difficult, self-appointed task with which they were
inextricably identified. Lomonosov on Peter the Great, or
Derzhavin on Catherine the Great expressed a fundamental
historical truth, in spite of all the exaggeration and bombast.
Yet, before leaving this topic, it would be appropriate at least
to mention some of the more prominent divergent interpretations which emphasize cracks, rifts, and contradictions between
and within the government and the educated public in eighteenth-
century Russia. At their best these opinions point to the complexity of historical reality which cannot be subsumed under
any formula. At their worst they represent exercises in abstract
theory which must find the play of the dialectic or a clear
differentiation between and a symmetrical alignment of the
forces of good and evil, regardless of the facts.

To start with, there is the problem of constitutionalism in
eighteenth-century Russia. While considering it does not take
us outside the thought of the Age of Reason, for a constitutional
monarchy could as well follow from that thought as could

[1] G. V. Plekhanov, *Istoriia russkoi obshchestvennoi mysli*, iii, Moscow, 1919, iii. 32.

enlightened despotism,[1] it is not irrelevant to an appreciation of
the relationship between the Russian educated public of the
period and its rulers. In a sense, modern constitutionalism
became part of Russian thinking once Peter the Great turned
to the West, for it long had been part of European political
ideology and practice. It is not really surprising, therefore, that
such a supporter of the reforming emperor and of the Russian
monarchy as the historian and administrator Tatishchev
believed nevertheless that that monarchy would profit from
the establishment of a senate of twenty-one members and an
assembly of 100, with elections held for high offices. It is not
surprising either, taking into account Peter the Great's succession law and the complex problem of succession in the years
following his death, that the small ruling group, the so-called
Supreme Secret Council, whom Tatishchev opposed, even
managed to impose a constitution upon Anne, daughter of Peter
the Great's half-brother Ivan V and widow of the Duke of
Courland, when it offered her the Russian throne in 1730. The
would-be empress had to promise not to marry and not to
appoint a successor. The Supreme Secret Council was to retain
a membership of eight and to control state affairs: the new
sovereign could not without its approval declare war or make
peace, levy taxes or commit state funds, grant or confiscate
estates, or appoint anyone to a rank higher than that of colonel.
The guards as well as all other armed forces were to be under
the jurisdiction of the Supreme Secret Council, not of the
empress. Anne, who had very little to lose, accepted these
drastic limitations, thus establishing constitutional rule in
Russia.

Russian constitutionalism, however, proved to be extremely
short-lived. Because the Supreme Secret Council had acted in
its own narrow and exclusive interest, tension ran high among
the gentry. Some critics, such as Tatishchev, spoke and wrote
of extending political advantages to the entire gentry, while
others simply denounced the proceedings. Anne utilized a
demonstration by the guards and other members of the gentry,
shortly after her arrival, to tear up the conditions she had accepted, asserting that she had thought them to represent the desires

---

[1] Better, according to many specialists, Soviet and other, who prefer to begin
their Enlightenment to the Left of enlightened despotism.

of her new subjects, whereas they turned out to be the stratagem of a selfish cabal. And she abolished the Supreme Secret Council. Autocracy came back into its own. In retrospect, it is difficult to find in the 'constitutional' episode of 1730 anything beyond a bid for power of a very narrow ruling clique dominated by the Golitsyn and the Dolgorukii families.

Yet 'the conditions' briefly imposed by the Supreme Secret Council on Empress Anne represented the only clear appearance of constitutionalism on the Russian eighteenth-century political scene. Otherwise, it is appropriate to speak only of projects and possibilities, and the constitutional nature of even these projects remains in doubt. Thus the famous memorandum of 28 December 1762 presented by Count Nikita Panin, brilliant courtier, diplomat, and tutor of Grand Duke Paul, to Catherine II who had just ascended the throne, has been interpreted by some scholars as an effort, similar to that of 1730, to limit the power of the sovereign. But different readings of it, such as that of the latest student of the matter, Professor David Ransel, are at least as convincing: 'Far from being an attempt to wrest control of affairs from the autocrat, the project represented rather an effort by Panin to secure his own threatened position by legitimizing it in the context of an established state council.'[1] It is especially notable that the guards, who repeatedly decided the succession to the throne in Russia in the eighteenth century and who brought both Elizabeth and Catherine II to power, sponsored no constitutional programmes, if one is to dismiss the inconsequential rumblings of 1730. As a principal explanation of this general acquiescence to autocracy, it has been argued that Russia during the eighteenth century, and especially during its second half, was dominated by an alliance between the ruler and the gentry with an implicit division of power: the landlords occupied a highly privileged economic and social position made possible by serfdom; the monarchs retained autocratic political authority. In any case,

---

[1] David Ransel, 'Nikita Panin's Imperial Council Project and the Struggle of Hierarchy Groups at the Court of Catherine II', *Canadian Slavic Studies*, vol. iv, No. 3 (Fall 1970), pp. 443–63; quoted from pp. 443–4. For an English translation of the text of the memorandum, as well as key documents *re* the crisis of 1730, see Marc Raeff, *Plans for Political Reform in Imperial Russia, 1730–1905*, Englewood Cliffs, N.J., 1966. Raeff described the memorandum as an effort to bring 'order and coherence to the process by which the monarch reached basic policy decisions' (p. 53).

constitutionalism played a very minor role in the Russian politics of the period. The rulers on their part, it might be added, in spite of Catherine the Great's praise of liberty and even republicanism, were more than willing to let sleeping dogs lie. They were fully satisfied with enlightened despotism.

Of course, the fact that Russia remained an autocracy in the eighteenth century did not in itself guarantee a monolithic unity between the government and the educated public. Numerous scholars, including Soviet specialists as a group, have emphasized precisely the rifts and the division both between the rulers and the intellectuals and among the intellectuals themselves. On the whole, while granting the gentry domination of Russia during the century and the formidable obstacles to fundamental economic, social, and political change, they stress the orientation of the progressive Russian intellectuals of the Age of Reason towards such change, their radical and at times revolutionary nature. They emphasize not co-operation with but struggle against the government on the part of the educated public. They view the Russian Enlightenment as a battle-field, not a classroom.

At its broadest, it has been asserted that the Russian Enlightenment was both independent of and superior to the French Enlightenment. It was superior because it was deeper and more radical. Whereas Western *philosophes* expressed the class interests of the rising bourgeoisie, progressive Russian thinkers of the period reflected the position of the exploited Russian peasantry which had revolted under the leadership of Emelian Pugachev against the established order. Indeed the achievements of the Russian Enlightenment included its unremitting struggle against the bourgeois character and ideology of the French Age of Reason. It is in this framework that Makogonenko presented Novikov as a great cultural hero, and in the process he even managed to interpret Fonvizin's notorious reactionary letters from France as a penetrating criticism from the Left of the bourgeois world of the French Enlightenment.[1] As usual, Soviet writers gave no explanation at all as to how a peasant rebellion becomes transformed into the philosophy of the Age of Reason.

[1] Makogonenko, op. cit. The remarkable discussion of Fonvizin's letters is on pp. 386–8, where Makogonenko's strange thesis does stand out in spite of important qualifications.

Nonsensical and at present largely abandoned even by their proponents, such and similar views are worth mentioning because they constitute the logical extreme, so to speak, of much of the Soviet scholarship in the field.[1]

Less extreme, most Soviet scholars have preferred to link the Russian Enlightenment to gentry liberalism or to 'an emerging, anti-serfdom, bourgeois according to its objective content'[2] position rather than directly to Russian peasants and Pugachev. They persistently concentrate nevertheless on the rifts between the intellectuals and the government and indeed on a continuous struggle between the two. Thus the history of Russian journalism in the reign of Catherine the Great has been presented as largely a camouflaged attack on the empress, the court, and the authorities in general, with the enormous amount of outspoken praise and support of the ruler, the state, and its policies neglected, minimized, distorted, or explained

---

[1] In addition to emphasizing the political, social, and economic radicalism of the representatives of the Russian Enlightenment, Soviet scholars have stressed the advanced nature of their religious views. In particular, they have concentrated on the progress of these intellectuals beyond deism to atheism, as well as on the general spread of unbelief in eighteenth-century Russia. Their arguments in this case do not affect the position of Russia within the general European Enlightenment, for different kinds of religious modernism and scepticism could be found in that Enlightenment; on the whole, they also fail to carry conviction. Thus the leading practitioner of the genre, Iu. Ia. Kogan (see esp. his *Ocherki po istorii russkoi ateisticheskoi mysli XVIII v.*, Moscow, 1962), lists assiduously police cases related to neglect of or challenge to church ritual and churches, usually some form of verbal protest or abuse, although he is concerned to avoid the Old Believers, who opposed the Orthodox Church for other than atheistic reasons. Fortunately tsarist authorities often took a lighter view of the matter than Kogan, urging such mitigating circumstances as drunkenness. Logically extended, Kogan's method could prove, for example, that armies are typically composed of pacifists. As to leading intellectuals, such as Lomonosov, Kogan emphasizes their frequent adherence to the theory of two truths, the religious truth and the scientific truth, and insists that, because of the incompatibility of the two, this objectively represents an essentially anti-religious position, an argument which would have been valid if the point at issue were Kogan's perception of the subject and not Lomonosov's. Many Soviet scholars are particularly weak when dealing with religious matters because of their reliance on a primitive, pre-Freudian psychology; e.g. they fail to see that a direct challenge to God could be as much part of a religious dialogue as evidence of irreligion. Atheism might have had a considerable number of adherents among the educated public of eighteenth-century Russia, but they are more likely to be found not among the leading progressive thinkers of the age, such as Lomonosov, Novikov, or Radishchev, but in the milieu of sceptical Voltairian aristocrats. It is not even at all clear where Catherine the Great herself belonged in this matter.

[2] This description of the viewpoint belongs to Beliavskii: M. T. Beliavskii, *Krestianskii vopros v Rossii nakanune vosstaniia E. I. Pugacheva*, Moscow, 1965, p. 27.

away as a device to protect the writer. Even when correct or at least plausible in specific cases—and issues which hinge on an innuendo, a hint, an indirect suggestion, or on double talk are frequently bound to be difficult to resolve—this approach tends to put out of focus the total picture of Russian journalism of the period. It misleads the reader as to the actual over-all content and argument of the famous periodicals of that time, and it is particularly damaging to any balanced appreciation of the provincial press.[1] *Mutatis mutandis* Soviet scholarship often achieves similar results in other areas of Russian intellectual and cultural development in the eighteenth century. Moreover, granted all the bitterness and the agony of the Russian intellectuals of the period, their experience did not lead to a novel ideological position. In other words, they remained adherents of enlightened despotism, although they developed reservations and at times felt disappointment in regard to Catherine the Great as the ideal enlightened despot. This is not a matter of dispute: it is the consensus of Soviet scholarship that all the leading representatives of the Russian Enlightenment, even Novikov, with the sole exception of Alexander Radishchev, were dominated by the concept of enlightened despotism and did not progress beyond it.

Soviet specialists have shown the same tendency to raise personal frustrations and quarrels to the level of a fundamental, dialectical struggle in their treatment of the foreign, especially German, participation in the development of modern Russian culture. Of course, the issue of the Russian ability to produce cadres of native scholars and scientists was an important one. It is also true that experts from abroad frequently demonstrated their ignorance of Russian life and people and their feelings of apartness and superiority. But none of this justifies the depiction of these immensely helpful foreigners as a hostile element

[1] Little is known about journals or about publishing in general in the Russian provinces in the eighteenth century, although there is good reason to believe that the provincial literary milieu was more conservative than that of St. Petersburg and Moscow. For an informative introduction to the end of the period, see A. V. Blium, 'Izdatelskaia deiatelnost v russkoi provintsii kontsa xviii–nachala xix, vv. (Osnovnye tematicheskie napravleniia i tsenzurno-pravovoe polozhenie)', *Kniga, issledovaniia i materialy*, vol. xii, Moscow (1966), pp. 136–59. The interesting material in the article includes Blium's calculation that 43 per cent of publications in the Russian provinces at the time were translations, compared with 'approximately one-third' for the empire as a whole (p. 142).

engaged in a relentless combat against the native Russian genius and determined to thwart it.[1] Even the question of elucidating the origin of the Russian state, prominent since the days of Lomonosov and particularly susceptible to national ignorance and prejudice, cannot be properly understood as a contest between Russians and Germans. While the original formulation of the so-called 'Norman theory' of a Scandinavian origin of the first Russian state belonged to German scholars working in Russia and poorly acquainted with the Russian past, largely *terra incognita* at the time, as the debate developed different positions easily crossed ethnic lines. Thus it was a German historian in Russia, J. Ewers, who early in the nineteenth century challenged the Scandinavian interpretation with his Khazar thesis, whereas M. Pogodin, a son of a serf and very much a native Russian, stood out for decades as the most determined champion of Normanism.[2] For the great majority of other conflicts, in or out of the Academy of Sciences, ethnic allegiance had no direct relevance at all, and these conflicts can be best understood in terms of pressing controversial issues in the particular fields and disciplines on the one hand, and of individual personalities, careers, and circumstances on the other.[3] It hardly needs adding that controversies between Russian and German scholars did not affect the basic ideological outlook of the period, whether in regard to Enlightenment or enlightened despotism. The orientation of the Russians has been the subject of this entire chapter. As to foreign specialists, the only reason for their presence in Russia was enlightenment, and that presence depended entirely on the will of the Russian monarchs and government.

In the last analysis, Alexander Radishchev must be distinguished as the only eighteenth-century Russian intellectual whose explosive protest burst the bonds of the Russian Enlighten-

[1] Few Soviet scholars occupy so extreme a position, but very many tend in that direction. Typically, they discuss 'good' as well as 'bad' foreigners, and make some allowance for contributions by the former. The difficulty lies, however, not in the precise membership of the two groups, but in the formulation of the problem.

[2] For an introduction to the historiography of the question, see N. Riasanovsky, 'The Norman Theory of the Origin of the Russian State', *The Russian Review*, vol. 7, No. 1 (Autumn 1947), pp. 96–110.

[3] The 'German question' in the Academy of Sciences and in the Russian scholarly world of the Enlightenment in general is treated sensitively and judiciously in A. Vucinich, *Science in Russian Culture*, vol. i, *A History to 1860*, Stanford, 1963.

ment, with its exclusive reliance on the enlightened despot, although certainly not of the Enlightenment in general. Much has been written about Radishchev's allegiance to the European Age of Reason and, conversely, of his specifically Russian concerns and attitudes. Both approaches, of course, are justified. Educated at the University of Leipzig and thoroughly versed in the literature of the times—pre-revolutionary Russian scholars noted that he even forgot Russian in part, to the detriment of his later career and literary activity—Radishchev belonged to the later, more radical, phase of the Enlightenment exemplified by such thinkers as Rousseau and Mably, although he reflected other currents of the age as well. The remarkable similarities of *A Journey from Petersburg to Moscow* to Raynal's *History of the Indies* is only one striking example of Radishchev's Western links. Yet Radishchev's deserved fame rests on his all-out attack on the Russian institution of serfdom, which he assailed not only in his celebrated literary venture, but also in a plan for serf emancipation with an accompanying land settlement, and which preoccupied him both before and after his exile to Siberia. A fundamental challenge to serfdom in 1790 meant also an attack on Catherine the Great, who kept repeating that Russian serfs with good masters were the happiest people in the world, and on the entire established system in Russia, and indeed the *Journey* developed such an attack. What is more, however, Radishchev's hope and ideal resided not in a more successful version of enlightened despotism, but in a republic with full liberties for the individual. The wheel had finally turned. Still, pioneering and daring though he was, Radishchev did not embody the consistent revolutionary of the Soviet version. His cry of impending disaster was a warning, not a call to rebellion. With all his sympathy for the Russian peasants, he looked at them only from the outside, as a landlord, government official, or intellectual. Revolutionary populism belonged to a later age.

Because the solidity and support of the Russian monarchy in the eighteenth century derived largely from its close alliance with the gentry, certain specialists have pointed to the corrosive impact of the emergence of an educated layer of the *raznochintsy* —that is, people of mixed background below the gentry, such as sons of priests who did not follow the calling of their fathers,

offspring of petty officials and lower rank army men, or individuals from the masses who made their way up through education
and effort. While, of course, it had been generally known that
during the Enlightenment many Russian painters, architects,
and other artists had risen from peasant backgrounds, that a
number of writers came from clerical families, or that Lomonosov himself was of peasant stock, and while Soviet scholars
even emphasized the struggles and the roles of these lower-class
individuals, it was the merit of the late M. M. Shtrange to put
the information together into an integrated account of 'the
Russian democratic intelligentsia in the eighteenth century'.[1]
In the 1750s and 1760s, through the institutions of higher and
specialized learning, including the cadet corps, the *raznochintsy*
rose to play a significant role in the intellectual and cultural life
of the country and in part in its administration, especially in
the Senate chancery. By their very nature these new proto-
bourgeois intellectuals were more democratic, critical, and
radical, as well as more patriotic and authentically Russian,
than their gentry counterparts. Led by Lomonosov, Shtrange
continues, they displayed a great activity and offered rich
promise for the subsequent evolution of Russia.

Yet at the time at least the promise was not fulfilled. Already
in the 1760s there began 'an offensive of the ruling circles'
against the intelligentsia from the *raznochintsy*. Aided by the
death of Lomonosov in 1765, it consisted of a much stricter
control of educational institutions and of a greater emphasis on
social origin there as well as in the service. The offensive
proved successful: the *raznochintsy* were suppressed and scattered;
Shtrange even notes some suicides and 'early deaths'. In the
end, he has to concede, the role of the intelligentsia from the
raznochintsy in eighteenth-century Russia was aborted, while its
contribution 'did not exceed the framework of the Enlightenment'.[2] Or, to quote the judgement of the leading present
specialist on the *raznochintsy*, Professor G. N. Vulfson of the
University of Kazan:

It must be admitted that government measures in that direction

[1] M. M. Shtrange, *Demokraticheskaia intelligentsiia Rossii v* XVIII *veke*, Moscow,
1965. Based on this book is M. Laran, 'La Première Génération de l'"intelligentsia"
roturière en Russie (1750–1780)', *Revue d'histoire moderne et contemporaine*, vol. xiii
(Apr.–June 1966), pp. 137–56. Shtrange's use of the word 'intelligentsia' is, of
course, anachronistic.   [2] Shtrange, op. cit., p. 274.

produced results: they delayed the growth and decreased the specific weight of the intelligentsia from the *raznochintsy* during the end of the eighteenth and the first half of the nineteenth centuries. The autocracy did everything to prevent the transformation of the intelligentsia of the *raznochintsy* into an independent force. And, indeed, it did not become such a force either in the eighteenth century or in the first half of the nineteenth.[1]

The last point, it might be added, is strikingly illustrated by the fact that in a search for radicalism in the Russian Enlightenment one still has to turn to such members of the gentry as Novikov and, especially, Radishchev. Government repression, emphasized by Soviet scholars, might have played a part in checking the intelligentsia from the *raznochintsy*. Yet, during the Age of Reason it was also controlled, in a sense, by the concept of enlightened despotism itself, a logical alliance between modernizing rulers and an emerging educated public.

Still other examples of tensions and conflicts between the government and the intellectuals in eighteenth-century Russia could also, of course, be found. But the fundamental pattern of a monolithic support of the state by the educated public remained essentially unimpaired. As reiterated in this study, Russian government and society followed the path of the Enlightenment in a remarkably united, conscious, and in many ways successful manner.

To be sure, neither the achievements nor the prospects were ideal. Rational criticism, effective and highly desirable though it was, especially for a modernizing country, tended to penetrate too far for the security of the established order. Radishchev had already challenged serfdom, and other such challenges were bound to follow. Education, too, the glory and the hope of the Enlightenment, raised difficult questions. While Peter the Great, a heroic champion of light in a realm of darkness, simply drove everyone he could reach to study useful things,

---

[1] G. N. Vulfson, 'Poniatie "raznochinets" v xviii–pervoi polovine xix veka (Nekotorye nabliudeniia)', *Ocherki istorii narodov Povolzhia i Priuralia*, Issue I, Kazan, 1967, p. 124. In this uniquely informative article the author traces the appearance of the word to 1711 and the emergence of the social category in the subsequent decades with its gradual liberation from the poll tax accomplished by the beginning of the 1760s. For an interesting account of 'non-gentry' historiography in eighteenth-century Russia, see S. L. Peshtich, *Russkaia istoriografiia XVIII veka*, Part II, Leningrad, 1965, esp. ch. VIII.

Catherine the Great had to consider the social consequences of education. Whom was she going to educate and how much? Here even Voltaire could not help her, for he had not solved that problem either. Enlightened despotism itself, although firmly grounded in the thought of the Age of Reason, was only one possible alternative in terms of that thought. Moreover, the justification for a ruler resided no longer in a religious or historical sanction, but simply in his ability to get the job done.

It is a truism, however, that history does not stand still, in the West any more than in Russia. While the empire of the tsars was following the path and the logic of European Enlightenment, that Enlightenment itself was changing. Not only was radicalism increasing, a disturbing development for an autocracy such as Russia, but stranger transformations were revealing themselves, as if forces pent up by eighteenth-century reason were finally breaking into the open. Fashionable literature, as much as Rousseau's philosophy—and, of course, the two cannot be entirely separated—oozed with sensitivity and emotion. Pseudoscientific and occult teachings of all sorts were becoming the rage of emancipated minds.[1] In some important ways the Enlightenment was going full circle.

The Russians, of course, trod the same curving line, attuned more than ever to developments in the West. In 1792 Nicholas Karamzin's *Poor Liza* marked the triumph of sentimentalism in Russian literature, with many writers eager to imitate its newly celebrated author. Tears and sighs bid to replace satire as the order of the day. Many varied, complex, and conflicting trends of the late eighteenth century found particular expression in Russian Freemasonry. Freemasonry came to Russia from Great Britain, Germany, Sweden, and France. Although the first fraternal lodges appeared at the time of Empress Elizabeth, the movement became prominent only in the reign of Catherine the Great. Then it consisted of about one hundred lodges located in St. Petersburg, Moscow, and some provincial towns, and of approximately 2,500 members, almost entirely from the gentry. In addition to the contribution made by Freemasonry

---

[1] On new rages see, for instance, R. Darnton, *Mesmerism and the End of the Enlightenment in France*, Cambridge, Mass., 1968. Auguste Viatte's two volumes remain a rich and suggestive account of occult trends in the late Enlightenment and their evolution in the early nineteenth century: A. Viatte, *Les Sources occultes du romantisme: illuminisme-théosophie, 1770–1820*, Paris, 1928.

to the life of polite society, specialists distinguish two main trends within that movement in eighteenth-century Russia: the mystical, and the ethical and social. The first concentrated on such elusive and essentially individual goals as contemplation and self-perfection. Rather than simply following reason, its devotees sought 'true knowledge', 'the awakening of the heart', or 'the inner essence of man'. The second reached out to the world and thus constituted the active wing of the movement. It was the socially oriented Freemasons centring around the University of Moscow and led by Novikov who engaged in education and publishing on a large scale, establishing private schools and the first major programme of publication in Russia outside of the government. But it is wrong to contrast the two groups too sharply, or to argue, for example, that Novikov cleverly utilized his addle-brained colleagues in the interests of the Age of Reason. The genius of the time was to combine, not to separate, the two approaches.

New developments in the late Enlightenment involved shifts in position on the part of many Russian intellectuals as well as generational conflicts. Soviet scholars have deplored a decline in radicalism and in political interest in general. Critics were becoming moralists or even mystics. Self-improvement was rapidly gaining adherents as a substitute for social change. The new generation did not have the simple belief in reason of the old. This view is well supported. Yet, to suggest the complexity of the period, one might cite a different example of generational misunderstanding and criticism, with radicalism this time on the side of the new generation, not the old. Catherine the Great noted on the margin of Radishchev's *Journey from Petersburg to Moscow*: 'The author says: Enquire of your heart; it is good. What it commands, that you should perform. And he tells us not to follow our reason.—This proposal can scarcely be reliable!'[1]

The Bastille was stormed on the fourteenth of July 1789. The ensuing French Revolution provided a climax to the Enlightenment such as few ideologies, or periods, could claim. Many theories suddenly became exhilaratingly—or terrifyingly— real. In France itself, the Revolution, practice and theory, became constantly more radical until the fall of Robespierre

[1] Lang, op. cit., p. 186.

and the end of Terror in 1794. Elsewhere the governments and gradually the educated publics too began to rally against the French Revolution and everything it stood for.

Educated Russians shared with other Europeans the excitement of the French Revolution. The calling of the Estates General received the approval of Catherine the Great herself, who liked to believe that the French were belatedly following the lead of her *Instruction*. Many of her subjects applauded the early developments in Paris. In fact, this Russian support of the Revolution lasted, apparently, for an extensive period of time. 'The news of the adoption by the National Assembly of the Constitution of 1791, which put an end to absolutism in France, received in Russia the approval of a considerable part of Russian society.'[1] It was only the fall of Louis XVI in August 1792, the proclamation of a republic, and the execution of the king on 21 January 1793 that led to an almost uniformly adverse reaction in Russia. Over a sequence of years, some prominent Russian intellectuals, like their counterparts in Germany, England, and elsewhere, experienced under the impact of the French Revolution a major shift of position from the Left to the Right. Karamzin might serve here as the leading, but by no means isolated, example.

The government, for its part, did not wait: Catherine the Great's early sympathetic interest in the developments in France was replaced by worry, fear, and rage. A feeling of betrayal by the spirit of the age probably added to her violent and tangled emotions. It was after the outbreak of the French Revolution that, in a travesty of justice, Radishchev was sentenced to death for his inopportune *Journey from Petersburg to Moscow*—although the sentence was commuted to Siberian exile—that Novikov and his fellow Masons also suffered, that edicts against travel and other contacts with the revolutionary West appeared in profusion. Catherine the Great broke diplomatic relations with France after the execution of Louis XVI, and, but for her death, might have joined a military coalition against that revolutionary country. The unexpected death of the empress in November 1796, following a stroke, gave the crown finally to her son Paul, whom Catherine had for decades

[1] M. M. Shtrange, *Russkoe obshchestvo i frantsuzskaia revoliutsiia 1789–1794 gg.*, Moscow, 1956, p. 182.

successfully kept away from the throne. While Paul too believed in enlightened despotism, represented by such rulers as
Peter the Great and Frederick the Great, his emphasis was
entirely on the prerogatives and power of the autocrat.[1]
Moreover, in practice Paul's reign quickly developed into a
devastating, and even insupportable, petty tyranny.

It is appropriate to end a chapter on the Russian Enlighten-
ment with the French Revolution having run its tragic course,
Paul I occupying the throne of the tsars, Russian armies
marching with their allies to restore legitimacy and order in
Europe, and the Russian educated public terrified by the
French assault on the sovereign and the upper classes alike, in
fact on the entire *ancien régime*. Yet the outlook of the Age of
Reason had such strength and pertinence in Russia that it was
to stage a full come-back, giving the Petrine empire a second
Enlightenment, or a post-Enlightenment, if you will, in the
reign of Alexander I.

[1] For the preliminary results of Roderick E. McGrew's full study of Paul I's
ideology see 'A Political Portrait of Paul I from the Austrian and English Diplomatic Archives', *Jahrbücher für Geschichte Osteuropas*, Dec. 1970, pp. 503–29.

2

The Reign of Alexander I, 1801–1825

> *'The opinions and sentiments which had seemed to me so admirable in Alexander when he was Grand-Duke did not change when he became Emperor; they were somewhat modified by the possession of absolute power, but they remained the foundation of all his principles and thoughts. They were for many years like a secret passion which one dares not acknowledge before a world incapable of comprehending it, but which constantly dominates us and colours our actions whenever its influence can make itself felt.'*
>
> Czartoryski[1]

THE death of Paul and the accession of Alexander to the throne struck Russians like a bolt from the blue just when the oppression and terror of Paul's reign seemed to have reached the zenith. As one eye-witness who hurried to his Moscow home at the news described the general reaction:

I ran more than I walked; still, I looked attentively at all the people I came across, those in simple peasant coats as well as the well-dressed ones. It was noticeable that the important news had been carried to all parts of the city and was no longer a secret for the most common people. This is one of those recollections which time can never destroy: mute, general joy illumined by the bright spring sun. Having returned home, I could not at all find out the facts: acquaintances constantly came and went, all talked at the same time, all embraced as on Easter Sunday; not a word about the departed in order not to dim even for a moment the heartfelt joy,

---

[1] A. Gielgud, ed., *Memoirs of Prince Adam Czartoryski and His Correspondence with Alexander I*, London, 1888, i. 256.

which shone in all the eyes; not a word about the past, only about the present and the future.[1]

Thus was inaugurated, to cite Pushkin's winged phrase, 'the beautiful beginning of the days of Alexander'. While Derzhavin, who had a true sense of poetic balance, wrote of a silencing of the North Wind and of a closing of 'a threatening, frightening orb', most poets and poetasters simply dissolved in ecstasy and expectation at the coming of Alexander. Nothing about the immediate past, only about the present and the future. One specialist counted over fifty published poems glorifying Alexander I's accession to the throne, declared that 'the number of those remaining in manuscript cannot be totalled', and reproduced opinions of contemporaries to the effect that no other inauguration inspired so much poetry and that, intoxicated by the event, even people hitherto 'entirely foreign to literature' composed poems.[2] Bad poetry and other signs of the joy of the educated public told an important story. They welcomed the return of Enlightenment to Russia after the tensions and persecutions of the last years of Catherine the Great's reign and unmitigated oppression under Paul. Indeed, as extravagantly as in any fairy tale, Prince Charming himself replaced the tyrannical monster on the Russian throne. The monolithic unity of the government and the educated public in Russia was probably never stronger, nor the belief in Enlightenment and enlightened despotism firmer, than in the remarkable year 1801.

The early measures of the reign fed this general euphoria.

After all, the new tsar declared that, promoting zealously the 'inviolable felicity' of all his subjects, he intended to rule following the guidance of 'the action of law alone'. After all, in the first days of the reign he freed from prison and returned from exile some 500 human beings who fell victim at the time of Catherine and Paul (A. N. Radishchev was among those fully amnestied), while the total number of persons who according to the ukase of 15 March 1801 recovered their service and civil rights, extended to twelve thousand.

---

[1] F. F. Vigel, *Zapiski*, Part I, Moscow, 1891, pp. 177–8. The Easter Sunday theme is repeated in, e.g., Karamzin: R. Pipes, *Karamzin's Memoir on Ancient and Modern Russia: A Translation and Analysis*, New York, 1966, p. 136. 'In houses and on the streets people cried with joy and embraced one another as on Easter Sunday.'

[2] A. V. Predtechenskii, *Ocherki obshchestvenno-politicheskoi istorii Rossii v pervoi chetverti XIX veka*, Moscow–Leningrad, 1957, pp. 64–5.

After all, one after another there appeared the tsar's ukases, from which it could be concluded that the government had taken the liberal road in politics: on 15 March, the escapees hiding abroad were amnestied; on 16 March, the prohibition against importing goods from abroad was lifted; on 19 March, there followed the ukase that the police must not cause 'injuries and oppressions'; on 22 March, those travelling into Russia and out of Russia were permitted freely to cross the border; on 31 March, the prohibition against importing books into Russia from abroad was repealed, and it was permitted 'to unseal' private printing establishments; on 2 April, the Secret Expedition was abolished, and it was stated in the ukase that 'in a well-organized state all crimes must be encompassed, judged and punished by the general power of law'; on 28 May, it was forbidden to announce in the press the sale of human beings without land; on 5 June, the creation of a Commission to formulate laws was proclaimed, and so on.[1]

But eliminating the worst excesses of Paul's reign or prohibiting press announcements of sales of serfs without land while these sales continued, could at best supply an introduction to a programme of Enlightenment, of rational, liberal reform. It remained to be seen what the new government was really going to do. Moreover, whereas both Alexander I with his associates and the educated public were considering this crucial issue within the framework of the thought of the Enlightenment, that framework itself was experiencing change, both in general and specifically with regard to Russia.

Of course, much in the second Russian Enlightenment stayed, or appeared to stay, as before. The optimism and the enthusiasm, so characteristic of the Age of Reason, not only returned to Russia after the death of Paul I, but made 1801 their banner year. The passion for education, central to the eighteenth century in all of Europe, found its logical Russian culmination in the reign of Alexander I. Caustic criticism of the established order in Russia and a faith in rational progress were as characteristic of the new emperor and his advisers as of his illustrious grandmother. And yet things had also changed. Most importantly, a hundred years after Peter the Great it was no longer possible to satisfy the requirements of the age and indeed to win its plaudits merely by opening Russia to the West and by championing Western ideas and ideals. The

[1] Vl. Orlov, *Russkie prosvetiteli 1790–1800-kh godov*, 2nd edn., Moscow, 1953, p. 227.

problem of the Russian performance, the extent to which Russia, government, society, and people in fact measured up to the principles of the Enlightenment could not be indefinitely ignored. Furthermore, with the French Revolution much of Europe was set in motion, politically, socially, and economically, and in contrast to the earlier decades of the century, it was now Russia that appeared to be standing still. Back in 1785, Catherine the Great had become enraged when, after purchasing and obtaining Diderot's library, she had found the following comment on her *Instruction* by her erstwhile admirer: 'Everything that you say here is so beautiful; why is it then that you do the opposite?'[1] The significance of Diderot's pointed question grew with the years. Just and firm laws, civil rights, and general happiness have never been easy to translate from theory into practice, least of all in a country still dominated by serfdom. If Alexander I had a chance to bring Russian reality markedly closer to his ideal vision, it was a difficult, late, and perhaps last chance.

To complicate matters further, enlightened despotism itself did not look quite the same in the early nineteenth century as in the eighteenth. On the one hand, the first years of Alexander's reign probably witnessed its greatest sway over educated Russians. The charming and liberal new emperor was all things to all men, and the promise of his rule seemed almost infinite. The French Revolution, by terrifying all but the most radical in Russia, served to emphasize the advantages of legitimate progress. Yet, on the other hand, Europe had changed irreversibly since 1789. Where Peter the Great built his state on the model of the more efficient contemporary European monarchies, and Catherine the Great liked to contrast her own liberalism with the restrictive measures of the French government, Alexander's immutable autocracy tended to suggest Turkey rather than the transformed and transforming polities of the West. If enlightened despotism still had relevance to Russia and the Russian future, the hour, once again, was late.

In addition to the rising hostile forces on the outside, there was corruption within the gates. The late Enlightenment in

---

[1] Quoted from W. F. Reddaway, ed., *Documents of Catherine the Great: The Correspondence with Voltaire and the 'Instruction' of 1767 in the English Text of 1768*, Cambridge, 1931, p. 327.

Europe had a strikingly radical tone, and the educated Russians of the early nineteenth century had been brought up on that Enlightenment in theory as well as on the French Revolution and its aftermath in practice. Scholars who minimize this development on the ground that Western radicalism simply did not apply to Russia take too pragmatic a view of human thought and human aspirations. Even arguments about the precise meanings of Russian terms can be misleading, because much of the discussion was carried on in French. Alexander I was representative of his generation. While Peter the Great was never troubled by the despotic nature of his power, and Catherine the Great exercised that same power firmly and skilfully, albeit paying extensive lip-service to the more liberal ideas of the Age of Reason, Alexander I was not certain how Russia should be governed. Although he remained an autocrat, he was to return time and again to the concept, and hopes, of a constitution. Not only constitutionalism in general but even republicanism found support among Russians nurtured by the late Enlightenment. Characteristically, the supporters included not only many of the Decembrists but also, in an abstract sense, the emperor himself in his youth and the leading conservative ideologist and historian, as Karamzin became in the new reign.[1]

Alexander I was twenty-three-years-old when he ascended the Russian throne. His personality and manner of dealing with men had thus already been formed, and it is the psychology of the emperor that has fascinated those who became acquainted with him, both his contemporaries and later scholars. Moreover, there seems to be little agreement about Alexander I beyond the assertion that he was the most complex and most elusive figure among the emperors of Russia. This unusual sovereign has been called 'the enigmatic tsar', a sphinx, and 'crowned Hamlet'. Striking contradictions or alleged contradictions appear in the autocrat's character and activities. Thus Alexander I was hailed as a liberal by many men, Thomas Jefferson

---

[1] Karamzin believed that the republican form of government was the best, but, because it depended on the virtue of the citizens, it was frequently impracticable, certainly so in Russia. See especially R. Pipes, 'Karamzin's Conception of the Monarchy', *Harvard Slavic Studies*, vol. iv (1957), pp. 35–58; and Pipe's discussion of Karamzin's political ideas in *Karamzin's Memoir on Ancient and Modern Russia*, esp. p. 90.

among them, and denounced as a reactionary by numerous others, including Byron. He was glorified as a pacifist, the originator of the Holy Alliance, and in general a man who did his utmost to establish peace and a Christian brotherhood on earth. Yet this 'angel'—an epithet frequently applied to Alexander I, especially within the imperial family and in court circles—was also a drill sergeant and a parade-ground enthusiast, given to uncontrollable rages over military trifles. Some students of Alexander I's foreign policy have concluded that the tsar was a magnificent and extremely shrewd diplomat, who consistently bested Napoleon. Napoleon himself, it might be added, called him 'a cunning Byzantine'. But other scholars, again on good evidence, have emphasized the Russian ruler's mysticism, his growing detachment from reality, even hinting at madness.

Various elements in the emperor's background have been cited to help account for his baffling character. There was, to begin with, Alexander's difficult childhood and boyhood, in particular his ambiguous relations with his father, Paul, and his grandmother, Catherine the Great, who hated each other. Alexander spent more time with Catherine than with his parents, and he learned early the arts of flattery, dissimulation, and hypocrisy, or at least so his boyhood letters indicate. He also developed a penchant for secrecy. The empress took a great liking to Alexander from the very beginning and apparently wanted to make him her successor, bypassing Paul. Quite possibly only the suddenness of her death upset this plan. Moreover, Catherine the Great took a personal interest in Alexander's education, which was guided by the ideas of the Enlightenment. A prominent Swiss philosopher and liberal, Frédéric-César de La Harpe, acted as the grand duke's chief tutor and became his close friend. Through La Harpe and the Catherinian court in general the future monarch grew a devoted disciple of the Age of Reason. By contrast, he learned relatively little about Russia. La Harpe, that 'very liberal and garrulous French booklet', as Kliuchevskii described the tutor, and his teaching had little in common with Russian reality. The contrast between theory and practice characteristic of Alexander I's reign has been attributed by some scholars to this one-sided education. The circumstances of Alexander I's accession to the throne have also been analysed for their effect on his character and rule. Alexander found himself in a precarious position during Paul's reign, especially because Paul thought of divorcing his wife and of disinheriting Alexander and his other sons by her. The young grand duke almost certainly knew of the conspiracy against his father, but the murder of Emperor Paul came to him apparently as a surprise and a shock. Certain critics attribute to the tragic circumstances of his accession Alexander I's strong feeling of guilt and his later mysticism and lack of balance.

Behind Alexander I's reactions to particular incidents and situations of his life there was, of course, his basic character. He remains a mystery in the sense that human personality cannot be fully explained. Yet his psychological type is not especially uncommon. The emperor belonged with those exceedingly sensitive, charming, and restless men and women whose lives display a constant irritation, search, and disappointment. They lack balance, consistency, and firmness of purpose. They are contradictory. Alexander I's inability to come to terms with himself and pursue a steady course explains his actions much better, on the whole, than do allegations of cynicism or Machiavellianism. As is characteristic for the type, personal problems grew with the passage of time: the emperor became more and more irritable, tired, and suspicious of people, more dissatisfied with life, more frantic in his search of a religious or mystical answer; he even lost some of his proverbial charm. He died in 1825, only forty-eight years old, possibly a suicide.

But death, and the Decembrists, were not on the immediate agenda when the young emperor ascended the throne. Following the welcome initial measures of his reign, Alexander I established in June 1801 the so-called Unofficial Committee of young advisers to consider fundamental reform. These advisers, all of whom shared with their sovereign progressive views of the age related to the late Enlightenment and the French Revolution, were Nicholas Novosiltsev, Count Paul Stroganov, Count Victor Kochubei, and a Polish patriot Prince Adam Czartoryski. La Harpe, who was at the time very close both to the emperor and to his friends, has occasionally been presented as, in effect, another member of the Committee. Novosiltsev and especially Stroganov had even spent some time in revolutionary Paris and could claim the Jacobin Gilbert Romme as their personal tutor. Czartoryski, a Pole, came from a somewhat different background and invariably concentrated much of his attention on his native land; yet he too responded fully in his own way to the liberal spirit of the age and was to be associated with the Polish constitution of 1815. Least is known about the precise opinions of Kochubei, but apparently he blended naturally with the group. The members of the Unofficial Committee reflected in a striking manner the abstract rationalism and the optimism of the Age of Reason. For years they had been talking and writing of civil rights and constitutions and of their speedy introduction to transform societies. Enthusiasm ran rampant. Yet, like their young emperor, these youthful advisers stood far from Russian reality. It is noteworthy that, with the partial exception of Stroganov, there is no record of their having considered prior to 1801 the issue of serfdom, or any other major Russian social issues for that matter. More pragmatic, if more conservative, were the older representatives of what has been described as 'the Senate party' whom the new monarch had asked to deliberate on the nature and functions of the Senate. They suggested an aristocratic constitution based on a greatly strengthened elected Senate with the right of remonstrance and some limitation on the power of the autocrat. But this approach promised a narrow gentry oligarchy rather than a fulfilment of the Age of Reason. The Unofficial Committee was in a political impasse from the start.

In the last analysis, it is not really surprising that, avoiding the difficult and divisive problem of constitutionalism, Alexander I and his associates turned for major achievement to another area of activity, so very prominent in the Enlightenment, education. It was during the first years of the reign that they scored their greatest successes in that area. With the creation of the Ministry of Education in 1802, the empire was divided into six educational regions, each headed by a curator. The plan called for a university in every region, a secondary school in every provincial centre, an improved primary school in every district, and at least one parish school for every two parishes. By the end of the reign the projected expansion of the three upper tiers had been largely completed: Russia then possessed six universities, forty-eight secondary state schools, and 337 improved primary schools. Besides, French *émigrés* escaping the Revolution, as well as the Jesuits who were active in Russia between 1796 and their expulsion in December 1815, also contributed to the education of the country through a few select boarding schools, private tutoring, and their general influence in polite society. Shortly after his accession to the throne, Alexander I founded universities in Kazan, Kharkov, and St. Petersburg—the latter, however, first appeared as a pedagogical institute—transformed 'the main school', or academy, in Vilna into a university, and revived the German university in Dorpat which, with the University of Moscow, made a total of six. In addition, a university existed in the newly acquired Grand Duchy of Finland: originally in Abo—called Turku in Finnish—and from 1827 in Helsingfors, or Helsinki. Following a traditional European pattern, Russian universities enjoyed a broad measure of autonomy. While university enrolments, except for the University of Moscow, numbered usually a few hundred or less each, and while the total of secondary school students rose to only about 5,500 by 1825, these figures represented undeniable progress for Russia.

Moreover, private philanthropy emerged to supplement the government efforts. It played an important part in the creation of the University of Kharkov, and it established two private institutions of higher education which were eventually to become the Demidov Law School in Iaroslavl and the Historico-Philological Institute of Prince Bezborodko in Nezhin. Karamzin's *Messenger of Europe* insisted that even modestly situated members of the gentry were to make their contribution to the spreading of education in their native land. They could provide scholarships for impecunious students training in the new institutions of higher learning to become teachers throughout the length and breadth of Russia. 'Each would be concerned with his particular protégé and would be proud of his achievement. The support of a student costs about 150 rubles a year: what other pleasure can be purchased so cheaply?'[1]

---

[1] Ts. Ts., 'O vernom sposobe imet v Rossii dovolno uchitelei', *Vestnik Evropy*, No. 8 (Apr. 1803), p. 325. My suggestion that the government turned to education partly to avoid, implicitly, political issues, finds an explicit parallel in this article so far as the educated public was concerned. The Russian gentry was to support poor students instead of seeking 'institutions of general utility' and 'inventing plans'—

The educational policy of the first years of Alexander's reign came as a culmination of the thought and efforts of the Russian Enlightenment, and it was received as such by at least some of the Russian educated public. To quote from *The Messenger of Europe* in 1803:

On January 24, Alexander's august hand signed the immortal ukase concerning the establishment of new schools and the spreading of learning in Russia. This fortunate emperor—for doing good to millions is the greatest blessedness on earth—solemnly called popular education an important part of the state system dear to *his* heart. Many sovereigns had the glory of patronizing learning and talents; but probably no one issued such a thorough, all-encompassing plan of popular education as the one of which Russia can now be proud. *Peter* the Great established the first Academy in our fatherland, Elizabeth the first university, the Great *Catherine* town schools, but *Alexander*, multiplying universities and secondary schools, says in addition: *let there be light also in the huts!* A new, great epoch is beginning henceforth in the history of the moral formation of Russia which is the root of state glory and without which the most brilliant reigns represent only the personal glory of the monarchs, not of the fatherland, not of the people. Russia, strong and fortunate in many respects, remained abased by a just envy, seeing the triumph of enlightenment in other countries and its weak, unsteady flicker in the vast Russian lands. Romans, already conquerors of the world, were still despised for their ignorance by Greeks, and not by might, not by victories, but only through learning could they escape at last the name of barbarians.

The name of *Peter* and of *Catherine* will for ever shine at the head of the history of reason and enlightenment in Russia; but what they could not accomplish, that is being done by Alexander, who has the happiness of reigning after them, and in the nineteenth century. Heaven left for *him* the glory and the opportunity of crowning their immortal work.

Let us anticipate the voice of posterity, the judgement of the historian and of Europe, which at present is watching Russia with the greatest curiosity; let us say that all our new laws are wise and humane, but that this edict on popular education is the *strongest* proof of the

'Vain labour! Let us leave it to the government to establish and to introduce: let us be content with the honour and the glory of assisting it in its holy intentions' (p. 323). Once Russia was educated, gentry 'projects' and 'inventions' themselves would be more felicitous. On *Vestnik Evropy*, see: A. G. Cross, 'N. M. Karamzin's "Messenger of Europe" (*Vestnik Evropy*), 1802–3', *Forum for Modern Language Studies*, vol. v, No. 1 (Jan. 1969), pp. 1–25.

heavenly goodness of the monarch, who wants *all his* subjects to be grateful, who loves *all* equally, and considers *all* human beings.

The establishment of village schools is incomparably more useful than all the secondary schools, for they are true *popular* institutions, the true foundation of the enlightenment of a state. The subject of their study is *the most important one* in the eyes of the philosopher. Between people who can only read and write and the totally illiterate there is a much greater distance than between the uneducated and the leading metaphysicians of the world. *The history of reason* presents *two* main epochs: the invention of the alphabet and of the printing press; all the others were their consequences.[1]

Paeans to Alexander's educational policy, perhaps especially when they stressed his concern with enlightening the common people—actually, as it turned out, the weakest part of the programme[2]—expressed in a striking manner the thought of the Age of Reason. They also testified to a substantial unity of belief and approach between the new emperor and his enlightened advisers on the one hand and the Russian educated public on the other during the first years of the nineteenth century.

With both government and society active, these years saw a remarkable quickening of a many-sided discussion of education in Russia, following a partial freeze under Paul. It was then that such intellectuals as Alexander Bestuzhev (the father of four Decembrists), Ivan Pnin, Basil Popugaev, Alexander Vostokov, and Ivan Born wrote works like 'Concerning Education', 'An Essay on Enlightenment in Relation to Russia', and 'On the Well-being of Popular Bodies' (Popugaev's treatise included chapters 'About the Influence of Enlightenment on Governing', 'About Popular Enlightenment and Its Results',

---

[1] 'O novom obrazovanii narodnogo prosveshcheniia v Rossii', *Vestnik Evropy*, No. 5 (Mar. 1803), quoted from pp. 49–50, 51, 53, and 56.

[2] Even the original plan called for the central government to finance the upper two tiers of educational institutions, but for the local authorities to provide for the lower two. Eventually least was done for parish schools. To quote the latest historian of Russian education: 'In the first year of Alexander's reign, while his advisers were seriously concerned with the peasant question, educational designs also included the rural masses. Both La Harpe and Maximilian von Klinger, the director of the cadet corps, urged the extension of enlightenment to the villages. When emancipation of the serfs proved impossible except in several minor ways, state instruction for the peasantry was discarded in favor of private, gentry, communal and ecclesiastical enterprise. This meant its effective abandonment.' P. Alston, *Education and the State in Tsarist Russia*, Stanford, 1969, pp. 24–5.

'About the Necessary Connection between Laws and Enlightenment', and 'About Enlightenment and the Personal Worth of
Those Governing'), or addressed the newly founded Free
Society of Lovers of Literature, the Sciences and the Arts on the
same or similar topics. 'Enlightenment is the true purpose of
our life. In achieving it we learn human worth and grandeur.'[1]
The discussion of education by Russian intellectuals followed
the broad current of the Age of Reason and occasionally, as in
Popugaev's insistence on classless, democratic schools, reflected
faithfully the more progressive Western trends. Here again the
range of thought of the educated public paralleled closely
government resources. It was the Jacobin Romme, Stroganov's
and Novosiltsev's tutor, who helped Condorcet draft the school
bill presented to the National Assembly in 1792.

Not only was formal schooling increasing in Russia, but the
Russian public was also becoming better educated in a broader
sense. In particular, it was reading more books. *The Messenger
of Europe* published by Karamzin, himself one of the leading
practitioners and promoters of literature of his age, pointed to
that development with pride at the same time that it was
celebrating Alexander's educational reforms. The article,
'About the Book Trade and the Love for Reading in Russia',
in the May 1802 issue of the journal, began as follows: '25 years
ago there were two bookstores in Moscow which did not sell
even 10,000 roubles worth of books a year. Now there are
twenty, and together they gross annually around 200,000
roubles. How many lovers of reading, then, have been added
in Russia?'[2] After noting the great role of Novikov in the
dissemination of reading matter, the article asserted that it was
unlikely that 'in any land the number of the curious grew as
rapidly as in Russia'.[3] Of course some members of the gentry
still would not subscribe to newspapers, but on the other hand
many from the lower classes did subscribe, even occasionally

---

[1] From Born's speech quoted in Orlov, op. cit., p. 233. Orlov's book provides a
good introduction to these 'Russian enlighteners of the 1790–1800s'; pp. 209–80
deal with the Free Society of Lovers of Literature, the Sciences and the Arts
(Volnoe Obshchestvo Liubitelei Slovesnosti, Nauk i Khudozhestv).

[2] N., 'O knizhnoi torgovle i liubvi ko chteniiu v Rossii', *Vestnik Evropy*, No. 9
(May 1802), p. 57. *Vestnik Evropy* commented on the spread of reading in Russia on
numerous occasions (cf., e.g., 'Pismo k izdateliu' in Part I for 1802, pp. 3–8).

[3] Ibid., p. 58.

a group of illiterates with only one of them able to make out the letters. 'Our book trade cannot as yet be compared to the German, the French or the English; but what is it that one cannot expect in time, given the annual successes of the trade? Bookshops already exist in almost all provincial towns; to every fair the treasures of our literature are brought together with other goods.'[1] Pedlars carried them from village to village. As to the favourite reading, 'I asked many booksellers about that, and all answered without hesitation: "novels!"'[2] But even translated novels represented a step forward. 'The worst novels contain a certain logic and rhetoric: one who reads them will speak better and in a more connected manner than a total ignoramus, who had not opened a book all his life. Besides, novels today are rich in all kinds of knowledge.'[3] Also, on balance, they exercised a moral, rather than an immoral, influence, and nurtured sensitivity and sentiment. 'In a word: it is good that our public reads at least novels!'[4]

If reading novels represented the first step, other Russians were progressing further up the ladder of enlightenment. As a leading writer and intellectual of the age, Prince P. Viazemskii, observed—commenting more specifically, it is true, on the later years of Alexander's reign: 'Contemporary writers, I suppose, have not surpassed their predecessors, but present-day readers are more sensible and more numerous. And that is enough to consider our century superior to earlier times.'[5] Or, in the words of a modern authority: 'The culture of the beginning of the nineteenth century expressed itself with the greatest force not in supreme creations of the human mind, but in a sharp rise of the average level of spiritual life. . . . That which had still appeared natural and normal to their fathers, began in the early nineteenth century to seem shameful to dozens and hundreds of members of the Russian gentry.'[6]

An important accomplishment in its own right, the growth of the Russian educated public and of its concerns made the issue of political and social reform in the empire of the tsars more pressing. Following the disappointment of their early hopes,

[1] N., op. cit., p. 59.   [2] Ibid., p. 60.
[3] Ibid., p. 62.   [4] Ibid., p. 64.
[5] P. A. Viazemskii, *Zapisnye knizhki (1813–1848)*, Moscow, 1963, p. 65.
[6] Iu. M. Lotman, 'Poeziia 1790–1810-kh godov', *Poety 1790–1810-kh godov*, Leningrad, 1971, p. 11.

Alexander I and his friends of the Unofficial Committee, as well as his later assistants, settled down to an essentially conservative approach. The emphasis came to be on law, justice, the *Rechtsstaat*, on a rational, legal organization and procedure to replace arbitrariness in government, rather than on any advanced constitutional schemes. As formulated by a leading Soviet specialist: 'In 1801–1820 Russian autocracy tried to create a new form of monarchy, which would juridically limit absolutism, yet in fact retain the monocratic authority [*edino-lichnuiu vlast*] of the sovereign.'[1] Similarly, the outstanding American scholar of Alexander's reform, Professor Marc Raeff, presented the entire activity of the chief statesman of the reign, Michael Speranskii, as a determined effort to rationalize the administration and establish legality in Russia, not to infringe upon autocracy.[2] Indeed in Speranskii's own words his project was intended merely 'to dress autocratic rule in all, so to speak, external forms of law, while retaining in essence the same power and the same scope for autocracy'.[3]

Nor should partial reform, let alone any opportunity to develop into an authentic *Rechtsstaat*, be minimized in the conditions of Russia in the beginning of the nineteenth century. During the years of the Unofficial Committee, 1801–5, the government not only made major advances in education and even enacted some liberal legislation in regard to serfdom, but it also tried to modernize and improve the administrative machine itself. Thus, the Senate was restored, or perhaps promoted, to a very high position in the state: it was to be the supreme judicial and administrative institution in the empire, and its decrees were to carry the authority of those of the sovereign, who alone could stop their execution. Peter the Great's colleges, which had a chequered and generally unhappy

[1] N. M. Druzhinin, 'Prosveshchennyi absoliutizm v Rossii', *Absoliutizm v Rossii* (*XVII–XVIII vv.*), ed. by N. M. Druzhinin, N. I. Pavlenko, and L. V. Cherepnin, Moscow, 1964, p. 457. On this entire approach, with special reference to 'the Senate party', see the following penetrating study: G. G. Telberg, 'Senat i pravo predstavleniia na Vysochaishie ukazy', *Zhurnal Ministerstva Narodnogo Prosveshcheniia*, New Series, Part XXV (Jan. 1910), pp. 1–56.

[2] See esp. Raeff, *Michael Speransky, Statesman of Imperial Russia, 1772–1839*, The Hague, 1957; and also my review of this in *Journal of Modern History*, vol. xxx (Sept. 1958), pp. 291–2.

[3] Speranskii to Alexander I in 1809; quoted from N. P. Eroshkin, *Istoriia gosudarstvennykh uchrezhdenii dorevoliutsionnoi Rossii*, Moscow, 1968, p. 150.

history in the eighteenth century, were gradually replaced in 1802 and subsequent years by ministries, with a single minister in charge of each. At first there were eight: the ministries of war, navy, foreign affairs, justice, interior, finance, commerce, and education. Later the ministry of commerce was abolished, and the ministry of police appeared.

The second period of reform in Alexander I's reign, 1807–12, corresponded to the French alliance and was dominated by the emperor's most remarkable assistant, Michael Speranskii. Speranskii, who lived from 1772 to 1839, was a fully self-made man. In contrast to the members of the Unofficial Committee as well as to most other associates of the sovereign, he came not from the aristocracy but from poor village clergy. It was Speranskii's intelligence, ability to work, and outstanding administrative capacity that made him for a time Alexander I's prime minister in fact, if not in name, for no such formal office then existed. Brought up through the bureaucracy, Speranskii was much more realistic and practical than the dilettanti of the Unofficial Committee. At the same time, proficient in languages and a man of great learning, he absorbed and reflected exceptionally well the theory and practice of government in Napoleonic Europe. In Speranskii the *esprit de système* of the Age of Reason found its best Russian representative.

Yet only partial reforms were enacted. In 1810, on the advice of Speranskii—actually this was the only part of his constitutional plan that the monarch translated into practice—Alexander I created the Council of State modelled on Napoleon's *Conseil d'État*, with Speranskii attached to it as the Secretary of State. This body of experts appointed by the sovereign to help him with the legislative work in no way limited the principle of autocracy; moreover, the Council tended to be extremely conservative. Still, it clearly reflected the emphasis on legality, competence, and correct procedure so dear to Speranskii. In the eulogistic words of a British historian:

But from the time when it was instituted, there was a right and a wrong way of conducting government business in Russia; and it is significant that, whereas later all the principal reforms were passed by regular procedure through the Council of State, nearly all the most harmful and most mischievous acts of succeeding governments were, where possible, withdrawn from its competence and passed only as executive regulations which were nominally temporary. Speranskii gave the bureaucracy a conscience, and henceforward it knew when it was not following it.[1]

Speranskii also reorganized the ministries and added two special agencies to the executive, one for the supervision of government finance, the other for the development of transport. A system of annual budgets was instituted, and other financial measures were proposed and in part adopted. Perhaps still more importantly, Speranskii did yeoman's work in strengthening Russian bureaucracy by introducing something in the nature of a civil service examination and trying in other ways to emphasize merit and efficient organisation. The remarkable statesman was not alone in his efforts. It is noteworthy, for example, that the former members of the Unofficial Committee proceeded to occupy a whole series of top government positions, frequently reorganizing and improving departments and functions under their jurisdiction.

Yet, what was accomplished represented only a very small part of what Speranskii had projected for Russia. The scope of his vision can be seen best in the thorough constitutional proposal submitted in 1809 to the emperor at the emperor's request.[2] In his customary methodical manner, the statesman divided the Russians into three categories: the gentry; people of 'the middle condition', that is, merchants, artisans, and peasants or other owners of property of a certain value; and, finally, working people, including serfs, servants, and apprentices. The plan also postulated three kinds of rights: general civil rights; special civil rights, namely exemption from regular service and the right to obtain populated estates; and political rights, which depended on a property qualification. The members of the gentry were to enjoy all the rights. Those belonging to the middle group received general civil rights and political rights when they could meet the property requirement. The working people too obtained general civil rights, but they clearly did not own enough to participate in politics.[3] Russia

---

[1] B. Pares, *A History of Russia*, New York, 1953, p. 308.

[2] 'Plan gosudarstvennogo preobrazovaniia grafa M. M. Speranskogo', *Ulozhenie gosudarstvennykh zakonov 1809 g.*, St. Petersburg, 1905, pp. 1–120.

[3] Literally, article 63 of Speranskii's project defined and apportioned rights as follows: '(1) General civil rights which belong to all subjects. (2) Particular civil

was to be reorganized on four administrative levels: the *volost*—a small unit sometimes translated as 'canton' or 'township'—the district, the province, and the country at large. On each level there were to be the following institutions: legislative assemblies—or *dumy*—culminating in the state *duma* for all of Russia; a system of courts, with the Senate at the apex; and administrative boards, leading eventually to the ministries and the central executive power. The state *duma*, the most intriguing part of Speranskii's system, showed the statesman's caution, for in addition to the property restriction imposed on its electorate, it depended on a sequence of indirect elections. The assemblies of the *volosti* elected the district assemblymen, who elected the provincial assemblymen, who elected the members of the state *duma*, or national assembly. Also the activities of the state *duma* were apparently to be rather narrowly restricted. But, on the other hand, the state *duma* did provide for popular participation in the legislative process. As to Speranskii's entire grandiose structure, it represented, in a sense, a far-sighted outline of the Russian future. Only that future took extremely long to materialize, offering—in the opinion of many specialists—a classic example of too little and too late. Thus Russia received district and provincial self-government by the so-called *zemstvo* reform of 1864, a national legislature, the *Duma*, in 1905–6, and *volost* self-government in 1917.

An emphasis on effective, rational administration, on legality, perhaps even on civil rights, but not on popular participation in government, has been appropriately considered, as already indicated, the hallmark of Speranskii's approach to reform and indeed of the entire approach of those in charge of Russia during the rule of Alexander I. But this leitmotiv did not constitute the entire composition. Throughout Alexander's reign, in contrast, for example, to those of both his predecessor and his successor, true constitutionalism remained a living issue. To repeat, according to the overwhelming testimony of those

rights which are to belong only to those who will be prepared for them by their manner of life and upbringing. (3) Political rights which belong to those who possess property.' See *M. M. Speranskii. Proekty i Zapiski*, Moscow–Leningrad, 1961, p. 186. Speranskii's clever distinctions, notably his postulation of a particular civil right to own populated estates, represented his allowance for Russian reality, in the first place serfdom, which nevertheless remained incompatible at heart with his project.

who knew him, Alexander before his accession to the throne favoured constitutionalism and even spoke of a republic. Czartoryski commented on 'grand ideas of the general good, generous sentiments, and the desire to sacrifice to them part of the Imperial authority, and resign an immense and arbitrary power in order the better to secure the future happiness of the people'.[1] When Alexander became emperor, his first impulse was to translate his ideals into reality, and the members of the Unofficial Committee called to assist the new sovereign shared, as we know, his views and sentiments. After concepts of the Age of Reason proved to be too abstract and Russian conditions intractable, the Sovereign quickly lost his enthusiasm for fundamental change and concentrated on very partial reform. He never gave Russia a constitution. Yet he could never forget constitutionalism either. Time and again the emperor would return with urgency and ardour to constitutional projects only to leave them short of execution, in a peculiar historical display of persistent non-adjusting response.

Although Speranskii might well be considered the outstanding exponent and promoter of the *Rechtsstaat* in Russian history, his great plan was also a constitutional project. With all its limitations, his state *duma* did provide for popular participation in legislation. That, together with his insistence on the division of powers, strict legality, and certain other provisions such as the popular election of judges, if successfully applied, would have in time transformed Russia.

Alexander I's interest in constitutional projects continued during the second, largely reactionary half of his reign. He sponsored the French Charter of 1814. In 1815 the Kingdom of Poland received a constitution, a remarkably liberal document for its time. In March 1818, in a celebrated address to the Polish Diet the emperor spoke of extending the benefits of 'free institutions' to the other parts of his empire. Also in 1818, and in the two following years, Novosiltsev, at the monarch's urging, prepared a constitution for the entire empire.[2] This *Constitutional Charter of the Russian Empire* emphasized very

[1] A. Gielgud, ed., op. cit., i. 324–5.
[2] 'Gosudarstvennaia ustavnaia gramota Rossiiskoi Imperii' was published as an appendix to Shilder's (or Schilder's) standard court history of Alexander I: *Imperator Aleksandr I, ego zhizn i tsarstvovanie*, St. Petersburg, 1898, iv. 499–526. See also G. Vernadsky, *La Charte constitutionelle de l'empire russe de l'an 1820*, Paris, 1933.

heavily the position and authority of the sovereign and bore
strong resemblance to Speranskii's scheme in its stress on
legality and rights and its narrowly based and weak legislative
assembly. In fact, Novosiltsev's project was more conservative
than Speranskii's. Still, it too provided for a legislature, a *sejm*,
with elected members. Novosiltsev differed from Speranskii's
rigorous centralism in allowing something to the federal
principle: he wanted the Russian Empire, including Finland
and Russian Poland, to be divided into twelve large groups of
provinces which were to enjoy a certain autonomy. The emperor
was characteristically enthusiastic about the new plan. As the
writer Viazemskii, who in his official capacity had helped
Novosiltsev draw up the plan, described an audience with the
emperor in a palace study in St. Petersburg, in 1819:

> after the political education which he had given to Poland he turned
> to the political reform which he was preparing for Russia. He said
> that he knew about my participation in the editing of the project
> of the Russian constitution, that he is satisfied with our work, that
> he will take it to Warsaw and pass his critical comments to Novosilt-
> sev, that he hopes without fail to bring this matter to a desired
> conclusion, that at the present time only a shortage of funds, needed
> for such a state measure, is delaying the realization of a thought which
> is to him sacred . . .[1]

The reader is free either to accuse the emperor of hypocrisy or
to lament another instance of financial stringency stunting the
historical evolution of Russia. In fact, Professor George Vernadsky argued, a point contested by Soviet scholars,[2] that Alexander I not only graciously accepted Novosiltsev's project, but
proceeded to implement it in part. He put Alexander Balashov
in charge of five provinces, thus creating as a model one of
the twelve units proposed by Novosiltsev. Certain appropriate
institutional changes in the provinces followed. Only after
Alexander I's death was the experimental unit abandoned, and
the old system of administration fully re-established. Even as he
was leaving in the autumn of 1825 on a journey south, a journey
from which he was not to return alive, the emperor kept talking,

---

[1] Viazemskii, op. cit., p. 148.

[2] For an explicit criticism of Vernadsky's assertion, see Predtechenskii, op. cit.,
pp. 393–4.

notably to Karamzin, about giving 'fundamental laws' to Russia.[1]

In the end, of course, autocracy survived the reign of Alexander I. So did serfdom. In a way, this conformed to a certain historical logic, for throughout the eighteenth century in Russia social consciousness and especially a desire for radical social change lagged behind political thought. If the Russian government and educated public of that age proved their devotion to enlightened despotism, they were at least aware of its rich potentialities and progressive implications, as evidenced both by Catherine the Great's *Instruction* and the contributions of the writers from Feofan Prokopovich through Derzhavin and Karamzin. The emphasis on service to the state, rule of law, and general happiness naturally pointed to political reform, even if nothing is allowed for Rousseau and other radicals who also received a hearing in Russia. By contrast, there was very little fundamental discussion of the social problem. Many students of Russian history have commented on the enormous blind spot which serfdom constituted for educated Russians. Moralizing criticism of the vices and excesses of individual landlords aside, it took Radishchev to challenge the institution of serfdom as such. Others preferred to ignore it, and they included, as we have already seen, both Alexander and his friends of the Unofficial Committee before they were called to direct the destinies of Russia.

Again, however, the nineteenth century was not, could not be, exactly like the eighteenth. The utter incompatibility of serfdom with any kind of enlightened state and society became more obvious than ever. Following the French Revolution even the vestiges of serfdom disappeared in much of western and central Europe, with eastern Europe next in line as the principal battleground for the abolitionists. In Russia, as Semevskii and other specialists have indicated, criticism of serfdom grew apace.[2] The initial impulse of Alexander I and his advisers, especially Stroganov, once they had to face the issue, was to

---

[1] The fullest account of Alexander I's last months, as well as of his life in general, is to be found in Shilder, *Imperator Alexsandr I.*

[2] See especially the classic work in the field: V. I. Semevskii, *Krestianskii vopros v Rossii v XVIII i pervoi polovine XIX veka*, St. Petersburg, 1888. The first volume deals with the eighteenth century and the first quarter of the nineteenth, the second with the reign of Nicholas I.

abolish serfdom. And when they retreated from such a formidable action, the emperor tried at least some partial legislation.

In 1801 the right to own estates was extended from the
gentry to other free Russians. In 1803 the so-called 'law concerning the free agriculturists' went into effect. It provided
for voluntary emancipation of the serfs by their masters,
assuring that the emancipated serfs would be given land and
establishing regulations and courts to secure the observance of
all provisions. The newly emancipated serfs were to receive in
many respects the status of state peasants, but, by contrast with
the latter, they were to enjoy stronger property rights and
exemption from certain obligations. Few landlords, however,
proved eager to free their peasants. To be more exact, under the
provisions of the law concerning the free agriculturists from
the time of its enactment until its suspension more than half
a century later on the eve of 'the great reforms', 384 masters
emancipated 115,734 working male serfs together with their
families. Even these figures overstate, in a sense, general gentry
participation in government action, for the initiative of the law
itself belonged to a single man, Count Serge Rumiantsev, who
also emancipated on particularly liberal terms a considerable
number of his own serfs. It should be added that Druzhinin
and other Soviet scholars have disproved the frequently made
assertion that Alexander I gave no state peasants, with state
lands, into private ownership and serfdom; only such estates
were designated hereditary leases rather than outright gifts.

Indeed, throughout the reign Alexander I's attitude toward
the emancipation of serfs bore a striking resemblance to his
attitude toward constitutional reform. There were the liberal
beliefs, hopes, even promises. Plans and projects appeared and
were given close attention, in the second as well as in the first
half of the reign. In fact, 1820 was a year when the government
seemed to be particularly concerned with serfdom. Time and
again it looked as if the vicious circle of suggested reform and
indecision would be finally broken and fundamental change
introduced. Yet in the end serfdom survived largely intact. In
the appreciative words of Semevskii:

A very favourable circumstance for the solution of the peasant
problem was the fact that emperor Alexander himself desired, as we
know, the liberation of the serfs. In Paris, at Madame de Staël's, he

had given a promise to destroy serfdom. He ordered to pay out from the resources of his chancery 200 *chervontsy* for the making of two medals to be awarded for the best solutions to the problems (concerning the relative advantage of serf and free labour and concerning separating peasants from factory workers) proposed by the Free Economic Society in 1812. He directs Arakcheev and Kankrin to compose projects changing the life of peasants; to him Miloradovich hands N. I. Turgenev's memorandum on that subject; all these projects he carefully gathers later to select everything that is best in them; during his reign the emancipation of the peasants in the Baltic provinces takes place, an emancipation which, although it was to cause later much misery to the emancipated, was based on principles which then seemed to many to be just; finally, he with great firmness stops the granting of inhabited estates into hereditary possession, in spite of the fact that even such enlightened men as Mordvinov wanted the parcelling of all state lands to the most eminent Russian families.[1]

As already indicated, the last point of this intriguing list of accomplishments has been in effect disproved by subsequent research. Several other points refer to schemes never carried out and indeed kept in great secrecy. The one important enacted reform on the list, the emancipation of the serfs in the Baltic provinces, proved to be, as Semevskii noted, a dubious blessing. Because serfs were emancipated without land in Estonia in 1816, in Courland in 1817, and in Livonia in 1819, their general position in certain important ways was made only worse by the reform. As in the case of the Polish constitution, this major change was introduced in a non-Russian part of the empire, while in the historic Russian lands serfdom and autocracy continued to rule in 1825 as in 1801.

A consideration of Alexander I's attitudes toward autocracy and serfdom militates against the traditional sharp division of his reign into the liberal first and the reactionary second halves. As we have seen, no major change was enacted in either half, while projects abounded in both. Still, in certain ways the years 1812–15 did constitute an important divide, with the following period unlike the preceding.

The year 1801 had witnessed the height of Alexander's popularity in Russia, 1815 marked the zenith of his standing in Europe in general and the world. After the epic victory of 1812,

[1] Semevskii, op. cit., i. 482–3.

the Russian emperor pursued Napoleon across the Continent, entered Paris, and, together with his allies, drew up in Vienna a global peace settlement. Throughout the years highlighted by his dramatic relations with Napoleon, Alexander I had attracted the attention, often favourable attention, of European public opinion.[1] Following the defeat of the master of Europe, admiration and enthusiasm for the Russian victor knew almost no bounds. Perhaps shamefully but understandably, the French led the way. It was none other than Rouget de Lisle, the creator of 'La Marseillaise', who eulogized the Russian sovereign, imploring him to 'restore to the Bourbons their throne, to the lilies their splendour'.[2] At its meeting of 21 April 1814 the *Institut de France* expressed its warm gratitude to Alexander I for bringing back to France the fruits of civilization in search of which Peter the Great had once visited their land.[3] There was a proposal to honour the Russian monarch, together with the emperor of Austria and the king of Prussia, on the *colonne Vendôme* and on the *Arc de triomphe de l'Étoile*, and to transform the Madeleine into a church of Saint Louis and Saint Alexander.[4] For a time at least the magic of Alexander appeared to combine power, order, the restoration of legitimate rulers and traditional values with magnanimity displayed in the French settlement, liberalism exemplified by the Polish constitution, and Christian peace and brotherhood proclaimed in the Holy Alliance. Probably few Russians by 1815 could be as unreservedly enthusiastic and optimistic about their emperor as were his

[1] Including French opinion. 'The cult of Alexander was born in Paris at the same time as in St. Petersburg': Charles Corbet, *L'Opinion française face à l'inconnue russe (1799–1894)*, Paris, 1967, p. 57. Corbet's extremely informative book treats Alexander I in separate sections, devoted to French opinion on Russia during the Consulate and the Empire, and during the Restoration. See also, e.g., Éphraim Harpaz, *L'École libérale sous la Restauration: le 'Mercure' et la 'Minerve', 1817–1820*, Geneva, 1968, pp. 207–9, for a later French evaluation of Alexander's policies. Russia was considered a land of opportunity for enterprising Frenchmen. Around 1802 two theatrical sketches on the Paris stage bore the same title: 'Let Us Go to Russia'. As a song in one of them put it, with particular reference to actors:

Allons en Russie.	Let's go to Russia.
On y prise le talent,	They appreciate talent there,
Tout nous y convie,	There everything suits us,
On y paye argent	There they pay solid
Comptant.	Money.

Corbet, op. cit., p. 60.

[2] Ibid., p. 95.   [3] Ibid.   [4] Ibid., n. 1.

Western admirers. Yet in Russia too, perhaps in Russia especially, the struggle against Napoleon constituted a deep experience and made many members of the educated public think of a renewal and of advancing, not of a return to the past. Although the Unofficial Committee had failed to transform Russia, and although Speranskii had been dismissed, there again seemed to be every opportunity for reform, with the Russian position in the world stunningly powerful and secure. Alexander was offered a second, or was it a third, chance.

That he never took advantage of that chance has been subject to different explanations. Some specialists have stressed the very success and importance of the Russian emperor in international relations as distracting him from home affairs and directing his mind and effort along other channels. Even physically he came often to be absent from his native land. Furthermore, international politics became increasingly complicated, demanding, and disappointing. As at home Alexander promised too much to too many men, and he obviously could not keep all the promises. Specialists have tried hard to trace his manœuvring between legitimism and liberalism, reaction and revolution, around or under the influence of Metternich. His problems were not unrelated to his predicament inside Russia. To quote the conclusion of a recent study of the foreign ministers of the emperor: 'They all were caught in the unreconciled dilemma between Alexander's enlightened aims, with which they had to sympathize to succeed, and his fundamental quest for peace and social stability—in whose interest he might pursue the most despotic conduct—to which they had to be willing to submit.'[1]

Many scholars have pointed also to the emperor's growing spiritual search, a kind of mysticism, and detachment from reality as affecting in an important, perhaps decisive, manner the policies of the second half of his reign. Again personal predilections combined intricately with the mood of a generation. That Alexander I lacked stability and that he was in constant quest of reassurance and security was evident throughout his life. In particular, much to the embarrassment of the

---

[1] Patricia Kennedy Grimsted, *The Foreign Ministers of Alexander I: Political Attitudes and the Conduct of Russian Diplomacy, 1801–1825*, Berkeley and Los Angeles, 1969, p. 303.

Orthodox establishment, he kept being attracted to sectarian religious groups, such as the Quakers, as well as to individual prophets and especially prophetesses.[1] After the defeat of Napoleon, the emperor's own mood of mystical, or quasi-mystical, elation found great resonance in the general European upsurge of religion and religiosity, mysticism, pseudo-mysticism and occultism of all sorts, which became prominent, as indicated in the preceding chapter, in the late Enlightenment and rose to what was probably its zenith around 1815. Uniquely placed in Europe and the world, Alexander, additionally inspired by such extravagant admirers as Baroness Julie de Krüdener,[2] could develop even Messianic thoughts, while his language and manner baffled at times his more prosaic assistants or observers. No wonder that the declaration of the Holy Alliance which issued from that mood was described by Castlereagh as 'a piece of sublime mysticism and nonsense'.[3] But Alexander I's spiritual orientation, supported by certain currents of the time, affected the domestic as well as the foreign policy of the second half of his reign. It enabled the Bible Society to spread its activities in Russia, and such men as Prince Alexander Golitsyn, Michael Magnitskii, and Dmitrii Runich to engage in an obscurantist purge of Russian education, most notably of several universities. By contrast, it militated against all liberal reform.

Preoccupied with foreign policy or given to mysticism, the once enthusiastic emperor continually neglected Russian affairs. In fact, discouragement and neglect have themselves been adduced as the primary explanation of Alexander I's treatment of domestic matters during the second half of his reign. This attitude also enhanced the importance of the monarch's chief assistants. While Speranskii was Alexander I's outstanding associate in the first half of the reign, General Alexis Arakcheev came to occupy that position in the second

[1] Prophetesses consulted by the Russian sovereign are still being discovered by such careful researchers as Professor G. de Bertier de Sauvigny. (See his article on Madame La Bouche in *Le Figaro littéraire*, 10 Dec. 1960, pp. 5–6.)

[2] On this, the most celebrated of Alexander's prophetesses, see, e.g., E. J. Knapton, *The Lady of the Holy Alliance, The Life of Julie de Krüdener*, New York, 1939. Knapton's book has the virtue of understatement where exaggeration is common.

[3] I am quoting this very well-known phrase from Harold Nicolson, *The Congress of Vienna. A Study in Allied Unity: 1812–1822*, London, 1946, p. 253.

half—and the difference between the two men tells us much about the course of Russian history in the first quarter of the nineteenth century. Arakcheev, who had been a faithful servant of Paul, was brutal, rude, and a martinet of the worst sort. He became Alexander's minister of war and eventually prime minister, without the title, reporting to the sovereign on almost everything of importance in the internal affairs of Russia and entrusted with every kind of responsibility. Yet the rather common image of the evil genius Arakcheev imposing his will on the emperor badly distorts the relationship. In fact, it was precisely the general's unquestioning and prompt execution of Alexander's orders that made him indispensable to the monarch who was increasingly peremptory and at the same time had lost interest in the complexities of home affairs.

Although Arakcheev left his imprint on many aspects of Russian life during the second half of Alexander's reign, his name came to be connected especially with the so-called 'military settlements'. That project apparently originated with Alexander, but it was executed by Arakcheev. The basic idea of military settlements was suggested perhaps by certain Turkish or Austrian practices, a book by a French general, or the wonderful precision and order which reigned on Arakcheev's estates—where, among other regulations, every married woman was commanded to bear a child every year—and it had the appeal of simplicity. The idea was to combine military service with farming and thus reduce drastically the cost of the army and enable its men to lead a normal family life. Indeed, in some of their aspects the military settlements could be considered among the emperor's enlightened, humanitarian endeavours. The reform began in 1810, was interrupted by war, and attained its greatest impetus and scope between 1816 and 1821, with about one third of the peace-time Russian army established in military settlements. Troubles and uprisings in the settlements, however, checked their growth. After the rebellion of 1831 Nicholas I turned definitely against the reform, but the last settlements were abolished only much later. Alexander I's and Arakcheev's scheme failed principally because of the extreme regimentation and minute despotism that it entailed, which became unbearable and resulted in revolts and most cruel punishments. In addition—as Professor

Pipes has forcefully pointed out—Russian soldiers proved to be
very poor material for this venture in state direction and
paternalism, resenting even useful sanitary regulations.[1] Whatever the theory of military settlements, their practice produced
disaster.

To sum up, Alexander I's failure to reform Russia, and in
particular to grant his people a constitution and to abolish
serfdom, can be attributed to numerous reasons. To many
scholars psychological, personal factors in the character and life
of 'the enigmatic emperor' loomed large. Time and again
students of the reign have noted his secretiveness and suspiciousness, his lack of firmness and of persistence, his mysticism or his
apathy, his inconclusive playing and replaying of the constitutional and the abolitionist themes only up to a certain point—
like a broken record. Some have argued more bluntly that, the
emperor's theoretical views aside, in practice he was determined
not to part with any of his power, thus dooming constitutional
projects. Poland was the exception that proved the rule, because
Alexander I, in spite of his liberal rhetoric, resented constitutional limitations of his authority in the kingdom and violated
them. And in general he acted throughout his reign like a wilful
tyrant who brooked no contradiction.

There were, certainly, other reasons working against fundamental reform. From the very beginning of the reign Alexander
I and his friends of the Unofficial Committee were apprehensive
of 'the Senate party' and proposals of change emanating from
that direction. A constitution could mean victory for an oligarchy and the end of enlightened policy, in particular with
regard to peasants. A constitution could destroy the prospects
of emancipation. Later the orientation of such gentry groups
as the one around *The Spirit of Journals* (*Dukh Zhurnalov*),
published from 1815 to 1820, confirmed the emperor's suspicions. In the end, Alexander I, of course, chose neither horn of
the dilemma, and thus left the possible implications of a choice
to historical speculation.

Even more important than the problem of division among
possible supporters of reform was the question of their total
strength and of the position of their cause in Russia. From the

---

[1] R. Pipes, 'The Russian Military Colonies, 1810–1831', *Journal of Modern History*, vol. xxii (Sept. 1950), pp. 205–19.

time of Peter the Great, modernizing the country had been the work of a small, although growing, minority. In the early nineteenth century, too, Russia remained overwhelmingly illiterate and generally backward. Moreover, its dominant class, the gentry, had excellent reasons to maintain and protect the *status quo*, especially serfdom. While some liberal historians, such as Professor Michael Karpovich, have taken a sanguine view of the possibilities of fundamental reform in the reign of Alexander I, most specialists have remained unconvinced. Both Russian and non-Russian students of the period have pointed in particular to the backwardness of Russia, to the fact that the country was not prepared to follow the liberal evolution of Western societies. Soviet scholars have also emphasized the fake elements in Alexander I's liberalism, at times treating his entire recourse to the Enlightenment as sheer demagoguery. Even those of them who grant some substance and progressive meaning to the emperor's views and policies are careful to emphasize their basic limitations[1] Autocracy and particularly serfdom could not be destroyed by sentimental talk.

Yet doubt lingers. Although it is extremely likely that most Russian landlords were opposed to the emancipation of the serfs in the reign of Alexander I, it is also likely that they were opposed to it in 1861. As to constitutions, once enacted, they sometimes acquire lives of their own. In the wistful words of a British scholar:

If, during the two centuries which divide the Russia of Peter the Great from the Bolshevik revolution, there was any period in which the spell of the authoritarian past might have been overcome, the forms of the state liberalized in a constitution and the course of Russian development merged with the historic currents of the west, it is the earlier part of the reign of Alexander I. Or so, for a moment, one is tempted to think.[2]

[1] As an example of the more positive Soviet approach, see the interesting article: I. A. Fedosov, 'Prosveshchennyi absoliutizm v Rossii', *Voprosy Istorii*, No. 9 (1970), pp. 34–55. Professor Fedosov argues that in Russian history there were two genuine periods of enlightened despotism, which he defines in terms of a progressive centralization of authority at a certain stage of the evolution of a feudal state: from the 60s to the late 80s of the eighteenth century, and the beginning of the nineteenth century. The first years of Alexander I's reign thus still had a progressive significance, for absolutism had not yet outlived its usefulness for the historical development of Russia, but that usefulness ended by 1815.

[2] R. D. Charques, *A Short History of Russia*, New York, 1956, p. 151.

The Russian educated public celebrated Alexander I's accession to the throne, applauded his educational reforms, and, together with the emperor and his advisers, was thrilled by the prospect of imminent progressive change. Later, under imperial leadership, it played its part in the epic struggle against Napoleon until final victory. It was only after the Congress of Vienna and Waterloo that the paths of the government and of at least the more radical segment of 'society' began perceptibly to diverge. Alexander I, as we have seen, fell into inactivity and reaction, even if he never quite abandoned his hopes of transforming Russia. The radicals responded, in the end, with the Decembrist rebellion. That the close similarity, even virtual identity, of beliefs and interests characteristic of the relationship between the Russian monarchs and their enlightened subjects in the eighteenth century and reaffirmed so strikingly in 1801 and the years following, culminated in an uprising and in executions, has remained a tragedy of Russian history and a challenge to scholars. To explain what occurred, specialists often stress the impact of the Napoleonic wars, of Russian officers becoming acquainted with western Europe, of their nationalism and patriotism, of their determination to bring the benefits of liberalism to their native land. Military *coups*, it has been added, had proved repeatedly successful in post-Petrine Russia and were the style in contemporary Europe, from Spain to Greece. Kliuchevskii and others have written of the last uprising of the guard.[1] Yet even more important than these special considerations was the general nature of the Decembrist generation. 'Because of the time lag between Russian and Western intellectual life, the Decembrists resembled in many ways the generation of Frenchmen that had led the first years of the Revolution.'[2] The Russian Enlightenment was finally bearing its full fruit. Of course, Russia was not France, and one might speculate that something like Speranskii's or Novosiltsev's constitution would have satisfied the Decembrists and marked for a long time the high point of liberalism in Russian history. Of course, Russia was not France, so that when

---

[1] V. Kliuchevskii, *Kurs russkoi istorii*, St. Petersburg, 1911–21, v. (?) 211.
[2] Marc Raeff, *The Decembrist Movement*, Englewood Cliffs, N.J., 1966, p. 22. A thirty-page introduction precedes this useful collection of Decembrist material translated into English.

the government refused to follow the logic of the Enlightenment and the Decembrists insisted on that logic, it was not a sovereign who mounted the scaffold, but Paul Pestel, Conrad Ryleev, Peter Kakhovskii, Michael Bestuzhev-Riumin, and Serge Muraviev-Apostol.

Soviet scholars in particular have insisted on close links between the Decembrists and the Russian educated public at large. The point is well taken provided one emphasizes general liberal beliefs and mood rather than any active opposition to the government. Literature continued to play a leading role in the education of the Russians, 'The cultured society of the beginning of the nineteenth century was permeated with literature through and through. Therefore it is not necessary for us, at least as far as the first decades are concerned, strictly to divide the circles and the *salons* of the period into the literary and the non-literary ones.'[1] Many Decembrists, represented tragically by Ryleev, were themselves men of letters, especially poets, for theirs was a poetic age. All read and heard literature. Answering question seven of the investigation, 'when and from where did you acquire liberal ideas?' Michael Bestuzhev-Riumin listed the tragedies of Voltaire, his study of natural, civil, and Roman law, as well as of political economy, and his interest in Western publicists, then continued: 'At the same time everywhere I heard the verses of Pushkin which were read with enthusiasm. All of this more and more strengthened my liberal opinions.'[2] Pushkin's verses were most apropos as most popular, but liberal poems were written at the time by many prominent and less prominent literary figures, including those who were later to become conservatives. Alexander Griboedov, too, like Pushkin, was very close to the Decembrists, and the Decembrists were in many ways very close to Griboedov. In any case, Chatskii in *Woe from Wit* expresses in a marvellously acid and brilliant manner the critical spirit of the Decembrist generation determined to expose the ramshackle Russian establishment to the annihilating glare of enlightened reason. The Decembrist movement emerged from this liberal and critical literary milieu, the last phase of the Russian Enlightenment. In fact, excising the early Decembrist circles from their

[1] M. Aronson and S. Reiser, *Literaturnye kruzhki i salony*, Leningrad, 1929, p. 24.
[2] Raeff, op. cit., pp. 56–7.

environment gives the movement a somewhat artificial clarity and precision.

The first of the so-called Decembrist societies was formally organized in January 1817 in St. Petersburg. Its members, aristocrats and officers of the guard most of whom had taken an active part in the recent war with Napoleon, were only a handful. They adopted the name of the Union of Salvation for their organization. The activity of the members was limited to discussion and the enrolment of new members, while the purpose of the Union never emerged clearly. Pestel, for one, wanted constitutional government, emancipation of the serfs, and many other reforms. But the average ideal was probably limited to the instructions which called upon each member 'to lead a virtuous life, resist all evil in the state, proclaim abuses of the authorities, find new reliable members and watch the conduct of his fellow-members'.[1] The organization was very formal. Members were divided into three classes: the Boyars, the six founders who elected the Supreme Council; the Elders, later members who were informed of the aims of the society; and the Brethren who were on probation. Awe-inspiring oaths completed the similarity to the Masons and other secret societies. Vague in content and rigid in form, the Union of Salvation could accomplish little. But in 1818 it was reorganized, renamed the Union of Welfare, and effectively reactivated. The Union of Salvation itself, unimportant in its own right, marked nevertheless the first stage in the Decembrist movement and the entrance of such men as Paul Pestel and Nikita Muraviev into Russian history.

The Union of Welfare was closely modelled after the Tugendbund, a national organization of intellectuals set up in Germany in 1808 for the purposes of a moral reawakening of the country and the struggle against Napoleon. It has been noted, however, that whereas a member of the Tugendbund had to emancipate

---

[1] Quoted from A. Mazour, *The First Russian Revolution 1825. The Decembrist Movement: Its Origins, Development and Significance*, Berkeley, Calif., 1937, p. 70. Professor Mazour's book is the only general study of the Decembrist movement in English. In Russian the literature on the subject, both published materials and secondary works, is huge. For a standard Soviet treatment see esp. M. V. Nechkina, *Dvizhenie dekabristov*, Moscow, 1955. For bibliography: N. M. Chentsov, *Vosstanie dekabristov—bibliografiia*, Moscow–Leningrad, 1929; and M. V. Nechkina and R. G. Eimontova, *Dvizhenie dekabristov—ukazatel literatury, 1928–1959*, Moscow, 1960.

his serfs, a member of the Union of Welfare promised merely to treat them humanely; also, in contrast to the German organization, there was no special emphasis on loyalty to the ruling house in the Russian society. The entrance ritual and the formality of the Union of Salvation were abolished. Male sex and moral integrity became the only requirements for membership. The four branches of activity expounded in the Green Book, the constitution of the Union of Welfare, were philanthropy, education, justice, and national economy. Members had to work in one of these fields, to promote hospitals, schools, or insurance companies, depending on their interest. They were to study their fields thoroughly, seek public office, and perform all their duties to the best of their abilities. Indeed, the Union of Welfare hoped in time to suffuse, supervise, and control philanthropy, education, justice, and economic life in Russia, always for their more successful development and the greater good of the country. Actually, the new society acquired two centres, one in St. Petersburg and a more active one in Tulchin, in the Ukraine, the headquarters of the Second Army. Its mainstay remained the liberal military élite.

Although materials from this period of the movement are relatively scarce, specialists have done much to reconstruct the thought of the members of the Union of Welfare during the three years of its existence, 1818–21. Pestel and a number of his colleagues continued to develop more radical views and to concentrate their interest on the actual governance of the country. Following Michael Novikov's lead, Pestel evolved into a determined republican, and he managed not only to assert his republican preference in his southern group but even to impose it upon his St. Petersburg colleagues during a visit to the capital in early 1820. It has been claimed that the Union of Welfare became in effect a subversive, revolutionary organization, that the parts of its constitution and operating procedure dealing with illegal aims and activities simply have not reached us, even that the Green Book was a device to mislead the gullible. There is no evidence for these statements. The Green Book spoke repeatedly and consistently of aiding the government, and there were apparently sincere proposals to submit it for imperial approval, although that step was never taken. Officially at least the view which the Union of Welfare took of its own activity in Russia and of its relationship to the government can perhaps be best seen from the following provision in its constitution.

Any member has the right to organize or be a member of all societies approved by the government, but he must inform the Union of everything that takes place in them and, imperceptibly, he should influence them in the direction of the Union's goals. Members, however, are forbidden to join societies prohibited by the government, because the Union is acting for the good of Russia and, consequently, for the aims of the government and does not wish to subject itself to the latter's suspicion.[1]

Yet even if the Union of Welfare itself essentially remained in the age-old tradition of loyalty to enlightened despotism, it became clear by 1821 that that tradition could not contain many of its members, that the Decembrist movement had to evolve further.

To revitalize the activity of the group and probably to get rid of undesirable members, a general meeting of the Union of Welfare was held in January 1821 in Moscow. The southern centre was represented by two rank-and-file emissaries whose journey to the old capital at the time would not draw suspicion. Officially the Union of Welfare was dissolved at the Moscow Conference; yet in fact its more radical members were to continue their activities, in a more vigorous as well as fully clandestine manner.

As usual, the southerners proved the more active. Before long, the Tulchin centre had two important branches: at Vasilkov headed by Serge Muraviev-Apostol and Michael Bestuzhev-Riumin, and at Kamenka, where Prince Serge Volkonskii and Basil Davydov were the leaders. In 1823 the Vasilkov group came into contact with a secret Polish organization, which had as its aim the independence of Poland. The Southern Society of the Decembrists made an agreement with the Poles, promising Poland independence on several conditions, in return for Polish help in the projected rebellion. The Poles were to arrest and possibly murder Grand Duke Constantine, resident in Warsaw and considered heir to the throne,

---

[1] Raeff, op. cit., p. 77. See Nechkina, op. cit. i. 227–37, for a somewhat tendentious account of the efforts during those years of individual Decembrists to influence the government, notably towards emancipation.

to immobilize the Lithuanian army corps, and to render all other assistance possible to the rebellion. The Poles were to be notified at least two weeks in advance. When the revolts in the north and in the south did occur, their unexpectedness and the general lack of co-ordination prevented any Polish participation.

The Southern Society also came into contact with, and indeed absorbed, a noteworthy Russian organization: the Society of the United Slavs. The United Slavs had been founded in 1817 by two brothers, Andrew and Peter Borisov, and their membership derived from lower and broader strata of society than that of the aristocratic Decembrist organizations proper. In the words of the leading specialist on the United Slavs:

It is possible to sketch four basic types of the Slavs: a lieutenant or generally a military man of a low rank, without land and 'without peasants'; a member of the gentry possessing a paltry estate or some two or three serfs without land; a military man of low rank in retirement, engaged in private service, having found employment with some rich count, also, of course, without land and without peasants; and, finally, a non-gentry employee in a chancery or some other office. Typically, all live from salary.[1]

In consonance with their humbler social background, the United Slavs were closer to the soldiers than were the aristocratic Decembrists proper and, according to doubtful assertions of Soviet scholars, they even showed certain inclinations towards a reliance on the broad masses and the concept of a popular revolution. But their views were not nearly as well developed or formulated as those of the Decembrists, a fact which has contributed to the rather futile controversy concerning the exact nature of their beliefs and the extent and character of their liberalism or radicalism. The United Slavs did possess, however, a few concepts which were peculiarly their own, notably their political goal of a democratic federation of all Slavic peoples, among whom they included even the Hungarians.

The Southern Society absorbed the Society of the United Slavs in part because of the intellectual superiority of the

---

[1] Nechkina, op. cit., ii. 154. I found the best, indeed devastating, critique of Nechkina's views concerning the United Slavs, in particular of her belief that they tended to favour a popular revolution, in Ms. Carol Shelly's paper, 'The Society of the United Slavs: A Re-evaluation', written in 1968 for the seminar of my colleague Professor Martin Malia.

former. Led by Pestel, it acquired a rich, well-formulated, and striking programme which dealt in a confident, indeed dictatorial manner, with the future of Russia. If Speranskii represented best the *esprit de système* of the Age of Reason in the Russian government, Pestel performed that service for the Decembrists. It is Pestel's *Russian Justice* which he and his associates considered of decisive importance for the transformation of their country and which they kept moving from one hiding-place to another —in vain as it turned out—when the investigation and the arrests began, that constitutes, in spite of being incomplete, the main doctrinal legacy of the Decembrist movement.

Russian Justice began with a sociological introduction. Each society has its goal and chooses the methods to achieve it. In each society there are those who command and those who obey; similarly in each state there exist the government and the people. Every right must be based on a corresponding obligation. 'The state organization's true aim must necessarily be: the greatest possible happiness of the greatest number of people in the state.'[1] 'And that is the reason why the Russian people is not the possession or the property of some one person or family; on the contrary, the government is the property of the people and it has been established for the good of the people, and not the people for the good of the government.'[2] The remaining parts of the introduction described the division of functions of the government, the necessity of change for Russia, the importance of *Russian Justice* as the guide for the provisional government, and its content. '*Russian Justice*, therefore, is the Supreme All Russian Charter setting forth all the changes to be made in the state, all the things and rules subject to abrogation and elimination, and lastly, the basic rules and fundamental principles which are to serve as immutable guidelines in establishing the new order of government and in drafting the new Constitution.'[3]

The first and the second chapters of *Russian Justice* dealt with the territorial and ethnic composition and organization of Russia. Two principles were crucial in a consideration of this issue: the principle of nationality and the principle of conveni-

---

[1] Raeff, op. cit., p. 127.   [2] Ibid., p. 128.

[3] Ibid., p. 131. Raeff prefers *The Russian Law* to *Russian Justice* as translation for *Russkaia Pravda*.

ence. The choice between the right to nationhood and the claims of convenience depended on the political viability of a given ethnic group. 'In this manner, the races which because of their weakness are subject to a larger state and cannot enjoy their own political independence, and consequently must necessarily submit to the power or protection of a large neighboring state, may not invoke the right to nationhood, for in their case it is fictitious and nonexisting.'[1] Therefore, Russia was to absorb 'Finland, Estonia, Livland, Courland, White Russia, the Ukraine, New Russia, Bessarabia, the Crimea, Georgia, the entire Caucasus, the lands of the Kirghiz, all the Siberian peoples'[2] and other ethnic groups which could not enjoy their own independence. It would be best for them 'if, spiritually and institutionally, they unite with a great state and merge their nationality completely with that of the dominant people'.[3] Moreover, 'to establish firmly the security of the state' Russia was to annex Moldavia, some additional territories in the Caucasus, certain lands of the Kirghiz-Kaisak nomadic hordes, and a part of Mongolia, 'so that the entire course of the Amur River, from the Dalai Lake on, belong to Russia'.[4] Russia, however, was not to expand further. The Russian state was, of course, to be one and indivisible. For Russia in particular with its many peoples and cultures, federation would mean weakness, division, and the falling away of territories. 'The Fundamental Law of the Russian state rejects any thought of a federal organization as utterly ruinous and evil.'[5] Only Poland remained outside Pestel's relentless assimilation and centralization. Its size and historic past entitled it to nationhood, and its future was thus to be settled on the basis of nationality rather than that of convenience. Still, Pestel was willing to grant Poland independence only on condition that its political system be organized in the same manner as in Russia and that, again as in reformed Russia, its aristocratic and other estate privileges be abolished.

It was in the third chapter of *Russian Justice* that Pestel turned to Russian society itself. After discussing the estates, their selfish behaviour, and their divisive effect on the nation, he concluded: 'From all that has been said above, it follows

[1] Ibid., p. 134.   [2] Ibid., p. 135.   [3] Ibid., p. 134.
[4] Ibid., p. 136.   [5] Ibid., p. 137.

that the estates must be destroyed, that inside the state all men must form but a single estate which may be called civic estate, and all citizens of the state must have one and the same rights and all be equal before the law.'[1] Serfdom, appropriately, bore the brunt of the heaviest attack:

To own other men in property, to sell, pawn, give away, inherit men like things, to use them according to one's own caprice without their prior consent and exclusively for one's own profit, advantage, and at times whim, is shameful, contrary to humanity, contrary to the laws of nature, contrary to the Holy Christian faith, contrary at last to the will of the Almighty Who has declared in the Scriptures that all men are equal in His eyes and that only their deeds and virtues make for the difference in them. And for this reason there can no longer be in Russia the right for one man to possess and call another his serf. Slavery must be definitely abolished and the nobility must forever, without fail, renounce the vile privilege of owning other men.[2]

Yet as the rambling and even contradictory admonitions in the first draft indicate, Pestel wanted to proceed with caution as well as with 'unmerciful severity against all who violate public peace'.[3] Furthermore: 'Freeing the peasants from slavery should not deprive the nobility of the revenue they receive from their estates.'[4] The miserable household serfs were to be emancipated after either a term of service or a monetary payment. The military colonies were to be liquidated. Merchants and other Russians were to profit from the abolition of guilds and a general unshackling of economic life, with anyone free to engage in any enterprise. Indeed freedom was 'the prime necessity of the national economy'.[5] As to the clergy, Pestel considered it, characteristically, *'part of the government,* and its most respectable part. It is a branch of the state administration, a division of the bureaucracy, and the closer the bond between the clergy and the laity, the happier the nation, the more prosperous the state.'[6]

The fourth chapter, entitled 'Of the Nation from a Political Point of View', contained Pestel's remarkable scheme for the division of land as well as some discussion of citizenship and representative government. The land was to be divided into halves: one to be communally owned and inalienable, thus

---

[1] Raeff, op. cit., pp. 149–50.   [2] Ibid., pp. 150–1.   [3] Ibid., p. 153.
[4] Ibid.   [5] Ibid., p. 151.   [6] Ibid., p. 150.

guaranteeing every member of the commune, and by projection every Russian, a subsistence minimum of land; the other in private ownership with a view to individual initiative and exploitation. In addition, a minimum livelihood was to be assured to every Russian. Russia was to acquire a network of representative institutions and a full political life, affected neither by aristocratic privilege, nor by wealth, but exclusively by the talent and merits of the candidates and the confidence which they inspired in the electorate. 'The fear that the so-called populace will shake the state if it participates in the elections is completely unnecessary and groundless. The populace creates disorders only when it is oppressed or when the rich bribe and agitate it for their own ends.'[1]

The fifth chapter, the last one extant, 'Of the Nation from a Civil Point of View', dealt with a variety of matters such as civil rights, economic arrangements, and even taxation. Russians were to enjoy an unimpeded rule of law and full civil rights, although Orthodoxy was to remain the religion of the state. The government had the responsibility for public education, but parents had the alternative of educating their children privately. Universal military service was established. And it was declared—to remind us again of France—'The right of possession or ownership is sacred and inviolable; it must be established and preserved on the most firm, positive, and indisputable foundations.'[2]

Together with *Russian Justice* one should consider another brief work of Pestel, his *Constitution-State Ordinance*. It contained the specifics of Pestel's projected government organization: a popular assembly with legislative power, an executive body of five men elected for five years, a supreme council of one hundred and twenty which was to supervise the proper constitutional functioning of the state.

The Northern Society of the Decembrists had its own constitution for Russia, composed by Nikita Muraviev. It too abounded in the convictions and sentiments of the Age of Reason: 'All Russians are equal before the law'; 'Serfdom and

[1] Ibid., p. 155.
[2] Raeff omits this passage from his translation and summary. I am quoting from Iu. G. Oksman, *Dekabristy. Sbornik: otryvki iz istochnikov*, Moscow–Leningrad, 1926, p. 176. The full text of *The Russian Justice* is on pp. 135–79.

slavery are abolished. The slave who touches Russian soil becomes free'; 'Everyone has the right freely to express his ideas and feelings and communicate them by way of print to his countrymen'; 'All the existing merchant and craft guilds and corporations are abolished'; 'Every criminal case is tried before a jury'.[1] Most importantly: 'The people is the source of *sovereign power*; to it belongs exclusively the right to make fundamental statutes for itself.'[2] However, in contrast to Pestel, Muraviev favoured a constitutional monarchy, not a republic, with the powers of the emperor similar on the whole to those of the President of the United States. He offered but a beggarly allotment of land to emancipated serfs, and postulated high property qualifications for effective participation in the political process. As K. N. Levin and M. N. Pokrovskii put it, even the lowest landowner would have five hundred times the electoral rights, that is, the electoral weight, of a peasant who had never been a serf, while former serfs would simply be excluded from voting.[3] Pestel himself charged Nikita Muraviev with legalizing aristocracy. Again, contrary to the determined centralization of the southern leader, Muraviev made allowance for the federal principle, envisaging Russia as a federal rather than a strictly unitary state. In this respect as well as perhaps in its greater conservatism, Nikita Muraviev's constitutional project stood to Pestel's not unlike the way Novosiltsev's stood to Speranskii's.

The Southern and the Northern societies differed in another respect as regards the future of Russia. Whereas Pestel has been frequently accused of 'Napoleonic' tendencies, and, whatever the validity of these suspicions, did want the Provisional Government to reform the country in strict accord with *Russian Justice*, Nikita Muraviev was willing to leave the entire settlement to a constituent assembly. Indeed 'not a single trend within the Northern Society considered it necessary in the last analysis to force a constitution upon the state by revolutionary means, but left the working out of a constitution and its adoption to popular representatives'.[4]

---

[1] Raeff, op. cit., p. 105.   [2] Ibid., p. 40.
[3] K. N. Levin and M. N. Pokrovskii, 'Dekabristy', *Istoriia Rossii v XIX veke*, (Granat), St. Petersburg, n.d., i. 107.
[4] M. V. Dovnar-Zapolskii, *Idealy dekabristov*, Moscow, 1907, p. 419.

Yet by 1825 both societies were fully convinced that a military *coup* was required to overthrow the existing regime. Led by Pestel, the southerners spread their organization, counting on the increasing number of troops commanded by members of the conspiracy and plotting regicide and seizure of power at the time of Alexander's projected inspection of the Second Army. The northerners, moribund at first, began showing signs of activity from about the end of 1822, gradually increased their initially very small membership, and evolved on the whole towards a more radical position. If the southern leader, Pestel, proved to be the outstanding ideologist of the movement, its chief poet was the northern firebrand, Conrad Ryleev, and Ryleev's radicalism, as well as Pestel's, became an integral part of Decembrism and of its legacy for the future. Still, the rebellions which took place in 1825 were essentially unprepared. The conspirators were forced to hurry their action because the authorities were finally hot on their trail and, perhaps even more importantly, because of the sudden demise of the emperor.

Alexander I's unexpected death in southern Russia in December 1825 led to a dynastic crisis, which the Decembrists utilized to make their bid for power. The deceased monarch had no sons or grandsons; therefore Grand Duke Constantine, his eldest brother, was his logical successor. But the heir presumptive had married a Polish aristocrat not of royal blood in 1820, and, in connection with the marriage, had renounced his rights to the throne. Nicholas, the third brother, was thus to become the next ruler of Russia, the entire matter having been stated clearly in 1822 in a special manifesto confirmed by Alexander I's signature. The manifesto, however, had remained unpublished, and only a few people had received exact information about it; even the two grand dukes were ignorant of its precise contents. Following Alexander I's death, while Constantine in Warsaw declined any interest in the throne, Nicholas, the Russian capital, and the Russian army swore allegiance to Constantine. Constantine acted with perfect consistency. Nicholas, however, even after reading Alexander I's manifesto, also felt impelled to behave as he did: Alexander I's decision could be challenged as contrary to Paul's law of succession and also for remaining unpublished during the emperor's own reign, and unpopular Nicholas was under pressure to step aside in favour of his elder brother, who was generally expected to follow Alexander I on the throne. Only after Constantine's uncompromising reaffirmation of his position, and a resulting lapse of time, did Nicholas decide to publish Alexander's manifesto and become emperor of Russia.

On 26 December 1825—14 December, Old Style—when the guard regiments in St. Petersburg were to swear allegiance for the second time within a short period, this time to Nicholas, the Northern Society of the Decembrists staged its rebellion. Realizing that they had a unique chance to act, the conspiring officers used their influence with the soldiers to start a mutiny in several units by entreating them to defend the rightful interests of Constantine against his usurping brother. Altogether about three thousand misled rebels came in military formation to Senate Square—today Decembrist Square—in the heart of the capital. Although the government was caught unprepared, the mutineers were soon faced by troops several times their number and strength. The two forces stood opposite each other for several hours. The Decembrists failed to act because they were gathering some reinforcements and waiting for more, and especially because of their general confusion and lack of leadership; the new emperor hesitated to start his reign with a massacre of his subjects, hoping that they could be talked into submission. But, as verbal inducements and even cavalry charges failed and dusk began to gather on the afternoon of that northern winter day, artillery was brought into action. Several canister shots dispersed the rebels, killing sixty or seventy of them. Large-scale arrests followed. The rebellion in the south was an act of despair after that in the north had failed. Weakened by the prior arrest of Pestel, the desertion of the movement by Colonel Artamon Muraviev, and other unfavourable circumstances, the rebels, led by Serge Muraviev-Apostol, could muster only a little over a thousand men and engaged in fruitless marching and counter-marching until easily defeated in the first battle by a government force.

Investigation, trial, and punishment followed. The three main accusations against the Decembrists concerned their plans for the assassination of the emperor, the idea of a revolt, and the actual execution of military rebellions. In regard to the different charges the Decembrists were divided into those who merely knew about the crime in question and did not report it to the authorities, those who approved it, and those who acted to realize it.

Altogether there were brought to trial five hundred and seventy-nine persons, of whom two hundred and ninety were acquitted, of the remaining two hundred and eighty-nine men, one hundred and twenty-one were selected as the most responsible conspirators, one hundred and thirty-four were found guilty of minor offenses and, after military degradation, were scattered through various military units, or left under the surveillance of local police authorities, four were expelled from the country, twenty died before or during the trial; the fate of the other nine defendants is obscure. Of the hundred and twenty-one leaders, sixty-one were members of the Northern Society, thirty-seven of the Southern, and twenty-three of the United Slavs.[1]

Eventually, after Nicholas I mitigated the decisions of the court, five Decembrists were hanged, while others received sentences of hard labour and exile in Siberia. The execution itself was in part mishandled and the executioner had to renew his efforts, providing occasion for the famous quip by one of the victims to the effect that in Russia they could not even hang people properly.

Like eighteenth-century Russian intellectuals the Decembrists belonged wholly to general European culture and were carried by main currents of European thought. Not inappropriately, the leading ideologist of the movement, Pestel, came from a German family, professed the Lutheran faith, received much of his education and upbringing in Germany, and wrote habitually in French. To be sure, most Decembrists possessed no German or Lutheran background, but many of them rivalled Pestel in their adherence to French culture. As Dmitrii Zavalishin described the education of a Decembrist in words marvellously similar to Tolstoi's: 'Mother placed no value on the Russian language and other subjects; her entire concern was for foreign languages, especially for graceful pronunciation and *manière de parler* in French, and that we be *comme il faut*.'[2] No

---

[1] Mazour, op. cit., pp. 212–13. In addition, many soldiers who participated in the uprisings were transferred to the active army in the Caucasus; some were subjected to severe corporal punishment. Concerning their fate see, e.g., Nechkina, op. cit. ii. 411–16.

[2] D. I. Zavalishin, *Zapiski dekabrista*, St. Petersburg, 1906, p. 19.

wonder that French permeated Decembrist conversation, correspondence, and other writings, ranging from political tracts to Alexander Bariatinskii's poem to Pestel. More important still, the bulk of Decembrist writings, which was, after all, written in Russian, often appears to be only one remove away from the French and can occasionally be understood better after translation into the language of Voltaire.

Content corresponded to form. The Decembrists expressed splendidly late Enlightenment and the momentous years of revolutionary thought and practice, and constitution-making, that followed the fall of the Bastille. At least a dozen major thinkers of the Age of Reason exercised important influence on Pestel, while on the whole he can perhaps be best described as a Jacobin. Nikita Muraviev's constitution, in its turn, reflected, among other sources, the French constitution of 1791, the Spanish constitution of 1812, and the United States Constitution. As in the West, intellectual continuity was obvious and striking. For many Decembrists Voltaire remained the sire and guide that he had been to their fathers and grandfathers. Or, to take an example in a more limited field, Beccaria's enlightened thoughts on crime and punishment attracted Pestel as much as they had attracted Catherine the Great.[1] After its abortive effort in France, reason was finally to triumph in Russia. But the fact that the Decembrists shared to the full the progressive ideologies of the West, the only ones then available, did not detach them from their native land or make their thoughts and actions any less real or patriotic. Contrary to what the government claimed, they were not immature criminals, but remarkably well-educated, gifted, and precocious representatives of their generation, a true élite. Even in terms of careers they were faring excellently until the catastrophe of 14 December. Moreover, the Decembrists did their best to adapt the principles of the Enlightenment to Russia, mounting a frontal attack on serfdom and proposing many other eminently relevant and practical reforms, in the army and elsewhere. On the whole they represented the best and the most far-reaching response made, within the framework of the Enlightenment, by the Russian educated public to the needs of Russia.

[1] See especially T. Cizova, 'Beccaria in Russia', *The Slavonic and East European Review*, vol. xl, No. 95 (June 1962), pp. 384–408.

Whereas the Decembrist allegiance to the liberalism and radicalism of the Enlightenment cannot be seriously questioned, certain other aspects of their ideology remain controversial. Recent research has stressed the historical sense as well as the patriotism and nationalism of the movement, together with such specific characteristics as a penchant for traditional Russian terminology and a dislike of foreigners. In other words, Pestel and his companions were moving beyond the Age of Reason to romantic nationalism, and perhaps even achieving *also* a synthesis of the two.[1] Valuable in its modest way, this approach, however, has obvious limitations. Thus, while the Decembrists wanted to prevent the Russian sovereign from spending his time outside Russian borders, to nourish sacred patriotism, and avoid things foreign in the education of Russian children, and even to make foreigners then in Russia learn Russian—giving them the reasonable period of twenty years to accomplish that purpose—their xenophobia was emotional, immediate, and narrow in its scope rather than ideological and comprehensive. The intellectual world of the Decembrists was the cosmopolitan universe of the Enlightenment. The ideological exclusiveness and opposition of the Russian principles to those of the West belonged to a different age. Again, while the title of Pestel's *Russian Justice, Russkaia Pravda*, harked back to an eleventh-century Russian legal code associated with Iaroslav the Wise, its content, as we have already seen, spoke emphatically of the Age of Reason. The Decembrists did not remain unaffected by the newer intellectual currents, but they belonged to the Enlightenment.

The problem of the relationship of the Decembrists to the government continues to fascinate. Aristocrats and officers of élite regiments, members of the movement belonged to the top of Russian society. They resembled friends and advisers of Alexander I in their social background, French culture, general education, and in their ideology of the Age of Reason. Progressive reforms and constitution-making preoccupied both groups. The early Decembrist societies naturally wanted to further the

---

[1] See in particular S. S. Volk, *Istoricheskie vzgliady dekabristov*, Moscow–Leningrad, 1958; H. Lemberg, *Die nationale Gedankenwelt der Dekabristen*, Cologne–Graz, 1963. An emphasis on the patriotism of the Decembrists is a stock-in-trade of the Soviet historiography of the movement. Raeff discusses, although cautiously, the Decembrist synthesis.

good intentions of the government. Even later, when philan-
thropic associations were becoming conspiracies, Alexander I
made his famous comment on an informer's report to the effect
that it was not for him to punish these men and these ideas. The
provisional government to be formed after the Decembrist
victory was to consist of liberal statesmen of the empire, notably
Speranskii. Indeed, the Decembrist movement, or rather many
of its members, remained psychologically so close to the government and so permeated by the concept of enlightened despotism
that their position was ambivalent to the end. This psychological ambiguity helps to explain the critical collapse of the
Decembrist leadership, especially in the North, at the time of
the uprisings. Colonel Prince Serge Trubetskoi, who had been
elected 'dictator' for the occasion, and his ranking assistants,
Colonel Alexander Bulatov and Captain Alexander Iakubovich, all deserted the rebel cause. Trubetskoi and Bulatov swore
allegiance to Nicholas I; Iakubovich offered his help to the
emperor and generally behaved in the Senate Square in so
bizarre a manner as to suggest a mental breakdown. Both
Bulatov and Iakubovich might have come close to killing the
emperor in the Senate Square. Later Bulatov committed suicide
in prison. The Decembrists who did lead their troops in
rebellion on the fourteenth showed a crucial lack of initiative
during the hours of confrontation. It is generally agreed that
their one hope of success lay in quick and decisive action; but
nothing was done. And these were some of the bravest and the
most daring officers of Russia. The psychological ambiguity
must also account in large part for the collapse of the Decembrists during the interrogation and the trial, when so many of
them confessed and repented and also tried desperately to
enlighten the monarch about the true condition of Russia so he
would reform it. Nicholas I, it should be added, made full
and detailed use of this major psychological weakness of the
conspirators.

And yet the salient characteristic of the Decembrist movement was its rejection of autocracy and enlightened despotism.
Although very difficult emotionally, it can well be argued that
the step was a natural one to take, and even long overdue.
The year of the Decembrist rebellion marked, after all, the
hundredth anniversary of the death of Peter the Great; Russia

remained, however, a land of serfdom, poverty, and ignorance. If further urging was needed, the second half of Alexander's reign seemed to demonstrate conclusively the total unfitness of the government for introducing reform. Moreover, enlightened despotism represented only one path of progress according to the canon of the Age of Reason. Recent decades, by contrast, had stressed revolutions and dictatorships, ranging from the classic French example to heroic rebellions organized by liberal army officers in different countries of southern Europe. The Decembrists were determined to keep their appointment with history. What would have followed a Decembrist victory? What power other than enlightened despotism would have propelled Russia on the road of progress and reason? The question is, of course, speculative because it was the destiny of the Decembrists to start an intelligentsia in Siberia, not to change Russia. It is also speculative because, as already noted, there was no agreement within the movement on the shape of things to come: while Pestel and his companions considered *Russian Justice* as of the utmost importance as a blueprint for future Russia, the Northerners, although they possessed Nikita Muraviev's constitution, were apparently willing to leave the settlement to a constituent assembly. Still, one is left with a strong impression that the Decembrist model called for a simple substitution of their own power or, at the most, the power of other like-minded men for that of Alexander I and his associates. As in France and elsewhere, perhaps more than in France and elsewhere, a revolutionary government was going to accomplish what a traditional one had failed to do. Above their profound concern with civil rights, the unshackling of economic activities, and an effective participation by the people in the life of their country, the Decembrists saw the necessity of progressive reform in Russia, to be achieved by revolution if need be. If enlightened despotism had played out its role in the empire of the tsars, Enlightenment itself was making one last bid.

But the long Decembrist clinging to the monarch and the government could be a result not only of an intellectual tradition going back to Peter the Great, or of emotion, but also of a sense of reality. Once the Decembrists made the break, they were horribly isolated. They could not expect support from their own social stratum, because that stratum was already ruling Russia—quite literally ruling large parts of it, as in the case of Pestel's father, or of Zavalishin's. The Decembrist rebellion was, among other things, a remarkable generational revolt. Only ten Decembrists were over forty years old, only one over forty-six. Even more strikingly, in this thoroughly military uprising a mere lieutenant had to command troops in the Senate Square. A possible Decembrist appeal to the gentry as a whole was bound to suffer from the limited education of the gentry as well as from the emphasis of the Decembrists on the abolition of serfdom and their other attacks on gentry rights. Although Pestel, Nikita Muraviev, and their friends wanted to promote the middle classes in Russia, they had no connection with these classes, and their very hopes for them referred only to the future. Similarly, the Decembrists had no connection with the peasants and indeed were afraid of peasant rebellions and determined to keep the people quiet while transforming Russia— although the huge crowds in and around the Senate Square were certainly on the Decembrist side. Even soldiers were to follow their Decembrist officers because of discipline and personal loyalty, not out of ideological conviction. The military historian of the uprising, G. S. Gabaev, pointed out that the revolt of 14 December was staged by units whose honorary head was Grand Duke Constantine, as opposed to those whose patron was Grand Duke Nicholas.[1] An untrustworthy but appropriate story claimed that for soldiers in the Senate Square shouts for Constantine and constitution meant Grand Duke Constantine and his wife. In the South efforts to propagandize the soldiers for the Decembrist cause were few and late, although occasionally strikingly anti-monarchist. All in all, the balance of forces would seem to indicate that ultimately the Decembrists had very slight chances of success, even if they were to gain some initial advantage by decisive action in the capital. And as one turns from these more immediate considerations to the longer vistas of history, the importance of the Decembrists remains tied to the value one would attach to an example, a martyrdom, a legend.

[1] G. S. Gabaev, 'Gvardiia v dekabrskie dni 1825 goda', appendix to A. E. Presniakov, *14 dekabria 1825 goda*, Moscow, 1926, p. 170.

PART II

The Government and the Educated Public in Russia in the Age of Romanticism

---

At full height
Illumined by the pale moonlight,
With arm outflung, behind him riding,
See, the bronze horseman comes, bestriding
The charger, clanging in his flight.
Pushkin, *The Bronze Horseman*, trans. Oliver Elton

PART II

The Government and the Educated Public in Russia in the *Age of Reaction*

3

Nicholas I and Official Nationality
in Russia, 1825–1855[1]

*Our common obligation consists in this that the education of
the people be conducted, according to the Supreme intention
of our August Monarch, in the joint spirit of Orthodoxy,
autocracy, and nationality.*

Uvarov[2]

NICHOLAS I belonged to the Decembrist generation. Born in
1796, he saw service in the last stages of the war against
Napoleon and came to the West with the victorious Russian
army. His mother, Empress Mary, like Zavalishin's mother,
was especially concerned that her son learn French, and Nicholas became fluent in French as a child, while studying, in
addition, several other languages. A member of the reigning
house of the Romanovs, Nicholas I had even more foreign
relatives and friends than the Trubetskois. And yet ideologi-
cally and emotionally the new emperor stood at the opposite
pole from the Decembrists, his references—usually in French—
to his 'friends of the fourteenth' carrying an exclusively ironic,
indeed very heavily ironic, meaning. In contrast to Alexander
I, there was no sympathy, no ambivalence, no hesitation, no
remembrance of things past.

[1] This chapter is based on my work: *Nicholas I and Official Nationality in Russia,
1825–1855*, Berkeley and Los Angeles, 1959 (pb., 1967), the only book on the
subject.
[2] S. S. Uvarov, 'Tsirkuliarnoe predlozhenie G. Upravliaiushchego Ministerstvom Narodnogo Prosveshcheniia Nachalstvam Uchebnykh Okrugov "o vstuplenii
v upravlenie Ministerstvom"',' *Zhurnal Ministerstva Narodnogo Prosveshcheniia*, 1834,
Part I, p. 1.

The two monarchs represented the Russian version of general European history. Although brothers, they were nineteen years apart; when Alexander was a boy the thought of the late Enlightenment held hegemony in the Western world, when Nicholas was growing up Europe was split by a titanic struggle between Napoleonic France and the old order. One could choose with Pestel the French Revolution, or one could defend the establishment. A young Russian grand duke was much more likely to be found in the second camp; in fact, because of the milieu and the historical circumstances he hardly had a choice.

The ideology that eventually set out to do battle with the *philosophes*, the Jacobins, and Napoleon was a ramshackle affair. The need to intellectualize and explain followed belatedly the urgent necessity to defend. Still, as local forces rallied against the reality, or at least the threat, of French invasion and revolution, they inscribed, with a new devotion, native institutions and traditions on their banners. For Russia that meant autocracy and perhaps even serfdom. In opposition to the sceptical *philosophes* and 'the godless French' religion came back into its own, Orthodoxy in Russia, Catholicism or various forms of Protestantism elsewhere. As in the days of old, the cross was raised on high as the ultimate protection against new enemies, reason and revolution. To be sure, Louis XVIII simply could not be another Louis IX, and the literature of the period is full of sarcastic comment concerning Voltairian aristocrats who suddenly acquired religion, or sceptics who became traditionalists overnight. The paradox extended to the greatest voices of reaction, and notably to Joseph de Maistre himself.[1] It remains true nevertheless that in one way or another authorities and evidence were assembled or conjured up to combat the principles of the Age of Reason and their translation into practice. Moreover, the intellectual climate continued to change. Nationalism and romanticism rose to challenge in their own

---

[1] The latest major study of de Maistre even exaggerates the degree to which he remained a man of the Enlightenment: Robert Triomphe, *Joseph de Maistre: étude sur la vie et sur la doctrine d'un matérialiste mystique*, Geneva, 1968. See G. de Bertier de Sauvigny's review of this in *The American Historical Review*, vol. lxxv, No. 1 (Oct. 1969), p. 134. De Maistre spent the years 1803–17 as Sardinian ambassador in St. Petersburg. On that, see esp. M. Stepanov and F. Vermale, 'Zhozef de Mestr v Rossii', *Literaturnoe Nasledstvo*, vol. 29/30 (1937), pp. 577–726.

manner the *philosophes* and the French. German idealistic philosophy in particular, while organically linked to Kant and other thinkers of the Enlightenment, reacted against its predecessors and proceeded to draw a new intellectual map of the world. The proponents of restoration and reaction, in the German states, in Russia, and in other lands, borrowed selectively from, or made uneasy alliance with, these newer currents of thought and their champions to produce the peculiar intellectual amalgam of the European Right of the first decades of the nineteenth century.

In Russia Nicholas I was the model champion of restoration and reaction, and the doctrine of so-called Official Nationality was its canon.[1] The sovereign's utter meticulous devotion to the cause spoke for itself, while Serge Uvarov's brief principles encapsulated successfully the Russian version of the general European ideology of the Right. The thought of the Russian reaction, like that of the Russian Enlightenment, was, if anything, starker and sharper in outline than its Western counterparts. Nor should chronology mislead. It might be considered a paradox that Russia was directed in the actual struggle against Napoleon and at the Congress of Vienna by an ambivalent and tormented representative of the Age of Reason, while a dauntless champion of legitimism and reaction ascended the Russian throne only in 1825, with the doctrine of Official Nationality formally proclaimed only in 1833. Yet history is made of just such paradoxes, or responses to the challenges of yesterday even more than to those of today.

As man and ruler Nicholas I differed sharply from his brother Alexander I. By contrast with his predecessor's psychological contradictions, ambiguity, and vacillation, he displayed determination, singleness of purpose, and an iron will. He also possessed an overwhelming sense of duty and a great capacity for work. In character, and even in his striking and powerful appearance, Nicholas I seemed to be the perfect despot.

[1] The term 'Official Nationality'—*ofitsialnaia narodnost*—was not used by its proponents, nor by the early critics. Initiated by Professor A. Pypin, it obtained currency among historians late in the nineteenth century, and it has since become standard. See the important chapter on Official Nationality in A. N. Pypin, *Kharakteristiki literaturnykh mnenii ot dvadtsatykh do piatidesiatykh godov*, St. Petersburg, 1906, pp. 93–140. See also, e.g., P. N. Sakulin, 'Russkaia literatura vo vtoroi chetverti veka', *Istoriia Rossii v XIX veke* (Granat), St. Petersburg, n.d., ii. 445.

Appropriately, he profited little from most aspects of his education and always remained an army man, a junior officer at heart, devoted to his troops, to military exercises, to the parade ground, down to the last button on a soldier's uniform— in fact, as emperor he ordered alterations of the uniforms, even changing the number of buttons. Participation in the final stages of the war against Napoleon and a happy marriage to Princess Charlotte—Alexandra, after she became Orthodox—of the allied and also militaristic ruling house of Prussia, enhanced this fascination with the army, the roots of which, however, went, no doubt, much deeper than political considerations. As the sovereign himself tried to explain the matter:

Here [in the army] there is order, there is a strict unconditional legality, no impertinent claims to know all the answers, no contradiction, all things flow logically one from the other; no one commands before he has himself learned to obey; no one steps in front of anyone else without lawful reason; everything is subordinated to one definite goal, everything has its purpose. That is why I feel so well among these people, and why I shall always hold in honour the calling of a soldier. I consider the entire human life to be merely service, because everybody serves.[1]

And in the same spirit, the autocrat insisted on arranging and ordering minutely and precisely everything around him.

Engineering, especially the construction of defences, was Nicholas's other lasting passion. Even as a child 'whenever he built a summer house, for his nurse or his governess, out of chairs, earth, or toys, he never forgot *to fortify* it with guns—*for protection*'.[2] Later, specializing in fortresses, he became head of the army corps of engineers and thus the chief military engineer of his country; this was probably his most important assignment during the reign of his brother. Still later, as emperor, he staked all on making the entire land an impregnable fortress.

Devotion to defence implied pessimism. In contrast to the organic optimism of the Enlightenment and its expanding vistas, the new intellectual and emotional climate stressed

---

[1] Quoted from N. K. Shilder [or Schilder], *Imperator Nikolai Pervyi, ego zhizn i tsarstvovanie*, St. Petersburg, 1903, i. 147. This extremely valuable documentary emperor- and court-centred history does not unfortunately extend beyond 1831.

[2] Quoted from *Sbornik Imperatorskogo Russkogo Istoricheskogo Obshchestva*, xcviii. 36. Vol. 98 is the most important for the reign of Nicholas I in this fundamental collection of Russian historical materials; see also vols. 31, 74, 90, 113, 122, 131, and 132.

duty, endurance, holding the line, performing one's task to the end. And Nicholas I bore his immense burden faithfully for thirty years, into the catastrophe of the Crimean War. When his diplomatic system collapsed, the weary monarch commented: 'Nothing remains to me but my duty as long as it pleases God to leave me at the head of Russia.'[1] 'I shall carry my cross until all my strength is gone.'[2] 'Thy will be done.'[3] Rarely does one find such congruity between a historical period and a man's character and convictions.

The government ideology, which came to be known as Official Nationality, was proclaimed on 2 April 1833 by the new Minister of Education, Serge Uvarov, in his first circular to the officials in charge of the educational districts of the Russian empire. Uvarov (1786–1855), that 'fortunate and flexible nature'[4], a precocious product of the Enlightenment and even something of a free-thinker, as well as a scholar, a writer, and from 1818 the President of the Academy of Sciences, belonged to those liberal European aristocrats, who, in changed political circumstances, discovered religion, authority, and tradition.[5] Uvarov wrote to his subordinates:

Our common obligation consists in this, that the education of the people be conducted, according to the Supreme intention of our August Monarch, in the joint spirit of Orthodoxy, autocracy, and

[1] From a letter to Frederick William IV of Prussia of 26 Aug. 1854, published in an appendix to Schiemann's standard four-volume history of the reign of Nicholas I: *Geschichte Russlands unter Kaiser Nikolaus I*, Berlin, 1904–19, iv. 434–5.

[2] In a letter to Prince Michael Gorchakov, the commander in the Crimea; quoted in M. A. Polievktov, *Nikolai I. Biografiia i obzor tsarstvovaniia*, Moscow, 1918, p. 376. [3] Ibid.

[4] I borrowed the phrase from the eulogistic introduction by L. Leduc to S. S. Uvarov, *Esquisses politiques et littéraires*, Paris, 1848, p. 11.

[5] There is a remarkable consensus that Uvarov was an unprincipled, extremely vain, and egotistical, although brilliant, careerist. As one among many such judgements, see the discussion of the minister and his creed by the historian S. M. Soloviev, which reads in part: 'Orthodoxy—while he was an atheist not believing in Christ even in the Protestant manner, autocracy—while he was a liberal, nationality—although he had not read a single Russian book in his life and wrote constantly in French or in German.' S. M. Soloviev, *Moi zapiski dlia detei moikh, a, esli mozhno, i dlia drugikh*, Petrograd, n.d., p. 59. Archival sources agree with the published materials. A notable example is an evaluation of Uvarov and his activity by the head of the gendarmerie, Count Alexander Benckendorff: 'Otchet IIIgo Otdeleniia Sobstvennoi Ego Imperatorskogo Velichestva Kantseliarii i Korpusa Zhandarmov za 1839 god', Tsentralnyi gosudarstvennyi arkhiv Oktiabrskoi Revoliutsii, Fond No. 109, Opis No. 85, Edinitsa khraneniia No. 4. Henceforward: TsGAOR and the numbers.

nationality. I am convinced that every professor and teacher, being permeated by one and the same feeling of devotion to throne and fatherland, will use all his resources to become a worthy tool of the government and to earn its complete confidence.[1]

The minister proceeded to propound and promote his three cardinal principles throughout the sixteen years during which he remained in charge of public instruction in Russia. In reports to the emperor, as well as in orders to subordinates, he presented these principles invariably as the true treasure of the Russian people and the Russian state. For instance, Uvarov discussed the matter as follows in the survey of his first decade in office, submitted for imperial approval:

In the midst of the rapid collapse in Europe of religious and civil institutions, at the time of a general spread of destructive ideas, at the sight of grievous phenomena surrounding us on all sides, it was necessary to establish our fatherland on firm foundations upon which is based the well-being, strength, and life of a people; it was necessary to find the principles which form the distinctive character of Russia, and which belong only to Russia; it was necessary to gather into one whole the sacred remnants of Russian nationality and to fasten to them the anchor of our salvation. Fortunately, Russia had retained a warm faith in the sacred principles without which she cannot prosper, gain in strength, live. Sincerely and deeply attached to the church of his fathers, the Russian has of old considered it the guarantee of social and family happiness. Without a love for the faith of its ancestors a people, as well as an individual, must perish. A Russian, devoted to his fatherland, will agree as little to the loss of a single dogma of our *Orthodoxy* as to the theft of a single pearl from the tsar's crown. *Autocracy* constitutes the main condition of the political existence of Russia. The Russian giant stands on it as on the cornerstone of his greatness. An innumerable majority of the subjects of *Your Majesty* feel this truth; they feel it in full measure although they are placed on different rungs of civil life and although they vary in education and in their relations to the government. The saving conviction that Russia lives and is protected by the spirit of a strong, humane, and enlightened autocracy must permeate popular education and must develop with it. Together with these two national principles there is a third, no less important, no less powerful: *nationality*.[2]

[1] See p. 103 n. 2.

[2] S. S. Uvarov, *Desiatiletie ministerstva narodnogo prosveshcheniia, 1833–1843*, St. Petersburg, 1864, pp. 2–3.

AON

It was for his long service to the three sacred principles that Uvarov was made a count. Still more appropriately, Nicholas I granted him the words 'Orthodoxy, autocracy, nationality' as his family motto.

Many poets, writers, professors, and journalists proved eager to echo Uvarov's battle cry, sometimes with a respectful bow in his direction. Professor Stephen Shevyrev, to give one example, followed the minister in 1841 in his analysis of Russia and the West for the first issue of *The Muscovite*. He asserted, in his usual ponderous and involved manner:

But even if we did pick up certain unavoidable blemishes from our contacts with the West, we have on the other hand preserved in ourselves, in their purity, three fundamental feelings which contain the seed and the guarantee of our future development. We have retained our ancient religious feeling. The Christian cross had left its sign on our entire original education, on the entire Russian life. . . . The second feeling which makes Russia strong and which secures its future well-being is the feeling of our state unity, again derived by us from our entire history. There is certainly no country in Europe which can boast of such a harmonious political existence as our fatherland. Almost everywhere in the West dissension as to principles has been recognized as a law of life, and the entire existence of peoples transpires in heavy struggle. Only in our land the tsar and the people compose one unbreakable whole, not tolerating any obstacle between them: this connection is founded on the mutual feeling of love and faith and on the boundless devotion of the people to its tsar. . . . Our third fundamental feeling is our consciousness of our nationality and our conviction that any enlightenment can be firmly rooted in our land only when it is assimilated by our national feeling and expressed by our national thought and national word. . . . Because of the three fundamental feelings our Russia is firm, and her future is secure. A statesman of the Council of the Tsar, to whom are entrusted those generations which are being educated, already long ago expressed them in a profound thought, and they have formed the foundation of the upbringing of the people.[1]

In addition to *The Muscovite*, a score or more other periodicals proclaimed 'Orthodoxy, autocracy, and nationality' as their articles of faith. They ranged from the fantastically reactionary,

[1] S. P. Shevyrev, 'Vzgliad russkogo na sovremennoe obrazovanie Evropy', *Moskvitianin*, Part I, pp. 292–5.

obscurantist, and nationalist *Lighthouse* to formal and pedantic government publications, such as Uvarov's own *Journal of the Ministry of Education*. A newspaper with a very wide circulation, *The Northern Bee*, published by the grammarian Nicholas Grech and the most notorious journalist of the period, Thaddeus, or Faddei, Bulgarin, was of particular assistance in disseminating the minister's views throughout the length and breadth of Russia. So was a similarly popular magazine, *The Readers' Library*, produced by another notorious and fantastic Pole, but also a gifted orientalist, Joseph, or Osip, Senkovskii. In fact, until the end of the reign of Nicholas I, Uvarov's brief formula dominated most of the Russian press. Books followed periodicals in spreading the government doctrine. The three sacred principles appeared in many different works, in and out of context, but they became especially common in textbooks and popularizations with a wide circulation.

Before long, 'Orthodoxy, autocracy, and nationality' came to represent much more than Uvarov's attempt at philosophizing, more even than the guiding principles of the Ministry of Education. The formula expanded in application and significance to stand for the Russia of Nicholas I. Military cadets were enjoined to become 'Christians', 'loyal subjects', and 'Russians' in that order.[1] The entire nation was to rally for 'faith, tsar, and fatherland', the phrase used, for instance, in the famous 1848 manifesto defying the revolutionary West.[2] The emperor himself dedicated his life to the service of Orthodoxy, autocracy, and Russia, and everyone else in the government was compelled to follow the monarch. At the same time a considerable part of the educated Russian public, led by prominent professors, writers, and journalists hoisted the three words as their banner. 'Orthodoxy, autocracy, and nationality' were interpreted to mean the past, the present, and the future of Russia, Russian tradition as well as Russian mission, Russian culture as much as Russian politics.

One attraction of Uvarov's formula was its apparent simplicity. It comprised only three terms, listed always in the

[1] Quoted from Polievktov, op. cit., p. 332.
[2] About the manifesto, see N. K. Shilder, 'Imperator Nikolai I v 1848 i 1849 godakh', first published in the *Istoricheskii Vestnik* for 1899 and later as an appendix to Shilder, op. cit. ii. 619–39. The text of the manifesto is given on p. 629.

same sequence. The content of the doctrine of Official Nationality depended on the meanings and the implications of these key concepts.

Orthodoxy, the first article of faith in the doctrine of Official Nationality, had several basic levels of significance and numerous connotations. In a deep personal sense it represented, as in the case of Nicholas I himself, the ultimate belief, hope and support of man. Indeed, it was his firm faith in God, Christ, the Divine Will, as revealed in the teaching of the Orthodox Church, that sustained the disappointed and at times desperate emperor in all the trials and tribulations of his hard life. Only Christ, only Orthodoxy, represented for the Russian monarch light, guidance, and salvation in this vale of sorrow and strife.

Imperial convictions were shared by many lesser adherents to the state ideology. As one of them, the poet Theodore Glinka, stated the matter:

> Extend to me Thy hand, Father, from heaven,
> Give me firmness on my slippery footing,
> Take away my suffering with a breath of Thy love
> And show me light in the dark steppe![1]

Or, in the words of another proponent of Official Nationality and a much greater poet, Basil Zhukovskii: 'The human soul needs God alone.'[2] Even Bulgarin, hardly a religious mind himself, fell in line with this view and affirmed: 'I do not claim a profound knowledge in the field of philosophy, and I confess openly that, having surveyed all philosophic schools and opinions, I find that true wisdom is contained only in the Gospel.'[3]

The most remarkable religious work to come from the proponents of Official Nationality was *Simple Talk about Complex Things* written by a leading historian and journalist of the government school, Michael Pogodin.[4] Although published in its author's old age, it represented faithfully his thinking during his entire life, consisting as it did largely of separate

[1] From the long poem 'Carelia' in F. N. Glinka, *Stikhotvoreniia*, Leningrad, 1951, p. 271.

[2] V. A. Zhukovskii, 'Vera i um. Istina. Nauka. Stati iz nenapechatannykh sochinenii', *Zhurnal Ministerstva Narodnogo Prosveshcheniia*, lxxxi (1854), Part II, p. 9.

[3] F. V. Bulgarin, *Salopnitsa*, St. Petersburg, 1842, p. 6.

[4] M. P. Pogodin, *Prostaia rech o mudrenykh veshchakh*, Moscow, 1875.

thoughts and short comments jotted down over a period of years and brought out in print without alteration. But in addition to reflecting Pogodin's personality and convictions, *Simple Talk* also presented in a typical manner a number of religious beliefs and attitudes common to many proponents of Official Nationality. One may note first the bluntness, crudity, and naïvety of Pogodin's entire argument. These qualities tended to characterize government ideologists in the field of religion as well as in other fields, setting their views apart from the brilliant religious thought of Khomiakov and his Slavophile followers. Together with the direct and artless approach, went a strong fideistic emphasis joined to a profound suspicion of all reasoning, even of theology. God emerged as the ultimate answer to man's quest, the beginning and the end of human wisdom, Alpha and Omega.

The philosophers recognize a certain creative force and cannot deny it intelligence; they revere it. This force is God. What is the highest, the holiest action of this force? Christianity. They bow, therefore, also before Christ, only covered by a different concept, in a different guise, under a different name. Is this not a misunderstanding?[1]

Short on theology, Official Nationality was long on moral fervour and moralizing. Throughout his life Nicholas I was bent on improving himself morally and spiritually, and the same was true of Pogodin and of numerous other adherents of the state creed. The emperor and his followers were convinced that Orthodoxy set the absolute ethical norm both for the individual and for the nation, and they took their moral obligations with the utmost seriousness.

Projected outward, self-improvement meant moralization and didacticism. The literature of Official Nationality teemed with moral lessons intended to edify and instruct the reader. Crude at best, these lessons became extremely cheap and vulgar when dispensed by such shady and facile journalists as Bulgarin with his innumerable moral tales. But, instead of Bulgarin, one might cite a true literary giant, Gogol, whose *Selected Passages from Correspondence with Friends*, published in 1847, gave an equally authentic, even exaggerated, expression to official

[1] Pogodin, op. cit., Part I, p. 42.

ideology and produced a scandal in Russian intellectual circles. For example, Gogol advised a landlord:

Take up the task of landlord as it should be taken up in the true and lawful sense. First of all, gather the peasants and explain to them what you are and what they are: that you are the landlord over them not because you want to rule and be a landlord, but because you are already a landlord, because you were born a landlord, because God will punish you if you were to exchange this condition for any other, because everyone must serve God in his own place, not someone else's just as they, having been born under authority, must submit to the same authority under which they were born, for there is no authority which is not from God. And right then show it to them in the Gospel so that they all down to the last one will see it. After that tell them that you force them to labour and work not at all because you need the money for your pleasures, and, as a proof, burn right there in front of them some bills, and make it so that they actually see that money means nothing to you. Tell them that you force them to work because God decreed that man earn his bread in labour and sweat, and right there read it to them in Holy Writ so that they will see it. Tell them the whole truth: that God will make you answer for the last scoundrel in the village, and that, therefore, you will all the more see to it that they work honestly not only for you, but also for themselves; for you know, and they know it too, that, once he has become lazy, a peasant is capable of anything—he will turn a thief and a drunkard, he will ruin his soul, and also make you answerable to God. And everything that you tell them confirm on the spot with words from Holy Writ; point with your finger to the very letters with which it is written, make each one first cross himself, bow to the ground, and kiss the book itself in which it is written. In one word, make them see clearly that in everything that concerns them you are acting in accordance with the will of God and not in accordance with some European or other fancies of your own.[1]

According to the proponents of Official Nationality, Orthodoxy was to permeate family life, schools, all of Russian society. In particular, 'the entire temple of popular education is to be sanctified by the altar of God, by the cross, and by prayers'.[2] The chief function of education was to produce right-minded

---

[1] 'Selected Passages from Correspondence with Friends' ('Vybrannye mesta iz perepiski s druziami'), vol. viii of N. V. Gogol, *Sochineniia*, ed. by V. V. Kallash, St. Petersburg, n.d.; quoted from pp. 121–2.

[2] S. P. Shevyrev, *Istoriia Imperatorskogo Moskovskogo Universiteta, napisannaia k stoletnemu ego iubileiu, 1755–1855*, Moscow, 1855, pp. 469–70.

subjects for the Russian empire, and Uvarov discussed this crucial matter in detail in some of his reports to the monarch.[1] Religion and morality appeared prominently in the official orders and regulations of the ministry of education and in other government literature. Indeed, right principles and good conduct held the centre of attention in the Russia of Nicholas I. The great poet Theodore Tiutchev expressed the official opinion when he observed that in Russia especially the government, as well as the Church, had to take charge of human souls.[2]

It is not difficult to understand why the appeal to 'Orthodoxy' in the doctrine of Official Nationality has frequently been considered a gigantic fraud. Religion was used to preach obedience to the emperor, the officer, and the landlord. The government which taught meekness and charity distinguished itself by despotism and brutality. Even the Church itself was effectively controlled by the state and generally did its bidding. Alexander Benckendorff, the chief of gendarmes, reflected government thinking when he remarked concerning the establishment of a new university in Kiev: 'Kiev was selected as the place for the new university, this city being, on the one hand, the ancient cradle of Orthodoxy, and, on the other, the headquarters of the First Army, which offered all the necessary facilities for the surveillance of a large gathering of young people.'[3]

The charges that Official Nationality misused religion are based on fact, and they are very important. Indeed, they cannot be gainsaid. Yet, they do not tell the full story. Nicholas I and many of his followers believed in Orthodoxy. They understood it in a limited manner, and their performance fell far short even of their understanding. But the ideal and the profession of faith remained. It fell to those living in the

---

[1] Uvarov's annual reports, as well as the orders and regulations mentioned in the following sentence, were published in *Zhurnal Ministerstva Narodnogo Prosveshcheniia*.

[2] F. I. Tiutchev, *Polnoe sobranie sochinenii*, St. Petersburg, 1913, p. 366. Cf. the remarkably similar educational theory and practice in the Austrian empire in the reign of Francis I (1806–35): R. Rath, 'Training for Citizenship in the Austrian Elementary Schools during the Reign of Francis I', *Journal of Central European Affairs*, vol. iv (July 1944), pp. 147–64.

[3] Shilder, op. cit. ii. 680. Benckendorff's 'Memoirs' for 1832–7 form an appendix to the volume.

twentieth century to witness the work of governments which denied moral principles as such.

Autocracy was the second article in the creed of Official Nationality. The law of the land declared: 'The Tsar of all the Russias is an autocratic and absolute monarch. God Himself commands us to obey the Tsar's supreme authority, not from fear alone, but as a point of conscience.'[1] Or, to quote from the military statutes dating back to the reign of Peter the Great:

Article 20. Whoever utters blasphemous words against the person of His Majesty, whoever deprecates His intentions and His actions and discussess them in an unseemly manner, he will be deprived of life by decapitation.—Commentary. For His Majesty is an autocratic monarch Who need answer to no one in the world for His actions, but Who possesses power and authority to govern His states and His lands, as a Christian ruler, according to His will and judgement.[2]

Even pithy, legal formulations of autocracy usually included two items: the absolute nature of imperial power, and the link between the emperor and God. For, in the last analysis, God provided the foundation for the authority of the tsar. Most proponents of Official Nationality were well aware of the connection. Such statements as 'the heart of the tsar is in the hand of the Lord', Pogodin's favourite, indicated this awareness. It also found expression in the constant joining of the images of the monarch and of God, one of the most common motifs in the poetry and the prose of Official Nationality. Typically, in such composite pictures the tsar was represented as the absolute ruler of his great realm yet begging guidance and support from the ultimate ruler of the world, God.

The belief in autocracy was also based on the conviction of the inherent weakness and even wickedness of man and of his resulting need for a strong, authoritarian rule over him. As is

---

[1] *Svod Zakonov Rossiiskoi Imperii*, St. Petersburg, 1832, vol. i, art. 1.

[2] Quoted in an appendix to Shilder, op. cit., i. 758. For the Swedish origin of the formulation, see P. N. Miliukov, *Gosudarstvennoe khoziastvo Rossii v pervoi chetverti XVIII stoletiia i reforma Petra Velikogo*, St. Petersburg, 1905, note on pp. 500–1. Cf., e.g., the 'small catechism' composed in 1832 for the education of the rebellious Poles and reproduced partly in Schiemann, op. cit. iii. 202 n. Examples: 'Question 5. What kind of obedience do we owe to the emperor? Answer: a perfect, passive, and boundless one in all matters. . . . Question 12. How does God consider a failure in respect and loyalty to the emperor? Answer: as the most horrible sin and the most dreadful crime.'

true of most conservative or reactionary teachings, Official Nationality was a profoundly pessimistic doctrine. Its low estimate of humanity fitted neatly into the Christian framework, if neglecting certain basic aspects of Christianity. One of Uvarov's favourite arguments, in his classical research as well as in his other writings, dealt with the fall of man from his initial state of grace, the fact 'which alone contains the key to all history'.[1] Similarly, Pogodin found everywhere 'proofs of the fall of man (which continues in us), of our impaired nature'.[2] Grech's *Memoirs* refer to mankind as a 'despicable and ungrateful tribe'[3] and note, in connection with Alexander I's sponsorship of the Bible Society, that 'human viciousness turns even a medicinal drink into poison, and by its machinations extracts damage and poison from the Word of God'.[4] Even Senkovskii's allegiance to Official Nationality has been credited to his sceptical view of the Russian people.[5] The same pessimism and disillusionment constituted fundamental traits in the personality of Nicholas I himself.

Because men were feeble and perverse, they had to be driven by a benevolent supreme authority in order to achieve desirable social ends. Pogodin combined loud praise of the Russian people, in line with new romantic philosophy, with some reservations on the subject. As early as 1826 he observed: 'The Russian people is marvellous, but marvellous so far only in potentiality. In actuality it is low, horrid, and beastly.' And he went on to assert that Russian peasants 'will not become human beings until they are forced into it'.[6] Grech proclaimed dogmatically: 'Men are not angels; there are many devils among them. Therefore, police, and a severe police, is a necessity both for the state and for all private individuals.'[7] He commented as follows on the reign of Nicholas I as contrasted to that of his predecessor:

Pepper too is required in a salad! Alexander was too meek,

[1] S. S. Uvarov, *Essai sur les mystères d'Eleusis*, Paris, 1816, p. 30.
[2] Pogodin, op. cit., p. 91.
[3] N. I. Grech, *Zapiski o moei zhizni*, Moscow, Leningrad, 1930, p. 209.
[4] Ibid., p. 365.
[5] D. Korsakov, 'Senkovskii, Osip Ivanovich', *Russkii biograficheskii slovar*, vol. 'Sabaneev' to 'Smyslov', St. Petersburg, 1904, p. 321.
[6] N. P. Barsukov, *Zhizn i trudy M. P. Pogodina*, St. Petersburg, 1888–1910, ii. 17.
[7] Grech, op. cit., p. 104.

replacing during the first years firmness of character with kindness and compassion. This is too good for the vile human species. Now there, I love our Nicholas! When he is gracious, he is really gracious; but when he hits, then willy-nilly they sing: 'God, save the Tsar!'. Truthfulness, directness, sincerity compose, in my opinion, the greatness of any person, especially of a tsar. Why be crafty, when one can issue orders and use the whip?[1]

While social betterment depended on government initiative, the state had a still more immediate and fundamental task to perform: to preserve law and order. Bulgarin wrote with unusual conviction:

It is better to unchain a hungry tiger or a hyena than to take off the people the bridle of obedience to authorities and laws. There is no beast fiercer than a raging mob! All the efforts of the educated class must be directed toward enlightening the people concerning its obligations to God, to lawful authorities and laws, toward the establishment of the love of man in the heart, toward the eradication of the beastly egoism inborn in man, and not toward exciting passions, not toward generating unrealizable hopes. Whoever acts differently is a criminal according to the law of humanity. One who has seen a popular rebellion knows what it means.[2]

The government knew. Nicholas I and his officials proceeded to emphasize above all the perfect maintenance of discipline and order, punishing relentlessly all opposition and disaffection. In theory too Tiutchev and other ideologists stressed the role of the Russian emperor as the mainstay of law, morality, and civilization against individual licence, subversion, and revolution.

Not only did an autocrat embody the ideal form of supreme rule, but at lower levels of government too everything depended on men, not on institutions or legal arrangements. Echoing Karamzin's earlier opinions, and in particular his emphasis on fifty good governors as the true need of Russia,[3] Pogodin explained the matter as follows:

There is no institution or law which cannot be abused, something that is being done promptly everywhere; therefore, institutions and

[1] Ibid., p. 211.

[2] F. V. Bulgarin, *Vospominaniia*, St. Petersburg, 1846–9, i. 14–15.

[3] Richard Pipes, *Karamzin's Memoir on Ancient and Modern Russia: A Translation and Analysis*, New York, 1966, pp. 192–5. Pogodin admired Karamzin, wrote about him, and was very well acquainted with his works. He probably read the secret *Memoir* when copies of it began to circulate in Russia in the 1830s.

laws are not as important as the people on whom depends their functioning.[1]

One educated, zealous, active superior—and the entire department entrusted to him is, under the system of publicity, aiding other departments by its example, organization and training of officials. One governor with such qualities—and one-fiftieth part of Russia is prospering, a second, a third—and all the people cannot recognize themselves, they will be the same and yet not the same in this general uplift.[2]

Human sinfulness and corruption demanded strong rule. Force had to be used whenever necessary. Yet the political and social ideal of Official Nationality was certainly not naked force, but rather a paternal or patriarchal relationship. Pogodin, the historian, again spoke for the government:

There it is, I shall add here, the secret of Russian history, the secret which not a single Western sage is able to comprehend. Russian history always depicts Russia as a single family in which the ruler is the father and the subjects the children. The father retains complete authority over the children while he allows them to have full freedom. Between the father and the children there can be no suspicion, no treason; their fate, their happiness and their peace they share in common. This is true in relation to the state as a whole, but one notices a reflection of the same law also in its parts; the military commander must be the father of his soldiers, the landlord must be the father of his peasants, and even servants in the house of every master were called children of the house in the expressive old language. As long as this union is sacred and undamaged, so long there is peace and happiness—as soon as it begins to waver, no matter where, there appear disorder, confusion and alarm.[3]

Gogol made the same general point: 'Do not forget that in the Russian language . . . a superior is called father.'[4] Nicholas I himself fully believed in paternalism. 'Tsar-father', the common popular term for the ruler of Russia, was more than a super-

---

[1] Barsukov, op. cit. v. 22.

[2] M. P. Pogodin, *Istoriko-politicheskie pisma i zapiski vprodolzhenii Krymskoi Voiny 1853–1856*, Moscow, 1874, p. 268. Except for 'the system of publicity' which found no favour in the eyes of the emperor, Pogodin's statement represented faithfully the convictions of Nicholas I and of his associates.

[3] M. P. Pogodin, *Rechi, proiznesennye v torzhestvennykh i prochikh sobraniiakh, 1830–1872*, Moscow, 1872, p. 90.

[4] Gogol, op. cit., p. 163.

ficial epithet in his reign, although its practical implications were often stern and even grim.

As Pogodin's discussion of 'the secret of Russian history' indicated, autocracy found justification not only in religion and in the nature of man, but also in history. Sharing in new currents of thought, the proponents of Official Nationality showed a remarkable awareness of history and the historical approach. Nicholas I read avidly everything dealing with the Russian past, both original documents and secondary works. It was in his reign that chairs of Russian history, as distinct from world history, were established in the universities of the empire, and large sums of money were devoted to the gathering and publication of source materials. Historians and historians of literature, such as Pogodin and Shevyrev at the University of Moscow and Nicholas Ustrialov at the University of St. Petersburg, made important contributions to the development and dissemination of the ideology of the state. Academic writing was supplemented by journalism and by fiction. The age of romanticism proved to be especially favourable in Russia, as elsewhere, to historical drama, novel, and story. Their quality ranged from such rare masterpieces as Pushkin's *Boris Godunov* to Michael Zagoskin's trite novels, Nestor Kukolnik's feeble plays, and even Bulgarin's insipid tales about the early Slavs. Most of these works were very poor history, but they helped to provide sustenance and form to the interest in the past which represented a distinct characteristic of the age. And many of them attained success with the public. History, in one way or another, became the centre of attention and controversy. 'The historian represented' —in the words of Pogodin—'the crowning achievement of a people, for through him the people came to an understanding of itself.'[1]

It is not surprising that, turning to history, the ideologists of Official Nationality, especially the more superficial among them, found the decisive role of autocracy, or at least of strong monarchical government, everywhere. Bulgarin's *Handbook* asserted that Rome had fallen because the Roman Senate had refused to recognize imperial succession as the hereditary right of a single family,[2] that Arabic caliphates had similarly

[1] M. P. Pogodin, *Historische Aphorismen*, Leipzig, 1836, p. 8.
[2] F. V. Bulgarin, *Rossiia v istoricheskom, statisticheskom, geograficheskom i literaturnom*

declined because their rulers had failed to maintain their proper authority,[1] that the superiority of the ancient Germans over their neighbours had stemmed from their possession of hereditary, not elected, chieftains.[2] 'The most secure foundation of states is hereditary succession to the throne of a single family. This has been proved by both Ancient and Modern History.'[3]

The work which presented best the salutary impact of autocracy on Russia was Karamzin's brilliant twelve-volume *History of the Russian State*, interrupted at the Time of Troubles by its author's death in 1826.[4] Karamzin held the position of official historian, and he also won immense favour with the reading public. Repetitions of his theme and variations on it became extremely common in the reign of Nicholas I. Autocracy received incessant praise for binding the Russians together and leading, or driving, them to new prosperity, power, and glory. Highly representative of this approach was Ustrialov's *Russian History* which Uvarov adopted as a textbook in the schools of the empire and which he commended enthusiastically in a report to the monarch.[5]

The entire history of Russia foreshadowed and justified Nicholas I's regime, its direct line of descent stemmed from Peter the Great. The proponents of Official Nationality, from the monarch himself downward, admired, almost worshipped, the titanic emperor. The historians among them, Pogodin, Shevyrev, and Ustrialov, paid special attention to his personality and reign. Pogodin, to take the most interesting example, fell in his youth, if not earlier, under the fascination of the great reformer, this 'Russian to the highest degree', the 'human god'.[6]

otnosheniiakh. Ruchnaia kniga dlia russkikh vsekh soslovii, St. Petersburg, 1837, History, Part I, pp. 10–11.

[1] Bulgarin, op. cit., Part III, pp. 178–81.
[2] Ibid., Part IV, p. 279.
[3] Ibid., Part I, p. 11.
[4] N. M. Karamzin, *Istoriia gosudarstva rossiiskogo*. Many editions.
[5] Uvarov, *Desiatiletie ministerstva narodnogo prosveshcheniia, 1833–1843*, pp. 97–8. Ustrialov's discussion of the reign of Nicholas I was corrected by the emperor in person.
[6] See especially Barsukov, op. cit. i. 56. 211; ii. 293. Shevyrev fell under the same spell as Pogodin. For instance, in 1829, at the age of twenty-three, he noted in his diary: 'Each evening certainly, and sometimes in the mornings too, I assign it to myself as an unfailing duty to read the life of Peter the Great and everything related to him.' And he added the categorical imperative: 'Be such a man as

Later, although specializing in an earlier period of Russian history, he taught a course on Peter the Great's reign, collected documents related to it, and wrote on the subject both as historian and publicist. The reforming emperor even inspired Pogodin to compose a tragedy in verse, 'Peter I', which dealt with a particularly painful episode of Peter's life, his condemnation of his own son Alexis to death, and which was written as an apotheosis of his sense of duty and of his services to Russia.[1]

Yes, Peter the Great did much for Russia. One looks and does not believe it, one keeps adding and one cannot reach the sum. We cannot open our eyes, cannot make a move, cannot turn in any direction without encountering him everywhere, at home, in the streets, in church, in school, in court, in the regiment, at a promenade—it is always he, always he, every day, every minute, at every step!

We wake up. What day is it today? January 1, 1841—Peter the Great ordered us to count years from the birth of Christ; Peter the Great ordered us to count the months from January.

It is time to dress—our clothing is made according to the fashion established by Peter the First, our uniform according to his model. The cloth is woven in a factory which he created; the wool is shorn from the sheep which he started to raise.

A book strikes our eyes—Peter the Great introduced this script and himself cut out the letters. You begin to read it—this language became a written language, a literary language, at the time of Peter the First, superseding the earlier church language.

Newspapers are brought in—Peter the Great introduced them.

You must buy different things—they all, from the silk neckerchief to the sole of your shoe, will remind you of Peter the Great; some were ordered by him, others were brought into use or improved by him, carried on his ships, into his harbours, on his canals, on his roads.

At dinner, all the courses, from salted herring, through potatoes which he ordered grown, to wine made from grapes which he began to cultivate, will speak to you of Peter the Great.

After dinner you drive out for a visit—this is an *assemblée* of Peter the Great. You meet the ladies there—they were admitted into masculine company by order of Peter the Great.

Christ, be such a Russian as Peter the Great.' N. Ch., 'Shevyrev, Stepan Petrovich', *Russkii biograficheskii slovar*, vol. 'Shebanov' to 'Shiutts', St. Petersburg, 1911, p. 22.

[1] But apotheosis was not enough. Nicholas I read the play and resolved: '*The person of Emperor Peter the Great must be for every Russian an object of veneration and of love; to bring it on to the stage would be almost sacrilege, and therefore entirely improper. Prohibit the publication.*' Barsukov, op. cit. iv. 13.

You receive a rank—according to Peter the Great's Table of Ranks.

The rank gives me gentry status—Peter the Great so arranged it.

I must file a complaint—Peter the Great prescribed its form. It will be received—in front of Peter the Great's mirror of justice. It will be acted upon—on the basis of the General Reglament.

You decide to travel abroad—following the example of Peter the Great; you will be received well—Peter the Great placed Russia among the European states and began to instill respect for her, and so on, and so on, and so on.[1]

Pogodin's preoccupation with Peter the Great was dull, blunt, crude, and obsessive; Pushkin's treatment of him was brilliant, graceful, sensitive, but also obsessive. The difference emphasized the chasm between awkward prose and magnificent verse, and, beyond that, between mediocrity and supreme genius. Yet both writers were under the spell of the great emperor, and the themes they kept repeating in their works showed profound similarities. Pushkin dealt with him in such accomplished pieces as 'Poltava' and 'The Bronze Horseman', as well as in notes, letters, and conversation. He was working on a history of Peter the Great when he was killed in a duel. Pushkin's Peter, as well as Pogodin's, was above all the glorious hero of Poltava, the almost superhuman leader of his country, who gave Russia new life and a new history, symbolized by St. Petersburg, Pushkin's beloved city. He stood for reform, light, progress, for the present strength of the nation, and for its future destiny. Still, Pushkin was concerned for the common man writhing in the clutches of the leviathan emperor and state. In his extensive study of the time of Peter the Great, the poet became increasingly impressed by the ruthlessness and cruelty of the overwhelming monarch and his measures. Pushkin's own life seemed to repeat the same tale: he found himself controlled, restricted, directed, and generally hounded at every turn by Peter the Great's state and by Peter's successor, another powerful and autocratic emperor, Nicholas I.

These elements, and, no doubt, many others, went into the making of Pushkin's masterpiece, 'The Bronze Horseman'. In this story of a poor, ordinary man, Eugene, who lost his beloved

---

[1] From the essay 'Peter the Great': M. P. Pogodin, *Istoriko-kriticheskie otryvki*, Moscow, 1846, pp. 340–2.

in a St. Petersburg flood, went mad, dared challenge the bronze statue of the builder of the city, and then ran in mortal terror pursued by it, the poet presented both the might and the harshness of Peter the Great and of Russian autocracy. While extending sympathy to the unfortunate Eugene, Pushkin depicted the Bronze Horseman as an infinitely majestic, an almost divine figure, the greatness and permanence of whose work the poet affirmed powerfully in the introduction. The astounding lines devoted to the emperor, not those describing Eugene, were to remain a treasure of Russian verse. Pushkin's tale is a tragedy, but its composite parts are not evenly balanced: above all rises the autocratic state sweeping on to its grand destiny, undeterred by the obstacles of nature, such as swamps and floods, and impervious to the pain, the sorrow, and even the opposition of the individual, exemplified by Eugene's miserable plight and his pathetic rebellion. Pushkin's 'Bronze Horseman', as well as his treatment of Peter the Great in general, represented his closest approach to the doctrine of Official Nationality. It was, so to speak, the poet's compromise with Russian historical reality: one course opened to those who were fortunate to survive 1825 unharmed.[1]

Peter the Great occupied a unique position in the ideology of Official Nationality. He was the founder and a kind of patron saint of Imperial Russia; it was his name that was paired most often with that of the ruling monarch, Nicholas. But there were other imperial predecessors who also deserved remembrance and praise, two especially: Catherine the Great and Alexander I. Catherine merited high consideration because of her achievements in diplomacy and war, and in spreading enlightenment in Russia. But Nicholas I disliked her as a person, and the treatment of her in official ideology remained formal and correct rather than warm and enthusiastic. Alexander I, on the other hand, was presented as an ideal Christian as well as a great ruler, Nicholas I himself in particular almost worshipping his elder brother. In the literature of Official Nationality, Alexander was eulogized as the saviour of Russia and the world from Napoleon, and as 'the angel' who brought humanity into

---

[1] My interpretation of 'The Bronze Horseman' is a common one. For a different view and rich material, see W. Lednicki, *Pushkin's Bronze Horseman. The Story of a Masterpiece*, Berkeley and Los Angeles, 1955.

warfare itself, whose manifestos directed his subjects to return good for evil, and who spared Paris even though the French had devastated Moscow. Politically he was pictured as a staunch conservative, a great builder and supporter of the legitimist alliance in Europe.

For autocracy had application even beyond Russian borders, where it became legitimism. Nicholas I and his followers considered themselves true defenders of the established, legitimate, international order against any transgression. As Tiutchev wrote in April of the cataclysmic year of 1848:

> In order to understand the meaning of that supreme crisis which has now gripped Europe, one should realize the following. For a long time now only two real forces have existed in Europe—revolution and Russia. These two forces are at present counterpoised against each other, and, perhaps, tomorrow they will join battle. No negotiations, no treaties are possible between them; the existence of one of them means the death of the other! On the outcome of the struggle which has begun between them, the greatest struggle which the world has ever witnessed, will depend for many centuries to come the entire political and religious future of humanity.[1]

The confrontation between Orthodox and autocratic Russia and the godless and revolutionary West thus summed up European history, politics, and beliefs; it defined the present and was bound to determine the future of Europe and even of humanity. Yet, as Tiutchev himself was only too well-aware, the official Russian creed contained still another principle, 'nationality'.

'Nationality', *narodnost*, was at the time and has since remained the most obscure, puzzling, and debatable member of the official trinity. While 'Orthodoxy' and 'autocracy' were relatively precise terms referring to an established faith and a distinct form of government, 'nationality' possessed no single, generally accepted meaning. It has been most often interpreted as merely an appendage to 'autocracy', an affirmation that the Russian people were happy, docile, and obedient subjects of their tsar and their landlords. According to this view, it served mainly as a propaganda device and possessed no significance of its own. Indeed, it has been equated by some simply with the defence of serfdom.

---

[1] Tiutchev, 'Rossiia i revoliutsiia', in Tiutchev, op. cit., p. 344.

This assessment of 'nationality' is largely valid, but incomplete. For in addition to its reactionary, dynastic, and defensive connotations, the term also had a romantic frame of reference. And on the romantic plane 'Russia' and 'the Russian people' acquired a supreme metaphysical, and even mystical, importance, leading to belief in the great mission of Russia, to such doctrines as Pan-Slavism and such practices as Russification. Theories attempting to buttress the antique Russian regime met German idealistic philosophy with its dizzying new vistas, restoration met romanticism. It followed logically that the two views of 'nationality', which we may call 'the dynastic 'and 'the nationalistic', were in essential contradiction to each other. This contrast and antagonism found expression in the strife between different groups of government ideologists. It was reflected more subtly in the change of position by certain proponents of the state views, while in still other instances the contradiction remained concealed and implicit. In general, the concept of nationality accounted for the tensions and conflicts within the government doctrine.

The dynastic view was represented by Nicholas I himself, as well as by most members of his government and his court. It also found expression in such a loyal newspaper as *The Northern Bee* with its well-known editors Grech and Bulgarin. The nationalist wing was led by the Moscow professors Shevyrev and, especially Pogodin, and it included the poet and publicist Tiutchev, as well as numerous participants in *The Muscovite*. The members of this latter group stood close to the Slavophiles, although they remained separated from them, primarily by the issue of the nature and role of the Russian state.[1] Moreover, judging by Barsukov's meticulous listing of Pogodin's contacts, nationalist student reactions, gendarmerie reports, and other evidence, they enjoyed considerable support among the Russian public. Indeed, the nationalists possessed, together with their much humbler background, a much wider appeal than the proponents of a dynastic orientation. But romantic, nationalist ideas penetrated even the Russian government, and that on an increasing scale, affecting some of

[1] On the relationship between this group and the Slavophiles, see N. Riasanovsky, 'Pogodin and Ševyrev in Russian Intellectual History', *Harvard Slavic Studies*, vol. iv (1957), pp. 149–67.

the ministers and other high officials, although they never grew strong enough to replace the essentially dynastic and *ancien régime* outlook of the emperor and of most of his aides. The proponents of the dynastic view centred in St. Petersburg, the capital; the nationalists, in Moscow.

Uvarov, in his key position of minister of education, reflected these opposing influences in a striking manner. An aristocrat by origin, an outspoken defender of serfdom, and a man fully identified with the existing Russian regime, he nevertheless patronized nationalistic professors, himself dabbled in quasi-romantic ideology in composing the famous triple formula, and wanted to play the role of an intellectual abreast of, and indeed leading, his time. The revolutions of 1848 made him recoil from nationalism and toe the line of extreme Russian reaction. Yet his support of official policy was found to be insufficiently complete and single-minded, and, in 1849, Uvarov was forced to resign his ministry.

The difference between the two points of view came out strongly, perhaps in an exaggerated manner, in the following question of terminology. Whereas Holy Russia was exalted as their key symbol by the nationalists, Bulgarin quoted Count Egor Kankrin, the Minister of Finance of German origin, as saying:

If we consider the matter thoroughly, then, in justice, we must be called not *Russians*, but *Petrovians*. . . . Everything: glory, power, prosperity, and enlightenment, we owe to the Romanov family; and, out of gratitude, we should change our general tribal name of *Slavs* to the name of the creator of the empire and of its well-being. Russia should be called *Petrovia*, and we *Petrovians*; or the empire should be named *Romanovia*, and we *Romanovites*.

And Bulgarin added his own opinion to the minister's suggestion: 'An unusual idea, but an essentially correct one!'[1]

---

[1] Bulgarin, *Vospominaniia*, i. 200–1. This was not the only proposal to rename Russia 'Petrovia'. A little later one historian even argued that, in recognition of the services of Nicholas I, the country should be renamed 'Nikolaevia'. R. M. Zotov, *Tridsatiletie Evropy v tsarstvovanie Imperatora Nikolaia I*, St. Petersburg, 1857, ii. 312–13. On 'Holy Russia' see esp. Michael Cherniavsky, ' "Holy Russia": A Study in the History of an Idea', *The American Historical Review*, vol. lxiii, no. 3 (Apr. 1958), pp. 617–37. Professor Cherniavsky stated his views in full in his controversial *Tsar and People: Studies in Russian Myths*, New Haven and London, 1961. I reviewed this in *Political Science Quarterly*, vol. lxxviii, No. 2 (June 1963), pp. 304–5. See

Yet, both the representatives of the dynastic orientation and the more nationalistically inclined supporters of the regime, both the Romanovites and the Russians, were in agreement concerning certain fundamental aspects of 'nationality'. They all emphasized that the subjects of the tsar felt and expressed overwhelming devotion to Orthodoxy and autocracy. Shevyrev, for instance, declared: 'I have become accustomed to feel, at the mention of the Russian people, a certain calm, and that not only back in my fatherland, but also all over Europe. The reason is that I indissolubly connect two concepts with the name of the Russian people: unqualified submission to the Church, and the same devotion and obedience to the ruler.'[1] Pogodin, in his turn, listed the fear of God, devotion to their faith, and piety among the distinguishing characteristics of the Russian people.[2] Tiutchev declared even more emphatically: 'Russia is above all a Christian empire. The Russian people is Christian not only because of the Orthodoxy of its beliefs, but also because of something even more intimate than belief. It is Christian because of that capacity for renunciation and sacrifice which serves as the foundation of its moral nature.'[3]

It was the nationalist Pogodin, with his 'secret of Russian history', who wrote probably most eloquently and most often about this remarkable love of the Russian people for their tsar. For instance, in 1841 he noted in his diary, in connection with Nicholas I's visit to Moscow: 'To the Kremlin. With the people. Thought about the idea of the tsar who, as far as we are concerned, cannot sin, against whom nobody complains, whom nobody accuses. This is an article of dogma, although not

also Alexander V. Soloviev, *Holy Russia: The History of a Religious-Social Idea*, 'S-Gravenhage, 1959.

[1] Quoted in A. G. Dementev, *Ocherki po istorii russkoi zhurnalistiki 1840–1850 gg.*, Moscow–Leningrad, 1951, p. 185.

[2] Pogodin, *Rechi, proiznesennye v torzhestvennykh i prochikh sobraniiakh, 1830–1872*, pp. 39–40. As a young man Pogodin had noted with pride that Russian soldiers away on a campaign preferred starvation to breaking a fast. Barsukov, op. cit. i. 94.

[3] Tiutchev, op. cit., p. 344. Ustrialov, dutifully underlining all the principles of Official Nationality, summarized the character of the Russian people as follows: 'profound and quiet piety, boundless devotion to the throne, obedience to the authorities, remarkable patience, a lucid and solid intelligence, a kind and hospitable soul, a gay temper, courage amidst the greatest dangers, finally, national pride which had produced the conviction that there was no country in the world better than Russia, no ruler mightier than the Orthodox tsar.' N. G. Ustrialov, *Russkaia istoriia*, 5th edn., St. Petersburg, 1855, ii. 15.

a written one. And I doubt that they understand it. How enormously much one can accomplish with this idea!'[1] Or, to cite Pogodin's fuller account of a similar visit by the heir to the throne, in 1837:

The doors of the Cathedral of the Assumption open; preceded by torches, the Metropolitan comes forth holding a Cross in his up-raised hands. Behind him the Grand Duke with uncovered head, with lowered eyes, followed by the worthy City Governor of Moscow, by the preceptors and the teachers, and by the most eminent statesmen. Oh, how handsome he was in this minute! What beauty radiated from his young, open face! How much goodness and happiness this gentle smile promised! . . . And what sacred thoughts awoke in a Russian mind. . . . The thought about him, and about the Russian people, the youngest son of humanity, firm and fiery when a skilful hand sets in motion the sacred strings of its heart, a fresh and energe-tic people which, at a signal from its tsars, is ready to fly to its death as to a nuptial feast, a people which has still retained all the freshness of feeling now when the time of raptures has passed for Europe, and the century has enveloped itself in egoism. 'Our father, our father!' exclaimed grey old men leaning on their crutches and trying to catch with their fading eyes the movements of the August Youth. 'Our father'—these simple words contain the entire meaning of Russian History. Do not boast to us, the West, of your famous institutions! We honour your great men and recognize duly their benefactions to humanity, but we do not envy them, and we point proudly to our own: unto the West that which is Western, unto the East that which is Eastern.[2]

The emphasis on the special character of the Russian people was joined to a general pride in Russia. Nicholas I and his followers stressed the virtues and the glory of the Russians, Russian history, institutions, and language. Language stood out as a vital issue because of its central position in the thought of the age, because of the common acceptance of, and even preference for, French in Russian educated society, and because of the multilingual nature of the Russian state. The emperor wanted the use of Russian in official reports, and even ordered that Russian be spoken at court functions.[3] The government,

[1] Barsukov, op. cit. vi. 4.   [2] Ibid. v. 4.

[3] Thus, beginning with the report for 1831 Russian replaced French as the lang-uage of the annual reports of the Third Department of His Majesty's Own Chancery which Count Alexander Benckendorff presented to the emperor. Nicholas I also sponsored 'nationality' by such means as the introduction of native Russian dress for ladies at the court—to everyone's delight, or so wrote the ubiquitous head of the

and especially the Ministry of Education headed by Uvarov, embarked on a great programme of spreading the knowledge of Russian in the non-Russian areas of the empire. Writers and journalists enthusiastically supported the same cause. Shevyrev even tried in a characteristically romantic fashion to establish the nature of his countrymen on the basis of their tongue: 'Language is the invisible image of the entire people, its physiognomy.'[1] Others usually limited themselves to denouncing the use of French by their compatriots and to praising their native tongue. Occasionally, as in the case of Gogol, these praises rang sufficiently loud and clear to break out of their milieu and join the voicies of great Russian writers of other generations, such as Lomonosov and Turgenev:

Finally, our extraordinary language itself is still a mystery. It contains all tones and all shades, all transitions of sounds, from the hardest to the softest and the most tender. It has no limits, and, being alive as life itself, it is able to garner riches every minute, obtaining, on the one hand, solemn words from the church-Biblical language, and, on the other, selecting at will neat expressions from its countless dialects scattered over our provinces. It is thus able, in one and the same speech, to attain heights inaccessible to any other language and to descend to the simple level tangibly felt by even the densest person. A language which is in itself already a poet. . . .[2]

gendarmerie: 'On the sixth of December of the past year of 1833, there appeared for the first time in the Palace our Ladies and the Empress Herself in national costume and in Russian headdress. The beauty of this attire aside, it evoked, because of the feeling of nationality, a general approval.' ('Otchet IIIgo Otdeleniia Sobstvennoi Ego Imperatorskogo Velichestva Kantseliiarii i Korpusa Zhandarmov za 1834i god', TsGAOR, 109, 85, 2, pp. 3–4). Benckendorff's general judgement on the matter deserves attention: 'one can firmly state that no characteristic of the Reign of the present Sovereign obtained for Him so much love, so many praises, so much general approval as His constant effort, from the very first day of His Reign, to glorify everything Russian, to sponsor everything Native [*Otechestvennoe*] and gradually to extirpate the slavish imitation of foreigners' (ibid., p. 3).

   [1] See his lecture on 'The Russian language—an expression of the spirit and the character of the Russian people' in S. P. Shevyrev, *Lektsii o russkoi literature*, St. Petersburg, 1884, quoted from p. 5. Cf., e.g., parallel efforts of the Slavophile Constantine Aksakov, to which Shevyrev referred in his lecture. Actually, Shevyrev's analysis proved to be in character, very 'professorial' and not very exciting: Shevyrev stressed such traits as the phonetic richness of the Russian language and the resulting ability of the Russians to learn other tongues and assimilate enlightenment from all European countries; the emphasis on the present tense as indicative of the concrete, practical nature of the Russians; and the role of aspects in condensing or expanding action, just as Russian historical development often proceeded by bursts.

   [2] Gogol, op. cit., p. 219. Although Gogol was born in 1809 and Turgenev in

In spite of its sterling character and peerless language, the Russian people was assigned a narrowly circumscribed role by all proponents of Official Nationality. The Russians were to act within the confines of an autocratic regime, to remain obedient and grateful children of their tsar, as well as devoted and heroic soldiers of their officers. Still, even in this estimate of the Russian people differences appeared between those who thought in terms of the traditional dynastic state and those who burned with the new flame of nationalism. The first group tended to be entirely reactionary in its approach: serfdom was defended as an indispensable pillar of Russian society, the education of the tsar's subjects was not to exceed what was proper for their social position, and in general they were to be kept in their place and to remain merely pliant material in the hands of their masters. The nationalist ideologists of the state accepted on the whole the existing Russian order, but they also envisioned some possible modification of it, such as the abolition of serfdom. They wanted to spread education among the masses, to make all people active and enthusiastic participants in the destinies of Russia. They believed in a popular autocracy, in a real union in thought and action between the tsar and his humble subjects. And they came to be opposed to aristocracy, as an obstacle to this union and a class phenomenon which had no place in the true Russian society.

Social and economic reaction in the reign of Nicholas I centred largely on the issue of the defence of serfdom. As Uvarov, who in this debate represented the extreme Right, formulated the matter: '*Political religion, just as Christian religion, has its inviolable dogmas: in our case they are: autocracy and serfdom.*'[1] He referred to this controversial subject very often and on at least one occasion discussed it in detail with a few friends who had gathered at the minister's estate of Poreche. Pogodin, one of the guests, wrote down fifteen separate headings

1818, it is appropriate to speak of different generations. As to Lomonosov, his extravagant praise of the Russian language is a useful reminder that there indeed already was a national consciousness, as well as an emphasis on language, in eighteenth-century Russia. For a rich and judicious account of the subject, see Hans Rogger, *National Consciousness in Eighteenth-Century Russia*, Cambridge, Mass., 1960. National consciousness, however, became much more pronounced and acute, in both the government and the educated public, in the reign of Nicholas I.

[1] Barsukov, op. cit. iv. 98.

under which Uvarov explained the problem of serfdom, arguing for the retention of that institution. The minister claimed
that there was no need for abolition, and he stressed the enormous practical difficulties of such a reform, but his main
emphasis remained on the indissoluble link between autocracy
and serfdom.[1]

Education served as another area of reactionary theory and
practice in the reign of Nicholas I. The emphasis lay, again, on
keeping the masses in their proper place. As Uvarov explained
the activity of his ministry to the emperor:

The difference in the needs of the different estates and conditions
of people leads inevitably to an appropriate delimitation among
them of the subjects of study. A system of public education can be
considered to be organized correctly only when it offers opportunities to each one to receive that education which would correspond
to his mode of life and to his future calling in society.[2]

Others, in and out of the government, were more outspoken
than the urbane minister. Benckendorff, the chief gendarme,
bluntly told the emperor:

Russia is best protected from revolutionary disasters by the fact that
in our country, from the time of Peter the Great, the monarchs have
always been ahead of the nation. But for this very reason one should
not hasten unduly to educate the nation lest the people reach, in
the extent of their understanding, a level equal to that of the
monarchs and then attempt to weaken their power.[3]

---

[1] 'The question of serfdom is closely linked to the question of autocracy and
even monarchy.

'These are two parallel forces which have developed together. Both have the
same historical beginning; both have equal legality . . . Serfdom, whatever one
may think of it, does exist. Abolition of it will lead to the dissatisfaction of the
gentry class which will start looking for compensations for itself somewhere, and
there is nowhere to look except in the domain of autocracy . . . Peter I's edifice will
be shaken . . . Serfdom is a tree which has spread its roots afar: it shelters both the
Church and the Throne.' This private talk of Uvarov, as recorded by Pogodin and
reproduced in Barsukov's work, is our best source of information concerning
Uvarov's views on serfdom. There was, of course, no public discussion of serfdom in
the reign of Nicholas I. Barsukov, op. cit. ix. 305–8. See also, e.g., S. P. Melgunov,
Epokha "ofitsialnoi narodnosti" i krepostnoe pravo', in *Velikaia Reforma. Russkoe
obshchestvo i krestianskii vopros v proshlom i nastoiashchem*, ed. by A. K. Dzhivelegov,
S. P. Melgunov, and V. I. Picheta, Moscow, 1911, iii. 1–21.

[2] Uvarov, *Desiatiletie ministerstva narodnogo prosveshcheniia, 1833–1843*, p. 8.

[3] Shilder, op. cit. ii. 287.

Gogol's obscurantist position in education, which included the affirmation that the great majority of the people should remain illiterate and that the masses 'in truth should not even know whether there are any books except church books',[1] created a scandal among Russian intellectuals. The lexicographer and minor writer Vladimir Dal produced a similar controversy when he, much like Gogol, declared publicly that education was more likely to spoil than to improve the peasants, at least for the time being.[2]

By contrast, the nationalists had more confidence in the Russian people and happier plans for them. Though no ardent emancipationist, Pogodin argued against Uvarov in favour of abolishing serfdom, added highly critical comments to his account of the minister's defence of that institution, and welcomed the great reform when it finally came. So did Shevyrev and Tiutchev, each contributing a poem to the great occasion.[3] In education, too, Pogodin urged the interests of the people, arguing that general education was a necessity if Russia were to survive as a modern state. His admonition became a shrill cry in the dark days of the Crimean War.[4]

Pogodin believed that true Russian society had to be classless. Aristocracy was evil because it could shackle the people and threaten the monolithic nature of the Russian state. Talent had to have opportunities for advancement, no matter where that talent originated. It is worth noting that Pogodin himself began life as a serf. Moreover, in addition to the leaders which it could produce, the people itself was important. Whether in the form of a *zemskii sobor*, or by other means, the people could advise and support the tsar, could back him fully and directly in all his undertakings. 'In other words: we think that every supreme authority, even the wisest, will become still wiser when assisted by the voice of the entire people.'[5] And Pogodin liked

---

[1] Gogol, op. cit., p. 125.

[2] About this controversy see Dementev, op. cit., pp. 374–5.

[3] Shevyrev, '19 February' (S. P. Shevyrev, *Stikhotvoreniia*, Leningrad, 1939, pp. 197–8), and Tiutchev, 'To Emperor Alexander II' (Tiutchev, op. cit., p. 197).

[4] See esp. Pogodin, *Rechi, proiznesennye v torzhestvennykh i prochikh sobraniiakh, 1830–1872*, p. 240; Pogodin, *Istoriko-politicheskie pisma i zapiski vprodolzhenii Krymskoi Voiny, 1853–1856*, pp. 218–19, 286.

[5] Pogodin, *Rechi, proiznesennye v torzhestvennykh i prochikh sobraniiakh, 1830–1872*, p. 388. Pogodin prefaced this statement with the assertion that it did not contradict at all the principle of autocracy. Here, as in so many other places, Pogodin's views

to repeat the famous democratic dictum: *vox populi, vox Dei.*[1]

The Baltic Germans represented an issue over which the nationalist and the dynastic outlooks clashed sharply. These descendants of the Teutonic Knights enjoyed an exceptional and dominant position in their provinces, and they also played a major role in the Russian state at large, occupying many important posts, expecially in the diplomatic service, in the army, and at court. The Baltic barons provided solid support for Nicholas's entire system, and they earned the emperor's high regard. Yet they became anathema to the rising nationalist spirit. Pogodin followed the Slavophile George Samarin in violent attack on this dangerous 'foreign' element.[2] He demanded the abolition of the special privileged status of the Germans in their corner of the empire as unnecessary, oppressive, archaic, and insulting to the Russian people and the Russian state. He urged further a rapid Russification of the Latvian and Estonian majority of the provinces which, he claimed, hated its ruthless German masters and longed for closer ties with the Russians. Only thus could the area be safeguarded from the German menace:

The Russification of the Ests, the Livs, and the Kurs is a political necessity, and one must be blind not to see that! . . . The Slavs have let slip the Oder, the Vistula, the Pregel, even the Memel—it is necessary, then, to insure in good time the Dvina . . . That is, it is necessary at any price to Russify the Letts and the Ests, and as quickly as possible. *Caveat consules, ne quid respublica detrimenti capiat,* I exclaim to our statesmen.[3]

The issue of the Baltic Germans raised the question on which the two trends within Official Nationality diverged the most: the position of Russia in the world. To be sure, all proponents of the government doctrine thought naturally in terms of a dichotomy between Russia and the West. 'The West and Russia,

overlap with those of the Slavophiles, whose thought will be considered in the next chapter.

[1] e.g., Pogodin, *Istoriko-politicheskie pisma i zapiski vprodolzhenii Krymskoi Voiny, 1853–1856*, pp. 139, 191, and *Stati politicheskie i polskii vopros (1856–1867)*, Moscow, 1876, p. 164.

[2] See esp. Pogodin, *Ostzeiskii vopros. Pismo k professoru Shirrenu*, Moscow, 1869.

[3] Ibid., pp. 108–11.

Russia and the West—here is the result that follows from the entire past; here is the last word of history; here are the two facts for the future.'[1] But for Nicholas I and most of his assistants this meant battle against revolution in defence of the established order and in full alliance with conservative forces in the German states and elsewhere. For Pogodin, Tiutchev, and some other romantic intellectuals of the Right, on the other hand, Russian 'nationality' was even more a promise of the future than a call of the past or a condition of the present. For them Russia expanded to become Slavdom, Russian destiny advancing to the Elbe, Vienna, and Constantinople. A Pan-Slav Russian empire was to replace those of Austria and Turkey which had played out their historical roles. The Messianic Russian future called for an adventurous, aggressive, even revolutionary foreign policy which represented the very opposite of the conservative and legitimist orientation of Nicholas I and his government. The contrast between the two views became especially startling in the trying months of the Crimean War, which also marked the end of Nicholas I's reign.

Official Nationality was part and parcel of European reaction, and all of its intellectual proponents were intimately connected with the West and Western culture. In fact, with the single important exception of Karamzin, no Russian writer influenced them as much or as significantly as did dozens of Western ones. A certain crudeness and lack of talent of the school served only to emphasize the derivative nature of its thought.[2] Even Shevyrev's extravagant account of the decline of the West was borrowed, in part, from a French publicist, Philarète Chasles.[3] When after the revolution of 1848, the government decided to isolate Russia completely from the intellectual development of the rest of Europe and proceeded to institute a ban on philosophy, Professor Alexander Nikitenko noted in his diary: 'Again a persecution of philosophy. It has been proposed to limit its teaching in the universities to logic

[1] S. P. Shevyrev, 'Vzgliad russkogo na sovremennoe obrazovanie Evropy', *Moskvitianin*, No. 1 (1841), p. 219.
[2] The issue here is of talent as ideologists; as literary figures Gogol or Tiutchev were, of course, supreme.
[3] Shevyrev, op. cit., especially pp. 242–5. See also P. B. Struve, 'S. P. Shevyrev i zapadnye vnusheniia i istochniki teorii-aforizma o "gnilom" ili "gniiushchem" Zapade', in *Zapiski Russkogo Nauchnogo Instituta v Belgrade*, Belgrade, 1940.

and psychology, entrusting both to the clergy. The Scottish school is to serve as the foundation.'[1]

The impact of the West varied, of course, in each individual case, being decisively affected by such factors as Uvarov's thoroughly cosmopolitan education and interests, Pogodin's and Shevyrev's voracious academic learning and eager travels abroad, Tiutchev's residence abroad, including some twenty years in Munich where he came to know Schelling well personally, Grech's German background and Lutheran faith, Zhukovskii's immersion in romantic literature and his marvellous ability to translate and adapt Western originals from many lands, or the aristocratic upbringing in the tradition of legitimism, Restoration, and the Prussian alliance of Nicholas I himself. Particular differences and nuances were almost countless. Yet at least one more general point has to be made. The nationalists had an extremely high opinion of German idealistic philosophy, above all of Schelling, and they were profoundly affected by that philosophy. Nicholas I and most of his dynastically oriented followers, on the other hand, paid no attention to Schelling and were suspicious and critical of the entire German school. Uvarov occupied, again, an ambivalent position. It was at this intersection of opinion most especially that old reaction met new romanticism.

Second-rate at best intellectually, Official Nationality proved historically important for one reason: for thirty years it governed Russia. In particular, Nicholas I's reign reflected in a striking manner both the character and the principles of the ruler, that 'most consistent of autocrats'.[2] Nicholas's regime became pre-eminently one of militarism and bureaucracy. The emperor surrounded himself with military men to the extent that in the later part of his reign there were almost no civilians among his immediate assistants. Also he relied heavily on special emissaries, most of them generals of his suite, who were sent all over Russia on particular assignments, to execute immediately the will of the sovereign. Operating outside the regular administrative system, they represented an extension, so to speak, of the monarch's own person. In fact, the entire

[1] A. V. Nikitenko, *Moia povest o samom sebe i o tom 'chemu svidetel v zhizni byl.' Zapiski i dnevnik. (1804–1877 gg.)*, 2nd ed., St. Petersburg, 1905, i. 395.
[2] Schiemann, op. cit., vol. ii, p. xii.

machinery of government came to be permeated by the military spirit of direct orders, absolute obedience, and precision, at least as far as official reports and appearances were concerned. Corruption and confusion, however, lay immediately behind this façade of discipline and smooth functioning.

In his conduct of state affairs Nicholas I often bypassed regular channels, and he generally resented formal deliberation, consultation, or other procedural delay. The importance of the Committee of Ministers, the State Council, and the Senate decreased in the course of his reign. Instead of making full use of them, the emperor depended more and more on special devices meant to carry out his intentions promptly while remaining under his immediate and complete control. As one favourite method, he made extensive use of *ad hoc* committees standing outside the usual state machinery. The committees were usually composed of a handful of the most trusted assistants of the emperor, and, because these were very few, the same men in different combinations formed these committees throughout Nicholas's reign. As a rule, the committees carried on their work in secret, adding further complication and confusion to the already cumbersome administration of the empire.

The first, and in many ways the most significant, of Nicholas's committees was that established on 6 December 1826 and lasting until 1832. Count Victor Kochubei served as its chairman, and the committee contained five other leading statesmen of the period. In contrast to the restricted assignments of later committees, the Committee of the Sixth of December had to examine the state papers and projects left by Alexander I, to reconsider all major aspects of government and social organization in Russia, and to propose improvements. The painstaking work of this select group of officials led to negligible results: entirely conservative in outlook, the committee directed its effort toward hair-splitting distinctions and minor, at times merely verbal, modifications; and it drastically qualified virtually every suggested change. Even its innocuous 'law concerning the estates' that received imperial approval was shelved after criticism by Grand Duke Constantine. This laborious futility became the characteristic pattern of most of the subsequent committees during the reign of Nicholas I, in spite of the fact that the emperor himself often took an active part in their proceedings. The failure of one committee to perform its task merely led to the formation of another. For example, some nine committees in the reign of Nicholas I tried to deal with the issue of serfdom.

His Majesty's Own Chancery proved to be more effective than the special committees. Organized originally as a bureau to deal with matters that demanded the sovereign's personal participation and to supervise the execution of the emperor's orders, the Chancery grew rapidly in the reign of Nicholas I. As early as 1826, two new departments were added to it: the Second Department was concerned with the codification of law, and the Third with the administration of the newly created corps of gendarmes. In 1828 the Fourth Department was formed for the purpose of managing the charitable and educational institutions under the jurisdiction of the Dowager Empress Mary. Eight years later, the Fifth Department was created and charged with reforming the condition of the state peasants; after two years of activity it was replaced by the new Ministry of State Domains. Finally, in 1843, the Sixth Department of His Majesty's Own Chancery came into being, a temporary agency assigned the task of drawing up an administrative plan for Transcaucasia. The departments of the Chancery served Nicholas I as a major means of conducting a personal policy which bypassed the regular state channels.

The Third Department of His Majesty's Own Chancery, the political police—which came to symbolize to many Russians the reign of Nicholas I—acted as the autocrat's main weapon against subversion and revolution and as his principal agency for controlling the behaviour of his subjects and for distributing punishments and rewards among them. Its assigned fields of activity ranged from 'all orders and all reports in every case belonging to the higher police' to 'reports about all occurrences without exception'![1] The new guardians of the state, dressed in sky-blue uniforms, were incessantly active:

[1] Quoted from I. M. Trotskii, *Trete otdelenie pri Nikolae I*, Moscow, 1930, pp. 34–5. Recently two books were published in English on the Third Department, the first stressing the general cultural setting and the second administration and functioning: Sidney Monas, *The Third Section: Police and Society in Russia under Nicholas I*, Cambridge, Mass., 1961; P. S. Squire, *The Third Department: The Establishment and Practices of the Political Police in the Russia of Nicholas I*, Cambridge, 1968.

In their effort to embrace the entire life of the people, they intervened actually in every matter in which it was possible to intervene.
Family life, commercial transactions, personal quarrels, projects of
inventions, escapes of novices from monasteries—everything interested the secret police. At the same time the Third Department
received a tremendous number of petitions, complaints, denunciations, and each one resulted in an investigation, each one became
a separate case.[1]

The Third Department also prepared detailed, interesting,
and remarkably candid reports for the emperor, supervised
literature—an activity ranging from minute control over
Pushkin, to ordering various 'inspired' articles in defence of
Russia and the existing system—and fought every trace of
revolutionary infection. The two successive heads of the Third
Department, Count Alexander Benckendorff and Prince Alexis
Orlov, probably spent more time with Nicholas I than any of
his other assistants; they accompanied him, for instance, on
his repeated trips of inspection throughout Russia. Yet most of
the feverish activity of the gendarmes seemed to be to no purpose. Endless investigation of subversion, stimulated by the
monarch's own suspiciousness, revealed very little. Even the
most important radical group uncovered during the reign,
the Petrashevtsy, fell victim not to the gendarmerie but to its
great rival, the ordinary police, which continued to be part of
the Ministry of the Interior.
    The desire to control in detail the lives and thoughts of the
people and above all to prevent subversion guided also the
policies of the Ministry of Education, and in fact served as an
inspiration for the entire reign. As in the building of fortresses
the emphasis was defensive: to hold fast against the enemy and
to prevent his penetration. The sovereign himself worked
indefatigably at shoring up the defences. He paid the most
painstaking attention to the huge and difficult business of
government, did his own inspecting of the country, rushed to
meet all kinds of emergencies, from cholera epidemics and riots
to rebellions in military settlements, and bestowed special care
on the army. Beyond all that, and beyond even the needs of
defence, he wanted to follow the sacred principle of autocracy,

[1] Trotskii, op. cit., p. 111.

to be a true father of his people concerned with their daily lives, hopes, and fears.

Education continued to attract the attention of the emperor and his assistants. During the thirty years of Official Nationality, with Uvarov himself serving as Minister of Education from 1833 to 1849, the government tried to centralize and standardize education; to limit the individual's schooling according to his social background, so that each person would remain in his assigned place in life; to foster the official ideology exclusively; and, especially, to eliminate every trace or possibility of intellectual opposition or subversion.

As to centralization and standardization, Nicholas I and his associates did everything in their power to introduce absolute order and regularity into the educational system of Russia. The state even extended its minute control to private schools and indeed to education in the home. By a series of laws and rules issued in 1833–5, private institutions, which were not to increase in number in the future except where public schooling was not available, received regulations and instructions from central authorities, while inspectors were appointed to assure their compliance. 'They had to submit to the law of unity which formed the foundation of the reign.'[1] Home education came under state influence through rigid government control of teachers: Russian private tutors began to be considered state employees, subject to appropriate examinations and enjoying the same pensions and awards as other comparable officials; at the same time the government strictly prohibited the hiring of foreign instructors who did not possess the requisite certificates testifying to academic competence and exemplary moral character. Nicholas I himself led the way in supervising and inspecting schools in Russia, and the emperor's assistants followed his example.

The restrictive policies of the Ministry of Education resulted logically from its social views and aims. In order to ensure that each class of Russians obtained only 'that part which it needs from the general treasury of enlightenment', the government resorted to increased tuition rates and to such requirements as the special certificate of leave that each pupil belonging to the

---

[1] Shevyrev, *Istoriia Imperatorskogo Moskovskogo Universiteta, napisannaia k stoletnemu ego iubileiu. 1755–1855*, p. 483.

lower layers of society had to get from his village or town before he could attend secondary school. Members of the upper class, by contrast, received inducements to continue their education, many boarding schools for the gentry being created for that purpose. Ideally, in the government scheme of things—and reality failed to live up to the ideal—children of peasants and of the lower classes in general were to attend only parish schools or other schools of similar educational level; students of middle-class origin were to study in the district schools; while secondary schools and universities catered primarily, although not exclusively, to the gentry. Special efforts were made throughout the reign to restrict the education of the serfs to elementary and 'useful' subjects. Schools for girls, which were under the patronage of Dowager Empress Mary and the jurisdiction of the Fourth Department of His Majesty's Own Chancery, served the same ideology as those for boys. Educational opportunities for women were limited, it goes without saying, not only by their social origin but also by their sex. In particular, they had no access to higher education.

The inculcation of the true doctrine, that of Official Nationality, and a relentless struggle against all pernicious ideas constituted, of course, essential activities of the Ministry of Education. Only officially approved views received endorsement, and they had to be accepted without question rather than discussed. Teachers and students, lectures and books were generally suspect and required a watchful eye. In 1834 full-time inspectors were introduced into universities to keep vigil over the behaviour of students outside the classroom. Education and knowledge, in the estimate of the emperor and his associates, could easily become subversion. With the revolutionary year of 1848, unrelieved repression set in. 'Neither blame, nor praise is compatible with the dignity of the government or with the order which fortunately exists among us; one must obey and keep one's thoughts to oneself.'[1]

Still, the government of Nicholas I made some significant contributions to the development of education in Russia. It should be noted that the Ministry of Education spent large

---

[1] This imperial marginal comment is quoted from Paul Milioukov [Miliukov], Ch. Seignobus, and L. Eisenmann, *Histoire de Russie*, Paris, 1932–3, ii. 785. For the context, see Barsukov, op. cit. x. 525–38, esp. p. 538.

sums to provide new buildings, laboratories, and libraries, and
other aids to scholarship such as the excellent Pulkovo observa-
tory; that teachers' salaries were substantially increased—
extraordinarily increased in the case of professors, according
to the University Statute of 1835; that, in general, the government of Nicholas I showed a commendable interest in the
buildings and equipment necessary for education and in the
material well-being of those engaged in instruction. Nor was
quality neglected. Uvarov in particular did much to raise
educational and scholarly standards in Russia in the sixteen
years during which he headed the ministry. Especially important proved to be the establishment of many new chairs, the
corresponding opening up of numerous new fields of learning
in the universities of the empire, and the practice of sending
promising young Russian scholars abroad for extended
training. The Russian educational system, with all its fundamental flaws, came to emphasize academic thoroughness and
high standards. Indeed, the government utilized the standards
to make education more exclusive at all levels of schooling.
Following the Polish rebellion, the Polish University of Vilna
was closed; in 1834 a Russian university was opened in Kiev
instead. The government of Nicholas I created no other new
universities, but it did establish a number of technical and
'practical' institutions of higher learning, such as a technological institute, a school of jurisprudence, and a school of architecture, as well as schools of arts and crafts, agriculture, and
veterinary medicine.

But, demanding and decisive in little things, Nicholas I
could not even approach major reform. Serfdom provided the
crucial issue. The emperor personally disapproved of that
institution: in the army and in the country at large he saw only
too well the misery it produced, and he remained constantly
apprehensive of the danger of insurrection; also, the autocrat
had no sympathy for aristocratic privilege when it clashed with
the interests of the state. Yet, as he explained the matter in 1842
in the State Council: 'There is no doubt that serfdom, as it
exists at present in our land, is an evil, palpable and obvious to
all. But to touch it *now* would be a still more disastrous evil . . . .
The Pugachev rebellion proved how far popular rage can go.'[1]

---

[1] *Sbornik Imperatorskogo Russkogo Istoricheskogo Obshchestva*, xcviii. 114–15.

In fact throughout his reign the emperor feared, at the same time, two different revolutions. There was the danger that the gentry might bid to obtain a constitution if the government decided to deprive the landlords of their serfs. On the other hand, an elemental popular uprising might also be unleashed by such a major shock to the established order as the coveted emancipation.

In the end, although the government was almost constantly concerned with serfdom, it achieved very little. New laws either left the change in the serfs' status to the discretion of their landlords, thus merely continuing Alexander I's well-meaning but ineffectual efforts, or they prohibited only certain extreme abuses connected with serfdom such as selling members of a single family to different buyers. Even the minor concessions granted to the peasants were sometimes nullified. For instance, in 1847, the government permitted serfs to purchase their freedom if their master's estate was sold for debt. In the next few years, however, the permission was made inoperative without being formally rescinded. Following the European revolutions of 1848, the meagre and hesitant government solicitude for the serfs came to an end. Only the bonded peasants of western Russian provinces obtained substantial advantages in the reign of Nicholas I. They received this preferential treatment because the government wanted to use them in its struggle against the Polish influence which was prevalent among the landlords of that area.

Determined to preserve autocracy, afraid to abolish serfdom, and suspicious of all independent initiative and popular participation, the emperor and his government could not introduce fundamental reforms. Important developments did nevertheless take place in certain areas where change would not threaten the fundamental political, social, and economic structure of the Russian empire. Especially significant proved to be the codification of law and the far-reaching reform in the condition of the state peasants. The new code, produced in the late 1820s and the early 1830s by the immense labour of Speranskii and his associates, marked, despite defects, a tremendous achievement and a milestone in Russian jurisprudence. In January 1835 it replaced the ancient *Ulozhenie* of Tsar Alexis, dating from 1649, and it was destined to last until

1917. The reorganization of the state peasants followed several years later after Count Paul Kiselev became head of the new Ministry of State Domains in 1837. Kiselev's reform, which included the shift of taxation from persons to land, additional allotments for poor peasants, some peasant self-government, and the development of financial assistance, schools, and medical care in the villages, received almost universal praise from pre-revolutionary historians. However, the leading Soviet specialist on the subject, Professor N. M. Druzhinin, claimed, on the basis of impressive evidence, that the positive aspects of Kiselev's reform had a narrow scope and application, while fundamentally it placed an extremely heavy burden on the state peasants, made all the more difficult to bear by the exactions and malpractices of local administration.[1] Finance minister Kankrin's policy, and in particular his measures to stabilize the currency—often cited among the progressive developments in Nicholas I's reign—proved to be less effective and important in the long run than Speranskii's and Kiselev's work.

But even limited reforms became impossible after 1848. Frightened by European revolutions, Nicholas I became completely reactionary. Russians were forbidden to travel abroad, an order which hit teachers and students especially hard. The number of students without government scholarships was limited to three hundred per university, except for the school of medicine. Uvarov had to resign as Minister of Education in favour of an entirely reactionary and subservient functionary, Prince Plato Shirinskii-Shikhmatov, who on one occasion told an assistant of his: 'You should know that I have neither a mind nor a will of my own—I am merely a tool of the emperor's will.'[2] New restrictions further curtailed university autonomy and academic freedom. Constitutional law and philosophy were eliminated from the curricula; logic and psychology were retained, but were to be taught by professors of theology. In fact, in the opinion of some historians, the universities themselves came close to being eliminated, and only the timely intervention of certain high officials prevented this disaster.

---

[1] N. M. Druzhinin, *Gosudarstvennye krestiane i reforma P. D. Kiseleva*, Moscow–Leningrad, 1946–58.

[2] Nikitenko, op. cit. i. 441.

Censorship reached ridiculous proportions, with new agencies appearing, including the dreaded 'censorship over the censors', the so-called Buturlin committee. The censors, to cite only a few instances of their activities, deleted 'forces of nature' from a textbook in physics, probed the hidden meaning of an ellipsis in an arithmetic book, changed 'were killed' to 'perished' in an account of Roman emperors, demanded that the author of a fortune-telling manual explain why in his opinion stars influence the fate of men, and worried about the possible concealment of secret codes in musical notations.[1] Literature and thought were virtually stifled. Even Pogodin was impelled in the very last years of the reign to accuse the government of imposing upon Russia 'the quiet of a graveyard, rotting and stinking, both physically and morally'.[2] It was in this atmosphere of suffocation that Russia experienced its shattering defeat in the Crimean War.

As already indicated, Official Nationality not only dominated Russia for thirty years, but also found application in foreign policy. Indeed it had emerged as part of the reaction of established European regimes against the French Revolution and Napoleon and thus had been international from the beginning. Nicholas I was determined to maintain and defend the existing order in Europe, just as he considered it his sacred duty to preserve the archaic system in his own country. He saw the two closely related as the whole and its part, and he thought both to be threatened by the same enemy: the many-headed hydra of revolution, which had suffered a major blow with the final defeat of Napoleon but refused to die. In fact, it rose again and again, in 1830, in 1848, and on other occasions, attempting to reverse and undo the settlement of 1815. True to his principles, the resolute tsar set out to engage the enemy. In the course of the struggle, the crowned policeman of Russia became also the 'gendarme of Europe'.

Although not to the exclusion of other considerations, this determined championing of legitimism—that international variant of autocracy—and established order explains much in

---

[1] Nikitenko, op. cit., pp. 393–417, and M. O. Gershenzon, ed., *Epokha Nikolaia I*, Moscow, 1911, p. 105 *re* musical notations. Nikitenko himself served as a censor.

[2] Pogodin, *Istoriko-politicheskie pisma i zapiski vprodolzhenii Krymskoi Voiny, 1853–1856*, p. 259. Cf., however, the over-all increase in publication during those years discussed in ch. V.

Nicholas I's foreign policy in regard to such crucial developments as the Münchengrätz and Berlin agreements with
Prussia and Austria, Russian policy towards the revolutions of
1830 and 1848, including large-scale military intervention in
Hungary in 1849, and the Russian emperor's persistent
hostility to such products of revolutions as Louis-Philippe's
monarchy in France and the new state of Belgium. The great
Polish uprising of 1830–1 only helped to underline to the monarch the direct connection between European revolution and
revolt in his own domains, and, long after the military victory,
the suppression of the Polish danger remained his constant
concern. From Don Carlos in Spain to Ernest Augustus in
Hanover, Nicholas I was ready to support, or at least sympathize with, all manifestations of European reaction.

Yet, even for Nicholas I not every issue could be entirely
clear. Unusually complex and difficult in his reign was the so-
called Eastern Question which led to a war between Russia
and Persia in 1826–8, to the battle of Navarino in 1827 and a
war between Russia and Turkey in 1828–9 in connection with
the Greek struggle for independence, to such striking diplomatic developments as the Treaty of Unkiar Skelessi of 1833,
the Treaty of London of 1840, and the Straits Convention of
1841, and which finally exploded in the Crimean War. Still,
although the last word on the Russo-Turkish relations in the
first half of the nineteenth century has not been said, it would
seem rash to dissociate Nicholas I's policy in the Near East
from his general orientation. The Treaty of Adrianople of
1829 represented a moderate settlement which might have
saved the Ottoman empire from destruction. The Treaty of
Unkiar Skelessi, whatever its exact nature and implications,
resulted from Nicholas I's quick response to the sultan in his
hour of need against Mohammed Ali of Egypt, another
revolutionary rebel in the eyes of the tsar. Even Nicholas's
eventual interest in partitioning the Turkish empire can be
construed as a product of the conviction that the Porte could
not survive in the modern world, and that therefore the leading
European states had to arrange for a proper redistribution of
possessions and power in the Balkans and the Near East in
order to avoid popular self-determination, anarchy, revolution,
and war. In other words, Nicholas I's approach to Great

Britain can be considered sincere, and the ensuing misunderstanding thus all the more tragic. However, one other factor
must also be weighed in an appreciation of Nicholas I's Near
Eastern policy: Orthodoxy. The Crimean War was provoked
partly by religious conflicts. Moreover, the tsar himself retained
throughout his reign a certain ambivalence toward the sultan.
He repeatedly granted the legitimacy of the sultan's rule in the
Ottoman Empire, but remained, nevertheless, uneasy about
the sprawling Muslim state which believed in the Koran and
oppressed its numerous Orthodox subjects. To resolve the
difficulty, on one occasion Nicholas I actually proposed to the
Turkish representative that the sultan become Orthodox![1] Once
the hostilities began, the Russian emperor readily proclaimed
himself the champion of the Cross against the infidels.

The reign of Nicholas I resembled in many important and
less important ways that of his older brother and predecessor.
Neither sovereign challenged the fundamental Russian realities
of autocracy and serfdom. Both, however, enacted certain more
modest and limited reforms. Nicholas I's reorganization of
state peasants can be considered as a rather substantial contribution to the kind of partial improvement in peasant life
inaugurated by such measures of Alexander I as the law
concerning the free agriculturists. Similarly, Speranskii's
codification of Russian law represented a logical continuation
of the work of that same Speranskii and others who tried to
improve the structure and functioning of the Russian government in the earlier reign. In foreign policy the younger brother
was only too conscious of continuity with the older, of the
legacy of the Congress of Vienna and the alliance system. In
terms of principles, Nicholas I maintained the Russian tradition
of the emperor as both the all-powerful head and the first
servant of the state, and he admired Peter the Great even more
fervently than had his predecessors. Even as to character,
it is worth remembering that Alexander I too was a perfectionist
and a drill sergeant, suspicious, given to rages, and determined to keep all authority to himself in matters great and small.
Both militarism and obscurantism existed in Russia before 1825
as well as after.

But the difference was also important. It was as if Nicholas I's

---

[1] Shilder, op. cit. ii. 271–2.

rule reproduced and developed comprehensively and consistently many basic aspects of his brother's rule. Alexander's reign, however, like the emperor's baffling and contradictory character, had another side, which Nicholas's regime and Nicholas conspicuously lacked. Alexander I was an autocrat, but an autocrat in love with constitutions. He was a despot, but a despot who believed in Enlightenment. Even his foreign policy could not be simply summarized as legitimism and a defence of the *status quo*. Whereas Alexander I talked to Prince Peter Viazemskii and others about his determination to introduce Novosiltsev's constitution in Russia, a project that was for him 'sacred', Nicholas I, after the recapture of Warsaw, wrote as follows to Prince Ivan Paskevich, the Russian commander, concerning that same constitution which the Poles had found and published:

Chertkov brought me a copy of the constitutional project for Russia found in Novsiltsev's papers. The publication of this paper is most annoying. Out of a hundred of our young officers ninety will read it, will fail to understand it or will scorn it, but ten will retain it in their memory, will discuss it—and, the most important point, *will not forget it*. This worries me above everything else. This is why I wish so much that the guards be kept in Warsaw as briefly as possible. Order Count Witt to try to obtain as many copies of this booklet as he can and to destroy them, also to find the manuscript and send it to me . . .[1]

Novosiltsev, to be sure, remained as a senior statesman of the empire. Indeed the efforts and aspirations of such figures as Novosiltsev, Kochubei, and Speranskii himself, under Alexander I and under Nicholas I, illustrate admirably the continuity, but also the change, between the two reigns.

By foreclosing one main line of development Nicholas I transformed enlightened despotism into despotism pure and simple. Instead of reason and progress Russians were to rally around Orthodoxy, autocracy, and nationality. Instead of winning a future, they were to defend a past. Was it really worth defending? The Russian educated public could not answer this question in simple terms, and certainly no longer in those of the Enlightenment, for its own thinking was undergoing even deeper and more varied changes than government thought.

[1] Ibid. ii. 390.

4

The Educated Public in the
Reign of Nicholas I

*Every age, every nation contains in itself the possibility
of original art, provided it believes in something, provided
it loves something, provided it has some religion, some
ideal.*
Khoviakov[1]

A Change of Scenes

IT is not known exactly when the Age of Reason came to its
end. Perhaps it never has, for it certainly remains a major
force in the world today. Yet, already in the eighteenth century
the fundamental outlook of the Enlightenment had to with-
stand many and varied challenges. Because reason was its key
concept, the new attacks on reason carried the greatest threat.
Whether promoting a religion of the heart, intuition, or even
the pseudoscientific obsession of mesmerism, numerous newly
popular doctrines tended to destroy the very basis for rational
man, society, and the universe. But it was German idealistic
philosophy that predicated its own advance on a most thorough
and comprehensive demotion of eighteenth-century reason.
That reason was proclaimed to be limited and superficial, a
lower mode of cognition at best, a mere *Verstand*, to be surpassed
by and absorbed into the higher knowledge of *Vernunft*. One-
sided rationalism became the main charge levelled by romantic
intellectuals against the Enlightenment. Moreover, German
idealistic philosophy developed, in a sense, as a sequence of

[1] A. S. Khomiakov, *Polnoe sobranie sochinenii*, Moscow, 1900–14; quoted from
iii. 96.

renewed attempts to overcome that persistent eighteenth-century reason: thus Fichte accused Kant of rationalism, Hegel accused Fichte, and Schelling Hegel. Later the Slavophiles were to include Schelling in the condemnation, and to equate the West with one-sided rationalism.

Whatever the vices of the eighteenth-century concept of reason, it had the virtues of seeming lucidity and general applicability. Its relevance, nature, and uses appeared perfectly clear, indeed generally self-evident, to Catherine the Great, and only a little less so to Voltaire. It encompassed all and belonged to all. By contrast, the new emphasis on knowledge in depth rather than mere understanding, on imagination, or on the integrating artistic vision made the subject as important as the process or the object of thought. In the last analysis, the philosopher or the artist carried within himself the secret of cognition and creativity. The romantic age tended towards subjectivism in a still more fundamental, although frequently concealed, sense. In spite of Hume's philosophical critique and the authentic vein of scepticism present in the Age of Reason, the *philosophes* lived generally in a secure intellectual world which they had inherited from earlier centuries: neither the physical reality of the universe nor the basic intellectual and moral values were seriously questioned. But, in the long run, it was precisely this fundamental security that secularization and a reliance on the critical intellect had put in jeopardy. The romantic generation responded to the threat in several ways, most strikingly by apotheosizing the role of the creative individual. The ego in German idealistic philosophy or the thinker and the artist in romantic aesthetics were in effect creating the basic values of life and even, one could argue, the physical world itself.

The terms of intellectual discourse also changed. Although the usual contrasts between cosmopolitanism and particularism, between an atomistic and mechanistic world and one of organisms and organic growth, between harmony and strife, or between present-mindedness and historism can all be overdrawn, they help to illuminate the transformation of European thought. Especially important, in Russia as elsewhere, was the emergence of romantic nationalism. Not that eighteenth-century Russians lacked patriotism—or failed to address themselves to the issue of Russia and the West for that matter. But what used to be a pedagogical problem of learning and progressing according to the universal postulates of the Age of Reason became a metaphysical issue of establishing and asserting the true principles of the unique Russian national organism, of ensuring its historical mission. The titanically creative philosopher, poet, or artist of the romantic period was also the consciousness, almost an incarnation, of his nation; and it was the romantic concepts of the intellectual and the nation that stood out in glaring light on the new European scene.

It has been wisely remarked that as a rule people do not change their convictions: they die. Intellectual evolution proceeds by generations. Transformation, to be sure, is rarely completely sudden. Already in the eighteenth century, Russians, like other Europeans, turned to new trends, ranging from sentimentalism in literature to various forms of occultism associated with Freemasonry, in defiance of the strict canon of the Age of Reason. The French Revolution and its aftermath administered a major shock and made many educated Russians, together with their counterparts in the West, seek new orientations and moorings. Karamzin provided the outstanding example. A typical intellectual of the late Enlightenment and a leading writer of his generation, Karamzin became in the reign of Alexander I the official and highly influential historian of the Russian autocracy and the leading Russian ideologue of conservatism. His shadow loomed large long after his death in 1826. Yet in his heart and in his mind Karamzin remained a child of the Age of Reason, whose abstract political ideal was a republic of virtuous citizens and whose very writing style reflected the lucidity, simplicity, and rationality of a disciple of Voltaire. No wonder that Karamzin's junior contemporaries not only admired him, but also found some criticisms to make, for instance, to the effect that Karamzin's history dealt at length with the state, but omitted the people—that is, ignored the romantic revelation.

Younger men learned new ideas better than Karamzin. Recent research has established that Peter Chaadaev, who was born around 1794, possessed two libraries. He assembled the first during the first two decades of the nineteenth century and in 1821 sold it to his cousin by marriage, the Decembrist

F. P. Shakhovskoi. In 1822 he began to gather another library, making substantial acquisitions during his stay in western Europe in 1823–6; that library he kept until his death in 1856. The 'first library was a typical one for an enlightened Russian gentleman of Chaadaev's era. The emphasis upon rationalist literature reflects the usual so-called "Voltairianism" of Russian intellectuals during the late eighteenth and early nineteenth century.'[1] But the second library marked a new departure:

> One can classify the writers of the books in this library into about seven major categories. Taken altogether these categories clearly reflect a definite shift in Chaadaev's major reading interests when compared to the first library: 1) French Romantic social thinkers and historians, 2) Idealist philosophers, 3) English and Scottish empiricist philosophers, religious writers, and literary writers, 4) German church historians, biblical scholars, and literary writers, 5) Christian mystics, 6) Rationalists, and 7) Classical authors.[2]

Chaadaev learned the contents of his second library so well before he stated his own views in the late 1820s that the chronological divide between the two libraries can be said to constitute a part of the nebulous and uncertain border between Russian Enlightenment and Russian romanticism.

Chaadaev was not the only Russian to turn to romanticism. Although, as we have seen, the thought of the Age of Reason continued in the reign of Alexander I to dominate the minds of both the government and the educated public, and notably the Decembrists, new currents kept gaining strength to burst to the foreground after the demise of the emperor and the catastrophe in the Senate Square. In literature, Scott, Byron, and other romantic writers attracted enthusiastic readers. Russian authors responded on the whole quickly and effectively to new fashions. Already in 1822 Prince Peter Viazemskii welcomed Pushkin's 'Prisoner of the Caucasus' as a triumph of romantic poetry in Russia. He added that the triumph could be all the more complete because, unlike France, Russia had little or no classical tradition to defend.[3] Through the seminaries, the universities, and by means of

[1] Raymond T. McNally, *Chaadayev and His Friends. An Intellectual History of Peter Chaadayev and His Russian Contemporaries*, Tallahassee, 1971, pp. 167–8. For the two libraries see pp. 164–98.   [2] Ibid., p. 170.

[3] P. A. Viazemskii, 'O "Kavkazskom Plennike", povesti soch. A. Pushkina', *Syn Otechestva*, No. xlix (1822), pp. 116–19.

direct reading German idealistic philosophy began to spread in
Russia. By the end of the reign its devotees included not only
scattered individuals but a whole group of talented young
followers of Schelling who called themselves Lovers of Wisdom
and published the first Russian philosophical periodical,
Mnemosyne. In fact, in 1823–5 the divide between the Enlightenment and Romanticism in Russia ran especially along the
narrow gap separating the Decembrists from the Lovers of
Wisdom, two closely related élite groups of young men, alike in
social standing, education, ability, and promise, but with quite
different views of the world.[1]

The Beginnings of German Idealistic Philosophy in Russia

Kant first became known to Russians in the eighteenth century,
and there even was a proposal to elect him to the Imperial
Academy. The German educator and mystic, and an active
figure of the Russian Enlightenment, Johann-Georg Schwarz,
apparently included some of the ideas of the great German
thinker in his teaching of philosophy at the University of
Moscow in the late 1770s and the early 1780s. In the first
decade of the nineteenth century ten or twelve Russian
professors were paying attention to Kant in their lectures,
while several of his works appeared in Russian translation and
his teaching was discussed in critical articles.[2] Kant never
became very popular in Russia, but at least his name came to be
appreciated by the educated and his views entered the current
of Russian thought.[3]

The same was generally true of Kant's successor as the
leading German idealistic philosopher, Fichte, and of such

[1] Under the circumstances, the separation of the two groups could not be complete, and it did break down in the individual case of William Küchelbecker. Also,
a detailed analysis indicates that a few Decembrists were interested in Schelling,
although sometimes they were criticized for it by their fellows. (See A. A. Kamenskii, 'F. Shelling v russkoi filosofii nachala 19 veka', *Vestnik Istorii Mirovoi Kultury*,
1960, No. 5, Sept.–Oct., pp. 52, 57–8.) The Lovers of Wisdom, who were close to
the Decembrists personally, disbanded their group after the Decembrist rebellion
so as not to attract the attention of the government.
[2] The latest student of the subject emphasizes Russian criticism of Kant: A. A.
Kamenskii, 'I. Kant v russkoi filosofii nachala 19 veka', *Vestnik Istorii Mirovoi
Kultury*, 1960, No. 1, Jan.–Feb., pp. 49–64.
[3] Chaadaev's statement in a letter written in 1812 cuts both ways: 'Here is
a surprising fact—in Petersburg where so many people think that they understand
Kant, I could not find his major works . . .' McNally, op. cit., p. 234.

crucially important thinkers, although not idealistic philosophers, as Herder and Friedrich Schlegel. Herder, once a
teacher in Riga, did not accomplish his youthful desire of
devoting his life to Russia, but his influence in Russia as a German thinker was both early and significant, dating at least
from Radishchev's *Journey from Petersburg to Moscow*. Friedrich
Schlegel's impact on the entire Russian romantic age is
unusually difficult to disentangle from contributions of others;
yet his aesthetics, his theories of history, and many of his other
views keep occurring to the student of the Russian intellectual
life and culture of the period.[1]

But it was Schelling who in the new age came to dominate
Russian thought in a manner unprecedented since the time of
the great *philosophes*. Indeed the extent of the German thinker's
impact on Russia has proved difficult to explain, although a
number of specialists have addressed themselves to the problem.
For one thing, Russia was advancing intellectually: more
Russians could read Schelling with profit than could read Kant
a quarter of a century earlier. After the reform of 1814, ecclesiastical schools taught a considerable amount of modern philosophy. Probably more important was the very rich and varied
fare which Schelling offered—especially because the Russians did not have to limit themselves to the Schelling of a
given period, but could borrow from all his writings as these
appeared—while at the same time claiming to present a true
synthesis and a final revelation. Whereas professors of natural
science turned eagerly to Schelling's *Naturphilosophie*, poets,
writers, and intellectuals in general were especially impressed
by his aesthetics and views on history.[2] Both Schelling's bid to

[1] For one example of this presence of Friedrich Schlegel in Russian intellectual
history see the appendix on 'Khomiakov's *History* and Friedrich Schlegel's *Philosophy of History*' in my book on the Slavophiles: *Russia and the West in the Teaching
of the Slavophiles. A Study of Romantic Ideology*, Cambridge, Mass., 1952, pp. 215–18.

[2] Of course, the division was not at all airtight. Indeed it was a very great
Russian poet mentioned in the preceding chapter, Tiutchev, who gave to Schelling's *Naturphilosophie* probably its best expression in world literature. Cf., among
many passages and poems:

> Duma za dumoi, volna za volnoi—
> Dva proiavlenia stikhii odnoi!

> Thought after thought, wave after wave—
> Two manifestations of the same element!

F. I. Tiutchev, *Polnoe sobranie sochinenii*, St. Petersburg, 1913, p. 116.

explain in a comprehensive fashion the objective structure of the world on the one hand, and the subjective, religious, even mystical elements in his teaching on the other have been cited as particularly attractive to educated Russians. More recently Soviet scholars have stressed the significance and appeal of the dialectic which they find inherent in much of Schelling.[1] In any case a new master, very different from Voltaire, came to claim the allegiance of the Russians.

Although the first mention of Schelling in Russian literature goes back to 1797, the German philosopher was really introduced to the Russians in 1805, when Professor Daniel Kavunnik-Vellanskii's *Prolegomenon to Medicine* came out in St. Petersburg. Vellanskii, a physician, a surgeon, and for many years a professor of physiology and anatomy at the Medical-Surgical Academy in St. Petersburg, had been born in 1774, had studied under Schelling in Germany at the beginning of the nineteenth century, and returned to Russia his devoted follower. In lectures and books Vellanskii repeated the basic tenets of the *Naturphilosophie* of his master: the universe was one organic whole, man formed a parallel to nature, physiology and physics were analogous disciplines (Vellanskii also published a huge work on physics), efforts to understand should be directed towards the attainment of complete knowledge, and so forth. Unlike Vellanskii, Alexander Galich, professor of philosophy from 1814 at the Pedagogical Institute and from 1819 at the newly formed University in St. Petersburg, was something of an eclectic rather than a strict disciple of Schelling, but, again in contrast to Vellanskii, he went beyond the *Naturphilosophie* and described to his Russian listeners and readers some other doctrines of Schelling and Schelling's German followers. A pioneer in Russia in the field of the history of philosophy, Galich concluded his two-volume *History of Philosophic Systems*, published in 1818–19, with an exposition of Schelling's teaching. Galich even suffered for his convictions, his academic career being terminated in the obscurantist attack on education

---

[1] For an emphasis on the dialectic, see Kamenskii, 'F. Schelling v russkoi filosofii', especially pp. 47–9. As to the literature on the subject in general, there is much in numerous books dealing with Russian intellectual history, but only a single monograph devoted to Schelling in Russia: W. Setschkareff [Sechkarev], *Schellings Einfluss in der russischen Literatur der 20er und 30er Jahre des XIX Jahrhunderts*, Berlin, 1939.

during the last years of Alexander I's reign. The charges against Galich included the allegation that he preferred 'godless Kant to Christ, and Schelling to the Holy Spirit'.

In Moscow three professors were particularly prominent as disseminators of Schelling's theories. Ivan Davydov (1794–1863) taught philosophy, mathematics, and literature both at the University of Moscow and at the University Boarding School for the Gentry, where he had the gifted romanticist and future Lover of Wisdom, Prince Vladimir Odoevskii, among his students. Davydov's inaugural professorial lecture, in the spirit of Schelling, 'Concerning the Possibility of Philosophy as a Science', which he delivered in 1826, produced a great impression. Nicholas Nadezhdin (1804–56), a prominent figure in Russian literary and intellectual life, introduced Schelling's aesthetic doctrines into his lectures on Russian literature at the University of Moscow. Finally, Michael Pavlov (1793–1840), who taught physics, mineralogy, and agronomy at the University, was probably Schelling's ablest popularizer in Russia. It was Pavlov whom Herzen described in a memorable passage as a majestic figure standing at the doorway to the department of physical and mathematical sciences of the University of Moscow and arresting the students with the following challenging words: 'You want to know nature. But what is nature? And what does it mean to know?'[1] It is noteworthy that for Herzen's university generation science as well as philosophy often meant Schelling. In addition to the capitals, Schelling's influence spread to certain Russian provincial towns, in particular to such university centres as Kharkov, Kazan, and Kiev. In Kharkov, for example, Schelling obtained early recognition in the work of a German philosopher, Johann-Baptist Schad, while in Kazan Nicholas Lobachevskii's teacher of astronomy, another German, Professor Joseph Littrow, has been described as a Schellingian.[2]

The Lovers of Wisdom

Schelling's popularity in Russia spread beyond the strictly academic spheres and led to the foundation of the first Russian philosophic 'circle' and the first Russian philosophic review. In

[1] A. Gertsen, *Sochineniia*, Geneva, 1875–80, vii. 119.
[2] Kamenskii, op. cit., pp. 51–2.

1823 several young men, who had been discussing Schelling in a literary group formed around the poet and teacher Simeon Raich, established a separate society which had the study of German idealistic philosophy as its main object. They chose the name of 'The Lovers of Wisdom', insisted on secrecy, and grew to about a dozen members.[1] Prince Vladimir Odoevskii presided, the poet Dimitrii Venevitinov served as secretary, and Alexander Koshelev, Ivan Kireevskii, and Nicholas Rozhalin were also very active in the society, while those mentioned less frequently in connection with it included Stephen Shevyrev, Michael Pogodin, Peter Kireevskii, and Theodore Khomiakov, a brother of the Slavophile Alexis Khomiakov. A number of the Lovers of Wisdom studied, or at least informally attended lectures, at the University of Moscow and served in the Moscow Archives of the Main Collegium of the Ministry of Foreign Affairs, where they formed a remarkable cultural and social élite, 'the archivist youths' of Pushkin's catching phrase.

The Lovers of Wisdom reflected the new romantic temper of the age in a certain kind of poetical spiritualism which pervaded their entire outlook, in their worship of creativity and art, and in their adoration of nature, as well as in their disregard for the 'crude' aspects of life, including politics. In an attempt to disseminate the ideas of their Western masters, Schelling in particular, they began publishing the review *Mnemosyne*, which had only four issues and 157 subscribers, but marked the beginning of periodic philosophic publications in Russia. That the Lovers of Wisdom were indeed a seminal group can be best seen simply from the roster of its members and associates. Ivan and Peter Kireevskii, as well as several other Lovers of Wisdom, came to be connected with Slavophilism, and Ivan Kireevskii at least made contributions of

---

[1] The Russian word for 'the lovers of wisdom', *liubomudry*, comes from the Masonic and the mystical literature of the eighteenth century. 'It is to be found in Novikov, Radishchev uses it already in the sense of *philosophy* . . . Labzin gives it the meaning of *love of true wisdom* as opposed to the rationalist philosophy which pretended to possess that wisdom . . . In the twenties the term was frequently used, by Davydov among others, in the sense of *philosophy* . . .' A. Koyré, *La philosophie et le problème national en Russie au début du XIXe siècle*, Paris, 1929, note to p. 36. The 'secrecy' of the society, some of its external characteristics, and much of its spirit remind one of Russian Freemasonry. For a brief account of the society by a member see A. I. Koshelev, *Zapiski Aleksandra Ivanovicha Kosheleva (1812–1883 gody)*, Berlin, 1884, pp. 12 ff.

the greatest importance to the Slavophile teaching—indeed, he became the philosopher of Slavophilism. Pogodin and Shevyrev, as we have already observed, developed into the most comprehensive and significant theoreticians of Official Nationality. Moreover, these men never forgot the gods of their youth; German idealistic philosophy, especially as represented by Schelling, remained the central axis of their thought.

For two young Russian intellectuals, however, the time spent as Lovers of Wisdom was even more than fundamental preparation for later beliefs: it marked their primary contribution to the intellectual history of their native land. Venevitinov, 'the poet of thought' to his contemporaries, died in 1827 at the age of twenty-two, and bequeathed only some thirty-eight poems, a little poetic translation, and a few articles, such as 'Sculpture, Painting, and Music' or 'Morning, Noon, Evening, and Night', as a record of his view of the world. That view was thoroughly romantic: Venevitinov's favourite subjects included the aesthetic theories of the romanticists; the particular roles of the several arts and their relation to the highest art, that of poetry; man as the microcosm; analogy between man's life and human history; the golden age and the cycle of human history; the romantic, organic theory of nationality and nations; the return to original harmony on a new, conscious level through creative effort. Venevitinov had the highest appreciation of the West, but he was deeply perturbed by the imitative nature of Russian culture and went so far as to condemn all Russian literature as imitation. He even urged that Russia withdraw from contact with the West and develop a true culture of its own on the basis of a real awareness of the self and organic creativity. At the dawn of a new intellectual age, Dimitrii Venevitinov in the 1820s, like Nicholas Stankevich later in the 1830s exercised an attraction beyond tangible, objective reasons. The remarkable glow persists. In the words of perhaps the best twentieth-century historian of Russian literature:

Born in 1805, he died in his twenty-second year, carrying away with him one of the greatest hopes of Russian literature. His death was accidental—he caught a chill when driving home from a ball in the winter. It is impossible to predict what might not have come of him. He was a man of dazzling abundance of gifts—a strong brain, a born metaphysician, a mature and lofty poet—at twenty-one. His thirst for knowledge was truly Faustian, and his capacity of acquiring it reminiscent of Pico. At the same time he was a virile, attractive young man who loved all the pleasures of life. There was also in him an essential sanity and balance of all the functions of soul and body that remind one of Goethe. . . . His few philosophical and critical articles introduce us for the first time to a Russian mentality modified by the grafting on it of German idealism.[1]

In contrast to the secretary of the Society of the Lovers of Wisdom, Venevitinov, its chairman, Odoevskii, born in 1803, lived until 1869 and changed his views in a life-long quest for knowledge and truth. But his most important contribution to Russian thought was made early in his life. In the new intellectual environment, Odoevskii was the first Russian to make a critical philosophic appraisal of Western culture and to formulate on this basis a doctrine of Russian Messiahship. Of special interest here is Odoevskii's *Russian Nights*, a work strongly influenced by Schelling, conceived in the twenties, written in the thirties, but published in a complete form only in 1844, in the first volume of its author's collected works.

The West, Odoevskii argued, had accomplished marvellous things, but it had lost its balance, its harmony, and was in the throes of a most dangerous crisis caused by its inability to resolve the antinomy of man and society, of the private and the public. This failure had led to the perversion of science and art, to the loss of love and faith. Salvation, however, was possible. Throughout the history of the world such crises had been surmounted by the appearance of a saviour, of a new, fresh people destined to show again to humanity the true path from which it had deviated. For the West the saviour was Russia. In the time of Napoleon Russia had already saved the body of Europe; this was a symbol of the more difficult task yet to be accomplished, the salvation of the soul of Europe. History had prepared Russia for its glorious mission: before Peter the Great, Russia had been distinguished by its enormous size, gigantic strength, and versatile spirit, but it lacked organization and Western learning; Peter the Great had added the latter elements, and thus Russia attained a harmonious development unknown in the West. Russia was an organic society which knew no struggle between the people and the government,

---

[1] D. S. Mirsky, *A History of Russian Literature*, New York, 1949, p. 107.

preserved the principles of love and unity, and believed in the happiness of all and everyone. Russian spirit was characterized by a particular versatility, universality, and inclusiveness on which a truly harmonious life could be founded. Odoevskii's benevolent romantic idealism reflected faithfully the earlier and less exclusive stage of European romanticism. It also enabled him to resolve in a strikingly integrated and optimistic manner the perennial problem of the role of Peter the Great in Russian history which was to tear Russian intellectuals apart in the decades to come.[1]

The 'Thirties'

In Russia the 1830s began on the evening of 14 December 1825 and lasted until 1839, or 1840, or even a few years beyond that date. The accession of Nicholas I to the throne and the Decembrist catastrophe led not only to the voluntary dissolution of the Society of the Lovers of Wisdom, but to a general shock among the educated public and—some specialists would argue—to a form of intellectual paralysis. In any case serious political discourse became wholly impossible, while any substantial criticism of the government was likely to be treated as subversion. No wonder that students of the period emphasize a switch among Russian intellectuals from a socially conscious political and pragmatic orientation to a preoccupation with romantic abstractions and the self. But the concept of an ideological switch following the failure of the Decembrists needs careful qualification. As we have seen, the views that were to triumph

---

[1] V. F. Odoevskii, *Russkie nochi*, Moscow, 1913. The standard work on Odoevskii remains P. N. Sakulin, *Iz istorii russkogo idealizma. Kniaz V. Odoevskii*, Moscow, 1913.

The philosophical and generally ideological writings of the Lovers of Wisdom have been highly praised by specialists, although with some reservations and exceptions. Koyré stressed the fact that the Lovers of Wisdom were naïve dilettantes, but he added that that in itself was very much in the romantic tradition, and that in Russia, where philosophy was at its inception, nothing else could be expected. Odoevskii often depended on his teacher Davydov, Venevitinov on his teacher Pavlov, rather than on the German originals (Koyré, op. cit., pp. 137–52). For a highly appreciative approach, among a considerable number, to Odoevskii and his views, see, in addition to Sakulin, V. A. Riasanovsky, *Obzor russkoi kultury. Istoricheskii ocherk*, New York, Part II, Issue II, 1948, pp. 303–10. For a highly critical treatment: M. M. Kovalevskii, 'Shellingianstvo i gegelianstvo v Rossii', *Vestnik Evropy*, vol. xi, (Nov. 1915), pp. 166–70. Venevitinov has been favoured even by such hypercritical specialists as Shpet (G. G. Shpet, *Ocherk razvitiia russkoi filosofii*, Petrograd, 1922, pp. 324–33).

under Nicholas I had been in preparation in the reign of his brother. However progressive by other standards, it was the Decembrists who looked back to the Enlightenment, whereas the literati of the thirties marched more in step with their own time. Also, it was not so much a change of opinion within the same circle as a succession of groups. While many political liberals and radicals went to Siberia or were otherwise reduced to silence, the new romantic generation came fully into its own.[1]

The literature of the 'thirties' was colourful, bombastic, superficial, escapist, and 'positive'—the last point in particular by way of contrast to the later critical approach. Much of its inspiration sprang from such Western authors as Schiller, Hugo, and especially Scott, and more broadly from Western romanticism in general. When in Alexander Bestuzhev-Marlinskii the Russians acquired their own romantic story-teller, they praised him beyond all measure as 'the Pushkin of prose', a first-class genius without peer in literature.[2] Similarly sweeping and similarly transitory acclaim greeted such writers as the crude historical novelist Michael Zagoskin and the pretentious but feeble dramatist Nestor Kukolnik. Apparently, it was especially patriotic, nationalist motifs which elicited raves from the Russian educated public of the thirties. Genres of literature popular at the time also included Nicholas Pavlov's polished and readable society novelettes. One or two levels down, the indefatigable professor and journalist Joseph Senkovskii and other facile writers specialized in entertainment and total intellectual vacuity. The literary scene had certainly changed from the time of Novikov or even of Griboedov who died in 1829. As a Soviet critic remarked, 'at the time of the flowering of the realistic talents of the founders of Russian literature, Pushkin and Gogol', the Russian reading public was nevertheless transported by Zagoskin, Kukolnik, and Marlinskii, not to

---

[1] This is not to deny the fact that many educated Russians, such as Prince Peter Viazemskii or Pushkin for that matter, became more conservative and otherwise modified their views. But their main intellectual assumptions were those of an older generation and they could not become ideologues of the new.

[2] For Bestuzhev-Marlinskii's popularity in the 1830s see, e.g., the summary in 'Bestuzhev (Aleksandr Aleksandrovich)', *Entsiklopedicheskii Slovar* (Brockhaus-Efron), iiia.620–2. Alexander Bestuzhev, who used the pseudonym 'Marlinskii', was one of the famous Decembrist Bestuzhev brothers.

mention the lesser lights, that is, all the Zotovs, Zriakhovs, Voskresenskiis, Vonliarliarskiis, and their like.[1]

Romantic literary criticism also developed in Russia. The subjects of the tsar read avidly Western romantic critics and responded enthusiastically to such crucial events in the battle of the romanticists against the classicists as Hugo's preface to *Cromwell* published in 1827. Moreover, from the early 1820s Russia possessed a romantic critical school of its own, exemplified by the writings of the Lovers of Wisdom or by Orest Somov's far-reaching article 'On Romantic Poetry' which came out in 1823. Romantic ideology easily became complex, opaque, and vague, but it persistently emphasized the supreme role of art and the artist. And in maintaining this main thesis it came to conclusions different from and often opposed to those of the Enlightenment. The new vision, like other major visions of an age, found its expression in everything from immortal poetry to personal mannerisms.

As a perceptive and involved observer, Ivan Panaev, commented on the Russian cultural scene:

The thought that art must serve itself, that it constitutes a separate independent world of its own, that the more unengaged an artist is in his creations, the more objective as the expression went, the higher he is—this thought was the most striking and dominant one in the literature of the thirties. Pushkin was developing it in his melodious, harmonious verses, and he brought it to the point of crying egoism in his poem 'The Poet and the Rabble', which we all were declaiming with exaltation and considered virtually his best lyrical poem. Following Pushkin, all the notable literary figures of the time and the youth that milled around them were zealous, passionate defenders of art for art's sake.

During the last years of Pushkin's life, and even more sharply after his death, Kukolnik, who also belonged to the devotees of this theory, preached, as we have seen, in addition, that true art must not pay attention to everyday, contemporary, base life, that it must soar high above and depict only heroic, historical, and artistic personalities. Thence those long and most boring dramas of artists, cold as ice inside but with boiling passions on the surface, those pictures of enormous size with effective lighting—and the longer

---

[1] Aleksandr Ianov, 'Zagadka slavianofilskoi kritiki', *Voprosy Literatury*, No. 5 (May 1969), p. 94. To support his argument Ianov quotes from the Slavophile *Russkaia Beseda* of 1859, Part I.

and the more boring the drama was, the larger the canvas on which a painting was painted, the more people marvelled at the poet or the painter. Besides, Kukolnik put into circulation patriotic dramas with bombastic pronouncements in which Germans were thrown out of windows, accompanied by wild shrieks and applause from the gallery. And he developed by these works a senseless self-confidence, which was later to cost us so dearly, that Russians could cover the entire world with their hats alone. Polevoi rivalled him in this patriotism and even added to it a cheap, sentimental colouring. Both of them in ceaseless rivalry gathered the laurels of the stage.[1]

The romantic poet in the abstract lived in Russian poets in the concrete. Panaev, then young and under the spell of the spirit of the time and the soi-disant greatness around him, recorded the following episode during a long evening at Kukolnik's:

'Should I tell you, gentlemen, what troubles me?'—Kukolnik said in conclusion—'I shall be candid with you: I am disturbed by the thought that the Russian public has not yet grown up to an understanding of serious creations. Does it contain many like you? I think that I shall cease writing in Russian, I shall write in Italian or in French.'

These words had a shattering effect on all of us. 'Oh! oh! Just look at him!'—we thought, exchanging glances with one another, and we gazed at Kukolnik with a certain fear, as at a being completely out of the ordinary, superior . . . Next it seemed to me a little suspicious that one could command foreign languages as well as one's native tongue, but I immediately became ashamed of my doubt.

'This is painful, bitter for me'—continued the poet, and in his eyes, at least so it seemed to us, there were tears—'I love Russia ardently, but there is nothing to be done! still, I think, it will be necessary to abandon the Russian language . . .'

We began to beg the poet not to do this and not to deprive Russian literature and our dear fatherland of glory; we entreated him that in Russia too he will find many true adherents and admirers . . . As for ourselves, we almost swore him an oath of fidelity for life.

Kukolnik was silent for a long time. The bottle was empty. He leaned against the back of the sofa and closed his eyes.

After several minutes had passed he raised his eyelids and slowly examined all of us with his eyes.

[1] I. I. Panaev. *Literaturnye vospominaniia*, Moscow–Leningrad, 1950, pp. 140–1.

That gaze seemed to me to be so pregnant with meaning that I shuddered.

'I thank you, I thank you sincerely and from the bottom of my heart'—Kukolnik pronounced the words in a deeply moved voice— 'Not for myself I thank you, but for art, for the great cause of art which you make so passionately your own. . . . Yes, I shall write in Russian, I must write in Russian, for the simple reason that I can find such friends as you! . . .'[1]

Quite appropriately, Russian Bohemianism is generally dated from the 1830s and linked, in particular, to Kukolnik and to such companions of his as the leading painter Charles Brüllow.[2] In the words of two students of the structure of Russian cultural life, M. Aronson and S. Reiser: 'The literary and artistic Bohemia had its inception, it would seem, at N. V. Kukolnik's Wednesdays.'[3] 'This is a cult of high, pure art, a cult of the powerful individual talent, and at the same time a burning of life in drinking bouts and other pleasures with a marked philistine aroma. What is so characteristic here of the 'priests of art' is not the drinking parties themselves, nor the cult of 'art for art's sake'. The characteristic thing is the close link between creativity and Bohemianism, creation in the poisonous, intoxicated atmosphere of Bohemia, of 'Nestor's stock exchange' which knew no proprieties of the *salon* and which was connected by close ties to Glinka's operas, Brüllow's paintings, and Kukolnik's dramas.'[4] Compared with the *salons* of the Enlightenment, the new gatherings had a more plebeian, commercial, professional, and at the same time a more personal, subjective, emotional, and even wild character. Aronson and Reiser add that both Kukolnik and Brüllow died of syphilis.

But whatever the problems and the dangers of the new style in culture, they were not primarily political. Under Nicholas I's repressive control, the educated public of the 'thirties' remained remarkably quiescent. Searching studies by such specialists as

[1] Ibid., p. 42. Breaks in the original. It will be recalled that Byron too deplored a lack of understanding and appreciation which he experienced in his native land and threatened to abandon the English language and write instead in a foreign tongue, again in Italian. However, the threats which the two poets posed to their respective literatures were not comparable.

[2] Or 'Briullov', if we transliterate the Russian form of this German name, the original of which was, in fact, French, 'Brulleau'.

[3] M. Aronson and S. Reiser, *Literaturnye kruzhki i salony*, Leningrad, 1929, p. 73.

[4] Ibid., p. 295.

I. A. Fedosov have served only to emphasize the paucity of identifiable opposition during the first half of the reign.[1] The gendarmes themselves, as Alexander Benckendorff's annual reports to the emperor indicate, were even less successful than Fedosov in uncovering subversion. For example, in his account for 1833 Benckendorff wrote: 'The society by the name of Burschenschaft discovered by the high Surveillance among students at the University of Dorpat proved, upon investigation, to have no Political purpose at all and no criminal intentions of any kind.'[2] In the report for 1837 he noted that all the secret denunciations turned out to be false.[3] Indeed, with the major exception of the rebellious Poles, the subjects of the tsar displayed on the whole a most laudable patriotism and, especially, a boundless devotion to the person of the ruler. It was this almost religious belief in the ruler among the masses, together with the national pride of the Russians, that provided its firmest support to the throne. In any case: 'It has thus been proved that Russia recognizes Emperor Nicholas as *necessary* and *indispensable* to the maintenance of its well-being and prosperity.'[4] At times history even seemed to follow the doctrine of Official Nationality, with Russia enjoying an ever greater repose just when the West was surging towards new perturbations. In his account for 1834, Benckendorff declared: 'Although in the course of the last four years liberalism has spread greatly in many European countries, at the same time that spirit, according to the observation of the high Surveillance, not only has failed to gain strength among us, but, on the contrary, the number of free-thinkers in the political sense is declining with each day.'[5]

[1] I. A. Fedosov, *Revoliutsionnoe dvizhenie v Rossii vo vtoroi chetverti XIX v.* (*Revoliutsionnye organizatsii i kruzhki*), Moscow, 1958.

[2] 'Obozrenie raspolozheniia umov i razlichnykh chastei gosudarstvennogo upravleniia v 1833 godu', TsGAOR, 109/85/1, p. 203.

[3] 'Obozrenie raspolozheniia umov i nekotorykh chastei gosudarstvennogo upravleniia v 1837 godu', TsGAOR, 109/85/3, p. 88.

[4] 'Résumé de l'opinion publique en 1828', TsGAOR, 109/85/1, p. 25.

[5] 'Obozrenie raspolozheniia umov i razlichnykh chastei gosudarstvennogo upravleniia v 1834 godu', TsGAOR, 109/85/2, pp. 5–6. As a pendant to Benckendorff's happy report, one may quote Panaev: 'In general the writers of the thirties were not interested in any European political events. None of them ever took a look at any foreign newspapers. They reasoned that everyone should be occupied with his own affairs, and not interefere in those of others. "So, what is it to me"— Iakubovich used to say—"that the French have staged a fight among themselves,

The Rebel Lermontov

Still, even the thoroughly quiescent Russian 'thirties' had their drama and their protest. Characteristically, however, the traumatic event of the decade was not 'a journey from Petersburg to Moscow', nor a rebellion in the Senate Square, but the death of a poet. When d'Anthès-Heeckeren fatally wounded Pushkin in a duel in January 1837, several lines of outrage and lamentation converged. Pushkin was remembered by the Russian educated public as a liberal, a friend of the Decembrists, and it was this same reputation of liberalism that made him highly suspect in the eyes of the authorities. Moreover, the immortal poet had been an object of special attention on the part of the emperor, high government and court circles, the police, and the entire milieu of Official Nationality, and his tragic and untimely death could be interpreted as in large part a result of that attention. Also, it was a foreigner, a legitimist refugee supported by the Russian exchequer, who killed the supreme national Russian poet, the greatest pride of Russian literature. But above all there was a stunning sense of loss in a society and in an age which knew how to appreciate, although not preserve, their poets.[1]

Young Michael Lermontov's 'The Death of a Poet' expressed boiling emotions best. Yet, although this piece has become justly famous for its explosive denunciation of both the murderer and the circles surrounding Pushkin during the last years of his

chased away one king and obtained another, this does not make me either hot or cold. For our fellows, the writers, the appearance of some *Northern Flower* is a hundred times more interesting than all these political news. Why, let France even be swallowed by the earth. What business is it of mine?' Panaev, op. cit., pp. 74–5. The Iakubovich in question is apparently Lucian Iakubovich, a very minor Bohemian literary figure who died in 1839 at the age of thirty-four.

[1] The literature on Pushkin is, of course, immense. For a recent study of his death, see Walter N. Vickery, *Pushkin: Death of a Poet*, Bloomington, Ind. 1968. As to the widespread and powerful reaction of the educated public, evident from all kinds of materials, from poems, letters, and memoirs to gendarme reports, the following in its own strange way is not untypical. '"Tell me, doctor, is there any hope? Can I recover?" "None," answered Spasskii, "and so what? We all shall die, my dear fellow. Look, Pushkin too is dying. . . . Do you hear me, Pushkin? So it is surely all right for you and me to die." Svarratskii with a groan lowered his head to the pillow and died the same day and almost the same hour as Pushkin. Spasskii remarked on that subject. "Just think, what a lucky man! To die the same hour with such a person as Pushkin. Not everyone can manage that."' Panaev, op. cit., p. 55. Break in the original.

life, and although it has been constantly cited by Soviet critics as a sterling example of social consciousness and social protest, it is even more memorable as a timeless dirge, a lament for a loss beyond all measure.

> The sounds of marvellous songs have ceased,
> They will not be heard again:
> The abode of the singer is sullen and narrow,
> And there is a seal on his lips.[1]

Born in 1814 and a very precocious poet, Lermontov became in 1837 a central figure in Russian literature, both because of his resounding protest on the occasion of Pushkin's death and, more importantly, because he was Pushkin's most likely successor. Lermontov's great novel, *A Hero of Our Times*, which came out in book form in 1840, naturally attracted attention and controversy, and it continued and developed the young writer's rebellion against society. But it was a new, romantic, kind of rebellion. Instead of instructing the reader by means of the cardboard positive characters of eighteenth-century story and drama, or even by means of Radishchev's and Karamzin's sentimental travellers, Lermontov expressed himself through the person of Pechorin, an isolated, fundamentally flawed, demonic individual who carried disaster within him. Many Russians must have shared the anger and the bafflement of their emperor who complained: 'Such novels spoil the *mores* and spoil character. Because, although one reads such a piece with vexation, one is nevertheless left with a feeling of depression,

---

[1]
Zamolkli zvuki chudnykh pesen,
Ne razdavatsia im opiat:
Priiut pevtsa ugrium i tesen,
I na ustakh ego pechat.

M. Iu. Lermontov, 'Smert poeta', *Polnoe sobranie sochinenii* (5 vols.), ed. by D. I. Abramovich, vol. ii, St. Petersburg, 1910, p. 204. Tiutchev wrote an equally remarkable poem on Pushkin's death which ended:

Let Him judge your enmity	Vrazhdu tvoiu pust Tot rassudit,
Who hears spilled blood,	Kto slyshit prolituiu krov,
As to you, you, like first love,	Tebia zh, kak pervuiu liubov,
The heart of Russia will not forget!	Rossii serdtse ne zabudet!

F. I. Tiutchev, *Polnoe sobranie sochinenii*, St. Petersburg, 1913, p. 89 (the poem 'Na konchinu Pushkina'). Lermontov and Tiutchev reflected two different, even opposite orientations towards the Russia of Nicholas I, or they may be considered as representing, respectively, a romanticism of the Left and a romanticism of the Right, but above all they were in these pieces two supreme poets burying a third.

for in the end one begins to think that the world consists exclusively of this kind of individual, whose very best actions proceed from disgusting and false impulses.'[1]

Behind Pechorin there stood a 'Demon'. Throughout most of his life Lermontov had been writing and rewriting a magnificent long poem by that name full of romantic apartness, pride, and despair, and of stunning verses.

> I am he, whose gaze destroys hope,
> As soon as hope blooms;
> I am he, whom nobody loves,
> And everything that lives curses.[2]

This was rebellion, to be sure, but one not concerned with serfdom or constitutions.

Chaadaev

While many Russian writers and artists—from Lermontov to Kukolnik—were giving expression to the romantic age in their work and their lives, the more formal intellectual argument of the period moved in Russia from the Lovers of Wisdom to Peter Chaadaev and then to the Slavophiles and the Westernizers. In the new framework of German idealistic philosophy and romantic nationalism, the nature and destiny of their country remained the main preoccupation of Russian thinkers.

---

[1] Quoted from S. A. Andreev-Krivich, *Lermontov. Voprosy tvorchestva i biografii*, Moscow, 1954, p. 137. Andreev-Krivich's book, characteristic of a large body of Soviet research on Lermontov, discusses in the introduction the debate in the reign of Nicholas I between 'progressive' Belinskii and 'reactionary' critics concerning the social relevance of Lermontov's work, continues with six chapters of close analysis of the poet's 'Caucasian' writings, always emphasizing their realism and exactness of detail as against fancy and foreign literary influences, and concludes with a chapter on how Nicholas I persistently aimed to destroy Lermontov, a purpose finally accomplished when the great poet was shot in a duel in 1841.

[2]
> Ia tot, chei vzor nadezhdu gubit,
> Edva nadezhda rastsvetet;
> Ia tot, kogo nikto ne liubit,
> I vse zhivushchee klianet.

Lermontov, op. cit., p. 368. 'A Demon' with its variants occupies pp. 348–412.

Although poetry, especially great poetry, is essentially untranslatable, an English reader can obtain a certain introduction to the three greatest poets in that golden age of Russian poetry in *Three Russian Poets: Selections from Pushkin, Lermontov and Tyutchev in New Translations by Vladimir Nabokov*, New York, 1944. Nabokov concludes his brief note on Lermontov by stating that 'Lermontov remains for the true lover of poetry a miraculous being whose development is something of a mystery' (p. 38).

The Lovers of Wisdom, as we have already seen, tried to give an early, balanced solution to this difficult problem, as they attempted to combine their admiration of Peter the Great's reform with their regard for the Russian past and their enthusiasm for the thought, literature, and art of the West with their concern for the originality and authenticity of native Russian culture.

Chaadaev made his memorable contribution to the historiosophical debate in 1836. Actually, the first 'Philosophical Letter' was written in 1829; it was, incautiously, passed by the censor and published in Professor Nadezhdin's *Telescope* seven years later. Eschewing all balance, Chaadaev argued, in the teeth of Official Nationality and its crude and unmeasured glorification of its own version of the Russian way, that Russia had no past, no present, and no future.

One of the most deplorable things in our unique civilization is that we are still just beginning to discover truths which are trite elsewhere—even among people less advanced than we are in certain respects. That follows from the fact that we have never advanced along with other people; we are not related to any of the great human families; we belong neither to the West nor to the East, and we possess the traditions of neither. Placed, as it were, outside of the times, we have not been affected by the universal education of mankind. This admirable linking of human ideas throughout the passing centuries, this history of the human spirit which led the human spirit to the position which it occupies in the rest of the world today, had no effect upon us. What has long since constituted the very basis of social life in other lands is still only theory and speculation for us . . .

Look around you. Do we not all have one foot in the air? It looks as if we were all travelling. There is no definite sphere of existence for anyone, no good habits, no rule for anything at all; not even a home; nothing which attracts or awakens our endearment or affections, nothing lasting, nothing enduring; everything departs, everything flows away, leaving no traces either without or within ourselves. In our houses we are like campers; in our families we are like strangers; in our cities we are like nomads, more nomadic than the herdsmen who let their animals graze on our steppes, for they are more bound to their deserts than we to our cities.[1]

[1] Raymond T. McNally, translator and commentator, *The Major Works of Peter Chaadaev*, Notre Dame and London, 1969, pp. 27–8. The first 'Philosophical Letter' occupies pp. 23–51.

The Russians missed the stage of adolescence, crucial to a people, for it provides it 'with its most vivid recollections, its myths, its poetry, all its strongest and most fertile ideas. These are necessary bases of society.'[1]

The epoch of our social life which corresponds to this moment was filled by a dull and somber existence without vigor and without energy, in which the only thing that animated us was crime, the only thing that pacified us was slavery. No charming memories and no gracious images live in our memory, no forceful lessons in our national tradition. Glance over all the centuries through which we have lived, all the land which we cover, you will find not one endearing object of remembrance, not one venerable monument which might evoke powerfully bygone eras and might vividly and picturesquely depict them again for you. We live only in the most narrow kind of present without a past and without a future in the midst of a shallow calm.[2]

Peoples are moral beings just as individuals are. It takes centuries to educate them, just as it takes years to educate a person. In a sense, it can be said that we are an exceptional people. We are one of those nations which does not seem to form an integral part of humanity, but which exists only to provide some great lesson for the world.[3]

This absence of a real historical past was totally deplorable:

For us historical experience does not exist; ages and generations have flowed by fruitlessly for us. It would seem that in our case the general law of humanity has been revoked. Alone in the world, we have given nothing to the world, taken nothing from the world, bestowed not even a single idea upon the fund of human ideas, contributed nothing to the progress of the human spirit, and we have distorted all progressivity which has come to us. Nothing from the first moment of our social existence has emanated from us for man's common good; not one useful idea has germinated in the sterile soil of our fatherland; we have launched no great truth; we have never bothered to conjecture anything ourselves, and we have only adopted deceiving appearances and useless luxury from all the things that others have thought out.

One time, a great man wanted to civilize us, and in order to give us a foretaste of enlightenment, he threw us the cloak of civilization: we took up the cloak but did not so much as touch civilization. Another time, another great Prince, associating us with his glorious

[1] Ibid., p. 29.   [2] Ibid., p. 30.   [3] Ibid., p. 32.

mission, led us victoriously from one end of Europe to the other:
upon our return from this triumphal march across the most civilized
lands in the world, we brought only evil ideas and fatal errors which
resulted in an immense calamity which threw us back a half a
century. We have something or other in our blood which alienates
any real progress. Finally, we lived and do now live simply to serve
as some great lesson to far-distant posterity which will become aware
of it; today, in spite of what anyone says, we do not amount to a
thing in the intellectual order. I cannot stop being dumbfounded
by this void and this surprising solitude of our social existence.[1]

The secret of Russian sterility resided in the schismatic
separation of Russia from the universal Christian civilization
of the West. Certainly, Russians were Christians, but only in
the sense in which Abyssinians were Christians: both were off
the main creative, historical road of Christianity. 'In a word, the
new destinies of the human race were not accomplished in
our land. Though we were Christians, the fruit of Christianity
did not mature for us.'[2] Russia remained outside the European
community of nations: 'Remember that during fifteen centuries they had only one single idiom with which to address
God, only one single moral authority, only one single religious
conviction . . . it is Christianity which has produced everything
over there.'[3]

As Chaadaev summed up his philosophy of history and in
particular his view of the West:

The entire history of modern society occurs on the level of beliefs.
That is the essence of genuine education. Instituted originally on
this basis, education advanced only by means of thought. Interests
have always followed ideas there and have never preceded them. So,
beliefs have always produced interests and never have interests
produced beliefs. All political revolutions were in principle simply
moral revolutions. Man sought truth and found liberty and happiness.
This approach explains the phenomenon of modern society and its
civilization; it cannot be understood in any other way.[4]

Thus, despite all that is incomplete, vicious, evil, in European
society as it stands today, yet it is nonetheless true that God's reign
has been realized there in some way, because it contains the principle
of indefinite progress and possesses germinally and elementarily all

---

[1] McNally, op. cit., pp. 37–9. The references are, of course, to Peter the Great,
Alexander I, and the Decembrist rebellion.
[2] Ibid., p. 40.   [3] Ibid., pp. 43–4.   [4] Ibid., p. 44.

that is needed for God's reign to become established definitely upon earth one day.[1]

Russia, to repeat, was outside that society and that progress, a gap in the intellectual order of things.

In the conditions of Nicholas I's police state and in the intellectual climate of a rising romantic nationalism, Chaadaev's remarkable 'Letter' produced a shock and a scandal. The Russian educated public in general, with a few notable exceptions such as Alexander Herzen and Lermontov, reacted sharply against the insolent critic. The authorities, on their part, banned *The Telescope*, banished its editor Nadezhdin, dismissed the censor who had inadvertently let the 'Letter' through, and officially proclaimed Chaadaev insane. As Benckendorff instructed the governor-general of Moscow, mental derangement 'was the only reason for writing such nonsense . . . His Imperial Majesty orders you to entrust an able physician with Mr. Chaadaev's treatment and instruct the physician to visit Mr. Chaadaev absolutely every morning. . . . His Imperial Majesty wants you to send him a monthly report on Mr. Chaadaev's condition.'[2] A year later, sick or sound, Chaadaev modified his views in a piece entitled 'The Apology of a Madman'.

Again under the epigraph 'Adveniat regnum tuum'—'Thy kingdom come'—Chaadaev vented his bitterness against his narrow-minded and near-sighted calumniators, who failed to realize both that his letter was truly patriotic and that it possessed the still higher justification of speaking the truth. But the main thrust of the 'Apology' was to establish an exit from the nihilistic cul-de-sac of Chaadaev's original formulation. Peter the Great provided the escape.

For the past three hundred years Russia has been aspiring to identify herself with the West, she has been admitting her inferiority to the West, drawing all her ideas, all her teachings, all her joys from the West. For more than a century Russia has done better than that. The greatest of our kings, our glory, our demigod, he who began a new era for us, he to whom we owe our greatness and all the goods which we possess, renounced old Russia a hundred years ago in front of the entire world. With his powerful breath he swept away all our

---

[1] Ibid., p. 47.
[2] Ibid., p. 225. I have slightly changed Professor McNally's translation.

old institutions: he dug out an abyss between our past and our present, and he threw all our traditions into it; he went to make himself the smallest in the West, and he returned the greatest among us; he prostrated himself before the West, and he rose as our master and our legislator; he introduced Western idioms into our idiom; he moulded the letters of our alphabet upon those of the West; he disdained the clothes of our fathers and made us adopt Western dress; he gave his new capital a Western name; he threw away his hereditary title and adopted a Western title; lastly, he renounced his own name and wrote his signature with a Western name. Since that time, our eyes constantly turned towards the West, and we did nothing but inhale the emanations which came to us from there and nourish ourselves on them. As for our princes, who were always in advance of the nation, who always dragged us along the road of perfection in spite of ourselves, who always towed the country behind them, without the country doing anything at all, they themselves imposed Western customs, language and luxury upon us. We learned how to read from Western books, we learned how to speak from Westerners; as for our own history, it is the West which taught it to us; we drew everything from the West, we translated the whole West and were finally happy in resembling the West and proud when the West counted us among its own.[1]

So, he liberated us from all these precedents which encumber historical societies and impede their development; he opened our intelligence to all great and beautiful ideas existing among men; he handed us over totally to the West, such as the centuries have made it, and he gave us all its history for a history, all its future for a future.[2]

And, in what became Chaadaev's most celebrated sentence: 'In his hand Peter the Great found only a blank sheet of paper, and he wrote on it: Europe and the West; since then we belonged to Europe and to the West.'[3]

Russia, thus, entered history. Moreover, once it became part of the West, Russia found itself in a remarkably advantageous position. Chaadaev argued, in effect, several connected arguments. Russia possessed the freshness and enthusiasm of the newcomer, and it was unencumbered by the interests, traditions, and prejudices of the past. Besides, as a conscious and voluntary participant in the development of mankind, it could plan and measure its steps, and move steadily and advisedly towards

---

[1] McNally, op. cit., pp. 201–3.   [2] Ibid., p. 204.   [3] Ibid., p. 205.

its goal. Chaadaev—who was, after all, a transitional figure—wrote at times as a *philosophe* championing reason, and at others as a romantic intellectual profoundly aware of the crucial importance of the understanding of the self and of history for the accomplishment of destiny.

I think that if we have come after the others, it is in order to do better than the others, in order not to fall into their superstitions, into their blindnesses, into their infatuations. To reduce us to repeating the long series of follies and calamities which nations less favoured than ours had to undergo would be, in my opinion, a strange misunderstanding of the role which has been allotted to us. I find that our situation is a fortunate one, provided that we know how to evaluate it, and that the ability to contemplate and to judge the world from the heights of a thought freed from unbridled passions, from miserable interests which encroach upon it, is a lovely privilege. There is more: I have the inner conviction that we are called upon to resolve most of the problems in the social order, to accomplish most of the ideas which arose in the old societies, to make a pronouncement about those very grave questions which preoccupy humanity. I have often said, and I love to repeat it, that by the very force of circumstances we have been constituted as a genuine jury for countless trials being handled before the great tribunals of the world . . .

In our land, there are none of these passionate interests, these already-formed opinions, these inveterate prejudices: we approach each new truth with virgin minds. In our institutions, spontaneous works of our princes, in our customs which possess just a century of existence, in our opinions which still seek to become fixed upon the most significant things, nothing opposes the good things which Providence destines for humanity. It is enough for a sovereign will to be pronounced among us, in order to have all our opinions disappear, to have all our beliefs waver, to have all our minds open up to the new thought offered them. . . . History is no longer ours, it is true, but science is ours; we could not begin the whole work of humanity again, but we can participate in its latest works. The past is no longer within our powers, but the future belongs to us.

There is no possible doubt about it, the world is oppressed by its tradition; let us not envy the world for the limited circle in which it flounders; it is certain that in the heart of all the nations there is a deep feeling of their life of past accomplishments which dominates their present life, an obstinate memory of days gone by which fills their todays. Let them struggle with their inexorable past. . . . let us rejoice in the immense advantage of being able to march forward with the awareness of the route which we have to travel, by obeying only the voice of enlightened reason with a deliberate will. Let us realize that for us there exists no absolute necessity, that we are not, thank God, situated on the rapid slope which sweeps the other people towards the destinies of which they are unaware; that it is given to us to measure each step which we make, to reason out each idea which happens to graze our intellect, that we are permitted to aspire to types of prosperity which are vaster than the prosperity of which the most ardent ministers of the religion of progress dream, and that, in order to achieve definite results, we need only a powerful will, like the one which regenerated us recently.[1]

Chaadaev's first 'Philosophical Letter' is a study in dissolution. The Russian past, the Russian present, physical reality itself dissolve into nothingness. 'I cannot stop being dumbfounded by this void and this surprising solitude.' To repeat one passage among many: 'There is no definite sphere of existence for anyone, no good habits, no rule for anything at all; not even a home; nothing which attracts or awakens our endearment or affections, nothing lasting, nothing enduring; everything departs, everything flows away, leaving no traces either without or within ourselves.' The 'Letter' is written from 'Necropolis', and its crucial and most frequently repeated concept, its focal point, is 'nothing'. It would seem that Chaadaev was on the verge of suicide, when he composed his first 'Philosophical Letter'. It may be relevant that, in the opinion of many specialists, he did eventually take his own life.[2] A would-be suicide's vision formed a marvellous, stunning contrast to the crude affirmations of Official Nationality, and it became for ever one extreme way to look at Russia.

If I am correct, then, 'The Apology of a Madman' was as authentic and as much a product of Chaadaev's innermost perception and struggle as the first 'Philosophical Letter'. Great pressure had been brought to bear on the insolent critic to change his views: by the authorities certainly, and, more powerfully, by the outraged educated public to which Chaadaev himself belonged. But the important point was that the turn to Peter the Great gave life to Russia—and a lease

---

[1] McNally, op. cit., pp. 213–16.

[2] On Chaadaev's life, see esp. Charles Quénet, *Tchaadaev et les lettres philosophiques. Contribution à l'étude du mouvement des idées en Russie*, Paris, 1931.

on life to Chaadaev. Will and form stepped forth to master dissolution and chaos.

Chaadaev was a truly seminal thinker. If criticism is to be considered the hallmark of the Russian intelligentsia, this 'officer of the Hussars'—to quote from Pushkin's well-known poem—remains one of its most distinguished members, or forefathers in case a later dating of the intelligentsia is preferred. Indeed, in a very real sense a critique could not go beyond the first 'Philosophical Letter'. Herzen, then in exile in Viatka, wrote of 'a shot that rang out in the dark night', shattering the deadly calm of Nicholas I's Russia—'it forced all to awaken'.[1] More than a century later, a critic placed Chaadaev's vision—misguidedly, to be sure—at the basis of his own understanding of the problem of the relationship between Russia and the West in Russian thought.[2]

But Chaadaev also had major positive contributions to make to Russian intellectual history. A disciple of French Catholic thinkers, perhaps especially Lamennais, and of German idealistic philosophers, notably Schelling, he came to the conclusion that religious principles ruled history and even, in effect, that religious knowledge was the only genuine kind of knowledge. The former conviction inspired the first 'Philosophical Letter' with its hypostatization of the active principle of Catholicism. The latter issue, and its many aspects and problems, constituted the main substance of the other seven letters, which remained unpublished during their author's lifetime.[3] The Slavophiles and certain other Russian intellectuals disagreed with Chaadaev's religious preference but followed his peculiar religious approach to history, and were in their different ways as much concerned as the 'officer of the Hussars' with the relationship of religion to knowledge. Even Chaadaev's Catholic predilections could be found among a number of Russians who became Catholic in the reign of Nicholas I—a step which Chaadaev himself apparently never took—as well as later, in a full intellectual panoply, in Vladimir Soloviev.

[1] McNally, op. cit., p. 226.

[2] Alexander von Schelting, *Russland und Europa im Russischen Geschichtsdenken*, Berne, 1948.

[3] These letters can be found in English translation in McNally, op. cit., pp. 52–198.

Chaadaev is remarkable, too, for his glorification of Peter the Great. Although in this respect his contribution was neither pioneering, nor isolated, it stands out because of its fundamental sweep and imagination. Beyond the pseudoclassical bombast of the eighteenth century, or Pogodin's earthy and weighty historical arguments, Chaadaev's Peter the Great rises as a true creator *ab nihilo*, as an imposition of divine order upon chaos. No other writer had such a drastic perception of the reforming emperor, except perhaps Chaadaev's good friend, Pushkin.

The Slavophiles

Chaadaev knew better how to repel than how to attract. In a sense, Slavophilism, the most comprehensive and coherent romantic teaching to appear in Russia, can be considered a thunderous and sweeping rejection of the 'Philosophical Letter' and of the 'Apology of a Madman'. In direct opposition to Chaadaev's historical nihilism, the Slavophiles postulated a most glorious and most meaningful Russian past. In contradiction to his later eulogizing of Peter the Great as the man who, in effect, brought Russia into being, they considered the reforming emperor as the evil genius who turned his native land in the false Western direction. They matched Chaadaev's praise of the Catholic Church with an elaborate affirmation— even a creative theological affirmation—of Orthodoxy and with a relentless attack on Rome. But striking differences should not obscure the similarities. Above all, both Chaadaev and his Slavophile friends and opponents theorized within essentially the same framework of romantic historiosophy. Metaphysical principles determined historical development. Whether with a plus or a minus sign, Peter the Great changed the destinies of Russia. Moreover, even among romanticists Chaadaev on the one hand and Alexis Khomiakov (1804–60) and his associates on the other stood out for their emphasis on religion and its decisive significance in the life and history of man.

Nor should the impact of Chaadaev on Slavophilism be overestimated. Important as he was in the background of that teaching, its true source was the entire romantic age. In fact Slavophilism represented the fullest and most authentic ex-

pression of romantic thought in Russia. Its central dichotomy
was that of organic harmony against mechanistic division, of a
unity in love, full understanding and freedom against rationalism and compulsion, of the new ideal of romanticism against the
Age of Reason. Only the romantic ideal became Russia, and the
Age of Reason became the West.[1] It was to the service to that
ideal that Khomiakov's theology, Ivan Kireevskii's philosophical analysis, Constantine Aksakov's historical writing,
and other Slavophile works were all devoted.

Slavophilism, thus, expressed a fundamental vision of inte-
gration, peace, and harmony among men. On the religious
plane it produced, in particular, Khomiakov's concept of
sobornost, an association in love, freedom, and truth of believers,
which Khomiakov considered the essence of Orthodoxy.
However, although Slavophilism can be dated from 1839, the
Slavophile theologian defined and discussed this crucial concept
in full only on one occasion, in 1860, the year of his death. The
discussion took the form of a brief theological treatise published
as 'A Letter to the Editor of *L'Union Chrétienne* Concerning the
Meaning of the Words: 'Catholic' and '*Sobornyi*', with Special
Reference to the Speech of the Jesuit Father Gagarin'.[2]

Gagarin had accused the Orthodox Church in Slavic lands of
deleting the word 'Catholic' from the Creed and of replacing

[1] An early and incisive statement of this view can be found in F. A. Steppun,
'Nemetskii romantizm i russkoe slavianofilstvo', *Russkaia Mysl*, Mar. 1910, pp. 65–
91. My own fullest treatment of the Slavophiles was in my book *Russia and the West
in the Teaching of the Slavophiles. A Study of Romantic Ideology*. Cambridge, Mass., 1952.

[2] The 'Letter', first published in the *Union Chrétienne* in the original French,
appeared in a Russian translation in the second, the theological, volume of
Khomiakov's *Collected Works*. I am using the 5th edition of the volume: A. S.
Khomiakov, *Polnoe sobranie sochinenii*, vol. ii (Moscow, 1907), pp. 305–14. Actually Khomiakov employed the terms *sobornyi* or *sobornost* on remarkably few occasions.
In addition to the major discussion already mentioned, one may cite examples,
ibid., pp. 5, 12, 25, 70–1. In the first three cases the adjectival form of the word is
included as a part of the set description of the Church taken from the Creed. The
last instance is more interesting: the usage is more individual, and the key term
is the noun *sobornost*. *Sobor* was, of course, used often throughout Khomiakov's
writings to denote a church council. Because Khomiakov discussed the term
sobornyi only once, and that in the year of his death, one is tempted to suggest that
he had not realized its full potential value for his own theological doctrines until
he began to compose his rebuttal of Gagarin's speech and that he would have
employed it much more frequently had he lived longer.

See my article 'Khomiakov on *Sobornost*', *Continuity and Change in Russian and
Soviet Thought*, ed. by Ernest J. Simmons, Cambridge, Mass., 1955, pp. 183–96,
which I am reproducing here in part.

it with the adjective '*sobornyi*', corresponding to 'synodal', 'a vague and obscure term utterly incapable of rendering the idea of the universality'[1] of the Church. Khomiakov met the charge by arguing that '*sobornyi*' was precisely the right translation for 'Catholic', that, in fact, it gave a new insight into the true meaning of the Greek word itself. St. Cyril and St. Methodius, he claimed, selected this translation advisedly and for an excellent reason, even though they had several Slavic words meaning 'universal' at their disposal:

They stopped on the word *sobornyi*. *Sobor* expresses the idea of a gathering not only in the sense of an actual, visible union of many in a given place, but also in the more general sense of the continual possibility of such a union, in other words: it expresses the idea of *unity in multiplicity*. Therefore it is obvious that the word *katholikos*, as understood by the two great servants of the Word of God sent by Greece to the Slavs, was derived not from *kata* and *hola*, but from *kata* and *holon*; for *kata* often has the same meaning as our preposition 'according to', for instance: *kata Matthaion*, *kata Markon*, 'according to Matthew', 'according to Mark'. The Catholic Church is the Church *according to all*, or according to the *unity of all*, *kath' holon tōn pisteuontōn*, the Church according to free unanimity, according to complete unanimity, the Church in which all the peoples have disappeared and in which there are no Greeks, no barbarians, no difference of status, no slave-owners, and no slaves; that Church about which the Old Testament prophesied and which was realized in The New Testament—in one word, the Church as it was defined by St. Paul.[2]

It was this Church 'according to all', 'according to the unity of all' in love and freedom that Khomiakov preached all his life. 'The Church is one. Her unity follows of necessity from the unity of God; for the Church is not a multitude of persons in their separate individuality, but a unity of the grace of God, living in a multitude of rational creatures, submitting themselves willingly to grace.'[3] And again: 'The Church is a revelation of the Holy Spirit, granted to the mutual love of Christians, that love, which leads them up to the Father through His incarnated Word, Our Lord Jesus Christ.'[4]

---

[1] Khomiakov, op. cit., p. 305.
[2] Ibid., pp. 312–13.
[3] A. S. Khomiakov, *The Church Is One*, London, 1948, p. 14.
[4] Khomiakov, *Polnoe sobranie sochinenii*, ii. 220.

A man could fully realize himself only in the Church:

A man, however, does not find in the Church something foreign to himself. He finds himself in it, himself not in the impotence of spiritual solitude, but in the might of his spiritual, sincere union with his brothers, with his Saviour. He finds himself in it in his perfection, or rather he finds in it that which is perfect in himself, the Divine inspiration which constantly evaporates in the crude impurity of every separate, individual existence. This purification comes about through the invincible power of the mutual love in Jesus Christ of the Christians, for this love is the Holy Spirit.[1]

No external, legal expression of these bonds of love which formed the essence of the Church was necessary or possible: 'We confess the one and free Church. It remains one, although it has no official representative of its unity, and it remains free, although its freedom is not expressed by a division of its members.'[2] The Church meant life, and truth, and freedom, and love, but not authority:

No! The Church is not authority, just as God is not authority, just as Christ is not authority; because authority is something external to us. Not authority, I say, but truth, and at the same time the life of a Christian, his inner life; for God, Christ, the Church live in him a life which is more real than the heart which beats in his breast, or the blood which flows in his veins; but they live in him only inasmuch as he himself lives an ecumenical life of love and unity, that is, the life of the Church.[3]

Khomiakov emphasized that every single member of the Church formed an organic part of it. No man or group of men stood at its head; the Orthodox Church knew no pope in any form, but only Jesus Christ. There was no excessive differentiation between the clergy and the laity, no assertion that the hierarchy had the exclusive right of teaching, while the masses were entitled only to the passive reactions of listening and following. Khomiakov was overjoyed by the Encyclical of the Eastern Patriarchs in 1848 which was directed against the growing papal claims in the domain of the Christian dogma, and which proclaimed that both the immutability of the dogma and the purity of the rite were entrusted not to the hierarchy alone, but also to the entire people of the Church who were the Body of Christ. Similarly, in the organization of the Russian

---

[1] Ibid., p. 112.   [2] Ibid.   [3] Ibid., p. 53.

Church itself, Khomiakov favoured all popular elements, and was invariably opposed to centralization, regimentation, and bureaucracy, in fact, to the whole system represented by the Holy Synod and its management of the Russian Church. Bitterly criticized by Orthodox conservatives as well as by a number of Catholic writers, Khomiakov's theological views found some devoted admirers, such as George Samarin (1819–76), Khomiakov's disciple and himself a leading Slavophile, and the twentieth-century philosopher Nicholas Berdiaev. Today a reader acquainted with Khomiakov's religious works is strongly reminded of them as he reads the literature of the Catholic Left.

Characteristically, Khomiakov not only proclaimed the principle of *sobornost*, but used it immediately as a weapon against his opponents. The same 'Letter' that defined that crucial concept continued:

> Papists, you who claim the apostles to the Slavs as your own, repudiate them as fast as you can! You who broke the harmony of thought and the unity by changing the Creed without participation or counsel of your eastern brothers, how are you going to cope with the definition of the Church bequeathed to us by Cyril and by Methodius? . . . The Apostolic Church of the ninth century is neither the Church *kath' hekaston* (according to the understanding of each) as the Protestants have it, nor the Church *kata ton episkopon tēs Rōmēs* (according to the understanding of the bishop of Rome) as is the case with the Latins; it is the Church *kath' holon* (according to the understanding of all in their unity), the Church as it existed prior to the Western split and as it still remains among those whom God preserved from the split: for, I repeat, this split is a heresy against the dogma of the unity of the Church.[1]

Just as *sobornost*, 'this one word' which contains 'an entire confession of faith',[2] sums up admirably Khomiakov's writings about Orthodoxy in the course of some fifteen years, so the attack quoted above presents in a capsule form Khomiakov's tireless polemical activity against the Western creeds over the same period of time. For Khomiakov was overwhelmed, virtually obsessed by the idea that the one great turning-point in the history of Christianity was the break between the Western and the Eastern churches, and that the reason for this break

---

[1] Khomiakov, op. cit., p. 313.   [2] Ibid.

was the Western repudiation of what he came to designate as *sobornost* through the arbitrary addition of the *filioque* phrase to the common Christian Creed.[1]

Once the proud peoples of the West had thus wilfully and insolently rejected their Eastern brothers, once they had sinned against the sacred principle of *sobornost*, the die was cast, and the history of the West was determined for all ages. The Roman Catholics, after they separated themselves from the Church, that is, from the only free and true unity of all believers, had to find another basis for cohesion. They discovered it in the artificial, outward union of a strongly centralized, authoritarian system headed by a new and unique official, the pope. This external order and conformity of the Roman Catholic world, imposing as it admittedly was, could, however, merely hide but never remove the essence of the Roman Catholic heresy which lay precisely in the arbitrary disregard of the community of all believers in favour of a local opinion. Therefore, Roman Catholicism naturally gave rise to Protestantism. The Protestants came merely as a logical extension of the original Roman Catholic revolt against the Church: whereas Rome asserted the sufficiency of the opinion and of the judgement of the Western patriarchate apart from the totality of all Christians, they claimed the same sufficiency for the individual conscience. Both denominations argued by means of clever syllogisms; both substituted private, rational judgement for *sobornost*, the true community of life, love, faith, and understanding to be found only in the Church.

But this private, rational opinion, divorced from the living unity and wisdom of the Church, would not stop with Luther. Indeed, the decomposition of Protestantism was swift, sure, and frightful. 'In its final result Protestantism must pass into a purely philosophic analysis with all its consequences.'[2] 'Kant was a direct and a necessary continuer of Luther.'[3] He, in turn, had able followers in Hegel, Schelling, and other German idealistic philosophers, but it was quite beyond the capacity of those

---

[1] See especially the remarkable passage about the stranger in the West hearing the falsified Creed in ibid., pp. 48–9. For perceptive comment see V. V. Rozanov, 'Pamiati A. S. Khomiakova (1oe maia 1804g–1oe maia 1904g),' *Novyi Put*, Year II (June 1904), pp. 1–16, especially p. 15.

[2] A. S. Khomiakov, *Polnoe sobranie sochinenii*, Moscow, 1900–14, vii. 213.

[3] Khomiakov, op. cit., i. 298.

well-meaning gentlemen to retrieve the lost truth of *sobornost*. They could only stretch the fundamental rationalism and falsehood of Western thought to its logical *reductio ad absurdum* in their several systems. With the failure of philosophy, nothing was left to the West but complete negation and chaos.

Ivan Kireevskii (1806–56), 'the philosopher of Slavophilism', differed sharply from Khomiakov as a person and an intellectual. Khomiakov's robustness, energy, and optimism were entirely foreign to Kireevskii who was characterized by preciosity in thought, writing, and life, by a constant state of worry, and by dark pessimism interspersed with sweeping assertions of hope and confidence. Kireevskii's snobbery, exclusiveness, and dreaminess further accentuated the difference between the two leaders of Slavophilism. Whereas Khomiakov was all of a piece and never changed his views—in Berdiaev's words, 'he came into the world all prepared, armed and armour-plated'[1]—Ivan Kireevskii began as a devoted admirer of the West, while his turn to Orthodoxy had the force and strain of a conversion. Even more than other Slavophiles, Kireevskii had difficulty carrying out his plans and projects. He published very little, and his pieces remained, characteristically, unfinished. Yet his few scattered essays have established him both as a highly sensitive and intelligent literary critic and even, in the opinion of many specialists, as one of the few truly philosophical Russian minds.[2]

And Ivan Kireevskii's thought, in its own quite distinct way, was closely akin to Khomiakov's. 'The philosopher of Slavophilism' was primarily concerned with attaining 'the complete cognition of believing reason'.[3]

The main characteristic of religious thinking consists in the effort

[1] N. A. Berdiaev, *A. S. Khomiakov*, Moscow, 1912, p. 73.

[2] It is a tribute to the quality of Ivan Kireevskii's thought that in the last several years three major books on Ivan Kireevskii were published in the West: Eberhard Müller, *Russischer Intellekt in europäischer Krise: Ivan V. Kireevskij (1806–1856)*, Cologne–Graz, 1966; Abbott Gleason *European Muscovite: Ivan Kireevsky and the Origins of Slavophilism*, Cambridge, Mass., 1972; Peter K. Christoff, *An Introduction to Nineteenth-Century Russian Slavophilism. A Study in Ideas*, vol. ii: *I. V. Kireevskij*, The Hague, 1972. Dr. Müller's work is the most important one, representing the most thorough and exacting analysis of Kireevskii's thought available. See my review of it in *Jahrbücher für Geschichte Osteuropas*, vol. xv, No. 3, pp. 445–6.

[3] The phrase used, e.g., in I. V. Kireevskii, *Polnoe sobranie sochinenii*, Moscow, 1911, i. 264.

to combine into a single force all separate parts of the soul, to discover that internal centre of being, where intelligence, and will, and feeling, and conscience, and the beautiful, and the true, and the remarkable, and the desirable, and the just, and the merciful, and the entire range of intelligence merge into one living whole, and, thus, re-establish the substantial personality of man in its primeval indivisibility.[1]

By contrast, the West, to repeat Khomiakov's point, had been smitten by the disease of one-sided rationalism, and that fatal disease, again to reiterate Khomiakov, had already almost run its course.

It is painful to see what a subtle, but inevitable and justly sent madness now drives the Western man. He feels his darkness, and, like a moth, he flies into the fire, which he takes to be the sun. He cries like a frog and barks like a dog, when he hears the Word of God. And this gibbering idiot they want to upbraid in accordance with Hegel![2]

Khomiakov's theology and Ivan Kireevskii's philosophy were profoundly romantic. Yet their creators were very self-consciously Orthodox, and they became well-versed in Church doctrine and Church tradition which they considered to be the only truth. Under the circumstances, an analysis of the relationship between romanticism and Orthodoxy became a crucial issue in the study of Slavophile thought, leading to many arguments.[3] But whatever view one takes of the kernel of Slavophile inspiration, the application of the Slavophile teaching to the historical plane was strikingly romantic.

Khomiakov was convinced that he had discovered the essence of human history: 'Freedom and necessity compose the secret fundamental principles around which are concentrated, in various ways, all thoughts of man.'[4] Khomiakov called the first

[1] I. V. Kireevskii, op. cit. i. 275.
[2] Ibid. ii. 250.
[3] My own approach, as expressed in my works on the Slavophiles, emphasizes the romantic element as on the whole the more fundamental and probably the earlier of the two in Slavophile thought. This is not to deny the significance of the Doctors of the Church for Slavophile writings, in particular religious writings, all the more so because there is no absolute divide between Christianity and romanticism.
[4] Khomiakov, op. cit. v. 217. Khomiakov's world history, the only Slavophile work to deal at length with that subject, is a huge compilation of notes, arguments, hypotheses, and examples, which was published in three parts, after his death, to

principle the Iranian and the second the Kushite, for he believed that its original home had been in Ethiopia, and the
Bible referred to Ethiopia as 'the land of Kush'. The proponents
of the two principles formed two hostile camps, based on spiritual affinity rather than on blood ties or political allegiance, and
were engaged in a constant and manifold struggle for the world,
not only in Europe, Africa, and Asia, but also in the Americas,
and even in Australia and in Polynesia.

The Iranian principle expressed itself in the belief in creation
and in spiritual religion, in the alphabet, literature, and song.
The Bible belonged to it, and Christianity was its logical
culmination. Typically Iranian details included the legend of
the great flood and enmity against the serpent. The link which
united the Iranians was their faith, but they also belonged to
the same white race which alone preserved the tradition of true
spirituality.

The Kushites were mute men who believed in necessity,
and directed their efforts toward enormous constructions, such
as the pyramids of Egypt or the temples of southern India.
They were engaged in hewing out of stone rather than talking;
they wrote little, and they wrote only in hieroglyphics. They
worshipped the serpent. The Kushites were slaves of nature,
whether in the form of stone or in the sensuous form of a serpent.
They developed phallic religions; often they gave themselves
up to complete sensuality, as, for instance, in Indian Shivaism.
Sometimes, however, Kushitism evolved in what appeared to be

constitute the fifth, sixth, and seventh volumes of his *Works*. It is a first draft at best.
Khomiakov began to write his history probably in 1838, and he continued to work
on it intermittently until his death in 1860. The manuscript had no title, but
merely four letters at the top of the first page—'I, i, i, i', and no subdivisions. The
Slavophiles sometimes referred to Khomiakov's history as 'Semiramis', after Gogol
had on one occasion been struck by this name in the text and used it to denote the
entire work.

The guiding idea of Khomiakov's history was effectively summed up by George
Samarin: 'The struggle of *the religion of moral freedom* (the Iranian principle finally
realized in the plenitude of divine revelation preserved by the Orthodox Church)
with *the religion of necessity, material or logical* (the Kushite principle, the latest and
the most complete expression of which is presented by the newest philosophical
schools of Germany), this struggle, embodied in religious doctrines and in the
historical fate of the leading peoples of humanity—such is the basic theme, which
binds separate studies together into one organic whole.' Iu. F. Samarin, *Sobranie
sochinenii*, vol. i (2nd edn., Moscow, 1900), p. 251.

For a very high evaluation of Khomiakov's fantastic history by a twentieth-
century scholar, see A. Gratieux, *A. Khomiakov et le Mouvement Slavophile*, ii. 50–101.

the opposite direction. Thus Buddhism denied the world and all its attractions. In reality, Shivaism and Buddhism represented the two sides of the same medal: both were based on the same principle, on the recognition of necessity, be it in a sensuous abandon or in nirvana. Kushite elements penetrated into the Iranian tradition itself. They always revealed themselves in formalism, legalism, and necessity, as opposed to free creativity and life. Through the Kushite Roman state they entered the Roman Church, and from Roman Catholicism they were taken up by Protestantism.

Of the bearers of the Iranian principle, the Slavs were the most promising. Khomiakov's world history assigned an overwhelmingly important role to Slavdom, and many of his other writings, including much of his poetry, dealt with the same themes of Slavic greatness and Slavic mission. The Slavs had contributed the most important elements of European civilization, for which biased historians failed to give them credit. They built towns, introduced commerce and navigation, and developed arts and crafts. They were the most highly spiritual, the most artistic, the most talented people on the face of the earth. Keeping the concept of *sobornost* in mind, it is especially interesting to note that Khomiakov emphasized the peace-loving, fraternal, and communal qualities of the Slavs. Indeed, he presented them, by contrast with the Germanic conquerors and exploiters, as the epitome of a peaceful agricultural society based on the peasant commune. It was this brotherly living in love and concord that made the Slavs especially receptive to the Christian message, and promised them a unique Christian role in history.

The Russians were the greatest Slavic nation. They possessed an abundance of vital, organic energy, revealed in their unsurpassed language, in their glorious institutions, in the entire life of the people. They had the blessed Slavic qualities of humility, brotherhood, and love. Moreover, they succeeded in preserving their country and their way of life, while other Slavs were either conquered by the Muslim Turks, or, worse, seduced by the Catholic West. To Khomiakov, as well as to other Slavophiles, Russia prior to the reforms of Peter the Great was that land of spontaneity, freedom, and brotherly love which was their hope and their vision. It was that vision that inspired their unmeasured praise and their ardent defence of the Muscovite state, society, and culture. The historian Serge Soloviev and some other critics pointed out at the time that the Slavophile view of the Russian past had very little connection with any historical reality. And, indeed, it had come from quite other realms.

While Khomiakov wrote the Slavophile world history, Constantine Aksakov (1817–60) made the greatest contribution to the Slavophile elaboration of Russian history. Khomiakov's study stood apart, however, whereas Constantine Aksakov was assisted by other Slavophiles, more often in articles dealing with religion, literature, philosophy, education, or politics than with history proper. More derivative and cruder in his thought than either Khomiakov or Ivan Kireevskii, Constantine Aksakov possessed the consistency and sincerity of a fanatic. An off-spring of an old gentry family, unforgettably described by his father, the marvellous writer Serge (Sergei Timofeevich) Aksakov, and a product of the University of Moscow, he concentrated early on the Russian language, Russian literature, and Russian history. And if his contributions in all these fields failed to last, they at least conveyed unmistakably his main message.

Russian history, as all history, Constantine Aksakov insisted, was determined by basic principles: 'A fearsome play of material forces strikes one at first glance, but it is a mirage; an attentive gaze will see only one force, which moves everything, which is present everywhere, but which makes its way slowly— the idea . . .'[1] History was moral as well as metaphysical: 'The moral task of life belongs not only to every man, but also to nations, and every man and every nation performs it in its own manner, selecting this or that path for its accomplishment.'[2] Russia had its principles and its moral path: '*The history of the Russian people is the only history in the world of a Christian people, Christian not only in its profession of faith, but also in its life, or at least in the aspirations of its life.*'[3]

The Slavs had always been distinguished by their peaceful occupation of agriculture, their strong family ties, and their organization into communes. The idea of force, compulsion,

[1] K. S. Aksakov, *Sochineniia istoricheskie*, Moscow, 1861, p. 1.
[2] Ibid.   [3] Ibid., p. 19.

law was foreign to them. The commune meant a harmonious
social relationship, the very opposite of egoistic Western individualism; the communes were organic, not mechanical, and
they represented true growth and life. Small communes organically united into larger ones. The largest was Russia itself. But
because of the imperfection of human nature, the commune
needed something to keep order, and above all to protect it
from its warlike neighbours. So it invited the state to perform these functions. This was the celebrated calling of the
Varangians.

The calling was voluntary. The State and the Commune-Land did
not mix, but as separate units formed an alliance with each other.
The relations of the Land and the State were already defined by the
spontaneous calling: mutual confidence on both sides. Not war, not
enmity because of conquest, as was the case with the other nations,
but peace because of voluntary invitation.[1]

Russia was so different from the West that its history had been
sui generis 'from the very first instant'.

All European states are formed through conquest. Enmity is their
fundamental principle. Government came there as an armed enemy
and established itself *by force* among the conquered peoples . . .
The Russian state, on the contrary, was founded not by conquest, but by a *voluntary invitation* of the government. . . . Thus in the
foundation of the Western state: *violence, slavery, and hostility*. In the
foundation of the Russian state: *free will, liberty, and peace*.[2]

The historical development of the Russians had been guided by
their profound comprehension of the spiritual and the temporal
elements in human life and of their interrelation:

Having understood after the conversion to Christianity that freedom
is only of the spirit, Russia continually stood up for her soul, for her
faith. On the other hand, she knew that perfection was impossible
on earth, she did not seek earthly perfection, and therefore she chose
the best (that is the least evil) form of government and held to it
constantly, without considering it perfect. Recognizing the government freely, Russia did not rebel against it, and did not abase herself
in front of it.[3]

The Slavophiles wrote little about the first period of Russian
history, the Kievan, but they praised it highly. In his study

[1] Ibid., p. 4.   [2] Ibid., p. 8.   [3] Ibid., p. 10.

of *The Bogatyri of the Time of Grand Prince Vladimir According to Russian Songs,* Constantine Aksakov emphasized that these heroes of Russian folklore had been inspired by the true Orthodox faith and by their love for their families. They had been the valiant defenders of a happy society similar to a 'merry-go-round, moving harmoniously and melodiously, full of joy . . . This spirit permeates, this form marks everything that comes from Russia; such is our song itself, such is its tune, such is the organization of our Land.'[1]

After the Mongol invasion and the appanage period, Moscow united Russia around itself, thus performing its great historical task. The principles of Russian life remained inviolate. The free opinion of the Land, which had formerly expressed itself at numerous town meetings, the famous *vecha,* was directed instead to the *zemskii sobor* and the *zemskaia duma,* which spoke to the tsar with the voice of the entire Land. The spheres of activity of the State and of the Land remained strictly separate. The State used the necessary force and compulsion; the Land, that is, the people, enjoyed the free life of the spirit. This arrangement proved to be extremely satisfactory:

Throughout the whole course of Russian history, the Russian people never betrayed the government, never betrayed the monarchy. If there were disturbances, they concerned the question of the legitimacy of a particular ruler: of Boris, of the False Dimitrii, or of Shuiskii. But a voice never sounded among the people: we do not want monarchy, we do not want autocracy, we do not want the tsar. On the contrary, in 1612, having defeated the enemy and being left without a tsar, the people, unanimously and loudly, again called the tsar.[2]

The year 1612 was the favourite Slavophile year because they considered it to be the clearest affirmation of the true Russian principles: after the State had been betrayed and destroyed, when Russia was on the brink of annihilation from the hands of its foes, the Catholic Poles in particular, the Commune, the entire Land itself rose for its faith and its way of life, defeated all enemies, and re-established the old system. Then it again retired from political activity to its proper sphere of the spirit, and the first Romanovs continued in the manner of earlier Muscovite tsars.

[1] K. S. Aksakov, op. cit., p. 337.   [2] Ibid., p. 12.

Thus lived Russia, homogeneous, harmonious, and organic, without Western class divisions, without aristocracy and democracy, without enmity and compulsion. Russian society and Russian life were distinguished by simplicity, by a complete absence of theatrical effects, so prevalent in the West. Russian education was based on the true learning of the Orthodox Church.

All Holy Greek Fathers, not excluding the most profound writers, were translated, read, copied, and studied in the quiet of our monasteries, these sacred embryos of universities which were not to be . . . And these monasteries were in a living, continuous contact with the people. What enlightenment in our common people are we not entitled to deduce from this single fact![1]

And yet this order of things did not last, the harmony was broken, the organic, Russian way of life destroyed. Peter the Great appeared on the scene.

The Slavophiles could never quite understand what enabled Peter the Great to sweep away old Russia, and to institute an oppressive, mechanistic, rationalistic, Western regime in its stead. Constantine Aksakov, in particular, made of Peter the Great a titan, who introduced practically single-handed, everything evil, even serfdom, into Russia. Other Slavophiles, led by Ivan Kireevskii and Khomiakov, were more willing to concede that pre-Petrine Russia had defects which contributed to its demise. According to them, it showed a certain one-sided exclusiveness, a devotion to the form at the expense of the spirit, and it lacked consciousness of itself and of its mission.[2]

The Slavophiles were, of course, completely opposed to Peter the Great and his work, to contemporary Russian government and society. Peter the Great was a despot, who interrupted the organic development of the country, and who wanted to mould Russia like clay in accordance with his rationalistic and utilitarian notions, and in direct imitation of the West. His reforms robbed Russia of its independent role in history, and made it an appendage to the West, split the educated public from the people, and led to such evils as formalism and bureaucracy. St. Petersburg was a perfect expression of and the natural successor to his work. The new capital was the very essence of

[1] I. V. Kireevskii, op. cit. i. 119.   [2] See, e.g., ibid., p. 219.

rationalism, formalism, materialism, legalism, and compulsion: it was built out of nothing, without spiritual sanctification or historical tradition, even the ground on which it stood was Finnish rather than Russian; yet this artificial, foreign city ruled the whole land, entire Holy Russia, by means of its compulsory decrees borrowed from the West and quite inapplicable to the Russian way of life.

Although the Slavophiles frequently reacted to Peter the Great, St. Petersburg, and reformed Russia in general, to the entire St. Petersburg period of Russian history, simply with bafflement, exasperation, or rage, they also had to establish the historical role and significance of their enemy. Romantic historiosophy accepted nothing less. And indeed Khomiakov and his friends did their best to explain the fate of their country. In terms of the total development of Russia, the St. Petersburg stage had its proper logical and dialectical place:

Look at Germany. More than any other people of Europe she denied her nationality, was even partly ashamed of herself, and what happened? . . . Was this temporary renunciation really fruitless? No, Germany was rewarded by the fact that when she returned to self-consciousness and self-respect, she brought with her from the period of her humiliation the ability to understand other peoples much better than a Frenchman, an Englishman, or an Italian understands them. She practically discovered Shakespeare. We also renounced ourselves and humiliated ourselves more, a hundred times more than Germany, I hope, I am certain that when we return home (and we shall return home—and soon), we shall bring with ourselves a clear understanding of the entire world, such as the Germans did not even dream of.[1]

The St. Petersburg period thus represented the antithesis, the necessary second, negative, element in the dialectic of Russian history. Ineluctably, therefore, it led to the third, to the synthesis. Russia would then return to its organic development, to its true path in history, but on a higher, because conscious,

[1] Khomiakov, op. cit. iii. 210. St. Petersburg also served its purpose. 'Petersburg was and will remain exclusively the city of the government, and perhaps this split in the very centre of the state will not be useless for the healthy and intelligent development of Russia. The life of the power of the state and the life of the spirit of the people became divided even as to the place of their concentration' (Ibid., p. 27). Moscow, the city of the Slavophiles, was thus left free to develop the life of the spirit, 'the thought of the Russian society of tomorrow' (ibid., p. 434).

level.[1] 'In ancient Russia intelligence lacked consciousness.'[2] The Slavophiles could supply that consciousness, because they were the first to understand and reveal the true principles, the real essence of Russia. They would save the Russians from the fate of those peoples which 'disappeared from the face of the earth solely because they had unwittingly and instinctively asked themselves the question whether they were necessary to God or man, and had not been able to find a satisfactory answer'.[3] The Russia of the future will not mark a return to the dead past, but rather the attainment of a new and glorious life:

Then ancient Russia will be resurrected in an enlightened and harmonious form, in the original beauty of a society which unites a patriarchal local life with the deep meaning of the state representing the moral and the Christian person; but then it will be conscious of itself and not based on chance, full of living, organic forces, not wavering between existence and death[4]

The Slavophiles claimed to represent the bringing into consciousness, the all-important revelation of the ancient, deep, mighty, and mysterious essence of Russia, its true spirit. No romantic theory could ask or offer more. Through the Slavophile revelation, in the battle of civilizations the organic, Orthodox, Russian way would triumph over the materialistic and rationalistic principles of the West, both at home and abroad.[5] At home, to repeat, the negative Petrine stage would

---

[1] The Slavophiles constantly used the triadic pattern and some form of romantic dialectic, but without full consistency or precision. Note in particular the criticism of an expert to the effect that Khomiakov's general scheme resembled the Hegelian, but that his synthesis was not really a synthesis because one of the two contrasting elements was simply destroyed. D. I. Chizhevskii, *Gegel v Rossii*, Paris, 1939, p. 188.

[2] Khomiakov, op. cit. i. 24.

[3] Ibid. iii. 428.   [4] Ibid., p. 29.

[5] The motif of the battle of civilizations permeated not only Slavophile theoretical, critical, and historical writings of every kind, but even their literary works. Khomiakov's only two completed tragedies, *Ermak* and *The False Dimitrii*, are especially interesting in that connection. Written in 1829 and 1833 respectively, they preceded the formulation of the Slavophile ideology, and expressed in poetic language the views which later came to dominate Slavophile historical writing. The argument of *The False Dimitrii* may be summarized as follows: the False Dimitrii after many trials and tribulations is seated on the throne of Russia; he has to choose between the Russian and the Polish party, between Russian civilization and Polish; he chooses Poland; he dies a villain, and his cause is lost. The story of *Ermak* is a variation on the same theme: Ermak after many trials and tribulations conquers western Siberia; he has to choose between Russia, where he is wanted as a criminal, and Siberia, where he is promised power and glory, between

be overcome and Russia would attain a new conscious organic synthesis. Abroad—and the Slavophiles were very vague on this point—the Russian message of salvation might somehow bring life to the dying West. At least on the distant horizon one could detect *sobornost* for all.

Sobornost thus constituted both the goal of history and the standard of measure within its course. Iranians, more particularly Slavs, still more particularly Russians were the bearers of that concept or of something very closely akin to it. Organic unity in love and freedom formed their very essence.

The Russian people is not a people; it is humanity; it is a people only because it is surrounded by peoples with exclusively national essences, and its humanity is therefore represented as nationality. The Russian people is free, it has no state element in itself, it contains nothing relative. . . . *Freedom* is the general essence of the Russian, true freedom and the absence of conditionality everywhere.[1]

Appropriately, the Russian language was the most organic of all the languages:

Indeed the Russian word is not some chance growing together of national essences with different principles and character, as, for instance, are the French, the Italian and the English languages, but a living expression of original and independent thought; it is no more possible to tell a Russian 'speak thus' than it is to tell him 'think thus'.[2]

Slavic and Russian institutions reflected the character of the people. The family was especially important: it represented the bonds of unity and love in their most direct and obvious form, it provided the foundation for every healthy society, and its decay was a very significant feature of the decline of the West. The Slavs had a special predilection for the family, which formed the basis of their social life: 'They did not know the chance nature of the organization of military bands, founded on brute force and unchecked by any moral laws. Family sanctity and human feelings were developed in a simple manner

Russian civilization and Siberian; he chooses Russia; he dies a hero, and his cause is won. 'Siberian civilization', invented for the purpose, is competently represented by a shaman, who offers Ermak rule over the whole of Siberia and untold riches, power, and glory, if only he would renounce Russia and link his fortunes to the Siberian principle. *Dimitrii Samozvanets* and *Ermak* occupy, respectively, pp. 117–292 and 303–418 in Khomiakov, op. cit., vol. iv.

[1] K. S. Aksakov, op. cit., p. 630.   [2] Khomiakov, op. cit. iii. 452.

between the graves of the fathers and the cradles of the children.'[1] The family forged bonds of love in time as well as in space, it united successive generations and made tradition and society possible. Much has been written about the importance of family ties and feelings in the Slavophile outlook and teaching.[2]

Even more striking was the Slavophile glorification of the peasant commune. The commune was a priceless treasure. 'Western thinkers turn in a vicious circle solely because it is impossible for them to attain the idea of the commune.'[3] Constantine Aksakov insisted that: 'The commune is that highest true principle, which is not destined to find anything higher than itself, but which is destined only to flourish, purify, and elevate itself.'[4] His summary description of the commune was probably the most significant one in Slavophile literature:

A commune is a union of the people who have renounced their egoism, their individuality, and who express their common accord; this is an act of love, a noble Christian act, which expresses itself more or less clearly in its various other manifestations. A commune thus represents a moral choir, and just as in a choir a voice is not lost, but follows the general pattern and is heard in the harmony of all voices: so in the commune the individual is not lost, but renounces his exclusiveness in favour of the general accord—and there arises the noble phenomenon of a harmonious, joint existence of rational beings (consciousness); there arises a brotherhood, a commune—a triumph of human spirit.[5]

As Berdiaev commented: 'The Slavophiles were under the influence of their *narodnik* illusions. To them the commune was not a fact of history, but something imposing which stands outside the realm of history; it is the "other world" so to speak within this world.'[6]

[1] Ibid., p. 135.

[2] 'They were accustomed to breathe the air of complaisance of relatives, the atmosphere of amiability of the next of kin, that soft lawlessness without which kinship itself would be unthinkable; evidently it never entered their heads that any social group could be formed in a different manner, except by an evil design. Projecting their studies, their drawing-rooms, and their dining-rooms over the entire world, they wished to see all the world organized along the lines of kinship, as one enormous tea party of friendly relatives gathered in the evening to discuss some good question.' P. A. Florenskii, *Okolo Khomiakova*, Moscow, 1916, pp. 42–3.

[3] Khomiakov, op. cit. i. 50.

[4] K. S. Aksakov, op. cit., p. 291.   [5] Ibid., pp. 291–2.

[6] N. A. Berdyaev, *The Russian Idea*, London, 1947, p. 50.

The Slavophile insistence on civil liberties, on freedom for 'the life of the spirit', also followed from their central vision. Conscience obviously had to be absolutely free. In the words of Constantine Aksakov's younger brother, Ivan Aksakov (1823–86), who developed into a leading Slavophile and Pan-Slav journalist: 'The Church says concerning conscience: it is free because it is *mine, God's*; the state says: it is free because it is *not mine, not Caesar's.*'[1] Similarly, freedom of speech was another fundamental necessity. As Constantine Aksakov tried to explain to an uncomprehending government: 'Man was created by God as an intelligent and a talking being.'[2] Not limited to prose, he gave his best known poem a characteristic title: 'The Free Word'. The free word meant, of course, freedom of the press as well as of speech. The Slavophiles had good reason to protest against censorship, which interfered with their work and closed down most of their publications. But they assailed above all censorship as such rather than its specific tendency, and they constantly remonstrated against restrictions imposed on their opponents, whether the opponents were Russian radicals or spokesmen of the Baltic barons. Concern for 'the spirit' even led to the unqualified Slavophile rejection of capital punishment: 'Death penalty is legalized murder, but murder never the less . . . And when you say that a criminal cannot repent, you are judging the soul of man, a judgement which belongs only to God.'[3] And the Slavophiles were fundamentally opposed to serfdom—a subject discussed in most studies of Slavophilism, including my own.

The Russian lived in the Church, in the family, and in the commune. He was active in many spheres of life and especially in the realm of the spirit. But the field of politics, the domain of the state, remained foreign to him. The Slavophiles were anarchists of a peculiar kind: they considered all formalism and compulsion and therefore every form of state as evil, but they were convinced that the state could not be avoided. The best one could do, then, was to limit its scope, and that, as we have seen, was exactly what the Russians proceeded to do

---

[1] I. S. Aksakov, *Sochineniia*, Moscow, 1886–91, iv. 112.

[2] N. L. Brodskii, *Rannie slavianofily*, Moscow, 1910, p. 95. This includes Constantine Aksakov's celebrated memorandum, 'O vnutrennem sostoianii Rossii', and some of his editorials in *Molva*.

[3] Constantine Aksakov in Brodskii, op. cit., p. 117.

throughout their history, from the invitation of the Varangians in 862, to the election of Michael Romanov in 1613, and into the nineteenth century. 'History offers no other example of that kind; no other people desired the state so consciously, but on the other hand, no other people kept itself so consistently apart from the state.'[1]

In this remarkable arrangement, supreme right and value rested definitely with the people, whereas the state, the government, had been merely invited to assist the people. As Constantine Aksakov put it in his usual blunt manner:

It was clearly understood that the people did not exist for the state, but the state for the people. The principle of life, of moral achievement, of the spirit is undoubtedly to be found in the commune, in the people. The state is of secondary importance, and according to its very idea it cannot put a soul into the people, at best it can communicate to the people mechanical motion.[2]

Or as Khomiakov admonished a fellow Slavophile in a letter, after praising an article of Tiutchev: 'Reproach him for one thing, for his attack on the *souveraineté du peuple*. It indeed does contain the *souveraineté suprême*. Otherwise what is the meaning of the year 1612?'[3] Although the Slavophiles loved to discuss the year 1612, however, they were absolutely opposed to any formal guarantee of the supremacy of the people, any established machinery for the election or control of the tsars. This meant to them the worst kind of legalism of the Western type, an involvement of the people itself in politics, a corruption of the Russian soul.[4]

The Slavophiles believed in autocracy. This conclusion

---

[1] K. S. Aksakov, op. cit., p. 594.   [2] Ibid., p. 251 n.
[3] Khomiakov, op. cit., viii. 200–1.
[4] The Slavophiles were very hostile indeed to political democracy. For example: 'It is clear that the principle of majority is a principle which does not need harmony; it is a compulsory principle, which wins only through physical superiority; those who are *in the majority* overwhelm those who are *in the minority*' (K. S. Aksakov, op. cit., p. 292). Or: 'The essence of democracy is the most crude worship blinded by ambition of the principle of the state, of the external, material, compulsory, and relative truth, and the desire to introduce this principle into the inner life of the people' (ibid. ii. 87). In the words of Professor N. V. Ustrialov: 'If Slavophilism is characterized by a certain democratic element, its democracy is not formal, political, not state, legal, but mystical.' N. V. Ustrialov, 'Politicheskaia doktrina slavianofilstva. (Ideia samoderzhaviia v slavianofilskoi postanovke)', *Izvestiia Iuridicheskogo Fakulteta*, vol. i. Harbin (1925), p. 66.

followed logically from their premisses: if power was an evil burden, the fewer men who had to carry it the better. The Slavophiles stressed the difficulty and the responsibility, not the power and the glory, of the supreme rule, and they 'regarded the crown of the tsar as a certain kind of a martyr's crown, a sacrificial symbol of self-renouncement'.[1] Ivan Aksakov in particular emphasized the advantage of having a living man, a soul and a conscience, instead of formal institutions and legal bodies, at the head of the nation. The Slavophile predilection for paternalism and family relations could be easily extended to tsar-father and his Russian children. Autocracy was also dear to the Slavophiles as a great Russian tradition, as an organic element of Russian history and life. And yet, with all that, the Slavophile justifications of autocracy remained historical and functional, therefore relative, never religious and absolute.[2] Moreover, indispensable in its proper place, autocracy, government in general, was to be restricted to that place, to interfere as little as possible with the free life of the people.[3]

At the beginning of Alexander II's reign Constantine Aksakov presented to the emperor a memorandum expounding the nature and the proper roles of the Russian people and the Russian government. He asserted that 'the first relationship between the government and the people is the relationship of *mutual non-interference*',[4] and concluded as follows:

May the ancient union of the government and the people, of the state and the land be re-established on the firm foundation of true, fundamental Russian principles. To the government the unlimited freedom of *rule*, which is its exclusive possession, to the people the

---

[1] Ustrialov, op. cit., p. 57.

[2] Samarin was true to the Slavophile teaching when he wrote in regard to Church and state, more specifically the Church and different forms of government: 'The Church is indifferent to this form, to the question how power should be organized, to whom it should be entrusted; the Church restricts as little the freedom of political development as of the development of commerce or of language.' Samarin, op. cit. vi. 557–8.

[3] Quite logically, the Slavophiles preferred custom to law: 'Law and custom rule the social life of the peoples. Law, written and armed with compulsion, brings the differing private wills into a conditional unity. Custom, unwritten and unarmed, is the expression of the most basic unity of society. It is as closely connected with the personality of a people as the habits of life are connected with the personality of a man. The broader the sphere of custom, the stronger and healthier the society, and the richer and more original the development of its jurisprudence.' Khomiakov, op. cit. iii. 75.   [4] Constantine Aksakov in Brodskii, op. cit., p. 80.

full freedom of both external and internal *life*, which the government safeguards. *To the government the right of action,* and consequently of law; *to the people the right of opinion,* and consequently of speech.[1]

On other occasions too the Slavophiles kept emphasizing this division of spheres and the need for the government to remain strictly in its own area. '*Defence* in general, that is the meaning and the duty of the state. Its guardianship consists in providing greater comforts of life, and not at all in managing it. The state is in no way a preceptor . . .'[2] 'Its entire virtue must consist of its *negative* character, so that the less it exists as a state, the better it accomplishes its aim, as is the case in England.'[3] And to eliminate all possible doubt: 'The fewer points of contact the government has with the people, and the people with the government, the better.'[4] A repudiation of enlightened despotism could hardly be more complete.

The Slavophiles and Slavophilism constituted a remarkable phenomenon in the life and thought of the Russian educated public at the time of Nicholas I. Well known in Muscovite society, able, and tireless as well as relentless in argument, the champions of the new teaching won the attention and often admiration and respect even of their direct opponents.[5] While Khomiakov and his associates were frequently accused of sophistry and casuistry in buttressing their case or in demolishing the assertions of their antagonists, few doubted their fundamental sincerity or the fact that they spoke with their own

[1] Ibid., p. 96.
[2] K. S. Aksakov, op. cit., p. 552.
[3] I. V. Kireevskii, op. cit. ii. 272.
[4] K. S. Aksakov, 'Zamechaniia na novoe administrativnoe ustroistvo krestian v Rossii', *Rus* (1883), Nos. 3, 4, 5, p. 26.
[5] To quote Herzen's celebrated notice of the deaths of Khomiakov and of Constantine Aksakov: 'It is painful for those persons who loved them to know that these noble, tireless workers are no longer, that these *opponents*, who were closer to us than many of *ours*, no longer exist. The Kireevskiis, Khomiakov, and Aksakov *accomplished their task* . . . they stopped the stampeded public opinion and made all serious men think. With them begins *the turning-point of Russian thought* . . . Yes, we were their opponents, but very strange opponents: we had *one love*, but *not an identical one*. Both they and we conceived from early years one powerful, unaccountable, physiological, passionate feeling, which they took to be a recollection, and we—a prophecy, the feeling of boundless, all-encompassing love for the Russian people, Russian life, the Russian turn of mind. Like Janus, or like a two-headed eagle, we were looking in different directions while *a single heart was beating in us*.' A. I. Gertsen, *Polnoe sobranie sochinenii i pisem,* ed. by M. K. Lemke, Petrograd, 1915–25, quoted from xi. 11.

authentic voice. They were part and parcel of the inward intellectual emancipation of the Russians, of 'the marvellous decade' of the 1840s. That their doctrine was so outrageous to many of their compatriots only made it more prominent and the need to explain it and to respond to it more imperative.

One way to account for the Slavophiles was to take them at their own word. Khomiakov, Constantine Aksakov, and other members of the original group, together with their few disciples and more numerous later admirers, all believed that in some sense Slavophilism represented the true expression of Orthodoxy or of Russia. It was a genuine revelation of the spirit for its age and perhaps for eternity. This view may help us to understand the Slavophiles' image of themselves, and it may even prove useful in emphasizing such aspects of the movement as its connection with Orthodoxy, but its larger ramifications belong to the realm of faith rather than of historical analysis.

More mundane explanations were not slow to arise. Contemporaries quickly noted that the Slavophiles belonged to several old gentry families and formed a closely knit group of relatives and friends.[1] In the winter most of them resided in the same section of Moscow. The remainder of the year they spent usually on their estates. 'In a patriarchal milieu, holding strongly to ancient customs, permeated by the traditions and the legends of the past, in the country, in the bosom of nature, in quiet gentry nests, all the early Slavophiles grew up.'[2] The patriarchal, family element and the emphasis on a tight, organic group became a hallmark of Slavophilism and, for some critics, the key to the Slavophile view of the world.

Broader social interpretations also made their appearance. Proposed first by such writers as Plekhanov and V. D. Smirnov,[3] they assumed the central importance in Soviet historiography

---

[1] In my own book on the Slavophiles I classified only six men (Khomiakov, the Kireevskii brothers, the Aksakov brothers, and Samarin) as original Slavophiles and added a few immediate disciples and associates. Peter Kireevskii (1808–56), the gatherer of Russian folk songs, published almost nothing and remains an elusive figure, although he apparently was personally important in the movement. In the autumn of 1969 I was able to work with the Elagin–Kireevskii archival materials in Moscow and found some interesting biographical facts, for example, concerning Peter Kireevskii's illnesses and death, but nothing new on his thought.

[2] Brodskii, op. cit., p. x.

[3] V. Smirnov, *Aksakovy, ikh zhizn i literaturnaia deiatelnost*, St. Petersburg, 1895, pp. 19–20.

where the exact class nature of the Slavophiles became the focal point of analysis. Obviously, the Slavophiles were landlords, but it remained to determine what kind of landlords and how their agricultural interests were related to the general economic evolution of Russia. Thus N. Rubinshtein argued in a comprehensive evaluation that the Slavophiles represented the middle layer of the landowning class.[1] Together with other Russian landlords, they were horrified by the deepening of the class conflict in Russia and by the rise of the revolutionary tide in the West. Moreover, they had the ingenuity to erect intellectual defences against these grave dangers by asserting the uniqueness of Russia and the Russian way, which had nothing in common with the West. The Slavophile theory of the boundless attachment of the people to their unique head, the tsar, was a reflection of their views concerning their own estates: '*The devotion of the people to the monarchy in the Slavophile system was nothing but a projection into history of their own 'monarchy' as landlords.*'[2] Again, by their emphatic affirmation of the 'nonpolitical' nature of the Russian people, the Slavophiles tried to convince themselves and others that this people could not rise against either its tsar or its landlords. They had good reason to detest Peter the Great, because he had put Russia on the road to becoming an industrial Western country. The conflict between the Slavophiles and the government of Nicholas I arose from the fact that Slavophilism was an ideology of the middle layer of the gentry, whereas the government at the time reflected primarily the interests of the upper layer. The basic assumptions of the two sides were the same, but the Slavophiles were more progressive and demanded a faster development of the Russian economy. In particular, they advocated the emancipation of the serfs, because they had found hired labour to be cheaper than serf labour. The Slavophile protests against 'formalism', 'legalism', and bureaucracy arose from a desire for a greater measure of liberty in economic pursuits, which were hampered by various government restrictions. As to the peasant commune, the Slavophiles were quick to discover in their capacity as landlords

---

[1] N. Rubinshtein, 'Istoricheskaia teoriia slavianofilov i ee klassovye korni', *Trudy Instituta Krasnoi Professury. Russkaia istoricheskaia literatura v klassovom osveshchenii. Sbornik statei*, ed. by M. N. Pokrovskii, Moscow, 1927, i. 53–118.

[2] Ibid., p. 92.

that it offered, because of its tight organization and common responsibility, the best guarantee of a full performance of their obligations by the peasants. Similarly, they objected to government interference with the commune because the commune operated better and produced more profit when left alone. The ambivalent Slavophile attitude toward the West, which they hated but found indispensable, was a perfect reflection of the position of their class. Progressive landowners were bitterly opposed to the rising industrial society, but they were forced to borrow from that society for the sake of their agriculture, which was undergoing a rapid change from feudalism to capitalism. This was obvious, for instance, in the case of agricultural machinery, but it was in fact no less compelling in such matters as an increase in popular education, for otherwise the people could not operate the machines. The unavoidable contradiction in the relations with the West was, therefore, fundamental both in the Slavophile ideology and in the life of the class which it represented: the Slavophiles desired social development, but not class struggle, Western machines, but not Western ideas, factory goods, but not the proletariat; in short, they wanted capitalism, but not its consequences.

The sparse Soviet literature on Slavophilism has paid particular attention to classifying the Slavophiles somewhere along the line from sheer reactionary landlordism to more progressive and modern positions. Certain writers have given a greater emphasis than Rubinshtein to the entrepreneurial activities and the interest in technology and science of such Slavophiles as Alexander Koshelev (1806–83) and Khomiakov himself to argue for veritable bourgeois elements and aspirations in the Slavophile movement. Progressive agriculture, of course, went hand in hand with this broader technological and modernizing orientation.[1]

Yet, matching Slavophilism with a specific narrow class position has proved to be a remarkably difficult task. Not

[1] For the latest contribution to this 'liberal', 'bourgeois' explication of Slavophilism in Soviet literature, see E. A. Dudzinskaia, 'Burzhuaznye tendentsii v teorii i praktike slavianofilov', *Voprosy Istorii*, No. 1 (1972), pp. 49–64. The author was a student of Professor S. S. Dmitriev of the University of Moscow, who, albeit with careful qualifications, pioneered this approach. See esp. S. S. Dmitriev, 'Slavianofily i slavianofilstvo (Iz istorii russkoi obshchestvennoi mysli serediny XIX veka)', *Istorik Marksist*, Book 1/89, 1941, pp. 85–97.

surprisingly, therefore, some scholars who have not been willing to abandon a social interpretation, have tried to redefine it in broader terms. Thus a Polish specialist, Andrzej Walicki, maintained in a recent article that the Slavophiles can be understood best not as champions of the 'semi-liberal gentry' or another specific social group, but rather as defenders of the entire old order threatened by modernization, of *Gemeinschaft* against *Gesellschaft*, to borrow Tönnies's famous dichotomy which appears to be so strikingly applicable to the Slavophile teaching.

In spite of many utopian elements, Slavophilism was much more than mere fantasy or messianic myth; it was a serious attempt to think over from the conservative standpoint the most momentous problems of European and Russian life. The type of community advocated by the Slavophiles was by then vanishing not only in Europe but also in Russia. Precisely this fact, however, contributed most to the flowering of conservative romanticism—the owl of Minerva, as we are told by Hegel, takes flight only as the shades of dusk are falling. Indeed, the Slavophiles themselves were greatly indebted to the 'process of reflection', for it was only their European culture and the feeling that their ideals were in danger that enabled them to reflect about the nature of social bonds based upon nonreflection and upon the total absorption of individual consciousness into the supraindividual consciousness of the community.[1]

Or, to paraphrase the argument in line with my own emphasis, the concept of *sobornost* originated not in a desire to obtain better profits from the peasant commune, not even in a bid to exorcize the revolutionary threat, but in the deep devotion of the Slavophiles to the more personal and familial pre-industrial community challenged by the new, more rational, contractual, and formal industrial society.

Walicki's analysis reminds the reader of another basic aspect of Slavophilism: its intimate connection with the intellectual life of the West. Indeed, speaking of a connection may well misrepresent the case, because Slavophilism was part and parcel of European thought. Whether or not the Slavophiles theorized cleverly in terms of their class interest or detected and responded to fundamental economic and social change in

[1] Andrzej Walicki, 'Personality and Society in the Ideology of Russian Slavophiles: A Study in the Sociology of Knowledge', *California Slavic Studies*, vol. ii (1963), pp. 1–20.

Russia, there is no doubt that they reacted quickly and constantly to the stimulus of the West. From the time of Peter the Great the West represented a tremendous challenge to educated Russians, and eighteenth-century Russian literature, travel literature in particular, was already full of admiration, excitement, envy, and a desire to assert one's own value and identity produced by acquaintance, especially direct acquaintance, with foreign lands. But whereas in the Enlightenment self-assertion meant permeation with and development of the universal principles of the Age of Reason, in the romantic epoch it required the creation of an independent doctrine in dialectical opposition to other doctrines. Its aim was to defeat and supersede those others. The Slavophiles, of course, constructed just such a doctrine. In the process of construction, they remained keenly aware of the West and of its thought. To be more exact, the awareness preceded as well as accompanied the construction, as the remarkable letters of the Kireevskii brothers from Germany in 1829–30, that is, long before the formulation of the Slavophile teaching, attest.[1] The West, however, was not confined to territories and people beyond the border. It established St. Petersburg and the modern Russian state, and it also spoke with the voice of Chaadaev and, still more directly, with the voices of the Westernizers. Slavophilism can be best understood as a passionate response to all these voices, from Friedrich Schlegel's to Chaadaev's, from Hegel's to Herzen's, from Guizot's to Granovskii's.

That Slavophilism was of much more than passing significance has been confirmed by the interest in it in the twentieth century. The views of Khomiakov, Ivan Kireevskii, and their friends attracted the attention of such figures of the Russian cultural renaissance in the early years of the century as Nicholas Berdiaev who, after the October Revolution, helped to spread these views abroad. It was in particular the religious, philo-

---

[1] See also other quite comparable Slavophile letters, such as those of an even earlier date, Khomiakov's from Paris in the 1820s or, at the other end of the time span, Samarin's from Berlin in the 1870s. The Kireevskiis' correspondence has been prominently discussed in many works on the Slavophiles, including my book. Archival evidence gives further confirmation to its tone and mood. Thus the rather naïve Pogodin noted in his diary for 8 Nov. 1830: '[Ivan] Kireevskii returned to his family after he had heard of cholera. This is a useless knightly act. To him. He is denouncing Germany without stop. Now what do you know!' G. B. L., Otdel rukopisei, F231 Pogodin, M. P., razdel I, k. 38, No. 5, f. 55.

sophical, and, to a lesser extent, historiosophical doctrines of the Slavophiles that had a kind of revival in the twentieth century.

Moreover, quite recently, signs of a renewed interest in Slavophilism have appeared in the Soviet Union, both in formal scholarship and in such a Samizdat publication as *Veche*, not to mention Solzhenitsyn's views. Especially remarkable was the extensive discussion of the 'literary-aesthetic programme' of Slavophilism in *Voprosy Literatury* (*Problems of Literature*) in 1969.[1] While relatively little was said about Slavophile literary criticism or aesthetics proper, the discussion became the occasion for a major debate concerning the nature of Slavophilism and the correct Soviet attitude towards it. Four of the participants, including S. Mashinskii brought in to summarize and conclude the discussion, treated the Slavophiles on the whole in the established manner as class enemies and religious fanatics. But the other seven scholars offered kinder, and at times much more unusual, judgements.[2] Their approaches ranged from the customary cautious balancing and emphasis on 'further study' of Professor S. S. Dmitriev (mentioned above) to A. Ianov's far-reaching claims on behalf of Khomiakov, Constantine Aksakov, and their associates.

The discussion enabled several participants to make the point that ignorance and prejudice dominated the Soviet treatment of the Slavophiles. For instance, E. Maimin wrote:

We try—and in part contrary to the facts—to keep Pushkin at a greater distance from the periodical, *The Messenger of Moscow*,

[1] 'Literaturnaia kritika rannikh slavianofilov', *Voprosy Literatury*, 1969, Nos. 5 (May), pp. 90–135, 7 (July), pp. 116–52, 10 (Oct.), pp. 103–44, 12 (Dec.), pp. 73–140. The following contributions were published: an introduction (No. 5, pp. 90–1); A. Ianov, 'Zagadka slavianofilskoi kritiki' (No. 5, pp. 91–116); S. Pokrovskii, 'Mnimaia zagadka' (No. 5, pp. 117–28); B. Egorov, 'Problema, kotoruiu neobkhodimo reshit' (No. 5, pp. 128–35); A. Dementev, '"Kontseptsiia", "konstruktsiia" i "model"' (No. 7, pp. 116–29); A. Ivanov, 'Otritsatelnoe dostoinstvo' (No. 7, pp. 129–38); L. Frizman, 'Za nauchnuiu obektivnost' (No. 7, pp. 138–52); E. Maimin, 'Nuzhny konkretnye issledovaniia' (No. 10, pp. 103–13); V. Kozhinov, 'O glavnom v nasledii slavianofilov' (No. 10, pp. 113–31); V. Kuleshov, 'Slavianofilstvo, kak ono est . . .' (No. 10, pp. 131–44); S. Dmitriev, 'Podkhod dolzhen byt konkretno-istoricheskii' (No. 12, pp. 73–84); A. Ianov, 'Otvet opponentam' (No. 12, pp. 85–101); S. Mashinskii, 'Slavianofilstvo i ego istolkovateli (Nekotorye itogi diskussii)' (No. 12, pp. 102–40).

[2] The four were Pokrovskii, Dementev, Kuleshov, and Mashinskii, and the seven, Ianov, Egorov, Ivanov, Frizman, Maimin, Kozhanov, and Dmitriev.

mainly because many future Slavophiles collaborated in that journal. We interpret one-sidedly the relationship of the Slavophiles to Lermontov—in the name of, so to speak, Lermontov's 'purity'. We clearly undervalue I. Kireevskii's critical articles about Pushkin —in spite even of the fact that these articles belong to the 'pre-Slavic' period of I. Kireevskii's creative work. We say little about the poets-Lovers of Wisdom, and when we do speak about them we concentrate mainly on their mistakes and weaknesses, without noticing certain positive tendencies in their poetic search—and we do this again because many Lovers of Wisdom later turned out to be Slavophiles, and so on, and so forth.

As long as in scholarship negative formulas and accusatory labels hang over A. Khomiakov, I. Kireevskii, Iu. Samarin, and others, as long as we connect with them in our minds evaluations which discredit instead of characterizing them, nothing else can be expected.[1]

The Slavophiles especially deserved understanding, because they had much to offer to the reader. A. Ianov insisted that they postulated and carried to its extreme an idealization, almost an idolatry, of the common people, of the downtrodden masses of Russia, counterposing these masses to the evil and parasitic upper layers of society—the people versus the public—a remarkably social view of reality. When S. Pokrovskii replied that the Slavophiles glorified not the love of freedom of the people, not its struggle against its oppressors, but rather its alleged Christian patience and humility,[2] he was in turn attacked by A. Ivanov: 'The main trait which the Slavophiles valued in the Russian people was not at all humility, but communal spirit, as we would now say collective sense, opposed to the individualism and the egoism of the bourgeois West.'[3]

And in his 'Answer to Opponents' A. Ianov returned with renewed vigour to his main thesis of the populist and democratic nature of Slavophile teaching, denying in the process many criticisms of it as subjective and irrelevant:

Whom did they love, how did they love, did they love sincerely . . . And what does love have to do here, may I ask? Democracy is a *political* concept. And, accordingly, the democratic or undemocratic nature of ideologies is proved not by murky talk about who loves whom and in what manner, but by a concrete analysis of their

---

[1] Maimin, op. cit., p. 112.   [2] Pokrovskii, op. cit., p. 118.
[3] Ivanov, op. cit., p. 134.

political doctrines. Democracy when one speaks of the nineteenth century is the theory of the supremacy of the people, of popular sovereignty, or a political structure in which the people is recognized as the supreme source of all authority. Counterposed to democracy are those theories or political structures in which something other than the people is recognized as the source of authority—Lord God, Providence, the absolute idea, and the like. And if A. Dementev intended seriously to challenge the democratic nature of the Slavophiles, he should have proved that their political doctrine was not the doctrine of popular sovereignty, that they did not recognize the people as the source of authority (in this case autocratic authority). But, alas, this is beyond doubt. Just as the fact that in their ethical doctrine the people was considered as the source of morality. While in their gnoseology the people was considered the source of knowledge ('*sobornost*-type knowledge'). And they regarded folk poetry as the foundation of literature. And their theology reduced itself to the Old Believer thought concerning the immutability of the ecumenical tradition fixed in an age-old popular experience. And their sociology consisted in a study of this popular experience, embedded in the way of life, custom, traditions. And the most basic distinction between Russia and the West they found in the fact that in the West the traditional social layer, the preserver of tradition, was the aristocracy, and in Russia the common people.[1]

No wonder that in his critical concluding contribution to the discussion S. Mashinskii declared: 'It is necessary to follow strictly social-historical class criteria in evaluating complicated phenomena of the historical past—this constitutes one of the important methodological lessons of our discussion.'[2]

[1] Ianov, 'Otvet opponentam', p. 97. Without necessarily eliciting agreement, whether in regard to the Slavophile theology or to other aspects of the movement, Ianov's views and other views expressed during the discussion deserve attention, especially in the Soviet context. In that connection, it might be noted that the Slavophiles were repeatedly criticized for a functional, utilitarian concept of literature where ideology guided art. The discussion contained, of course, no defence of the religious Slavophile orientation as such, but even in that area some new notes were struck. L. Frizman wrote: 'We may sympathize with the struggle of the Slavophiles against serfdom and frown in dissatisfaction as we remember their apologetics for Orthodoxy. But in actual fact the Slavophiles attacked serfdom, among other reasons, also from the point of view of its immorality, its incompatibility with the teaching of Christ, and their sincere Orthodoxy (no matter how reactionary in itself) sharpened their hostility to serfdom.' Frizman, op. cit., p. 141.

[2] Mashinskii, op. cit., p. 140. Mashinskii too, however, called for an extended programme of studies of Slavophilism, and one can only welcome this and look forward to the results.

The Westernizers

The Westernizers left their mark in history in part as the celebrated antagonists of the Slavophiles. At least initially, the
Slavophiles were good personal friends of such men as Nicholas
Stankevich, Alexander Herzen, or Timothy Granovskii. They
read the same books, attended the same lectures, argued in the
same *salons*, even wrote in the same periodicals. They appeared
to be a single, friendly, although quarrelsome, society. Monday
evenings were usually spent at Chaadaev's, Friday at the
Sverbeevs', Sunday at the Elagins', Thursday at the Pavlovs'.

The whole large literary society of the capital [Moscow] assembled
there on Thursdays. There enthusiastic arguments continued late
into the night: Redkin with Shevyrev, Kavelin with Aksakov,
Herzen and Kriukov with Khomiakov. There the Kireevskiis used
to appear, also Iurii Samarin, then still a young man. Chaadaev
was a constant guest there, with his head as bald as his hand, his
unexceptionable society manners, his civilized and original mind,
and his eternal posing. This was the most brilliant literary time of
Moscow. All questions, philosophical, historical, and political, everything that interested the most advanced contemporary minds, were
discussed at these assemblies, to which the competitors came fully
armed, with opposed views, but with a store of knowledge and the
charm of eloquence. At that time Khomiakov led a fierce struggle
against Hegel's Logic . . . Similarly vehement disputations concerned
the key problem of Russian history, the reforms of Peter the Great.
Circles of listeners formed around the debaters; this was a constant
tournament in the course of which knowledge, intelligence, and
resourcefulness were all displayed . . .[1]

It was in these comfortable Muscovite *salons* in the 1840s that
the developing Slavophile teaching encountered the views of its
persistent opponents, grouped vaguely by contemporaries and
later writers under the name of 'Westernizers'.

But before the Westernizers could meet the Slavophiles on
something like even terms, they had undergone a considerable
intellectual evolution, which formed an important chapter in
the history of Russian thought. A coterie of friends which began
gathering around Nicholas Stankevich (1813–40) in the winter
of 1831–2 has been generally considered the first Westernizer

---

[1] B. N. Chicherin, *Vospominaniia. Moskva sorokovykh godov*, Moscow, 1929, pp. 5–6

circle. The original half a dozen young men were joined a little later by several more, including Vissarion Belinskii and Constantine Aksakov, and in 1835 by Michael Bakunin, Michael Katkov, and Basil Botkin. Still later Timothy Granovskii and the writer Ivan Turgenev were associated with the group. The circle was most active in 1833–7, until Stankevich's departure from Russia; 1839, when Belinskii left Moscow for St. Petersburg, has been cited as the terminal date of its effective existence.

In the words of the latest literary historian of Stankevich: 'The circle was a loosely organized intellectual fraternity with literary and philosophical interests. Its members met irregularly to read romantic literature—their own and others'—to discuss ideas, and to explore the philosophy of Schelling, Kant, Fichte, and Hegel.'[1] Indeed, the orientation, quite logically one might add, was that of the Lovers of Wisdom. To quote from Stankevich's 'Metaphysics' of 1833:

The knowledge which we have from our senses assures us that an external nature does exist. Nature is a single whole composed of many separate things. The life of nature moves within the separate things, but independently of them and almost always without their being conscious of it, and always without their participation, obeying its own laws, which are eternal . . . Although the separate things are not conscious of themselves, the life that is distributed among all these individual things must be conscious of itself since its movements have purpose. This life as a whole is consciousness.

The various species of things make up an ascending ladder through which life, conscious of itself as a whole, moves toward self-realization in individuals . . . In the case of man this universal life has at last become aware of itself in a separate individual creation. Thus man is not lost in the infinity of the universe . . . but in exactly the same way that nature is conscious of itself as a whole, he is conscious of himself as a separate entity. And therefore man is able to feel an identity between himself and the world reason, he can penetrate its laws, foresee its purposes and experience the beauty of creation. In this sense man is an image of the creator (the world reason).[2]

Or, again as expressed by Stankevich, this time in a letter to

---

[1] Edward J. Brown, *Stankevich and His Moscow Circle*, Stanford, Calif., 1966, p. 4.
[2] Quoted from Brown, op. cit., p. 15.

another member of the group, in 1838: 'Art is becoming divinity for me, and I keep repeating one thing: friendship . . . and art! That is the world in which man must live, if he does not want to be like an animal! that is the beneficial sphere in which he must reside to be worthy of himself! that is the fire with which he must warm and cleanse his soul!'[1]

It was not by chance that Stankevich paired friendship with art in his affirmation of supreme values. Friendship was a fundamental experience in German romanticism, a form of communion with spirit, almost a category of thought. And Stankevich's own impact on the Russian intellectual development was almost entirely personal. A thoroughly mediocre writer who produced little, a thinker of no true originality, not a publicist or a promoter, Stankevich had the gift of bringing talented people together and of affecting them. They remembered him until their deaths as a selfless champion of noble ideas, as a transparent figure who joined them and these ideas into one whole, as these ideas themselves. Stankevich was a romantic revelation. Intelligence, education, including highly successful studies at the University of Moscow, cultivation of mind and spirit, sensitivity and tact all went into the performance of Stankevich's difficult task. Appropriately, Stankevich had little else in life. He died in 1840 at the age of twenty-seven, from the great romantic disease consumption. According to the veteran Russian historian of literature S. Vengerov: 'His early death produced a shattering impression on his friends, but at the same time it brought to completion in an extraordinarily harmonious manner the beauty of his image.' Vengerov even adds: 'Et, rose, elle a vécu ce que vivent les roses—/L'espace d'un matin.' Very few images in Russian culture have been as compelling and as persistent as that of Stankevich.[2]

Yet Stankevich, that epitome of harmony and balance, and a true disciple of Schelling and Schiller, was evolving. On the

---

[1] Quoted from S. Mashinskii, 'Stankevich i ego kruzhok', *Istoriia Literatury*, No. 5 (1964), p. 135.

[2] 'And, rose, she lived what roses live—/The space of one morning.' Vengerov actually reproduced Malherbe's celebrated words as 'a rose lives' rather than 'roses live'. S. Vengerov, 'Stankevich (Nikolai Vladimirovich)', *Entsiklopedicheskii Slovar* (Brockhaus-Efron), xxxi. 423. The issue of the image of Stankevich with its attendant problems is central to Brown, op. cit. Cf. my review of this: *Slavic Review*, vol. xxvi, No. 2 (June 1967), pp. 338–9.

one hand, German idealistic philosophy and romanticism themselves were constantly changing, to the point of their eventual disintegration. On the other, Russian intellectuals had to keep facing the irrepressible reality of the condition of their country and their position in it. Hegel became more prominent in Stankevich's thought—an illustration of the notable Russian sequence where the major influence of Hegel followed, not preceded, that of Schelling. The dying Russian intellectual spent the last years of his life in Berlin, in the company of Hegel's student, Karl Werder. Moreover, there is some evidence that Stankevich was moving beyond Hegel. Thus, he became interested in the early works of Feuerbach. Commenting on Stankevich's letter to Bakunin in the last year of Stankevich's life, Professor Walicki concludes:

. . . Stankevich's intention is clear . . . he declared himself in favour of transforming philosophy into action and linked that postulate with Feuerbach's rehabilitation of feeling and sensuality and with the idea of a man of flesh and blood who not only thinks but lives a full life. It was a peculiarity of Stankevich's to avoid any criticism of Hegel and to stress that the 'transformation of philosophy into action' and even the 'liberation of sensual images' was made possible by Hegel's philosophy. Death prevented Stankevich from carrying out his plans . . .[1]

The seminal significance of the Stankevich circle was reflected in the influence which it exercised on Vissarion Belinskii (1811–48), who became the most famous Russian literary critic and one of the most important and, so to speak, founding members of the Russian intelligentsia. That influence was probably all the more powerful because Belinskii came to the brilliant circle from a relatively deprived background. A son of an impoverished and alcoholic provincial doctor, he grew up in the small town of Chembar—now Belinskii—in Penza province, in circumstances much rougher and cruder than those which surrounded such scions of the landed gentry as Stankevich, Constantine Aksakov, or Michael Bakunin. Although Belinskii did make his way to the University of Moscow, he was expelled from the University in September 1832, long before

[1] Andrzej Walicki, 'Hegel, Feuerbach and the Russian "philosophical left", 1836–1848', *Annali dell'Istituto Giangiacomo Feltrinelli*, Anno Sesto (1963), p. 108.

completing his course of studies, probably as punishment for his feeble tragedy, *Dmitrii Kalinin*, which attacked serfdom, but possibly also for academic reasons. From that time until his death of consumption in 1848, Belinskii, always financially embarrassed, supported himself by hectic and largely hack journalistic labour, in particular by reviewing books. His collected works are mostly such reviews of books.

Gaps in education must have been even more damaging to Belinskii's progress and self-assurance than social handicaps. Belinskii knew no German and was only learning French when he joined the polyglot Stankevich circle. He was thus uniquely dependent on those who did possess German, the authentic language of the romantic revelation, in particular on Stankevich and later on Bakunin. In fact, in a poetic contrast to uncounted Soviet scholars who claim for Belinskii supreme wisdom and originality, such specialists in the West as Professor Chizhevskii have discounted him as an ignorant and incompetent philosopher or even thinker. Neither approach does justice to its subject. While the virtues of Belinskii the philosopher should best be left to dogmatic Soviet writers, what remains important is not Belinskii's limitations in understanding German idealism, but the fact that that idealism determined his views. Stimulated by Stankevich's excellent aesthetic taste and understanding and the general atmosphere of the group, the young man from Chembar quickly developed into the leading literary critic of the Stankevich circle, reflecting on the whole faithfully its opinions and aspirations.

Belinskii's reviews picked up numerous themes of idealistic historiosophy and aesthetics and applied them to Russia. Characteristically, in this application the critic stressed both the cultural and historical poverty of his native land, the virtual absence of significant Russian literature, and his high hopes for progress in Russia and for the Russian future. Much of the emerging Westernizer position was at least implicit in Belinskii's literary criticism. As to individual elements, Belinskii always distinguished himself by the passion of his convictions, by arguing in terms of white and black, of love and hate. Even more conscious of the oppressive Russian reality than his friends, he reacted by occupying, following Fichte, an extreme idealistic position. As Belinskii kept insisting at that time, 'it was precisely the ideal life that was the real life . . . , while the so-called real life was negation, a phantom, nullity, emptiness'.[1]

But reality could not be simply conjured out of existence. The idealism of the Stankevich circle, so strikingly expressed by Belinskii, remained fundamentally unstable. As already indicated, Stankevich himself was groping for new solutions in the years and months preceding his death. In his turn, Belinskii, once his supreme disregard of reality became unbearable, tried to resolve the problem in a typically drastic, extreme, and sweeping manner. According to a reading of Hegel, and especially of his celebrated assertion that what was real was rational and what was rational was real, the real world was to be identified with the ideal world, whereas idealism as a separate and alienating category was to disappear. Nullity became everything for Belinskii, subjective idealism nothing. The reversal was complete, although still very much in terms of contemporary German philosophy. In his remarkable reversal Belinskii had an associate, even a guide, in the person of Michael Bakunin, who thrust himself forward to lead the Stankevich circle after Stankevich's departure from Russia in August 1837.

I arrive in Moscow from the Caucasus, Bakunin arrives . . . In the summer he looked through Hegel's philosophy of religion and philosophy of law. A new world opened to us. Might is right, and right is might—no, I cannot describe to you with what feeling I heard those words—this was liberation. I understood the idea of the fall of kingdoms, the lawfulness of conquerors. I understood that there is no savage material force, no rule of the bayonet and the sword, no arbitrariness, no change—and there ended my wardenship of the human race, and the meaning of my fatherland appeared to me in a new light . . .[2]

Michael Bakunin came from a prosperous and well-established gentry family, a real gentry 'nest', such as the ones usually encountered in Slavophile biographies. Bakunin never became a Slavophile. Instead he followed the path of German idealism to its decomposition in anarchism and pan-destruction to become one of the apostles of anarchy. In retrospect

---

[1] Quoted from G. V. Plekhanov, *V. G. Belinskii. Sbornik statei*, Moscow, Petrograd, 1923, p. 13.

[2] Ibid., pp. 15–16. Plekhanov's book contains one of the best discussions of the controversial issue of how Belinskii understood or misunderstood Hegel as well as of the entire episode of his 'reconciliation with reality'.

especially it is easy to see Bakunin as 'a romantic, mystical anarchist which he always was'.[1] Rebellion against authority proved to be essential to Bakunin's explosive and pathological character, and it found expression in many remarkable offensives, from the one against God to the one against Marx. But Bakunin's volcanic eruptions, just like Stankevich's 'harmony', were expressed for years in terms of German idealism, and indeed the idealistic and romantic background remained with Bakunin to his death. Moreover, Bakunin's development was not direct or simple. At the time he took over the leadership of the Stankevich circle and in the years immediately following he turned, like Belinskii—indeed leading Belinskii to whom he read Hegel—to apotheosizing reality. Both turnings were highly personal, a reason why the friends and associates of the two men generally did not join or even understand them. Yet, if in the case of Belinskii it might be appropriate to emphasize the dilemma of an extremely sensitive and sincere intellectual faced by the inequities of Russian life and the need to reconcile the ideal and the real, Bakunin's aim was in truth even more basic: the annihilation of his insufferable individuality and its absorption into a higher reality, an urge expressed repeatedly in his life as a pendant to his frenetic rebellion. Where Belinskii wanted to surrender the burden of his 'wardenship of mankind', Bakunin wanted to divest himself of individual existence as such.

A strange chapter in Russian intellectual history followed, extending from 1837 or 1838 to 1840. As Ivan Panaev, who lived then with Belinskii, recorded the thought, the mood, and the doings of the two great Russian radicals of the future:

> The arrival of Bakunin in Petersburg in the winter of 1840 gave Belinskii great joy. Bakunin visited us almost every day and, full of monarchical ecstasy according to Hegel, related to us various anecdotes concerning the emperor, which had been passed on to him by the adjutant Glazenap and he elevated these stories to the point of apotheosis. . . . To doubt the genius of Nikolai Pavlovich [the emperor] was considered a sign of ignorance. All this seemed a little strange to me; still, I too, following the authority of Belinskii and Bakunin, directed myself towards reverent admiration of the monarch. . . .

[1] P. V. Annenkov, *Literaturnye vospominaniia*, Leningrad, 1928, p. 506. This is the judgement of an informed contemporary.

We spent our entire time retelling to our friends the august words, speeches, and actions related to us by Bakunin; we went into raptures, dissolved in tenderness, and passionately filled the air with resounding verses.[1]

The verses were from Pushkin's famous nationalistic, bombastic, and arrogant poem, 'To the Slanderers of Russia', written in 1831 in response to the public support in the West of the Polish rebellion against Russian rule.

Belinskii's literary criticism during the period, beginning with an 1838 article on *Hamlet*, in which Hamlet was forced to accept reality in a triadic Hegelian manner, constitutes a more durable record of the entire episode. The most significant articles were those on Zhukovskii's poem 'The Anniversary of Borodino', on Theodore Glinka's *Sketches of the Battle of Borodino*, and on Goethe and his critic Menzel. The first two were published in 1839, the last in 1840. In accord with his new intellectual orientation, the critic praised such great reconcilers with reality as Homer, Shakespeare, and Goethe, while he turned against the rebels, including the once fervently admired Schiller. Two themes seemed most important to Belinskii. He affirmed Russian reality, above all the Russian political system, as usual totally and without any concession or compromise. And he insisted at the same time that art must be pure, unconscious, and unrelated to the pressures of practical life. The themes were, of course, intimately linked for Belinskii: it was the complete acceptance of reality that rendered social criticism unnecessary and even intellectually impossible, thus making art for art's sake the only meaningful art. The burden of the 'wardenship of mankind' vanished to be replaced by communion with the beautiful. The problem of the relationship of art to life remained fundamental to Belinskii's thought, and his elaboration of it was to be of great importance in Russian history; yet, at the time of the reconciliation, it was the critic's out-and-out support of the existing system that proved most shocking to his unsuspecting friends. In his review of Zhukovskii's 'Anniversary of Borodino' and the great celebration at Borodino, Belinskii wrote:

Yes, a great event took place in front of us, a *popular* event, but popular not in the sense in which this word is understood by the

[1] Panaev, op. cit., p. 232. Breaks in the original.

uninvited wardens of the human race, foreign criers. For us, Russians, there are no popular events which do not proceed from the living source of the supreme authority . . . Let our popular celebration be great, let the entire population of boundless Russia flow into it like the waves of an ocean; still, if this innumerable mass of people did not see in front of it its tsar, who in his calm, tsarist majesty greets its rapturous shouts, and on whose face it reads wrath, and kindness, and tsarist valour, and a great mighty spirit on which rests calmly and confidently its happiness in the present and its hopes for the future, then a celebration would not have been a celebration for it, but a meaningless gathering of idle people, and in a sacred event there would have been nothing sacred! That is why our old, our sovereign Kremlin becomes young and swirls with people, why the centuries-old 'hurrah' resounds there, when over the palace there waves a broad banner, a guarantee of the presence of him who is the life and the soul of his people. Yes, in the word 'tsar' there is marvellously blended the consciousness of the Russian people, and for it this word is full of poetry and of mysterious meaning. And this is not chance, but the most severe, the most rational necessity, which reveals itself in the history of the Russian people. The course of our history is the opposite in relation to European history. In Europe the starting-point of life has always been the struggle and the victory of the lower rungs of state life over the higher: feudalism struggled against kingly power and, defeated by it, limited it, turning into aristocracy; the middle estate struggled against both feudalism and aristocracy, democracy against the middle estate. Our case is the very opposite: with us the government has always marched ahead of the people, it has always been the lodestar pointing to its high destiny, the tsar's authority has always been a living source, in which the waters of renewal have never dried up, it has been the sun, the rays of which proceeding from the centre run down the joints of the gigantic corporate body of the state and permeate it with the warmth and the light of life. Our *freedom* is in the tsar, because our new civilization, our enlightenment comes from him, just as from him comes our life. One great tsar freed Russia from the Mongols and united its separated parts, another—an even greater one—brought it into the sphere of a new broader life; and heirs of both completed the work of their predecessors. And that is why every step forward of the Russian people, every moment of development in its life has been an act of the tsar's power. But this power has never been abstract and arbitrarily fortuitous, because it has always blended mysteriously with the will of Providence, with rational reality, guessing wisely the needs of the state, hidden in it even without its knowledge, and bringing them into consciousness. From this follows that marvellous sympathy which has united two principles into one whole, that constant and unconditional obedience to the tsar's will, as to the will of Providence Itself. Thus, let us not engage in discourse and reason concerning the necessity of an unconditional obedience to the authority of the tsar: this is clear enough by itself; no, there is something more important and more to the point: it is to bring into the general consciousness the fact that an unconditional obedience to the tsar's authority is not only our benefit and our necessity, but also the highest poetry of our life, our *nationality*, if one is to understand by the word 'nationality' a merging of private individualities through a general consciousness of one's state personality and identity. And our Russian popular consciousness is fully expressed and fully exhausted in the word 'tsar', in relation to which 'fatherland' is a subordinate concept, a result of a cause. Thus, time has come to bring into a clear, proud, *free* consciousness that which has been in the course of many centuries an immediate feeling and an immediate historical phenomenon: time has come to realize that we have a *rational* right to be proud of our love for the tsar, of our boundless devotion to his sacred will, as Englishmen are proud of their state statutes, of their civil rights, as the North American States are proud of their freedom. The life of any people is a rationally necessary form of the world idea, and this idea contains the meaning and the strength, and the might, and the poetry of the life of the people, while a living, rational consciousness of this is both the goal of the life of a people and at the same time its internal power.[1]

Belinskii's apotheosis of the tsar speaks for itself. One is left to wonder whether the critic thought of it when in the last months of his life he wrote his celebrated denunciation of *Selected Passages from Correspondence with Friends*, where Gogol had expressed identical sentiments. Belief in autocracy died hard in Russia.

But, of course, Belinskii's self-induced infatuation with Russian reality did not last. Conviction snapped at the point of human suffering, at the price exacted by Russian tsardom and the Hegelian absolute. The development of the critic's new rebellion can be traced in his correspondence in 1840 and 1841, in particular in letters to a friend, Basil Botkin, a member of the Stankevich circle and later a Westernizer, who was also interested in a reconciliation with reality. Already in a letter written

---

[1] V. G. Belinskii, *Polnoe sobranie sochinenii*, Moscow, 1953, iii. 246–7.

in mid-June 1840 Belinskii emphasized that his love for everything Russian had become a sadder feeling, one dominated by
suffering, not by a naïve enthusiasm. The essence of the Russian
people was great and boundless, but its manifestations in life
were base, dirty, and mean. In a letter of 4 October 1840 the
critic exploded:

I curse my base effort for reconciliation with base reality. Long live
great Schiller, a noble advocate, a bright star of salvation, an
emancipator of society from the bloody prejudices of tradition! May
reason live, may darkness perish! as great Pushkin used to exclaim.
For me now *human personality* is above history, above society, above
humanity. This is the idea and the thought of the century! My God,
it is frightening to think what happened to me—a fever or madness
—I am as if recovering.[1]

And later in this process of recovery, in a letter of 1 March
1841, in what was to become one of the most famous Belinskii
passages:

I have long suspected that the philosophy of Hegel is only a phase,
although a great one, but that the absolutism of its conclusions is not
good, that it is better to die than to be reconciled to them . . . The
individual with him is not an end in itself but a means for the
momentary expression of the universal, and with him the universal
is a Moloch in regard to the individual . . . I have particularly
weighty reasons for raging against Hegel, for I feel that I was faithful
to him (in sense) in reconciling myself with Russian reality . . . All
of Hegel's views on morality are downright nonsense, for in the
realm of objective thought there is no morality . . . The destiny of
the subject, of the individual, of the person, is more important than
the destinies of the whole world and the health of the Chinese
emperor (i.e. the Hegelian *Allgemeinheit*) . . . I thank you humbly,
George Frederick Hegel; I bow to your philosopher's gown. But
with all due respect for your philosophic philistinism, I have the
honour to inform you that if it were granted to me to climb to the
highest rung of the ladder of development, at that very point I
would ask you to account to me for all the sacrifices to the conditions
of life and history, all the victims of hazard, of superstition, of the
Inquisition, of Philip II, etc., etc. Otherwise I would throw myself
down head foremost from the highest rung. I do not want happiness,
even when it is offered free, if I am not certain about the fate of all
my brothers, my own flesh and blood. It is said that discord is the

[1] Quoted from Plekhanov, op. cit., p. 22.

condition of harmony. No doubt that is quite profitable and enjoy-
able for lovers of music, but certainly not for those whose fate it is to
express the idea of discord by their participation in it. . . . What good
is it to me to know that reason will eventually win and that the
future will be beautiful if destiny makes me a witness of the triumphs
of chance, irrationality, and brute force?[1]

Yet, as Plekhanov noted perceptively, Belinskii's rebellion
against Hegel did not lead to a complete emancipation from the
views of the German philosopher, either in the field of literary
criticism or more generally. And it certainly did not imply a
return to a position which the critic had occupied before he
made his bid for reconciliation. In particular, reality could
never again be dismissed as a phantom or a nullity. Instead,
Belinskii's relationship to it took the form of a tragic, even
desperate, personal struggle—perhaps a logical outcome for a
radical Westernizer of the 1830s and 1840s best exemplified in
the evolution of Alexander Herzen.

But Belinskii had a passionate need to believe and a great
capacity for enthusiasm. As we have seen, his attack on Hegel
was itself inspired by a new faith in the individual. He combined this faith with the principle of what he called 'sociality',
perhaps best described as a humanitarian concern for fellow
human beings.[2] In the names of the individual and of sociality
Belinskii reaffirmed his support of the great French Revolution
and of the entire progressive development in the West. As to
Russia, that country needed 'another Peter the Great', another
mighty effort to advance along the common road of civilized
humanity.

Bakunin's infatuation with tsardom and reality lasted no
longer than Belinskii's. After leaving Russia and arriving in
Berlin in 1840, Bakunin joined actively and enthusiastically in
German intellectual life, and he moved rapidly to the Left.
Bakunin's arrival and establishment in the Prussian capital

[1] As translated in Herbert E. Bowman, *Vissarion Belinski, 1811–1848. A Study in
the Origins of Social Criticism in Russia*, Cambridge, Mass., 1954, pp. 138–9, with,
however, some insertions from the letter omitted by Bowman and also some help
from the translation of the passage in Walicki, op. cit., pp. 115–16. The letter is
published in Belinskii, op. cit., Moscow, 1956, xii. 22–3.

[2] 'By its very awkwardness this Anglicized equivalent of Belinski's term *sotsial-
nost* may serve to suggest the novelty of Belinski's own word, in its turn an awkward
Russian equivalent of the French *socialité*.' Bowman, op. cit., note to p. 143.

corresponded with Arnold Ruge's publicistic activities, the appearance in 1841 of Ludwig Feuerbach's *Essence of Christianity*, and in general the emergence of the so-called Young Hegelians. The sustained effort of the Hegelian Left to interpret Hegel's teaching as a theoretical justification of radical action suited Bakunin to perfection: it left many of his Hegelian, metaphysical, and even mystical premisses intact, yet it offered him what he longed for most, rebellion. Fully converted in the winter of 1841–2 and never one to keep in the background, Bakunin published in October 1842, in Ruge's *Deutsche Jahrbücher*, a remarkable article entitled 'Reaction in Germany: from the Notebooks of a Frenchman', signed 'Jules Elysard'. Typically, he argued especially against the compromisers, the people in the middle. There could be no compromise. The issue of the day was the struggle between democracy and reaction. The victory of democracy would produce a new heaven and a new earth. In the meantime, however, only the struggle, only negation mattered. The article concluded:

> All peoples and all men are full of presentiments. Everyone whose living organs are not paralyzed sees with trembling expectation the approach of the future which will utter the decisive word. Even in Russia, in that limitless and snow-covered empire, of which we know so little and which has before it perhaps a great future, even in Russia the dark storm clouds are gathering! The air is sultry, it is heavy with storms!
>
> And therefore we call to our blinded brothers: Repent! Repent! The Kingdom of God is coming nigh.
>
> Let us put our trust in the eternal spirit which destroys and annihilates only because it is the unsearchable and eternally creative source of all life. The passion for destruction is also a creative passion![1]

Michael Bakunin was well on his way to becoming 'founder of nihilism and apostle of anarchy'.

When Belinskii repudiated his reconciliation with reality, he could become reconciled with Alexander Herzen. Born in the memorable year of 1812, an illegitimate but pampered son of a cultured and misanthropic landlord, Herzen combined in his childhood and boyhood social and perhaps emotional isolation with fluency in three languages, including his mother's German,

---

[1] As translated in E. H. Carr, *Michael Bakunin*, New York, 1961, pp. 115–16.

voracious reading, and the usual aristocratic education of private tutors. Next he studied successfully at the University of Moscow and at the same time organized a circle of young Russian intellectuals parallel to that of Stankevich. The group included Herzen's boyhood and lifelong friend, the poet Nicholas Ogarev (1813–77), the translator of Shakespeare Nicholas Ketcher, Nicholas Sazonov, Vadim Passek, and several others, all described brilliantly in Herzen's great autobiography, *My Past and Thoughts*. In 1834, however, Herzen was arrested when the government reacted very harshly to a few signs of disaffection among students. While in the case of Herzen next to nothing could be demonstrated beyond his interest in Saint-Simon, he had to spend ten months in prison and five more years in exile in provincial towns, distant Viatka from 1835 to the end of 1837, and after that Vladimir until early 1840. Prison and government service in the provinces both separated Herzen from his intellectual and social world and offered him a new look at Russia. They helped to intensify certain intellectual and psychological processes that had been developing in him. It was in May 1840 that Herzen, finally pardoned, came to St. Petersburg to resume intellectual life with his friends and acquaintances, including Belinskii, whose reconciliation with reality he had deplored but whom he was happy to welcome back into the ranks of the intellectual opposition.

Like Belinskii, Herzen became eventually a great radical as well as an inspiration both to the pre-revolutionary Russian intelligentsia, which he had helped to create, and to the educated Soviet public. It was Herzen who even as a boy promised revenge for the executed Decembrists and an uncompromising battle against autocracy. Also, in the hagiography of the Russian intellectual tradition few stories are better known than the boyhood oath of Herzen and Ogarev, taken on the Sparrow Hills overlooking Moscow, to dedicate their lives to a struggle for the liberty of Russia. Many commentators have added, correctly, that the boys lived up to their oath. Herzen himself emphasized that already his first circle, in contrast to the contemporary one of Stankevich, was oriented towards France, politics, and progress, not Germany and metaphysics. He and his associates were accused of being frondeurs and French. The reading of the French Utopian socialist Saint-Simon was the main charge which the authorities could level against Herzen, and it should be added that he read other progressive French writers equally voraciously. Appropriately, perhaps the best book about Herzen is entitled *Alexander Herzen and the Birth of Russian Socialism 1812–1855*.[1]

Still, the radical political and social orientation of Herzen should not be overemphasized, dated too early—a mistake probably committed by Herzen himself writing in retrospect—or, especially, taken out of the general context of his thought. Although in contrast, for example, to Stankevich, Herzen was apparently not predisposed to romantic metaphysics by nature, he became an intellectual in an atmosphere of German idealism and romanticism. Even his interest in Saint-Simon blended with that atmosphere. 'Young Herzen's main interest in Saint-Simon's doctrine was the philosophy of history, the revelation of a new religion and the announcement of a new "organic age". In Herzen's *Weltanschauung*, the influences of Saint-Simon and Pierre Leroux coexisted happily with the equally strong influences of Schelling and German romantic philosophy.'[2] And indeed Schelling, certainly Schiller, and some other German writers were at the foundation of Herzen's thought. Ogarev in his turn, it might be added, spent the years in the circle trying to formulate a philosophical system very much like Schelling's, while his 'poetry of reflection' gave an excellent expression to Russian idealism. 'Melancholy, disillusionment, impotent longing, wistful recollections of missed happiness, are his principal themes. The poetry of Ogarev is the poetry that might have been expected from a hero of Turgenev's novels.'[3] Moreover, Herzen and Ogarev lived their romantic convictions. Their celebrated friendship, to which they seemed to attach a supreme, even at times a metaphysical or quasi-religious importance, was itself a remarkable product of the age. Their loves were equally notable. In particular, Herzen's courtship of and marriage to Natalie Zakharina, during his exile, had almost cosmic overtones for the future great radical: Natalie became his reconciliation and his salvation, almost his religion and his philosophy, in a manner no Voltairian could comprehend.

[1] By Martin Malia (Cambridge, Mass., 1961).
[2] Walicki, op. cit., p. 118.
[3] Mirsky, op. cit., p. 139.

Ogarev in his own marriage followed Herzen's experience very closely, although with less *brio* than his friend.[1]

When Herzen came back from exile to St. Petersburg and, soon after, Moscow, he turned to a study of Hegel, so popular and controversial at the time. As in some other cases, his own typically exaggerated but immensely effective and memorable description of the intellectual scene is the one known best in historical literature:

There was not a paragraph in all three parts of the *Logic*, the two parts of the *Aesthetics*, of the *Encyclopaedia*, which was not taken by assault after the most desperate debates lasting several nights. People who were the closest friends broke off relations for entire weeks because they could not agree on a definition of the 'all-embracing spirit', or were personally offended by opinions about 'absolute personality' and its '*an sich* existence'. The most insignificant pamphlets appearing in Berlin and the other provincial and country towns of German philosophy in which there was any mention of the name of Hegel were sent for and read to shreds, till they were covered with spots, till the pages dropped out after a few days. Thus, just as Francœur in Paris was moved to tears when he heard that he was regarded as a great mathematician in Russia, and that all our young generation used his system of notation to solve differential equations, so might they all have wept for joy—all those forgotten Werders, Marheineckes, Michelets, Ottos, Vatkes, Schalles, Rosenkranzes, and Arnold Ruge himself . . . if they had known what duels, what battles they had started in Moscow between the Maroseika and the Makhovaia, how they were read, how they were *bought*.[2]

[1] 'The idea of Providence working through the love of Natalie was necessary to Herzen to rationalize the uncertainty of his existence into a higher certainty, his bondage into a higher freedom, and his impotence into a loftier strength—all safely beyond the contingencies of real life. In imagination, everything that had happened to him was made to seem the opposite of what it was in fact. The waste of five years and the capricious decrees of the government became a meaningful pattern of destiny. Isolation became union with God, and frustration self-fulfilment. Despair became hope, and pessimism optimism. In short, an absurd lot was transfigured into a higher glory.' (Malia, op. cit., p. 175.) Not only did Ogarev closely reproduce Herzen's emotional and intellectual experience, but so did, usually on a lesser scale, many other Russian—as well as non-Russian—romantics. Romantic love bid to be much more than a mere emotion: it presented itself as a supreme philosophical and religious value, a path of cognition, a means for union with God, and an affirmation of the world. It may not be irrelevant that the two Westernizers who attempted the most theoretically formal, as well as the most political, reconciliation with reality, Bakunin and Belinskii, were men unable to establish a relationship such as that between Herzen and his Natalie.

[2] Quoted from Malia, op. cit., pp. 202–3. Maroseika and Mokhovaia were

It was idealism with a vengeance. The Schellingian period in Russia looked tame or merely preliminary by comparison.

Herzen's study of Hegel led him, like Bakunin, to Left Hegelianism and, like Belinskii, to an affirmation of the individual, of human personality. In fact, he developed these views in part as a reaction to his friends' temporary reconciliation with reality, and ahead of those friends; also, he held them on the whole with more intellectual clarity. It was Herzen who referred to Hegelianism as 'the algebra of revolution' and in a series of remarkable articles in the early 1840s proceeded to criticize what he considered to be mistaken philosophical approaches and to delineate the desirable one. While still broadly speaking Hegelian, the articles indicated the road which the Russian radical had traversed almost to the end of idealistic philosophy. 'The world is complete only in action . . . the living unity of theory and practice.'[1]

Herzen thus represented the Westernizer Left in the celebrated running debate between the Slavophiles and the Westernizers which attracted the attention of educated Moscow at that time and which was mentioned at the beginning of this section. Bakunin was abroad; Ogarev studied in Germany from 1841 to 1846; Belinskii's voice gained in power and resonance, but he remained in St. Petersburg. Yet it was the Slavophiles rather than Herzen who were isolated in the debate, for Herzen found support among many so-called moderate Westernizers including such outstanding young professors at the University of Moscow as the historian Timothy Granovskii (1813–55), the philologist Dmitrii Kriukov (1809–45), and the legal scholar Peter Redkin (1808–91), who had attended Hegel's lectures in Berlin. Beyond that, and in very general terms, it would be fair to say that the Russian educated public was more Westernizer than Slavophile in its orientation and inclinations.

Granovskii, with Herzen the most prominent champion of the Westernizer cause, illustrated well both the course of Russian intellectual development and the liberal views of those who were not willing to go to the radical extreme of a

streets in Moscow. Herzen added: 'French literature was in disgrace, and in general everything French and along with it everything political.'

[1] Quoted from Malia, op. cit., p. 247.

Bakunin, a Belinskii, or a Herzen. A close friend of Stankevich, with whom he lived for a time in Berlin, Granovskii imbibed German idealism and romanticism. He became a specialist in European medieval history and an extremely popular professor at the University of Moscow. His public lectures in the winter of 1843-4 were a triumph and a great event both in the Slavophile–Westernizer controversy and in the general intellectual life of the old capital. Granovskii has been admired and praised as have very few other figures in the history of Russian thought and culture.[1] As in the case of Stankevich, his impact on those around him was very largely personal, moral and psychological as much as intellectual. His lectures and other remaining writings provide little or no indication of it. His contemporaries were themselves aware of the peculiar and essentially intangible nature of his appeal. As one of them remarked at the time of Granovskii's death: 'So now he is gone from us, and what remains after him will not give even the slightest idea of him.'[2] Granovskii stood out as a prophet of light and humaneness which shone to his listeners in his account of Western history and institutions. 'No one did more to introduce into the consciousness of society the idea of universal history as a progressive movement towards humaneness.'[3] It should be added that Granovskii's views both of the unity of history and of its development were strongly influenced by Hegel. But the popular historian would not follow Herzen into religious and political radicalism. Many other Westernizers were even more moderate than Granovskii, although they consistently upheld the West and the Western way as in some manner models for Russia.

The debate between the Westernizers and the Slavophiles which swirled for several years in Muscovite *salons* was many-sided and complex. In terms of philosophy, it has often been presented as a contest between the Schellingianism of the Slavophiles and the Hegelianism of the Westernizers. Yet the reality was considerably more complicated. The Slavophiles, to

---

[1] The admirers have included some of the best Russian historians and other scholars, both Granovskii's younger contemporaries and later specialists. See, e.g., Chicherin, op. cit., pp. 41–62, etc.; S. M. Soloviev, *Moi zapiski dlia detei moikh, a, esli mozhno, i dlia drugikh*, Petrograd, n.d., pp. 49–50. Cf. P. Vinogradov's judgement almost immediately below. [2] Quoted from Chicherin, op. cit., p. 45.
[3] P. Vinogradov, 'Granovskii (Timofei Nikolaevich)', *Entsiklopedicheskii Slovar* (Brockhaus-Efron), ix a 563.

be sure, had experienced a major impact of Schelling, but they were also affected by many other idealistic and romantic thinkers and were determined to present an original, Orthodox, and Russian ideology. As we have seen, the Westernizers too, for that matter, had been influenced by Schelling. As to Hegel, the Slavophiles, Khomiakov in particular, did mount a concentrated attack on that imperious German philosopher. Overcoming Hegel, however, was as much an internal issue in the Slavophile camp as a rallying cry in external war. Constantine Aksakov and especially George Samarin had been going through a Hegelian period. Samarin in particular wanted to use Hegelianism as the philosophical foundation for Orthodoxy, an exceptionally pernicious project in the eyes of Khomiakov.[1] The Westernizers, in their turn, had, as already indicated, great difficulties with Hegel. Those radically inclined were turning to Feuerbach, the Hegelian Left in general, and beyond. The more numerous moderates tried to adapt Hegelianism and combine it with other influences, depending in each case on individual circumstances. The 'marvellous decade' of the 1840s in Russia cannot be understood without making a huge allowance for German idealistic philosophy, but it is dangerous to draw symmetrical patterns in that muddy field.

In religion the two groups stood far apart. Although it can be argued that the most fundamental religious divide, that between belief and unbelief, emerged within the Westernizer camp, not between the Westernizers and the Slavophiles, the fact remains that Khomiakov and his friends placed Orthodoxy at the very centre of their philosophical and historical thought, whereas

---

[1] The relationship between idealistic philosophy and Christianity was, of course, a crucial intellectual question of the time. Russia again followed the general European pattern. As a pendant to Samarin's loud search one might mention, for example, the following quiet passage from the autobiography of the great historian, on the whole a very moderate Westernizer, S. M. Soloviev: '. . . Hegel turned the heads of all, although very few read Hegel himself, obtaining him only from lectures of young professors; serious students expressed themselves exclusively in Hegelian terms. My head too worked constantly; I would snatch several facts and immediately proceed to construct on their basis an entire edifice. Of Hegel's works I read only *The Philosophy of History*; it produced a strong impression on me; I even became a Protestant for a few months, but nothing else developed; the religious feeling was rooted too deeply in my soul; and now an idea occurred to me—to study philosophy and to use the means which it offers in order to buttress religion, Christianity; but abstractions did not suit me, I had been born a historian.' Soloviev, op. cit., p. 60.

their opponents, even when personally religious men, essentially ignored it in their theoretical constructions. From the Slavophile point of view at least, Slavophilism was a defence of religion and religious life and culture against rationalism and scepticism. As one Slavophile, Alexander Koshelev, explained the real difference between the two parties:

We all, and especially Khomiakov and C. Aksakov were designated as 'Slavophiles'. But this appellation did not at all express the essence of our school. True, we were always well-disposed towards the Slavs, tried to maintain contact with them, studied their history and their present condition, helped them as best we could; but this did not at all constitute the main, essential difference between our circle and the opposing circle of the Westernizers. Immeasurably more important differences separated them from us. They assigned religion a little place in the life and the understanding of only a poorly educated man; they accepted its sway in Russia only for the time being—as long as the people is unenlightened and weak in literacy. We, on our part, postulated the teaching of Christ, preserved in our Orthodox church, as the foundation of our entire way of life, our entire philosophy, and we were convinced that only on that foundation we should and could develop, improve, and occupy our proper place in the historic march of humanity. They expected light only from the West, glorified everything that existed there, tried to imitate everything that was established there, and forgot that we had our own mind, our own spatial, temporal, spiritual and physical peculiarities and needs.[1]

It was the religious concept of *sobornost*, the union of Christians in love and freedom, that the Slavophiles postulated as their ideal collectivity, the model for all other associations of human beings, and the answer to the championing of the individual by the Westernizers. The radical Westernizers at least were willing to accept the challenge to its extreme conclusions. Whereas for Khomiakov the Church meant freedom, Bakunin was later to make his celebrated declaration that if God existed, man was a slave. The differing views of man remained central to the Slavophile–Westernizer controversy, their expression ranging from Bakunin's titanism to Constantine Aksakov's images of happy peasants in ancient Russia. Some of the main positions and possibilities were immortalized in the works of a restless intellectual who became a writer in the 1840s, Dostoevskii.

[1] Koshelev, op. cit., p. 76.

The conflict between the Westernizers and the Slavophiles in interpreting Russian history is probably the best known of their many controversies, although there is actually a paucity of primary sources on the subject.[1] The Westernizers upheld the work of Peter the Great, and there remains glowing praise of the reforming emperor by such different people as Belinskii, Michael Katkov, Granovskii, and Serge Soloviev. Here the Westernizers followed the main, the overwhelmingly dominant, Russian intellectual and literary tradition, also promoted by the government and brilliantly re-emphasized by Pushkin and Chaadaev. Of course, Peter the Great meant different things to Nicholas I and his ideologues on the one hand and to the Westernizers on the other. To the emperor he represented above all the modern Russian state with all its power, glory, and responsibilities, now devolved upon Nicholas I himself. To the Westernizers Peter the Great signified primarily reform, progress, Russian advance to a better destiny. Both interpretations were entirely legitimate, so to speak. The salient fact is that they were fused together throughout the eighteenth century and into the nineteenth, but became clearly separate in the reign of Nicholas I. The Westernizer version pointed to a continuing advance along the Western path, to liberalism and constitutionalism. It was the Slavophiles who assailed the cult of Peter the Great in any form, branding, as we have seen, the famous emperor and his work as the negative stage of Russian history to be overcome by a return to the true Russian principles. Consistently they also denied the liberal approach of the Westernizers to contemporary Russia, as well as their aspirations for its future. Instead of the Western road of development, and in line with their views of the Russian people and the collective principle, they championed their concepts of ancient Russian institutions, such as autocracy, the *zemskii sobor*, the *zemskaia duma*, and, especially, the peasant commune. Although the Westernizer–Slavophile debate centred on extremely weighty problems, it often took the form of book reviews or other rather fugitive literary comment—not only because of the crucial importance of literature for the intellectuals of the age,

---

[1] The Slavophiles wrote very little on Peter the Great, or at least very little remains. The best source is Constantine Aksakov's historical writings, republished both as a separate book and as the first volume of his *Works*.

but also because literary criticism was allowed relative freedom in Russia—and it found its chief expression in talk, talk, talk, little of which unfortunately has been preserved.

The glow of the great debate persists in Russian intellectual history, in part, no doubt, because it brought together in confrontation a rich variety of opposite views held by some of the best intellectuals of Russia, 'fully armed . . . with a store of knowledge and the charm of eloquence'. By the same token, the direct confrontation could not last. The positions were too far apart, the emotions too strong. Various incidents served as pretexts for quarrels. There was, for example, a violent argument connected with the question of the participation of the Westernizers in *The Muscovite*. More bitterness was provoked by Granovskii's dissertation *Volin, Iomburg, and Vineta*, which proved that the famous Slavic town of Vineta was only a myth. The Westernizers accused Pogodin and Shevyrev, close to the Slavophiles, of denouncing Granovskii and thus preventing him from obtaining permission for a new review. Khomiakov's brother-in-law, the gifted poet Nicholas Iazykov, wrote abusive verses 'To those, who are not of us', and the ensuing argument almost resulted in a duel between Peter Kireevskii and Granovskii. Khomiakov opposed Granovskii on the subject of the Burgundian migrations and the nature of the Franks, and their dispute assumed a personal character. Reconciliations proved to be only temporary, and by 1846 the break was virtually complete. Even personal relations between the Westernizers and the Slavophiles were coming to an end.[1]

Nor could unity be preserved among the Westernizers. Especially symptomatic, as well as painful, was the separation of Granovskii and Herzen, each of whom had the highest regard for the other. But Granovskii could not abandon his belief in God,[2] and he also came to disapprove increasingly of Herzen's political and social radicalism. Until his death in

---

[1] Constantine Aksakov's formal partings from his Westernizer friends were particularly pathetic. A. I. Gertsen, *Sochineniia*, Geneva, 1875–80, vii. 306–7; Annenkov, op. cit., pp. 244–5 (1909 edn.).

[2] One is again reminded of the importance of the issue of religion in the evolution of Hegelianism and Left Hegelianism. For an excellent recent discussion of this, see William J. Brazill, *The Young Hegelians*, New Haven, 1970. For the broader European picture: H. G. Schenk, *The Mind of the European Romantics. An Essay in Cultural History*, London, 1966.

1855, he continued to occupy a moderate position which seemed increasingly irrelevant in Nicholas I's Russia. Idealistic philosophy apparently had lost much of its attraction for Granovskii, but although he too showed some interest in a more 'realistic' approach, he developed no new ideology to replace the old. Dejected, he gambled at cards. Other Westernizers, less liberal and less devoted to idealism than Granovskii, had correspondingly less to mourn or repudiate. Moreover, many of them lived to welcome the emancipation of the serfs and other 'great reforms' which gave a new lease on life in Russia both to liberalism and to intellectual development in general. Redkin, Serge Soloviev, Boris Chicherin, Constantine Kavelin, and others were to make a variety of contributions to Russian scholarship, thought, and culture. A few Westernizers, such as Basil Botkin and, especially, Michael Katkov, even went over to the far Right. As a spokesman of Russian nationalism and reaction too, Katkov continued to think in terms of the German idealism of his youth.[1]

Herzen remained very active during the 1840s. In 1845 he produced *Letters on the Study of Nature*, his most important philosophical work, in which he tried to combine idealism and empiricism as complementary approaches to reality. His interest in socialism continued, and it also showed a certain evolution:

> Thus, in the forties as in the thirties, Herzen took from the Western socialists only what was most congenial to his own thought, which was largely what was most general in theirs. Essentially, the socialism of his middle years boiled down to the abstract notion that the new world meant the combination of 'personality' with the commune, of individual liberty with democratic equality. Nonetheless, there are degrees of abstraction. His New Christianity of the thirties had been almost pure allegory; the 'principles' of 'individuality' and 'community,' which he now emphasized, though still abstract, were discernably related to social problems.[2]

It was also in the 1840s that Herzen made, in such novels as *Who Is to Blame?* and *Dr. Krupov*, significant contributions to Russian literature, these works too indicating a progression from

---

[1] The continuity in the fundamental structure of Katkov's thought is brought out well in Martin Katz, *Mikhail N. Katkov: A Political Biography, 1818–1887*, The Hague, Paris, 1966.

[2] Malia, op. cit., p. 325.

romanticism and sentimentalism to a special kind of sarcastic realism.[1]

Yet, idealism and romanticism died hard, and, above all, there was little to replace them. If Herzen was maturing as man and thinker, he was maturing essentially towards scepticism and despair. 'The heart of his thought is the notion that the basic problems are perhaps not soluble at all, that all one can do is to try to solve them, but that there is no guarantee, either in socialist nostrums or in any other human construction, no guarantee that happiness or a rational life can be attained, in private or in public life.'[2] In 1847 Herzen left Russia to publish eventually *The Bell* and become perhaps the most important, as well as the most celebrated, political *émigré* in Russian history.[3]

In the 1840s Belinskii developed into a great literary critic. Already the most prominent commentator on Pushkin, he proceeded to make basic evaluations of the contributions of Lermontov and of Gogol to Russian literature. He had the additional good fortune of welcoming the debuts of Dostoevskii, Turgenev, and Nekrasov. And he wrote ceaselessly on almost all other Russian writers and their writings. Belinskii's new organ, *The Contemporary*, gained increasing public support and even came to dominate the Russian literary scene.

It is customary to divide Belinskii's thought into three main periods: Schellingian idealism, Hegelian 'reconciliation with reality', and the last 'critical' or 'negative' stage until his death in 1848. This scheme, of course, is much too simple and neat. In addition to the contrasts between periods, there were great shifting enthusiasms, disappointments, and deviations within periods. The very last months of Belinskii's life, witnessed, apparently, another transition. The critic himself declared that

[1] For a perceptive recent treatment of this evolution, see Monica Partridge, 'Herzen's Changing Concept of Reality and Its Reflection in His Literary Works', *The Slavonic and East European Review*, vol. xlvi, No. 107 (July 1968), pp. 397–421.

[2] Isaiah Berlin, 'A Marvellous Decade. 1838–1848: The Birth of the Russian Intelligentsia', *Encounter*, May 1956, p. 29.

[3] Malia even overstates the significance of this momentous step: 'With Herzen's removal to the West the great adventure of his life began: emigration transformed him from a minor journalist, writing gnarled Hegelian treatises and second-rate social fiction for the Moscow intellectuals, into a major revolutionary figure. If he had not succeeded in escaping from Russia when he did, his place in history would have been modest indeed—that of a more radical Granovskii or of a sub-Belinskii.' Malia, op. cit., p. 335.

only he who did not seek truth made no mistakes. Or, to put it a little differently, Belinskii's 'consistency was moral not intellectual'.[1]

Yet the main outlines of Belinskii's beliefs emerge with sufficient clarity. 'Belinsky in his final phase was a humanist, an enemy of theology and metaphysics, and a radical democrat, and by the extreme force and vehemence of his convictions turned purely literary disputes into the beginnings of social and political movements.'[2] The critic did his best to build upon the legacy of Peter the Great, to further enlightenment and progress. 'Like everything else in contemporary Russia that is living, beautiful, and rational, our literature is a result of Peter the Great's reform.'[3] In spite of his passionate character and his propensity for extreme positions, Belinskii's view of progress in Russia was remarkably sane and even moderate. He stressed education and gradual development, including the growing role of the middle class. Also, he was entirely free of any idealization of the common people, of the peasants, brilliantly developed by the Slavophiles and destined to have, in particular through Bakunin and Herzen, a great career in Russian radical and populist thought.

It was to the progressive social and cultural role of Russian literature that Belinskii dedicated himself. As he wrote not long before his death:

> Whatever our literature might be, in any case its significance for us is much greater than it might appear: in it, and in it alone, are contained our entire intellectual life and the entire poetry of our life. Only in its sphere we cease being Ivans and Peters and become simply human beings, turn to human beings and interact with human beings.[4]

> Speaking about successes in the education of our society, we speak about the successes of our literature, because our education is the direct impact of our literature on the understanding and the *mores* of our society. Our literature has created the *mores* of our society, has already brought up several generations, each sharply distinct from the others, has laid the foundations for a *rapprochement* of the estates, has formed a kind of public opinion and has produced something like a special class in society, which is different from the

---

[1] Berlin, op. cit., Dec., p. 30.   [2] Ibid., p. 36.
[3] Belinskii, op. cit., vol. x, Moscow, 1956, p. 8.
[4] Ibid., vol. ix, Moscow, 1955, p. 430.

usual *middle estate* by the fact that it consists not only of the merchants and the burghers, but of people of all estates brought together by education, which in our case is concentrated exclusively on our love for literature.[1]

Belinskii's commentary on the Russian writers became famous for its passion, invective, and eulogy, and especially for its determination to treat works of literature in the broader contexts of society, history, and thought, and to instruct and guide the authors and the reading public. His extraordinary denunciation of Gogol for his *Selected Passages from Correspondence with Friends* constituted its fitting climax and monument. The critic had travelled a long way. It has been pointed out that whereas Belinskii began in the mid-1830s by asking the question whether a given work was art, a decade later he treated the perfect self-contained artist, Pushkin himself, as in effect *passé*. Still, utilitarianism never fully replaced idealism. As Belinskii wrote in his last major piece, his survey of Russian literature for the year 1847: 'It is impossible to break the laws of art with impunity. To copy faithfully from nature, it is not enough to be able to write, that is to master the art of a copyist or a scribe; it is necessary to bring the phenomena of the actual world through one's fantasy, to give them a new life.'[2] For Belinskii, as for most other Russians who were intellectually formed in the 1830s, art and artistic creativity remained supreme values. Radically different views belonged to a different generation.

Long after their celebrated debate with the Slavophiles and the entire 'marvellous decade' of the 1840s the Westernizers retained a central position in Russian thought and culture. Already in life but especially in death Belinskii and Herzen became gigantic figures towering over Russian liberalism and radicalism. Belinskii has been commonly described as the father of the dominant school of Russian literary criticism, which became in fact the main channel for progressive and oppositional thought in Russia. Herzen became linked for ever to political migration and the struggle against Russian autocracy from abroad. Yet by means of *The Bell* and later as a legend he maintained an immediate presence in Russia. Ogarev, although not really a giant, remained at the side of Herzen, the

[1] Ibid., p. 432.
[2] Ibid., vol. x, Moscow, 1956, p. 303.

pact between the two boys apparently lasting beyond the grave, symbolized today by the two statues in front of the University of Moscow. Bakunin, on his part, was an authentic titan, in death as in life. His mindless devotion to extremism circumscribed his appeal to the Russian educated public, resulting in a more selective following than in the case of a Belinskii or a Herzen. But he did play a major role in the Russian radical and revolutionary movement, and it was he of all the Westernizers who fully transcended national boundaries to become a leading figure of world anarchism. Granovskii and other moderates too received rich recognition. More important than direct praise was the fact that Russian intellectual development and scholarship evolved on the whole along Westernizer rather than Slavophile lines, thus sanctioning the side of Herzen and Granovskii in the great debate.

The October Revolution did not displace the Westernizers from their magisterial position in the Russian intellectual tradition, although it led to some significant shifts in perspective. As Soviet interpretations developed, they tended to draw a fundamental divide between the moderates and the radicals in the Westernizer camp, assigning the former, often together with the Slavophiles and other assorted members of the Russian educated public, to the general category of gentry liberalism. Nonsensical in terms of intellectual history, the realignment was intended to emphasize class division and class struggle in the evolution of Russia. However, although in the new view Granovskii and other moderates lost their former exalted standing, the position of the radicals was in effect enhanced. Not Bakunin's, to be sure: that genuine revolutionary in addition to his general wild anarchism managed to clash directly with Marx, and his reputation in the Soviet Union has suffered accordingly. Belinskii and Herzen, however, and with Herzen Ogarev, have been apotheosized as belonging to the very small group of supreme heroes of the Russian intellectual past. In the worst days of Stalinism and of the Zhdanovshchina, when almost every other subject became taboo, dissertations concerning the philosophical views of Belinskii and the pedagogical contributions of Herzen kept rolling off the presses. Nor has the flood stopped in a somewhat improved intellectual climate. In a different sense, in the West too since the Second World War

Westernizers have been found relevant by a number of perceptive commentators interested in such subjects as existentialist self-affirmation, generational conflict, or simply rebellion and freedom.[1]

The critical response to the Westernizers differed from that to the Slavophiles. For one thing, there was less effort to explain the emergence and the views of the former than of the latter, because they seemed so much more natural. True, the special and at times strange impact of German idealism was emphasized by a number of commentators, beginning with Westernizers themselves, such as Herzen and Ivan Turgenev. On the whole, however, the main current of Westernizer thought appeared to be simply a logical expression of the mind of educated Russia, and as such it needed no particular explication or justification. Only a few pre-Soviet, sometimes Marxist, writers and later Soviet scholars as a group tried to define the Westernizers in class terms and to situate them precisely in the evolution of Russian thought. As indicated, they generally wrote off the moderate Westernizers as mere gentry liberals, while extolling the radicals as 'revolutionary democrats' and true champions of the people, who, with their materialism, atheism, and incipient dialectic, reached the summits of progressive ideology of the 'pre-Marxist period'. Another shift in the appreciation of the Westernizers came from the comparative perspective. Whereas originally and for a long time the Westernizers and the emerging Russian intelligentsia as a whole were considered uniquely Russian phenomena, they are now seen as inevitable products of the general process of 'Westernization' or 'modernization' in underdeveloped countries. In this respect, the split between the government and the educated public in Russia in the 1840s and 1850s—to be discussed explicitly in the next chapter—had a wider significance.

The Petrashevtsy

The so-called Petrashevtsy appeared on the Russian scene later than the Slavophiles and the Westernizers, although still in the

---

[1] See, e.g., E. Lampert, *Studies in Rebellion*, London, 1957. I reviewed this in *The American Slavic and East European Review*, vol. xvii, No. 1 (Feb. 1958), pp. 129–30. Lampert's study is dedicated to Isaiah Berlin, whose own works, cited in part above, often emphasize the abiding significance of the writings of the Westernizers and especially of the problems which they tried to face.

234 The Educated Public in the Reign of Nicholas I

1840s, and their intellectual roots differed from those of the earlier groups. The simple story of the circle of the Petrashevtsy is reasonably well known.[1] The circle was an informal gathering of some twenty-five young men, who used to assemble in St. Petersburg at Michael Butashevich-Petrashevskii's on Fridays and engage in long and varied discussions and debates. The first meetings took place late in 1845, the last on Friday, 22 April 1849. The latter date marked the abrupt end of the circle, because the government, which had been watching the Petrashevtsy for some time through its able spy P. D. Antonelli, finally struck, arresting over forty persons. Twenty-three members of the group were eventually put on trial, and all, with the exception of one who died in prison and one who went insane, were sentenced to death. At the place of execution the sentence was commuted to various terms of hard labour and other punishments, but not before the expectation of immediate death had produced an ineffaceable impression on the mind and spirit of Fedor Dostoevskii, who was one of the condemned. Some of the Petrashevtsy returned to European Russia after serving their terms in Siberia, and a few of them, notably Dostoevskii, achieved prominence. Others, Petrashevskii himself included, died in Siberia.

The Petrashevtsy were an informal group, without an effective programme or organization. This, together with the youth of the members, and the paucity of written material surviving the circle, has led some specialists to minimize the importance of the Petrashevtsy and of their thought. Such an attitude, however, is hardly warranted by the facts. Although young, many of the Petrashevtsy were well educated and very well read, and they included such interesting thinkers as Petrashevskii himself, Nicholas Danilevskii, Alexander Khanykov, and Nicholas Speshnev, as well as such gifted writers as the poet Alexis Pleshcheev, Michael Saltykov, and, of course, Dostoevskii. Petrashevskii, the leader of the group, was evidently a bizarre, eccentric, and even somewhat emotionally

[1] A brief account and evaluation are provided in my article 'Fourierism in Russia: An Estimate of the Petraševcy', *The American Slavic and East European Review*, vol. xii, No. 3 (Oct. 1953), pp. 289–302, which I am reproducing here in part. A recent full study is George Weider, 'The Petrashevsky Circle and the Rise of Opposition to the Government in St. Petersburg, 1848–1849', unpublished Ph.D. thesis, University of California, Berkeley, 1971.

unbalanced individual, but he also possessed high intelligence, excellent education—he was a brilliant graduate in law of the University of St. Petersburg—a wide range of interests, and an overwhelming devotion to his ideas. As a writer, Petrashevskii has certain merits: he is learned, clever, and forceful. His defects, notably his enormous self-confidence and his passion for excessive precision and detail, should probably be ascribed as much to the very nature of Fourierism to which he adhered as to his personal peculiarities.

A student of the ideology of the Petrashevtsy has to labour under certain handicaps: in contrast to the Decembrists, the Petrashevtsy left no constitutions and no political programme; in contrast to Herzen, Bakunin, and other radicals, Petrashevskii and the Petrashevtsy wrote no books expounding their political, social, or economic views. One has to rely heavily on the records of the trial, on occasional memoirs of members of the circle, and on certain accounts by their contemporaries. The crucial trial materials provide a wealth of information, but they are not complete; some important items, including the Speshnev dossier, are missing.[1] One can turn also to a few works of fiction, and to the remarkable *Pocket Dictionary of Foreign Words*. That dictionary, published by the unsuspecting Captain N. Kirilov, was skilfully utilized by Kirilov's employee, Petrashevskii, as a ready vehicle for the dissemination of the latter's radical ideas. Not only words pregnant with socialist implications, for instance, 'Owenism', but even the seemingly innocuous ones, such as 'oratory' or 'naïvety', were made to serve Petrashevskii's purpose. The innocent appearance of the book, the blundering on the part of a censor, and Petrashevskii's inclusion of some flamboyant praise of the Russian government and Russian life in his critical articles resulted in permission to publish the dictionary. Only several weeks later the government saw its mistake, stopped further publication, and made an attempt to purchase every copy of the dictionary. On 3 February 1853, 1,599 such copies were burned.[2]

In 1845 the Petrashevtsy established a library of Western literature, which Petrashevskii managed to obtain through

---

[1] *Delo Petrashevtsev*, Moscow–Leningrad, 1937–1951.

[2] Petrashevskii participated in the second unfinished edition of the dictionary (Apr. 1845), while Valerian Maikov was primarily responsible for the first edition.

a bookseller, and the records of this loan library provide interesting information about the favourite reading of the circle. Saltykov, for instance, took out works of Considérant, Adam Smith, Proudhon, Vidal, Pereire, and two issues of the 'Revue 1846', probably the *Revue Indépendente* published by Pierre Leroux, George Sand, and Louis Viardo. Dostoevskii checked out of the library Louis Blanc's *Histoire de dix ans*, a book by Proudhon, a book by Paget, Cabet's *Le Vrai Christianisme suivant Jésus Christ*, Strauss's *Vie de Jésus*, and Beaumont's *Marie ou l'esclavage*. Nicholas Speshnev was interested in Pellarin's study of Fourier, and in the writings of Vidal, Cabet, Proudhon, Marx, N. Turgenev, and Beaumont. Also in demand were the works of Bayle, Condorcet, Benjamin Constant, Feuerbach, Lamennais, Michelet, Morelli, Muiron, Quinet, Raspail, Sismondi, and, of course, Fourier.

The Petrashevtsy did not exact conformity from members of their group. Indeed they differed profoundly on a number of fundamental issues. In particular, their appreciations of Fourier and of Fourier's importance in relation to other thinkers and schools of thought, especially to other radical and socialist teachers and teachings, were quite varied. Still, most Petrashevtsy can be correctly designated Fourierists, whether in the total sense or, more frequently, because they accepted at least Fourier's fundamental psychological, economic, and social views.[1] Some Petrashevtsy had been attracted to Fourier by the

[1] Fourier believed that, because the world had been created by a benevolent deity and yet wallowed in misery, men had obviously failed to carry out the divine plan. The plan was discovered by Fourier, and it had to be translated into practice. Happiness would then replace misery, unity would replace division. Harmony would replace Civilization. The transformation would occur through the release of man's thirteen passions, instilled by God but repressed in Civilization: the five senses; the four 'group', or social, passions of ambition, friendship, love, and family feeling; the three 'series', or distributive, passions, that is, the 'cabalist' or passion for intrigue, the *papillone* (butterfly) or passion for diversification, and the 'composite' or passion for combining pleasures; and, finally, the passion for unityism or harmony, which synthesizes all the others. To accomplish the release of the passions, humanity would have to be organized into phalanxes of about eighteen hundred men, women, and children. In each phalanx different characters and inclinations would be scientifically combined in a complex and finely graded system of groups and series so that each person could give full expression, in his work and in his other activities, to all his passions, tastes, and capacities, and avoid everything that did not suit him. A single trial phalanx would prove its absolute superiority as a mode of life within weeks or, at the most, months and, through the resulting imitation, abolish Civilization in a year or two. See my book *The Teaching of Charles*

lectures of Victor Poroshin, professor of political economy at the University of St. Petersburg. Their enthusiasm for the strange French thinker paralleled similar reactions by groups of intellectuals in many countries. Still, it could be argued that for Russia at the time, heavily burdened and immobile, the prospect of a Fourierist palingenesis was especially appealing.

The Petrashevtsy repeatedly described Fourier as 'the genius among geniuses', as the regenerator of mankind. To quote from Petrashevskii's speech at the dinner which marked Fourier's birthday anniversary: 'The social science of the West said its last word, gave us the forms in which must be moulded the final development of mankind. Three-quarters of the work has been done by our predecessors, by our elder brothers in the common faith we have in human progress. The genius of Fourier freed us from the great work of invention, gave us the true doctrine.'[1] At the same dinner Alexander Khanykov, apparently the most orthodox Fourierist in the circle, described Fourierism in a manner worthy of its originator:

The law of the series, gentlemen, is the complete expression of harmony in all the possible motions that can appear to observation, revealing everywhere the purpose, grouping all objects around the purpose in a predestined and necessary way, analysing them according to the four methods, which, as you know, have their specific characters, avoiding at the same time simplism, for the law of the series is a complex law which considers movement in every possible direction: in the ascending and the descending—in the direct and the reverse; in the direct—the dominating and the dominant; in the reverse—the dominating and the dominant. Into the law of the series, to use the strict language of our school, mathematics itself, all known laws of thinking, the laws of harmony enter as particulars. Its essential, profound nature is its unity, its solidarity, the natural connection of all phenomena; for all phenomena are expressed in no other way but in the series. The passions, brought under the serial law, find their purpose in the harmonious, unityistic development of themselves—which is the highest truth, the unconditional freedom, happiness, reasonable necessity. The passions, considered

Fourier, Berkeley and Los Angeles, 1969. A very rich bibliography on Fourier and Fourierism, including Fourierism in Russia, with listings in original languages, can be found in I. I. Zilberfarb, *Sotsialnaia filosofiia Sharlia Fure i ee mesto v istorii sotsialisticheskoi mysli pervoi poloviny XIX veka*, Moscow, 1964.

[1] *Delo Petrashevtsev*, i. 522.

together with all the phenomena of our planet, are basic or pivotal in their serial expression, that is, all phenomena are nothing but symbols of our passions.[1]

After his arrest, Petrashevskii testified: 'To read his [Fourier's] critical analysis of the life of society ... is the same as to be born anew.'[2] And truly Fourierism had become the foundation of Petrashevskii's thought. A cursory glance at Petrashevskii's articles in the *Pocket Dictionary* discovers abundant evidence of the influence of Fourier. For instance, in the article on the 'organization of production' Petrashevskii described Fourier's celebrated scheme of the proportional division of profit among labour, capital, and talent, referred to Fourier and to Fourier's particular works, and declared that the system of Fourier was superior to others because it did not sacrifice any one factor of production to another and thus permitted true solidarity.[3] The article on 'morality' clearly stated Fourier's fundamental views on that subject:

The true morality or ethical teaching is just one; that name can be applied only to that teaching which derives its principles not from numerous a priori suppositions, apparently necessary for the pacification of the human spirit, *but from an experimental study of human nature and a strict analysis of all its needs,* that teaching which does not deny a single one of those seemingly contradictory, but none the less normal (see that word) demands, and which considers it a sacred duty of every man to strive for an all-around development of these demands.[4]

Even the discussion of 'naïve' announced that: '*Naïvety* (the simplicity of the soul and the simplicity of the heart), in the sense in which it is now usually understood, can have a place in life until the forms of social organization are brought into a full harmony with the demands of human nature.'[5] The article on 'natural condition' spoke of the coming golden age and mentioned Fourier's *Traité de l'association domestique et agricole* as well as his *Théorie de l'unité universelle*, and so on. Fourier's criticism of the contemporary position of women and of the institutions of marriage and the family was clearly reflected in the dictionary articles of Petrashevskii on such topics as 'monogamy' and

---

[1] *Delo Petrachevtsev*, iii. 19–20.   [2] Ibid. i. 76.

[3] N. Kirilov, *Karmannyi slovar inostrannykh slov, voshedshikh v sostav russkogo iazyka*, St. Petersburg, 1845, pp. 316–19.

[4] Ibid., p. 203.   [5] Ibid., p. 211.

'odalisque'. It might be added that, unrestrained by censorship at their private gatherings, such Petrashevtsy as Khanykov were willing and eager to follow Fourier to his extreme conclusions on the subject of women and the family.[1]

Like their master Fourier, the Petrashevtsy often delighted in discussing the details, the minute particulars, of the coming social order. For instance, A. P. Beklemishev presented the following argument in favour of the phalanx:

Two hundred families have two hundred kitchens, each kitchen obviously must be heated. Find out some time how much wood is necessary for that, let us say in a month, and inquire from some innkeeper who prepares food for a thousand men, how much wood he needs for that period of time. You will see that in the first case ten times more wood will be used, and the wood is becoming more expensive by the year, and the impassable forests are becoming more sparse by the year. Living together offers even more advantages in that respect than the cooking of food in an inn, where the heat of the kitchen is lost, while in a building of two hundred united families this heat is also used to warm the upper stories. For a kitchen kettles, pots, pans and various utensils are necessary, every family must have them; in the case of communal living four or five huge pots will suffice. To prepare food for two hundred families one is simply forced to rely on two hundred male or female cooks; but for two hundred united families five or six cooks will, of course, be adequate. Finally, the purchase of supplies in large quantities costs less than in small. Of course, peasants purchase few supplies, but the fact of their separate living does not allow them even to utilize their own products—for instance, a peasant cannot eat beef because it is unprofitable for a single family to slaughter a bull, or even a calf, or a pig. Why is it that our peasants do not make cheese? Because a single poor family cannot obtain everything necessary for cheese-making and because the expenses will not be covered by the gains. But bring these families together, and they, without increasing their expenses, will eat beef, veal, and pork, will make cheese and sell it. Under present conditions the peasant eats dry bread six days a week. Why? Because he cannot bake every day for two or three persons; in the case of union, however, bread will be baked every day at the rate of approximately twenty loaves.[2]

Beklemishev went on to cite examples of more economical

[1] See especially the denunciation of the family in Khanykov's dinner speech: *Delo Petrashevtsev*, iii. 19.
[2] Op. cit. ii. 343.

cooking in boarding schools and in army camps, and then turned to an equally thorough discussion of the subject of the laundry.

The tone, the mood of the circle of the Petrashevtsy was devoutly Fourierist, and this emotional allegiance of the members of the circle to the gospel of their French prophet is quite as impressive as their intellectual acceptance of his taxing doctrines. With Fourier the Petrashevtsy believed in a set course of history. With Fourier they possessed a naïve optimism and a faith in the impending blessed transformation of human life. Petrashevskii, repeating Fourier, stated that the millennium would come within a few years after the establishment of the first phalanx. He hoped to end his own days in a phalanx. There is even a story that Petrashevskii once tried to establish a phalanx among his own serfs, but that the project failed before it had really started, because the communal building, the phalanstery, burned down. And he willed one-third of his estate 'to Considérant, the head of the Fourierist school, for the founding of a phalanstery'.[1]

At the Fourier birthday dinner on 7 April 1849 the Petrashevtsy decided to translate the writings of Fourier into Russian, and plans were made for the distribution of work among the members of the circle. Even in prison most of the Petrashevtsy admitted their interest in Fourier, some calling themselves Fourierists, and they tried patiently to explain the ideas of their master. Petrashevskii himself in a written address to the emperor implored him to establish a phalanx in some central location, preferably near Paris, and by that act surpass Peter the Great in glory, for Peter worked only in the interests of his own nation whereas Nicholas would become a benefactor for the entire world.[2] This address, however, was one of the last sparks of Petrashevskii's hope and optimism. More often his prison

[1] *Delo Petrashevtsev*, i. 183–4.
[2] Ibid., 44–6. Petrashevskii tried hard and repeatedly to enlighten his judges about socialism as a whole as well as about Fourierism. For example: 'Cast your eyes at the houses of the Lord, where everyone prays gratis, at public festivals, at asylums, barracks, public educational institutions, and so on: everywhere, where there exists some advantage accessible to the many, you will find the spirit of socialism' (ibid., p. 95). Several of the arrested Petrashevtsy produced, on demand, outlines of Fourier's system which were even more comprehensive and better constructed than Petrashevskii's summary. See especially those written by Danilevskii and Beklemishev (Ibid. ii. 290–319 and 350–62 respectively).

thoughts turned to Siberia, to hard labour, or to death. There is something profoundly tragic as well as strikingly ridiculous in the image of Petrashevskii dreaming about the future, dreaming how in a chain-gang: 'Perhaps fate . . . will put me next to a hardened criminal, on whose conscience there are ten murders . . . Sitting down during the break for the noontime meal of dry bread, we shall start a conversation; I shall tell him how and why misfortune struck me . . . I shall tell him about Fourier . . . about the phalanstery.'[1]

Still, although devoted to Fourier, the Petrashevtsy could not remain Fourierists in the abstract: they had to respond to Russian reality in general and the intellectual life around them in particular. Neither aristocratic nor socially prominent, but frequently well educated, the Petrashevtsy, typically, occupied relatively minor positions in the imperial bureaucracy. Their location in the capital offered them a good vantage point to observe the government and even the country. Their eyes could not be always riveted on the phalanx.

Very much in the spirit of the time, however, a major battle within the circle was fought not over the functions of the imperial bureaucracy or the role of education in Russia, but over religion. Like the Westernizers, the Petrashevtsy were rent by the issue of belief versus atheism. The problem was complicated in their case by the outlandish religious views of Fourier which only the most orthodox disciples of the fantastic French master could bring themselves to accept. Not surprisingly, many Petrashevtsy had to establish a certain distance between themselves and their teacher on some matters, sometimes very consciously so. As Petrashevskii wrote to Constantine Timkovskii, who vacillated between straight Fourierist orthodoxy and a somewhat more independent position:

You proclaimed yourself a Fourierist . . . but when one declares oneself a partisan of a system it does not mean that one has to agree to it unconditionally; that one has to believe in what cannot be reasonably proved; that one has to accept hypotheses the aim of which is to round out the system, to make it more symmetrical, and which . . . may be rejected without damage to the understanding of the essence . . .[2]

---

[1] Op. cit. ii. 84.
[2] Op. cit. i. 530.

A 'hypothesis' dismissed by Petrashevskii and many of the Petrashevtsy was precisely Fourier's remarkable religious doctrine. From the age of twenty Petrashevskii was a convinced atheist. Speshnev, Felix Tol, Basil Golovinskii, and a number of other members of the group shared his view. Timkovskii, originally a religious man, was eventually turned by them into an atheist. By contrast, some 'purists' in the circle, led by Khanykov, accepted Fourier's system in its entirety.

There is evidence that several Petrashevtsy attacked religion both in conversation and in more formal addresses to their fellows. In the *Pocket Dictionary* Petrashevskii could not, of course, openly espouse atheism, but sometimes he found ways of expressing his views on the subject in a manner which satisfied both the censors and his own sense of humour. For example, in the article on 'optimism' we read:

Thus, for instance, atheism (*see that article*), that is, the teaching which denies the existence of God and the presence of omnipotent divine providence, bases itself on facts which it thinks are directly opposed to the idea of the divine, such as the death of children in the wombs of their mothers, death of anybody at all prior to his full physical and mental development, and, in one word, the perishing of any being before it had reached its normal development, that is, before it had accomplished its purpose, for that perishing represents an unproductive, or a less than maximally productive, expenditure of the living forces of nature, an expenditure which cannot be justified on any grounds of practical utility or edification. These facts, as well as other similar facts, have constantly remained the stumbling block and the temptation for thinkers who have tried to reconcile evil with eternal goodness, the foreknowledge of the Creator with the freedom of the will . . . (See articles 'theology', 'theosophy'.)

Optimism, as one of the external forms of the system of deism, merits attention also because it demonstrates the instability of the foundations of a rational (that is, a reasoned) approach to God and the impossibility of any veneration of God without an acceptance of positive revelations! . . . So deep and all-embracing is the significance of faith! Without faith there is no salvation![1]

In their political interests too most Petrashevtsy deviated from Fourierism. Fourier simply had not been concerned with politics—the foundation of a phalanx was bound to resolve all problems. The thought of Petrashevskii and many Petrashevtsy,

[1] Kirilov, op. cit., p. 290.

on the other hand, had a pronounced political character. The Petrashevtsy felt a violent hostility toward the government of Nicholas I and the condition of Russian society and life in general, but they went beyond mere emotion and outlined desired changes and reforms. Petrashevskii, Beklemishev, and Golovinskii in particular wanted to emancipate the serfs, and sketched projects of the emancipation. It is noteworthy that the serfs were to receive the land they were tilling, and that Petrashevskii at least did not deem it necessary to offer any recompense to the landlords.[1] Petrashevskii apparently was even more interested in a reform of the judiciary, in particular in the introduction of trial by jury, arguing that, once achieved, this 'would open everyone's eyes to other problems as well'.[2] The Petrashevtsy also engaged in vigorous discussions concerning the desired establishment of the freedom of the press, among other reforms.

Petrashevskii favoured a republic as the best form of government. One authority specifies that Petrashevskii championed a federal republic on the American model, and that de Tocqueville's *Démocratie en Amérique* was one of the most popular books among the Petrashevtsy, while Alexander Balasoglo, another member of the circle, preferred a strongly centralized state.[3]

The *Pocket Dictionary* contained as much political propaganda as Fourierism. The article on 'the national assembly', for instance, observed: 'In the countries where society is highly developed, for example in the United States of America, they [national assemblies] are not occasional but continuous or periodical phenomena.'[4] It then gave high praise to the famous National Assembly of the French Revolution and put the censors on the defensive by citing as an example of a Russian national assembly 'the Zemskii Sobor which elected the now reigning House of the Romanovs'.[5] The article on the 'innovator' argued for innovation and innovators as means of human

---

[1] For a highly critical discussion of the problem of the emancipation of the serfs in the movement of the Petrashevtsy, see L. Raiskii, *Sotsialnye vozzreniia Petrashevtsev*, Leningrad, 1927.

[2] Quoted from V. I. Semevskii, *M. V. Butashevich-Petrashevskii i Petrashevtsy*, Moscow, 1922, p. 162.

[3] Raiskii, op. cit., p. 79. See also *Delo Petrashevtsev*, i. 514–15; iii. 385–7.

[4] Kirilov, op. cit., p. 223.

[5] Ibid., pp. 223–5.

progress.[1] The discussion of 'opposition' gave Petrashevskii an opportunity to write as follows:

A well-organized opposition is an essential element in any well-organized government: it rises against all kinds of governmental and administrative abuses, it helps to establish firmly the political organism, supporting in it elements of life and of development. Parliamentary struggle which takes place due to the conflict (lack of solidarity) of interests leads to the development of the talent of the orator and to a comprehension of the general state interests; it is the most reliable means for practical training in the wisdom of statecraft; and it reveals to the court of fellow citizens all the demands, all the weaknesses, and all the ills of the social organism; it guards social reason (*esprit publique*) from apathetic stagnation and sickness—and by correcting the direction of administrative activity it protects the right of reason from the intrusion of rude licence, violence, chance; it eliminates noxious *routinism and old-believer sectarianism* from the administration.[2]

Even the analysis of 'oratory' contained a sweeping and thinly veiled condemnation of Russian society:

Would it not be strange to search for reason, for discoveries, for improvements and inventions useful to the whole of mankind where every demonstration of reason, every innovation is something illegal, immoral; where justice itself has never been fair; where the high court of society is nothing but an organ of preservation of every falsehood? Where, as it were, everything both man and nature, has been covered by the mould of stagnation and inactivity . . . where one set way, monotony, and lack of sense and more lack of sense is the law of social life . . . as is the case in Turkey and in China.[3]

The government certainly over-reacted to the Petrashevtsy. Trial records prove beyond doubt that the circle lacked virtually any organization and planning, let alone revolutionary organization or revolutionary planning. The Petrashevtsy never went beyond discussion. And even in discussion they found themselves divided several ways.[4] Still, their hostility to

---

[1] Kirilov, op. cit., p. 257.   [2] Ibid., p. 283.   [3] Ibid., p. 301.

[4] In addition to other divisions, many of them already mentioned, it is worth noting again that at least a few Petrashevtsy were not even Fourierists. Thus Speshnev, an intelligent, able, and radical member of the circle, chose to call himself a 'communist' rather than a Fourierist and at times argued for 'communism' as against Fourierism. The nature of his 'communism' is unknown, but it might have been derived from Weitling or Dezamy. Speshnev influenced some other Petrashevtsy, for instance, Timkovskii, who proposed to organize the society of the future half on 'communist' and half on Fourierist basis, and concluded

the regime of Nicholas I was bitter and uncompromising. Even when that hostility expressed itself entirely in talk, the government could well consider such talk ominous. Nicholas and his lieutenants were especially provoked by pronouncements against the emperor himself,[1] by the hopes of uprisings in the Urals and elsewhere entertained by certain members of the circle, by a propaganda pamphlet produced by a member, as well as by the general radicalism of the group. They saw correctly an unbridgeable gulf between Official Nationality and these young Petersburg intellectuals. Also, as far as any possible leniency was concerned, the Petrashevtsy were brought to account, so to speak, at the wrong time: after the revolutions of 1848 in Europe had led to the last and most oppressive stage of Nicholas I's reign.

The Last Years of the Reign of Nicholas I, 1848–55

As Annenkov wrote in his celebrated memoirs:

That year of 1847 was a surprising year. By a strange coincidence, it marked the appearance at the same time of some remarkable monuments of Russian literature. Then were finished and published: I. A. Goncharov's *A Common Story*, F. M. Dostoevskii's *Poor Folk*, D. V. Grigorovich's *Anton Goremyka*—works opening new roads to talents and announcing a flowering of literature in the near future which, however, was not to be, because of the events and circumstances that were to arrive soon.[2]

Annenkov emphasized in effect the impressive rise of a new realistic trend in Russian literature. The so-called 'natural school' emerged in the early 1840s, its prosaic, even 'physiological' depiction of everyday Russian life contrasting sharply

cheerfully that each part would have something to learn from the other. See Semevskii, op. cit., p. 126; *Delo Petrashevtsev*, i. 326. Petrashevskii reacted violently to Timovskii's insolent proposal (ibid. i. 533–5). Timkovskii himself, after his arrest, blamed this controversy on 'a misunderstanding' (ibid. ii. 432–4).

[1] A particularly violent attack on Nicholas I was made by an emotional member of the circle, Nicholas Mombelli, in his paper on 'The Foundation of Rome and the Reign of Romulus', read at a meeting of the Petrashevtsy: 'No, the emperor Nicholas is not a human being, but a monster, a beast; he is that Antichrist of whom the Apocalypsa speaks . . . How strangely the world is organized: one loathsome man and how much evil he can do, and according to what right?' *Delo Petrashevtsev*, i. 280.

[2] Annenkov, op. cit., p. 638.

with the preferences for poetry and artificiality of the 'thirties'. The school found its supreme master and model in Gogol, in particular in his story 'The Greatcoat' and in his novel *Dead Souls*, both published in 1842, although Gogol's own genius, to say the very least, was not confined to realism.[1] Welcomed and promoted by Belinskii, the 'naturalism' of the forties became the starting-point for a number of great Russian writers. Many others, not at all great, such as Jacob Butkov, made nevertheless their contributions to the development of the realistic trend. The Russian literature of the decade showed an increasing vitality, reflecting to some extent the remarkable intellectual ferment of those years.

However, what followed 1847 was, of course, not a cultural flowering, but revolutions on the European continent, a most severe repression in Russia, and, before long, the catastrophe of the Crimean War. One of Annenkov's most promising authors, Dostoevskii, found himself condemned to death and, after a reprieve, sent to hard labour in Siberia. As already indicated in the preceding chapter, the frightened Russian government introduced extreme measures to control universities, publication, and intellectual life in general. Even such a pillar of Official Nationality as Pogodin spoke of a resulting graveyard. The conservative professor of literature and censor, Alexander Nikitenko, concluded as he wrote about that period: 'The main failing of the reign of Nicholas consisted in the fact that it was all a mistake.'[2] Fear and paralysis gripped the Russian educated public, including such enthusiastic and committed intellectuals as the Slavophiles.[3] Moderate professors, such as Serge

---

[1] I summarized my views on Gogol as writer in my *History of Russia*, 2nd edn., New York, London, Toronto, 1969, pp. 397–8. I wrote there of 'the Gogol of the commonplace and the mildly grotesque, which he somehow shaped into an overwhelming psychological world all his own; the Gogol who wrote in an involved, irregular and apparently clumsy style, which proved utterly irresistible'.

[2] A. V. Nikitenko, *Moia povest o samon sebe i o tom 'chemu svidetel v zhizni byl'. Zapiski i dnevnik (1804–1877 gg.)*, 2nd edn., St. Petersburg, 1905, i. 553.

[3] Ivan Kireevskii spent the last years of his life in a state of constant fear, which, to be sure, reflected his personal psychology as much as the oppressive Russian reality. Other Slavophiles complained more of apathy. As Peter Kireevskii wrote in Apr. 1850, from Moscow: 'In Moscow there is nothing special, except for a special paralysis, as a result of which not only nothing is being done, but nothing vital is even being said; even Khomiakov and Aksakov now play cards!' G. B. L. Otdel rukopisei, F99 Elaginykh, Kireevskii, Petr Vasilevich, Pisma k Elaginoi, Ekaterine Ivanovne, ur. Moier, letter 17 dated 7 Apr. 1850.

Soloviev[1] and Boris Chicherin, left pathetic accounts of how the repression hit Russian higher education. Chicherin even decided that: 'The University of Moscow and indeed the entire enlightenment in Russia suffered a blow from which it never recovered. The high significance of the University of Moscow in the life of Russian society was lost forever.'[2] Another moderate Westernizer, Ivan Turgenev, commented on those memorable years as follows:

I cannot help repeating: those were oppressive times; the young people of today have never experienced anything of the sort. Let the reader judge for himself; in the morning you might have your proofs returned, all crossed over, deformed with red ink, as if covered with blood; you might even have been forced to visit the censor and, after presenting useless and degrading explanations and justifications, to listen to his unappealable, frequently mocking, verdict . . . In the street you come across the figure of Mister Bulgarin or his friend, Mister Grech; a general not even your superior but simply a general, would cut you short or, what is worse, would give you encouragement . . . Look around you with the eye of your mind: bribery flourishes, serfdom stands like a rock, the barracks occupy the foreground, there is no justice, rumours fly concerning the shutting of the universities, which were soon to be limited to a complement of three hundred, travel abroad has become impossible, one cannot order a worthwhile book, some kind of a dark cloud is all the time hanging over the so-called academic and literary department, and here in addition denunciations hiss and crawl; among the young there is no common bond, no common interests, fear and servility in all—one might just as well quit![3]

Educated Russians who had lived through the last stage of Nicholas I's reign never forgot it. Yet its importance should not be exaggerated. The entire rule of the inflexible emperor was remarkable for its consistency. Its final years accentuated certain trends and increased the oppression, but they brought no fundamental change in the policy and no new departure. Moreover, the split between the government and at least a part of the educated public had developed before 1848. Extreme reactionary measures could perhaps deepen it, or, conversely, hamper its growth, but they could not eliminate it or change its basic nature.

[1] Soloviev, op. cit., pp. 128–46.   [2] Chicherin, op. cit., p. 84.
[3] Quoted from Aronson and Reiser, op. cit., pp. 141–2.

5

The Split between the Government and the Educated Public

I do not know exactly, but something is wrong.

From the annual gendarme report for 1840[1]

THE modern Russian educated public was created by the reforms of Peter the Great. Throughout the eighteenth century

[1] 'Otchet III-go Otdeleniia Sobstvennoi Ego Imperatorskogo Velichestva Kantseliarii i Korpusa Zhandarmov za 1840 god', TsGAOR, 109/85/5, p. 147. Literally: 'I do not know, but something is wrong.'

The annual gendarme reports, to which I referred earlier in this study and which are especially useful for the present chapter, deserve notice. I read the reports beginning with the first one, for 1826, and ending with that for 1855 (except that I found no report for 1827—apparently none was written). The reports were presented to Nicholas I by the successive heads of the Third Department of His Majesty's Own Chancery, Count Alexander Benckendorff through the report for 1843, and Prince Alexis Orlov during the rest of the reign. Although neither truly intelligent nor really perceptive, Benckendorff covered much interesting ground in great detail, and with striking candour he reported *in extenso* criticisms of the emperor, the imperial family and imperial policies, as well as opinions and gossip concerning ministers and other officials. At his best Benckendorff seemed to have had a certain valuable intuitive feeling for the moods of the country. Orlov, by contrast, was terse, neither gossipy nor slanderous, and much more conventional in his views and comments. The reports for the thirty years of Nicholas I's reign provide a rich and frequently striking picture of the problems and deficiencies of the Russian empire, including the tremendous issue of serfdom. Incidentally, they give no support at all to the repeated allegations in historical literature that the gendarmes magnified these problems, and in particular that they saw subversion everywhere. In addition to the relationship between the educated public and the government which is my primary concern, the reports throw light on a variety of other topics. Obviously they represent a fundamental source, with a wealth of statistical material, for the history of the Third Department itself. More broadly, they contain intriguing information, including remarkably low if apparently incomplete crime figures, for the history of crime, as well as of attitudes towards crime, in imperial Russia. Because of the imperial instructions as well as his own nosiness, Benckendorff

and well into the nineteenth it co-operated most closely with the government for the sake of what both parties, inspired by the ideas and the hopes of the Age of Reason, considered to be the interests of Russia. When enlightened despotism failed in the task of enlightenment, the Decembrists tried to take matters into their own hands through military rebellion. Yet that daring step implied no basic intellectual change: reason and progress were to be imposed upon the Russians by their rulers, who would utilize the political form of a constitutional monarchy or a Jacobin republic or a dictatorship, rather than of the old autocracy.

The catastrophe in the Senate Square deprived the educated public of all initiative, and left the government, again, in complete control. Although, according to gendarme reports and other evidence, Nicholas I and his associates were greatly worried by the possibilities of subversion on the morrow of the Decembrist rebellion, and although they were to receive another major shock from the great Polish insurrection of 1830–1, the 'thirties', that is, roughly, the years from 1826 to 1840, were, to repeat, a remarkably calm and quiet period in Russia. Except for the rebellious and perhaps incorrigible Poles, the subjects of the tsar—so the gendarmes asserted—were vying with each other in loyalty and devotion to their august father. Indeed, 'liberalism . . . not only has failed to gain strength among us, but, on the contrary, the number of free-thinkers in the political sense is declining with each day'.[1]

The mood began to change around 1840. The gendarme report for that year warned:

and, therefore, it should not be passed over in silence that, although there are as yet no complaints against the person of the *Sovereign*, there is hidden everywhere a certain general dissatisfaction, which can be expressed in a statement written to the Chief of Gendarmes from Moscow: '*I do not know exactly, but something is wrong*', and this intervened or attempted to intervene in a great variety of matters. Reports include, for example, arguments, before 1830, for a reversal of the oppressive policy towards the Poles, and a certain defence of the Old Believers who must not be persecuted because such persecution infringes the principle of freedom of religious conscience. The gendarmerie was also particularly concerned with, e.g., military conscription and trade fairs in the empire, both of which it supervised, as well as with plays on the Russian stage and the number and activities of foreigners in Russia.

[1] 'Obozrenie raspolozheniia umov i razlichnykh chastei gosudarstvennogo upravleniia v 1834 godu', TsGAOR, 109/85/2, pp. 5–6.

expression we now hear often from the most gentle, the most well-intentioned people. Of course, nothing bad has as yet happened, but unfortunately this kind of an expression is a reflection of a state of mind and feelings which is less propitious than at any time during the entire last fifteen years, and which proves that all the estates in general find themselves in some sort of awkward condition, for which no one can account, even to oneself.[1]

The following year the report paid special attention to the army:

In general it has been noted that the spirit of the army is not at all what it used to be twenty-five or thirty years ago. One notices a certain despondency in the mass of officers, a certain lack of interest in their profession! A general passion to criticize all measures and a general fashion to complain about the burdens of the service, bad treatment and excessive severity exist. There is none of the former devil-may-care attitude, gaiety, or dash so characteristic of military calling . . . [2]

The turning-point, or at least the potential turning-point, detected by Benckendorff just as one decade replaced another, corresponds in time to better-established periodizations. As already mentioned, the forties witnessed the rise of the so-called 'naturalist' school of writers and, more broadly speaking, the emergence of a critical, 'negative' approach in literature in rivalry with and in succession to the 'positive' tone of the thirties.[3] After discussing the switch to realism of the memoirist and writer Ivan Panaev—cited often in the present study—a literary historian continues: 'Precisely at that time—at the divide between the 1830s and the 1840s—there occurred an

[1] 'Otchet IIIgo Otdeleniia Sobstvennoi Ego Imperatorskogo Velichestva Kantseliarii i Korpusa Zhandarmov za 1840 god', TsGAOR, 109/85/5, pp. 147–84.

[2] Ibid. 109/85/6, pp. 152–3.

[3] The leading specialist on the history of Russian towns, P. G. Ryndziunskii, observed that the new 'naturalist' literature, devoted usually to urban themes, arose together with the publication of official, descriptive scholarly studies of urban conditions, notably of *Materialy dlia statistiki Rossiiskoi imperii* (*Materials for Statistical Information concerning the Russian Empire*), the first volume of which came out in St. Petersburg in 1839, and the second in 1841. P. G. Ryndziunskii, *Gorodskoe grazhdanstvo doreformennoi Rossii*, Moscow, 1958, p. 191. Harvests were bad in the Russian empire in both 1838 and 1839. Misery was great around 1840, in particular in St. Petersburg.

analogous turn in the creative work of a whole series of most important Russian writers, Turgenev, Nekrasov, Goncharov, Herzen.'¹ By the end of the new decade Belinskii, and Gogol as interpreted by Belinskii, reigned supreme in Russian literature.

The evolution of Russian thought during the same years produced, as we saw in the preceding chapter, notable, although complicated and controversial, results. If 1840 is to serve as a divide, it marked, roughly, the appearance of the Slavophile ideology, which was soon to give battle to the more diffuse views of the Westernizers. The 'marvellous decade' encompassed that celebrated encounter, the development and consolidation of Slavophilism, and the frantic, gifted, and strident search of the Westernizers for their truth. Within a few years, Bakunin ended in anarchism and Herzen in a kind of personalist nihilism, while other members of the group came to disparate, although generally less devastating, conclusions. The Petrashevtsy too made their entry upon the scene in the second half of the decade to offer the Fourierist solution to the Russian impasse and to add their voice to the criticism of the established order. Russian intellectual life had developed and changed remarkably in the short span between the years of 1840 and 1850. And whether or not quantity had been transformed into quality, there was certainly much quality in the thought and the writings of the 'marvellous decade'.

To single out one important result of the rapid intellectual evolution of the Russian educated élite: by 1850, and even more by the time of Nicholas I's death in 1855, the simple faith in the principles of the Age of Reason and in enlightened despotism had been left far behind. The Lovers of Wisdom had already demoted both politics and eighteenth-century reason in favour of idealistic philosophy, artistic creativity, and culture. Chaadaev swept the slate clean, ruler, subjects, and all. True, later he restored and indeed elevated Peter the Great to an almost divine position, but he made no further effort to link the Petrine legacy to the needs of contemporary Russia. It is impossible to imagine Chaadaev in the role of a Novikov,

¹ I. Iampolskii, 'Literaturnaia deiatelnost I. I. Panaeva', which serves as an introduction to I. I. Panaev, *Literaturnye vospominaniia*, Moscow–Leningrad, 1950 (pp. v–lvi, quoted from p. xi).

publishing piles of useful literature for his semi-educated com-patriots. The Slavophiles, to repeat, offered their own solution to the problem of the nature of the relationship between the government and the people of Russia. They accepted and even affirmed autocracy, but they also insisted on the greatest possible separation between state and society. 'The first relationship between the government and the people is the relationship of *mutual non-interference.*' 'The State is in no way a preceptor.' 'Its entire virtue must consist of its *negative* character, so that the less it exists as a state, the better it accomplishes its aim, as is the case in England.' 'The fewer points of contact the govern-ment has with the people, and the people with the government, the better.' One could hardly repudiate enlightened despotism —or Nicholas I's regime—more effectively. The Westernizers showed less unanimity on this as on other matters. Yet at their extreme, Bakunin eventually reached the position of total anarchism and pan-destruction, whereas Herzen achieved last-ing and deserved fame as an uncompromising opponent of government oppression and a tragic champion of the individual. Quite as importantly, even those Westernizers, including Belinskii, who took a much more positive view of the Petrine state, often found themselves hopelessly alienated from that state. Finally, Petrashevskii, together with his associates, exhi-bited a bitter hostility towards the order of things in Russia, while he begged Nicholas I, in lieu of enlightened despotism, simply to establish a phalanx near Paris and thus transform life on our planet, a plea made by Fourier himself and by Fourierists countless times to would-be benefactors the world over.

The government found men, as well as ideas, highly suspect. Like many non-intellectuals, Nicholas I never distinguished sharply between the two, and perhaps with reason. The Lovers of Wisdom, to be sure, disbanded their society in time and caused no trouble. Chaadaev, however, insisted on making his statement and had to be proclaimed insane. The government was offended by the Slavophiles in more ways than one. In addition to expressing nonsensical but clearly critical and oppositionist views, they usually failed to serve the state either in the army or the bureaucracy. Scions of good landholding families, they seemed to be engaged in some kind of gentry *fronde.* As a reprisal and a security measure, the authorities interfered drastically with Slavophile publishing, while no member of the immediate group obtained a position in the imperial educational establishment, although Ivan Kireevskii, at least, certainly wanted to teach in a university. The Westernizers ranged from suspicious liberal professors who had to be watched constantly to outright rebels, such as Bakunin and Herzen. Belinskii, on his part, apparently died at the right moment, that is, just before his arrest. The Petrashevtsy were worse, if anything. Lacking organization and professing a peaceful ideology, they seemed nevertheless to threaten the government with their bitter hostility. Moreover, their appearance marked in a sense a new stage in the alienation of progressive intellectuals from the state. Whereas Chaadaev, like some of the Decembrists, stood at one time close to Alexander I, and whereas Nicholas I still could admonish Samarin in person and even be impressed by Bakunin's stunning written confession to the autocrat,[1] no such ties existed between the young men who gathered at Petrashevskii's on Fridays and the rulers of Russia. In fact—although at the time this, of course, could be at best sensed rather than known—the Petrashevtsy, and possibly even more so the members of a related circle organized by the poet Serge Durov, were in composition and attitude quite similar to the later revolutionary groups of the sixties and the seventies. While the Petrashevtsy were holding their meetings in St. Petersberg, authorities uncovered another subversive society, the Brotherhood of Cyril and Methodius, in Kiev, arresting its members in March 1847. These few members, who included the historian Nicholas Kostomarov and the great Ukrainian poet of serf origin Taras Shevchenko, believed in the Messianic role of the Ukrainians and in a free democratic federation of Slavic peoples centred on Kiev.[2]

How can one account for all these developments? What were the reasons which terminated, or at least so greatly impaired,

---

[1] Chaadaev, a hero of Napoleonic wars, served as adjutant to Prince Hilarion Vasilchikov, commander of the Guard Corps; Samarin's family belonged to court circles; Bakunin came from a well-established gentry family and at least began his career as a gentleman and an officer (see also Bakunin's admiration for the emperor and the imperial family during his 'reconciliation with reality').

[2] The best study of the Brotherhood of Cyril and Methodius is P. A. Zaionchkovskii, *Kirillo-Mefodievskoe obshchestvo (1846–1847)*, Moscow, 1959.

the more than century-old intimate alliance between the government and the educated public in Russia, transforming the apparently monolithic image of the 1830s, with the government in virtually complete control, into a picture of alienation and opposition?

Most pre-revolutionary Russian scholars blamed directly the government itself, and more specifically Nicholas I. With a characteristically liberal, and occasionally radical, bias they saw the educated public, in particular its intellectual leaders, as bearers of light and the conscience of Russia. These leaders naturally supported progressive Petrine reforms, and they offered their strong backing to the activities of Catherine the Great and the projects of Alexander I, although in these last two instances they might have been misled and mistaken to some considerable extent. But with Nicholas I co-operation ceased. The new emperor refused to solve the pressing problems of the country. Notably he would not abolish serfdom, and he established a regime of unbearable reaction, oppression, and militarism. The last harrowing years of his rule, which followed the revolutions of 1848 in many European countries, raised oppression to an insane pitch and made a fundamental break between the state and all aware and self-respecting Russians inevitable. One is reminded of Alexander Nikitenko's bitter comment that the main failing of the reign of Nicholas I consisted in the fact that it was all a mistake.

Nikitenko—who, it might be added, was not even a liberal but a conservative—and his numerous successors are hard to gainsay. Books have been written, and more books can easily be written on the errors, probable errors, and deficiencies of Nicholas I and his associates. Moral judgements aside, the reign did end with the Crimean catastrophe. Also, it would be odd to consider the attitude of an educated public towards its government without reference to that government's activities. Oppression can indeed produce alienation and opposition. And yet, at least in its simple form, the liberal view fails to carry conviction. For one thing, as already indicated, the last years of Nicholas I's rule were probably more painful than decisive in the relationship between the government and the educated public in Russia because the split between the two had preceded their onset. More importantly, Nicholas I was not called the most consistent of autocrats for nothing. The emperor's beliefs, aims, and policies remained essentially the same in the 1820s, 1830s, 1840s, and 1850s. It was the educated public that changed. In other words, if one is to argue that the alienation and split in question resulted from the activities of the government, one must present this argument in terms of shifting orientation and behaviour on the part of the intellectuals, not in terms of an obvious and direct reaction to oppression. Only then it might be possible to understand why similar conditions produced different results in successive decades.

The educated Russian public was affected, it goes without saying, by many factors of diverse kinds and potency. Among the most persistent and important was the course of Russian foreign relations and the role which Russia played on the world stage in an increasingly nationalistic age. Professor Peter Christoff has wasted much effort in his valuable books on the Slavophiles demonstrating that the hearts of his protagonists belonged to Russia. Soviet specialists keep insisting, again needlessly, on the patriotism of their radical heroes. In fact, every educated Russian—and many an uneducated one for not quite the same reasons—was a patriot in that bright and naïve dawn of romantic nationalism in Russia over which there shone the luminous light of 1812. That was true, in his own desperate way, even of the Chaadaev of the first 'Philosophical Letter' (and not only of the Chaadaev of 'The Apology of a Madman' or of the Chaadaev who fought at Borodino). Observers and later scholars noted, for instance, in what a united manner the Russian educated public reacted against the Poles when they staged their rebellion in 1830–1. Throughout his reign Nicholas I was concerned not by any lack of patriotism but by the nationalist wing within his own Official Nationality and by other nationalists outside government circles. Benckendorff kept citing so-called 'Russian patriots' or 'Muscovite patriots' as the greatest source of critical discussion and discontent in the country, at least outside Poland, and, conversely, he continually reiterated his belief that nothing gained the sovereign so much approbation and support as measures meant to enhance the Russian national spirit. A dedicated patriot himself, Nicholas I was also a convinced conservative or reactionary as well as the man actually responsible for state policies and their results. By temperament, conviction, and also certainly because of his position, he could not endorse the irresponsible nationalistic enthusiasms of many of his subjects. Tension and hostility, therefore, developed, reflected in the writings of the Slavophiles and of many other educated Russians, including representatives of the nationalist wing of Official Nationality. In respect to foreign policy and public opinion, Nicholas I was much less fortunate than Catherine the Great, whose enormous acquisitions could satisfy almost any appetite, or Alexander I who had striking ups and downs but saved Russia, triumphed over Napoleon, and became Agamemnon, the king of kings, 'the monarch of Europe'. The Crimean fiasco at the end of the reign constituted a terrible disaster for Russians in general, but especially for the nationalists among them. The government looked so strikingly isolated in 1855 precisely because it had lost all nationalist support.

In another respect too, in regard to the West, the decades of Nicholas I's rule proved to be on the whole disastrous as well as, once again, highly significant for Russian public opinion. As already mentioned, throughout the eighteenth century and the reign of Alexander I Russia enjoyed, so to speak, a good press, everything considered, in other European countries. Many disparate phenomena, ranging from Catherine the Great's skill in dealing with the *philosophes* to a virtual European idolatry of Alexander I following his victory over Napoleon, contributed to this favourable image. Most importantly, the cosmopolitan European Enlightenment welcomed Russia as a promising, as well as enthusiastic, disciple. By 1813 or 1815 the land of the tsars was, to all appearances, already repaying its debt, leading other countries in the overthrow of the Napoleonic tyranny and in the establishment of a new age of peace, stability, and happiness.

It was in the years following, and especially in the reign of Nicholas I, that the image of Russia changed. The change was primarily determined by the increasing polarization of European politics and by the logical alliance of the Russian empire with the Right. Nicholas I's personal devotion to the conservative cause and his directness and rudeness probably accelerated and sharpened the process. In any event, whereas Alexander I had been hailed as the liberator of Europe, Nicholas I came to be known as its gendarme. Consequently, whereas Catherine the Great had been eulogized by Voltaire, Diderot, and d'Alembert, among others, and whereas Alexander I had received praise, e.g., from Jefferson, all liberals and radicals denounced Nicholas I, his system, and his country. Nor was the condemnation limited to the Left, no matter how broadly defined. The most famous literary attack on the Russia of Nicholas I, *La Russie en 1839*, was mounted by Astolphe Marquis de Custine, a conservative French aristocrat.[1] After Russian troops in the summer of 1849 suppressed the Hungarian revolt against the Habsburg crown, hatred of Nicholas I and of Russia became in a sense part of the Hungarian national creed. While the Hungarians reacted to a single decisive intervention, the Poles remained a constant enemy and source of trouble for the Russian ruler and state. Following the defeat of their rebellion in 1830–1, many Poles migrated to the West, especially to Paris but also to London and other cities, where they formed effective centres of Polish nationalism and anti-Russian propaganda. Mickiewicz's great voice was only one of many calling attention to the tragedy of Poland and the brutality of its Russian oppressor. Violent denigration of Nicholas I reached remarkable extremes. To quote Lamennais in *Les Paroles d'un croyant*: 'And the old man saw the third one there. That one had driven God out of his heart, and in his heart, in the place of God, there was a worm which kept gnawing at it without stop; and when the agony became great, he babbled indistinct blasphemies, and his lips became covered with a reddish foam.'[2]

---

[1] A. Custine, *La Russie en 1839*, Brussels, 1843. Several editions appeared within a few years. In the words of a specialist: 'Even more than Tocqueville in the case of the United States, it contributed to the formation of [French] opinion on Russia.' André-Jean Tudesq, *Les Grands Notables en France (1840–1849)*. *Étude historique d'une psychologie sociale*, Paris, 1964, ii. 799. On Custine, see George F. Kennan, *The Marquis de Custine and His 'Russia in 1839'*, Princeton, N.J., 1971.

[2] Yves Le Hir, ed., F.-R. de Lamennais, *Les Paroles d'un croyant*, Paris, 1949, p. 234. *Les Paroles* were first published in 1834. A note explains: 'Without any doubt, Tsar Nicholas of Russia is meant here. On the ninth of May, 1833, Lamennais wrote to the Countess de Senft: "There resided in hell a horrible demon, born from a coupling of pride and impiety, and his name was *murder*. Because he spread dread in infernal regions and because at his appearance Satan himself felt a strange emotion as if pure, essential, infinite evil had passed in front of him, he banished him from his empire. Exiled, the monster assumed human form and found refuge on earth: here he is called *Nicholas*" ' (p. 241, n. 47, in the commentary to Ch. XXXIII).

258 *The Split between the Government and the Educated Public*

Nicholas I's unswerving opposition to nationalist revolts and all other revolutions in Europe did not even assure him the sympathy of the governing circles and social strata of various European countries. The emperor's closest foreign associates themselves, the rulers and governments of Prussia and Austria, were not in full accord with their mighty neighbour: the Prussians resented the fact that Nicholas I had taken the side of Austria during the momentous developments of 1848–50; the Austrians felt that their interests were in conflict with those of Russia in the Balkans; both chafed under Nicholas's over-bearing solicitude. The British, in addition to their general disapproval of Russian autocracy and its reactionary policies, became increasingly concerned with Russian aims in the Near East. Indeed a state of strident worry and excitement, almost panic, developed over the alleged Russian designs on the Ottoman Empire, Persia, and India itself. And, although these British complaints against Russia, in contrast to the complaints of the Poles or the Hungarians, were based much more on fiction than on fact, they had their weight and role in the evolution of public opinion and in international relations. Russophobia affected broad and varied layers of British society including its governing circles. One can see its work in a striking, perhaps exaggerated, manner by comparing the attitude to Russia on the part of Lord Palmerston to the earlier attitudes of the Duke of Wellington or even Lord Aberdeen.[1] Nicholas I did not obtain much sympathy in France either. Of course, he detested the French Revolution and the usurper Napoleon, narrowly basing his *rapport* with France on his support of Charles X and the legitimists. The legitimists, to be sure, re-ciprocated on the whole his friendly attitude, although even they were divided, and increasingly so after 1830–1, by the issue of Poland—Catholic, Francophile, and a mortal enemy of Russia. But the revolution of July 1830 overthrew Charles X, raising Louis-Philippe of the junior Orléans branch of the Bourbon family to the French throne. Nicholas I, who had known and admired Louis-Philippe, interpreted his accession

[1] The best work on the subject remains J. Gleason, *The Genesis of Russophobia in Great Britain. A Study of the Interaction of Policy and Opinion*, Cambridge, Mass., and London, 1950. See also, e.g., Monica Partridge, 'Slavonic Themes in English Poetry of the 19th Century', *The Slavonic and East European Review*, vol. xii, No. 97 (June 1963), pp. 420–41.

as a betrayal of the monarchical principle, and his personal hostility to the new ruler did much to spoil the relations between the two countries in the years following. (It was the liberals in Russia who applauded the July Monarchy.) Nor was the Russian autocrat kind to the heir of the next French revolution, Louis-Napoleon, especially after that prince-president made himself Emperor Napoleon III. 'The Russian party' in France came to be reduced to some old-line legitimists in their provincial chateaux.[1] Indeed, generally speaking, Russian diplomatic isolation in the Crimean War was fully paralleled by its isolation in European public opinion.

Russian intellectuals could and did react in a variety of ways to this massive Western criticism and condemnation of their government and their country. Those on the Right frequently chose defiance, which is so prominent in the political writings of Tiutchev or of Pogodin. It was Tiutchev, a diplomat with some twenty years of residence in Germany, who composed the remarkable lines:

> One cannot understand Russia by reason,
> Cannot measure her with a common measure:
> She is under a special dispensation—
> One can only believe in Russia.[2]

The Slavophiles—it is worth remembering—constructed an entire ideology to demonstrate that Russia and the West were activated by different and incompatible principles, and that, therefore, they could not be comprehended in the same way.

Most educated Russians, however, drew comparisons and suffered accordingly. The entire argument of the Westernizers, for example, implied trying to catch up with the West. To be sure, seeing and admitting Russian deficiencies did not have to imply being blind to those found abroad, and some progressive

---

[1] *Re* France, full treatments are to be found in Charles Corbet, *L'Opinion française face à l'inconnu russe (1799–1894)*, Paris, 1967, and Michel Cadot, *La Russie dans la vie intellectuelle française (1839–1856)*, Paris, 1967.

[2]   Umom Rossiiu ne poniat,
          Arshinom obshchim ne izmerit:
          U nei osobennaia stat—
          V Rossiiu mozhno tolko verit.

F. I. Tiutchev, *Polnoe sobranie sochinenii*, St. Petersburg, 1913, p. 202. Professor Vladimir Weidle (Veidle) analysed brilliantly the relationship between Tiutchev and Russia in 'Tiutchev i Rossiia', published in V. Veidle, *Zadacha Rossii*, New York, 1956, pp. 169–200.

Russian intellectuals, such as Herzen, criticized the West with a vengeance after they had left their native land. Like Chaadaev, they were to discover hope for Russia in its very youth and even in its historical backwardness. Yet in trying to understand the Russian intellectuals of the 1840s the salient point is to realize that the integrative framework of the Age of Reason was gone. Defiance, counter-attack, Utopian hopes, or an emphasis on separateness, could not restore the harmonious vision of the enlightened despot leading his people ever farther along the universal road of progress, a vision of their country once shared by the educated Russians with other enlightened Europeans. The new Western rejection of Russia thus cut deep to the fundamental intellectual assumptions of the epoch.

Both Russian foreign policy and opinion about Russia abroad affected the Russian educated public in the 1840s and 1850s. No doubt, it was also influenced by domestic developments, although there is no consensus in historical literature concerning the precise nature of these developments or of their possible impact. It has become customary to refer to a mid-century crisis of gentry agriculture as well as to indicate that serfdom had outlived its usefulness and was perhaps even in the process of destroying itself. Apart from a few doubters of the entire postulate, scholars have concentrated on trying to elucidate this fundamental impasse of Russian economy and society. Their efforts are all the more interesting to a student of Russian public opinion because they frequently claim a rather rapid deterioration of the situation in the country which might help to explain the swift and explosive contemporaneous intellectual evolution in Russia.

To focus better the enormous subject, which can be barely touched in this study, of serfdom and Russian economy on the eve of the emancipation, it would be useful to have recourse to the extensive and trenchant writings of two leading contemporary Soviet specialists, I. D. Kovalchenko and P. G. Ryndziunskii. Kovalchenko throughout his published work but especially in his book *Russkoe krepostnoe krestianstvo v pervoi polovine XIX v.* (*The Enserfed Peasantry of Russia in the First Half of the XIX Century*)[1] used statistical methods as well as an analytical

[1] I. D. Kovalchenko, *Russkoe krepostnoe krestianstvo v pervoi polovine XIX v.*, Moscow, 1967.

and polemical mind to restate in its extreme form the argument for the increase of landlord exploitation and the deterioration of the serf condition in the decades preceding reform. Serf holdings were brought down to the minimum subsistence level and the serf population of Russia could no longer reproduce itself, or, at least, it stopped increasing. At the same time, Kovalchenko insisted, peasant economy, as distinct from gentry economy, was the most productive, progressive, and generally important in the economic life of Russia. These basic facts led to the abolition of serfdom and also to the compromise emancipation settlement, which was intended to protect the interests of the gentry but had to allow something for the peasant economy because of its overwhelming significance for the country.

Ryndziunskii agrees with Kovalchenko to the extent that he too recognizes deterioration and crisis in the serf economy during the decades preceding the emancipation. But he views that crisis in quite a different light. Instead of Kovalchenko's relentless exploitation increasing to the point of self-destruction, a hardening and a tightening of serfdom, Ryndziunskii sees a general loosening of the social fabric, and in particular vast numbers of former serfs moving to the frontiers and into the suburbs of growing cities and towns to escape the oppression of landlords and regular government control. They were not returned to their masters because the old system, inefficient at best, was breaking down, and because indeed they were often of marginal and even negative value to their owners. A decline in the number of serfs could thus be interpreted as a progressive phenomenon, not as a gauge of murderous exploitation. Still, in Ryndziunskii's judgement, as in that of Kovalchenko, serfdom had largely outlived itself, although in not quite as dialectical a manner.[1]

Russian intellectuals in the reign of Nicholas I were, of course, deeply concerned with serfdom. Very broadly speaking,

---

[1] For Ryndziunskii's views see his book, *Gorodskoe grazhdanstvo doreformennoi Rossii* Moscow, 1958, and such articles as 'O melkotovarnom uklade v Rossii xix veka', *Istoriia SSSR*, No. 2 (1961), pp. 48–70. Ryndziunskii has debated the issue with Kovalchenko for years. See, e.g., P. G. Ryndziunskii, 'Ob opredelenii intensivnosti obrochnoi ekspluatatsii krestian tsentralnoi Rossii v kontse xviii-pervoi polovine xix v. (O state I. D. Kovalchenko i L. V. Milova)', *Istoriia SSSR*, No. 6 (1966), pp. 44–64).

it might be suggested that such Westernizers as Belinskii and Herzen saw it the Kovalchenko way, as a direct exploitation of men by men past all bearing. By contrast, the Slavophiles, somewhat like Ryndziunskii, stressed the social disorientation, and especially their conviction that serfdom represented compulsion and division in what should have been a free, united, and harmonious nation-wide commune of Russian Orthodox believers. In any case: 'By the middle of the nineteenth century, educated, or "enlightened" public opinion was, almost by definition, abolitionist opinion.'[1] The Decembrists, the Slavophiles, the Westernizers, the Petrashevtsy, some supporters of Official Nationality, particularly from its nationalistic wing, together with other thinking Russians, all wanted emancipation. Writers, from Radishchev through Pushkin to Ivan Turgenev, whose magnificent and unforgettable *A Sportsman's Sketches* began to come out in 1847, made their contribution to the same cause. The economic argument, derived largely from Adam Smith and the free trade school and emphasizing the advantages of free over bonded labour, received increasing attention and endorsement. Indeed, in this respect, as the aftermath of the emancipation was to demonstrate, enlightened Russian landlords proved to be much too optimistic as far as the economic prospects of their class were concerned. All in all, on the eve of the abolition of serfdom in Russia—in contrast to the situation with slavery in the American South—virtually no one defended that institution; the arguments of its proponents were usually limited to pointing out the dangers implicit in such a radical change as emancipation.[2]

Growing moral indignation against serfdom and opposition to it suggests a general awakening of sensibilities. Indeed, there is little doubt that such an awakening was taking place among the Russian educated public in the first half of the nineteenth

[1] Terence Emmons, *The Russian Landed Gentry and the Peasant Emancipation of 1861*, Cambridge, 1968, p. 33.

[2] To repeat what Nicholas I told the State Council in 1842, serfdom was a palpable evil obvious to all, but its immediate abolition could produce an even greater disaster in the nature of a Pugachev rebellion. Yet he set up numerous committees to consider serfdom, and the issue, although strictly secret, was never far from the attention of high government officials in his reign. Benckendorff, in his annual gendarme reports, condemned serfdom as a powder keg threatening state security and proposed twice, albeit cautiously, that the emperor move to abolish it (in the reports for 1834 and 1839).

century—following the trend in the eighteenth—and probably at an accelerating rate, although it is impossible to estimate its extent or its precise effects. In the annals of the Russian intelligentsia, the hagiographic image of Belinskii includes prominently his ability 'to make grown men cry'. And it was in the 1840s that the great critic acquired his sway over Russian intellectuals. Ivan Panaev's shock of awareness when as a young man he innocently mentioned that his mother had given a servant girl as a gift to a relative and was told by a friend that 'educated people are ashamed to talk about such matters aloud' because human beings are not things and even serfs have souls,[1] was being repeated many times over in Russia. The lack of freedom, which the Marquis de Custine found so oppressive that he made it the leitmotiv of his *La Russie en 1839*, was becoming increasingly difficult to bear for Russians, at least educated Russians, themselves. In that respect the 1840s and the 1850s were certainly different in degree, if not in kind, from the preceding decades.

Serfdom, to be sure, was not only a moral scandal, but also a fundamental economic reality of Russia. Gentry fortunes, linked intimately to that institution, could well worry members of the possessing class quite apart from any ethical implications of their situation. As the enormous indebtedness of the landlords to the state on the eve of the emancipation and other evidence indicate, landlord agriculture was in a condition of crisis in the mid-nineteenth century. Subjective and partial observations fill in the picture. Economic worries were prominent in the correspondence even of such generally successful landowners as the Slavophiles; scions of leading families, for example Prince Peter Viazemiskii, had to enter service to make ends meet; Boris Chicherin's account of social life in Moscow becomes— to the surprise of an unwary reader—a sequence of bankruptcies.[2] The Slavophiles and other concerned Russians kept emphasizing the baffling contrast between the size, the abundance of natural resources, and the large numbers and the great giftedness of the population of the country on the one hand, and the pervasive misery on the other. Whereas during the Age of

---

[1] Panaev, op. cit., p. 33.
[2] B. N. Chicherin, *Vospominaniia. Moskva sorokovykh godov*, Moscow, 1929, pp. 92–106. *Re* Viazemiskii's service, see below.

Reason education and work appeared to provide the correct
and comprehensive solution to the Russian riddle, in the 1840s
and 1850s that solution seemed no longer convincing to many
Russian intellectuals. The heightened interest in economic
theory and economic literature indicated a search for better
answers. Going beyond specific measures, such as tariff reform
or importation of agricultural machinery, some educated
Russians saw a total transformation of Russian society as the
only real way out of the morass. This was the message of the
Slavophiles with its insistence on a return to the true Orthodox
and Russian principle of *sobornost*, and, even more obviously,
of the devotees of Utopian socialism, whether in or out of
Petrashevskii's circle. Again, economic dissatisfaction and criticism, like moral awareness, grew in Russia, apparently, at an
accelerating rate, providing a more explosive setting for the
intellectual evolution in the decades immediately preceding
the emancipation than had existed earlier.

Service ranked with land and serfs in its importance for the
gentry. Although obligatory gentry service had been abolished
by Peter III in 1762—a measure which has elicited varied
evaluations, from Kliuchevskii's betrayal of Russian historical
principles to Leontovitsch's first fundamental step in making
Russia a free country[1]—many landlords had to serve to support
themselves and their families. Besides, state service, especially
in the army, remained an established pattern of the upper-class
way of life. More officials, as well as many officers, were constantly needed. Like numerous other major topics of Russian
history in the first half of the nineteenth century, the development of the bureaucracy needs much further study. No doubt,

---

[1] V. O. Kliuchevskii's views on Russian history were, of course, expressed most
fully in print in his *Kurs russkoi istorii*. I am using the five-volume, 1911–21 edition,
the first four volumes of which were published in Moscow and the fifth in Petersburg; the law of 1762 is discussed in v. 140–4. Many other works of Kliuchevskii
are also relevant here, not only major studies reconstructing over centuries
Russian society and institutions, but also such pieces as 'Eugene Onegin and His
Ancestors': V. O. Kliuchevskii, 'Evgenii Onegin i ego predki', *Ocherki i rechi*.
Vtoroi sbornik statei, Petrograd, 1918, pp. 66–87.

Victor Leontovitsch, *Geschichte des Liberalismus in Russland*, Frankfurt am Main,
1957. Leontovitsch's study begins with a mention of the law of 1762, and although
his own analysis starts after it, with the reign of Catherine the Great, the author's
heavy emphasis is on the liberation of the gentry as the first fundamental stage in
the development of Russian liberalism. I reviewed Leontovitsch's book in *Journal
of Central European Affairs*, vol. xviii, No. 3 (Oct. 1958), pp. 346–8.

the bureaucracy increased during that time—according to one authority, from approximately 38,000 men to 115,000, trebling while the population of the empire doubled.¹ No doubt, too, following the efforts of Speranskii and others, it became better organized, more professional in character, and probably more exacting toward its members. As Speranskii's own case so strikingly indicates, it continued to offer opportunities for advancement to able and persevering individuals from the lower classes, although in 1845 hereditary ennoblement was restricted to its upper five ranks (Peter the Great had specified the upper six). It held the gigantic country firmly together and governed it with considerable success. As illustrated by the activities of the Third Department, paternalism remained the dominant philosophy within its ranks. Not in vain did the imperial rescript of 1837 proclaim a governor to be 'the master [*khoziain*] of his province'.² It remains very difficult, however, to estimate the efficiency of this bureaucracy, although most estimates have rated it as very low, or to calculate its impact on the governed and on the officials themselves.

The last point is illumined in part by extensive, and frequently extremely negative, comments on state service scattered throughout gentry memoirs. The reactionary policies of the government in the reign of Nicholas I made joining the bureaucracy particularly unattractive. As Boris Chicherin, certainly no radical, presented the matter, reflecting the climate of the last years of the autocrat's rule:

And how could I, in the political conditions of the time, be enticed by service? To become a direct tool of the government, which was repressing mercilessly every thought and all enlightenment, and which I hated for that from the bottom of my soul; to crawl slavishly up the service ladder, pleasing superiors, never expressing my convictions, often doing what seemed to me to be the greatest evil— such was the service perspective which opened in front of me. I

¹ Hans J. Torké, 'Continuity and Change in the Relations between Bureaucracy and Society in Russia, 1613–1861', *Canadian Slavic Studies*, vol. v, No. 4 (winter 1971), p. 466. For a fuller treatment see Hans J. Torké, 'Das russische Beamtentum in der ersten Hälfte des 19. Jahrhunderts', *Forschungen zur osteuropäischen Geschichte*, vol. 13 (1967), pp. 7–345. I reviewed that study in *Jahrbücher für Geschichte Osteuropas*, vol. 17, No. 1 (Mar. 1969), pp. 114–15.

² Quoted from N. P. Eroshkin, *Istoriia gosudarstvennykh uchrezhdenii dorevoliutsionnoi Rossii*, Moscow, 1968, p. 181. Torké mentions in his *Canadian Slavic Studies* article (p. 470) that Catherine the Great used this term in her legislation of 1764.

turned away from it in indignation, but there was no other solution in sight.[1]

All ideology aside, the simple inefficiency and mismanagement of the government were frightening. The recollections, for example, of Philip Vigel or of Ivan Panaev—used extensively in this study—contain numerous grotesque bureaucratic episodes, including total waste of salaried bureaucrats. Herzen's celebrated memoirs have a more ominous ring, notably in the incident of the Jewish children dispatched without proper provision in the cold, in effect to their death.[2] Prince Peter Viazemskii served as a high official for over twenty years, but this long term did not make him feel comfortable in the service. Forced to abandon service once, primarily because of some private remarks disrespectful to Grand Duke Constantine, Viazemskii was readmitted in 1830 only after a confession of his errors (in fact two such apologetic documents because the first was not considered contrite enough) and assigned to the Ministry of Finance, not the Ministries of Education or Justice where he wanted to work. As he described his own position, and by extension Russian bureaucracy in general, in the middle of his peculiar *cursus honorum*:

28 October 1846. Strange is my lot: from being a publican I am becoming a usurer, from the vice-director of the department of foreign trade to the manager of the State Loan Bank. What is there in these positions, in these spheres of activity that is compatible with me? Absolutely nothing. All this is against my nature, and this is precisely why it must be that way, according to the Russian custom and system. Our government considers it to be a weakness, an example of noxious permissiveness to take into account the natural abilities and inclinations of the man who is being appointed to an office. Man is born to stand on his feet: that is precisely why he must be put on his hands and told: 'walk!' Otherwise what is the meaning of authority when it obeys the general order and course of things. In addition, a certain apprehension plays its part here: man in his proper place acquires a certain strength, a certain autonomy, but the authorities want mere tools, frequently crooked and uncomfortable to use, but for that reason all the more dependent on their will. What had been given me by nature, has been repressed or swept aside in the service: only my defects are called into action

[1] Chicherin, op. cit., p. 114.
[2] A. I. Gertsen, *Byloe i Dumy*, Parts 1–3, Moscow, 1958, pp. 235–6.

and find application. I have no ability at all for an *effective management of affairs*; accounts, book-keeping, figures is an incomprehensible lingo for me which makes my head spin and drains all my capacities, all my intellectual and spiritual strength: so that is exactly what I must be chained to by fateful chains. Were this a fortuitous incident, an exception that befell me—nothing to be done then, my misfortune, and that is that, apparently so the fates had prescribed for me. But the thing is that this is the general rule, and that my misfortune is at the same time the misfortune of entire Russia.[1]

Or, to put it very succinctly and with Viazemskii's brilliant wit at its best: 'Well, all right, let the poor in spirit have the heavenly kingdom, but why are they also given kingdoms on earth?'[2]

Yet, simply blaming the government, much as it deserved the blame, does not tell the whole story. Apparently there were failings also on the side of the gentry. In fact a clear distinction between the two is more than a little artificial, because it was the landlords who in their capacities as officials ran the state machine. Someone like Prince Viazemskii must have surely been on both sides of the bureaucratic tangle, even if he insisted on presenting himself merely as a victim of bureaucracy. Little is known and relatively little has been written about the social psychology of the Russian gentry, although recently a few efforts have been made to come to grips with the subject.[3] Of the various explanations of the general difficulties experienced by the gentry in the service, most suggestive is the emphasis on the rather archaic character and traditions of the landlord class and its inability to adjust effectively to modern trends. Life on an estate was very different from life in the St. Petersburg bureaucracy, and as government service became more professional and more exacting the gap between the two worlds widened. While it would be an exaggeration to refer to Oblomov's nurture as either the ideal type or the average of the gentry upbringing, Ivan Goncharov's immortal anti-hero, even if he is to be treated as a great caricature, does make one

---

[1] P. A. Viazemskii, *Zapisnye knizhki (1813–1848)*, Moscow, 1963, p. 299.
[2] Ibid., p. 64.
[3] See esp. Raeff, *Origins of the Russian Intelligentsia. The Eighteenth-Century Nobility*, New York, 1966. Also Michael Confino's critique of Raeff: 'Histoire et psychologie: À propos de la noblesse russe au xviiie siècle', *Annales. Économies. Sociétés. Civilisations*, Year 22, No. 6 (Nov.–Dec. 1967), pp. 1163–1205.

sympathize with Speranskii, Nicholas I, Kiselev and others who were trying to maintain and improve a functioning state apparatus. An exact perception of time, schedules, formal procedure, the prescribed correct way of doing things, all had to be taught and learned with a mighty effort. Perhaps historians have wondered too much why Nicholas I was so obsessed with discipline. Moreover, not only was discipline deficient in the gentry background, but also members of that class often reacted to its imposition with special resentment. Little kings at home, admired by their family and relatives, mostly women, and confident that they were superior in kind to their serf servitors and playmates, gentry children frequently lacked the presence of even the one obvious authority, their father, whose service obligations had taken him elsewhere. They ruled the roost. The awakening, whether in a military school or government office, was bound to be rude. And some of the bitterness must have remained to feed feelings of alienation and opposition in the Russian educated public. Insufficient opportunities in the service too could produce resentment. The crucial importance of patronage and connections aside, the very considerable expansion of bureaucracy during the period was uneven, with gluts as well as shortages of talent for employment and advancement. It was such a glut apparently that occurred in the 1840s and found some reflection in the talk and mood of the Petrashevtsy. Military service, although it also demanded discipline, was traditionally more to the gentry liking than office work. Yet its exceptional severity, beginning with the reign of Paul I and going through those of Alexander I and Nicholas I, contrasted unfavourably with the freer legendary epoch of Catherine the Great and Suvorov. Also, in the opinion of specialists, it was under Nicholas I that Russian military service became particularly stultifying at every level, repressing all initiative and imagination. And in war technology the Russians were falling behind the other leading European countries. To restate the obvious, in spite of an enormous imperial concern and effort, the Russian armed forces proved to be entirely unprepared for the Crimean War, turning the disgruntlement and the disappointment of those involved into a tragedy.[1] In general, it

---

[1] For a full scholarly account see John Shelton Curtiss, *The Russian Army under Nicholas I, 1825–1855*, Durham, N.C., 1965.

would seem that the difficulties and failures of the Russian gentry in the civil and in part military service in the decades preceding the emancipation derived primarily from the same basic character of the landlord class which made it impossible for it in the main to adjust successfully to the changed economic conditions which followed the abolition of serfdom. New demands did not suit the old way of life.

As one would expect, the frequent inability to work in a disciplined, effective, and sustained manner was not limited to the domain of state service, but broadly permeated the Russian educated public. It was, for example, the only negative trait of the Russian character discussed at length by the Slavophiles. Ivan Kireevskii described its spiritual background:

But it is necessary to confess that this constant longing for the integral wholeness of all moral forces could also have its dangerous side. For only in the society where all classes are equally permeated by the same spirit, where universally respected and numerous monasteries, these popular schools and the highest universities of a religious state, wholly control the minds; where, in consequence, men mature in spiritual wisdom can guide others not yet mature, only there such an attitude of man must lead him to the highest perfection. But when he is deprived of the guiding care of a higher mind, before his inner life had attained originality and maturity, his life may represent an unfortunate combination of excessive efforts with excessive prostrations. Therefore, we see sometimes that a Russian by concentrating all his strength on work can accomplish more in three days than a cautious German would accomplish in thirty; but, on the other hand, he cannot for a long time afterwards resume his work voluntarily. That is why in many cases a Russian, in such an immature state and deprived of a proper guide, may regulate his own work worse than the most mediocre German mind, which would measure for him the amount and the intensity of his efforts according to hours and tables.[1]

Russian laziness was most exasperating indeed. Khomiakov exclaimed angrily on one occasion: 'The faculties of the mind, given by God, are left in a peculiar state of criminal neglect, because of the eternal expectation of miracles. This is our disease.'[2]

The preceding pages may have concentrated too exclusively

---

[1] I. V. Kireevskii, *Polnoe sobranie sochinenii*, Moscow, 1911, i. 211–12.
[2] A. S. Khomiakov, *Polnoe sobranie sochinenii*, Moscow, 1900–14, viii. 142.

on the gentry in disregard of the fact that it was not at all coter-
minous with the educated public. Even in the mid nineteenth
century large strata of the gentry could not be considered
educated, while, conversely, members of the lower classes had
contributed to the intellectual and cultural development of
Russia from the days of Peter the Great, not to mention earlier
times. Church schools and the clerical estate were of fundamental importance in the spreading of enlightenment in the
country, ranging from bare literacy all the way to German
idealistic philosophy. A considerable part of the artistic intelligentsia in Russia emerged from serfdom. Non-serf lower orders
provided many distinguished figures, including Lomonosov.
The *raznochintsy*, people of mixed background below the gentry,
had their role and their stake in the Russian Age of Reason.
Moreover, the growth of precisely that group has been presented as a main motif of the intellectual and cultural evolution of Russia in the 1840s and 1850s.[1] A full allowance for this
approach would shift the search for the reasons for the split
between the Russian government and the Russian educated
public in the middle of the nineteenth century from an examination of the possible objective and subjective causes of gentry
discontent—my chief preoccupation so far in this chapter—to
a careful investigation of the class origins of the intellectuals
involved. As one Soviet historian put it to me: people of a
certain social background supported the monarchy in the
eighteenth century, in the mid nineteenth century, and in the
early twentieth century for that matter; the task of a scholar is
to trace the appearance and progressive evolution of new social
forces in the articulate intellectual and political life of the
country, and the concomitant growth of an opposition to the
throne and the established order.

But, whatever the validity of this view for the later history
of the Russian empire or for other societies, it does not seem to
fit Russia in the first half of the nineteenth century. There the
gentry continued to be the dominant class. Soviet historical
periodization itself classifies the state of the Romanovs of the

---

[1] As far as I am aware, this was best accomplished in V. R. Leikina-Svirskaia,
'Formirovanie raznochinskoi intelligentsii v Rossii v 40-kh godakh XIX v.', *Istoriia
SSSR*, No. 1 (1958), pp. 83–104. The author's useful statistics, however, at times
contradict her evaluations and conclusions.

time as still feudal, although in the last stages of feudalism, and feudalism implies a hegemony of landlords. The Russian liberation movement, in Lenin's own opinion, was in its gentry phase. More to the point, there is no substantial evidence that the emerging split between the government and the educated public in the reign of Nicholas I was connected with a democratization of that public.

Democratization itself is an involved and controversial subject. Although—as a brief consideration of the structure of Russian intellectual life will indicate—the Russian educated public kept increasing in numbers and activity, absorbing new elements from different social groups, that growth was uneven, and it does not suggest a momentous social change in the second quarter of the nineteenth century. In fact, the gentry was more prominent in Russian universities during the last years of Alexander I's reign and in the reign of Nicholas I than at any other time in history, because earlier, for one thing, it had shown an overwhelming preference for education in the home and in military schools. Characteristically, members of the gentry concentrated on political subjects, useful for future administrators, while sons of the clergy, for example, chose especially medicine, an established venue of upward social mobility for them. Even the total numbers of university students indicate relatively little change. These numbers increased notably during most of the reign, only to be cut back after 1848–9, so that the figures for 1855 resemble those for 1825. No additional universities were created by Nicholas I, although after the Polish rebellion the one in Vilna was replaced by a new one in Kiev. Writing, another major intellectual activity, was becoming a profession in Russia, rather than a pastime of the leisure class, but the great majority of writers, particularly the more important ones, were from the gentry. The bureaucracy itself, which kept growing in size, tended nevertheless to be composed in its upper echelons almost exclusively of people of gentry background, while advancement for others became in certain ways more difficult under Nicholas I.

Most important, whatever the exact numbers and distribution of non-gentry intellectuals, there is no reason to believe that they made the educated public in the reign of Nicholas I more radical. The great bulk of the intellectuals considered above were members of the gentry, even if such a recent and insecure arrival into that class as Belinskii is to be classified among the *raznochintsy*. When these same individuals become alienated from the government, one can hardly ascribe the alienation to a change in their social composition. It might be added that the few prominent figures of serf background, such as Nikitenko and indeed Pogodin, tended to take their stand on the Right rather than on the Left. Nor were the occasional scions of merchant families, for example Botkin or the remarkable poet Alexis Koltsov, notable for their radicalism.[1] Nicholas I and his associates, for their part, kept remembering the Decembrists and worrying about a gentry danger.

Although our knowledge is fragmentary at best, the few precise studies available serve to emphasize the importance of the gentry in the opposition to Nicholas I and his regime. L. I. Nasonkina, who investigated the University of Moscow from 1826 through 1831, concluded that on the whole political attitudes of students were not determined by their social origins, that many members of the gentry were among 'the progressives', and that gentry students retained their 'leading position' in the university.[2] Professor Daniel R. Brower analyzed two groups: the Petrashevtsy, and student activists at the University of St. Petersburg in the late 1850s—that is, immediately after the period of this study. In the process of research, just as Nasonkina for the University of Moscow, he was able to utilize relevant statistics for the University of St. Petersburg and the St. Petersburg Pedagogical Institute. 'The striking fact is that in both institutions sons of the nobility were never in those years as numerous proportionately as the sons of nobles in the group of radical intellectuals.'[3] Professor Brower commented as follows on his own results:

[1] One is reminded of Ryndziunskii's observation: 'Merchants did not manifest themselves in the abolitionist movement, and, therefore, their social views are not reflected in the materials illuminating that movement.' Ryndziunskii, *Gorodskoe grazhdanstvo doreformennoi Rossii*, p. 86.

[2] L. I. Nasonkina, *Moskovskii universitet posle vosstaniia dekabristov (1826–1831 gody)*, p. 6. I am very grateful to the author for allowing me to read her manuscript and for discussing it with me. The book was published in Moscow in 1972. (The published title does not include the dates.)

[3] Daniel R. Brower, 'Fathers, Sons, and Grandfathers: Social Origins of Radical Intellectuals in Nineteenth-Century Russia', *Journal of Social History*, vol. 2, No. 4 (summer 1969), p. 344.

The soundest conclusion to be drawn from the assorted and imperfect data presented here is that intellectual revolt came mainly from the 'upper classes' of Russia. The attempt to locate the time and circumstances when the 90 young radicals came to deny the justness of basic institutions of their society and to put their faith in a new order revealed above all that their revolt was only infrequently associated with oppression and hardship. They were men whose training was very advanced for the time, who had before them the possibility of respected and often well-paid careers, and who were in fact very intent on finding a meaningful and useful life. Some experienced real hardship, others suffered the humiliations of the weak in a society which favored the strong, but they were the minority. If traditional Russian values and behavior no longer satisfied these men, the responsibility lay above all with their own aspirations and beliefs, not with conditions around them.[1]

Whereas social composition *per se* is of little help in explaining the emerging split between the government and the educated public in Russia in the middle of the nineteenth century, the evolving structure of the intellectual life in the country might offer more promising leads. Although the number of universities did not alter in the reign of Nicholas I, at least they developed their work and became better established in Russian society and culture. Other institutions of higher learning and even more notably the secondary schools, the *gimnazii*, did increase in number, attracting ever more students. The Russian periodical press experienced a great expansion and differentiation reflecting much of the rich thought of the period. Writing and publishing in general became more professional and, obviously, acquired more readers. As most commentators have noted and as we have seen earlier, the intellectual development of the time centred frequently in ideological circles, which left their indelible mark on Russian thought and culture. Even a brief glance at some of these different elements of the Russian intellectual and cultural scene should give us a better conception of the Russian educated public, and it might aid our understanding of the growing dissatisfaction of that public with the established order.[2]

[1] Ibid., pp. 353-4.
[2] Much of the information in the following section was supplied by my research assistant, Mr. Gary Marker, who is writing a doctoral dissertation on the development of journalism and the book trade in Imperial Russia. I am very grateful to Mr. Marker for his help.

Except for the University of Moscow founded in 1755, no Russian universities were established before the beginning of the nineteenth century. It was during the early years of Alexander I's reign, as already mentioned, that universities came into being in Kazan and Kharkov, as well as in Vilna where 'the main school' was transformed into a university and in Dorpat where a German university was revived. The capital itself received a fully fledged university only in 1819 through an upgrading of its teachers' college, created originally in 1786 and reactivated in 1803. Another university existed in the Grand Duchy of Finland, annexed in 1809. In other words, it was under Alexander I and especially under Nicholas I, after the destructive activities of Golitsyn, Magnitskii, Runich, and their like, characteristic of the last years of Alexander I's reign, had ceased, that universities became a vital part of Russian life. The total number of students, not counting those in Finland, climbed from 2,618 in 1824 and a low of 1,985 in 1835 to 3,659 in 1855, in spite of another sharp decline following the European revolutions of 1848–9 and the resulting reactionary policies of the Russian government.[1] The University of Moscow remained by far the best attended of the six. Although, as indicated in an earlier discussion, the gentry was particularly prominent in the universities in the reign of Nicholas I, people of other social origins also played their part, and with the general development their participation increased in absolute terms, if not necessarily relative to the gentry. Higher education could also be obtained in half a score of specialized schools, ranging from the Institute of Mining opened in 1773 to that of Civil Engineers inaugurated by Nicholas I in 1842. Church academies and seminaries continued to represent a separate but important road towards specialized and advanced education in Russia. Secular secondary schools under the jurisdiction of the Ministry of Education grew both in number and in the number of students they accommodated under Nicholas I: from sixty schools and 14,000 students in 1825, without Poland and Finland, to seventy-seven and 17,817 respectively in 1855.[2] Cadet corps and other military schools long favoured by the gentry augmented the total.

---

[1] Nicholas Hans, *History of Russian Education Policy (1701–1917)*, London, 1931, p. 238. [2] Ibid., p. 235.

Although precision is difficult and anything like a full account impossible by the very nature of the matter, it is hard to over-estimate the importance of universities, together with other institutions of advanced learning, for the intellectual and cul-tural development of Russia in the second quarter of the nine-teenth century. They constituted the main conduit of Western knowledge and thought into Russia. Moreover, the ability of the Russians to profit by what they received and even to con-tribute to the common treasure kept increasing. One of Uvarov's most fruitful undertakings was the sending of promising young Russian scholars for further training first to the German university of Dorpat, within the empire, and after a period in Dorpat to leading centres abroad. It was these young scholars returning to occupy university chairs after several years of advanced study at the very fountainheads of knowledge who did so much to vivify and bolster Russian academic and in-tellectual life. Whatever the general geography of Russia with its attendant problems, many of the lecture halls of the country were in effect located in Berlin, Munich, or Paris.

It is not at all surprising, therefore, that much significant thought in Russia had its starting-point at university lectures, whether those of Pavlov discussing the philosophy of Schelling at the University of Moscow or those of Poroshin explaining the views of Fourier at the University of St. Petersburg. Not only knowledge but inspiration too came from the universities, especially from the University of Moscow during its 'golden age', or at least so reads the testimony of intellectuals as dif-ferent as Herzen and Constantine Aksakov. Besides, while the university represented an important stage in Herzen's life, Granovskii's entire adult existence and role in Russia cannot be separated from his professorship at the University of Moscow. Much more than in the eighteenth century, the position of a university professor became a crucial post in the ideological advances and struggles of the romantic age. That many Russian intellectuals found the post congenial, is indicated, for example, by the fact that professorships became the favourite occupation, so to speak, of moderate Westernizers: not only Granovskii, but also Redkin, Kriukov, Chicherin, Kavelin, Serge Soloviev, and still other members and associates of the group occupied uni-versity chairs. That a preference for a professorship was not limited to the moderate Westernizers, however, is attested, for instance, by the fact that such stalwart contemporary ideologues of the doctrine of Official Nationality as Pogodin and Shevyrev were also primarily university professors.

The periodical press developed in the reign of Nicholas I much more strikingly than did higher education, and it reflected in a number of ways the remarkable evolution and growth of the Russian educated public. The history of journalism in Russia in the first half of the nineteenth century might be divided into two periods. The first spanned the years from 1801 to 1838. It witnessed a full recovery from the repression under Paul I, with journalistic activity far surpassing the highest levels attained at the time of Catherine the Great. Numbers, circulation rates, and the durability of journals all increased markedly. But it was the second period, from 1838 to 1855, that constituted a virtual journalistic explosion, the number, size, and also the reading public of the periodicals shooting way beyond anything in the Russian past.[1]

Active and successful publishers, such as Andrew Kraevskii and the already mentioned proponent of Official Nationality Senkovskii, became significant figures in Russian intellectual life. Others acquired popularity and occasionally fame writing for the journals; indeed their appeal sometimes determined the success of a particular periodical. They included not only the irrepressible and vacuous Senkovskii again, this time under the pen name of *Baron Brambeus*, but also serious writers like Nicholas Polevoi and especially Belinskii. Belinskii's role in Russian thought and culture can no more be separated from journalism than Granovskii's from university teaching. Because periodicals had to support themselves to survive in a limited and insecure market, publishers developed sensitivity, adaptability, and business sense. In fact, it has been suggested that journalism was the only industry in Russia in the second quarter of the nineteenth century which operated along sophisticated capitalist lines and responded promptly and effectively to market conditions.

---

[1] This description of the second period, including the last years of Nicholas I's reign, contradicts much contemporary and historical literature which emphasizes almost exclusively reaction and repression. And, of course, there was reaction and repression, which I discussed repeatedly in my own works. Yet sky-rocketing publication figures cannot be gainsaid, and historical analysis will have to adjust to them.

A student of intellectual history cannot fail to note that Russian journals were expounding increasingly pronounced and varied ideological positions. In spite of the concerted effort of Soviet scholars to emphasize division and struggle in the eighteenth-century periodical press, that press was actually characterized by a remarkable intellectual sameness which corresponded to the hegemony of the fundamental outlook of the Age of Reason. That uniformity cracked in the first quarter of the nineteenth century and collapsed in the second. In the reign of Nicholas I, the government doctrine of Official Nationality, championed in journalism in particular by the notorious trio of Bulgarin, Grech, and Senkovskii, found massive support in such publications as Bulgarin and Grech's newspaper *Severnaia Pchela* (*The Northern Bee*), Grech's periodical *Syn Otechestva* (*A Son of the Fatherland*), and Senkovskii's immensely popular but intellectually insignificant journal *Biblioteka dlia Chteniia* (*The Reader's Library*). *Zhurnal Ministerstva Narodnogo Prosveshcheniia* (*The Journal of the Ministry of Education*) and other official publications also represented, of course, the government point of view. Pogodin's *Moskvitianin* (*The Muscovite*), 1841–56, was rather more independent, combining the ideology of the nationalist wing of Official Nationality of its editor and his close friend Shevyrev with considerable Slavophile participation. There even appeared for some years in St. Petersburg an organ to the right of the government, a kind of unwitting parody of the doctrine of Official Nationality entitled *Maiak*, or, in full, *Maiak Sovremennogo Prosveshcheniia i Obrazovannosti* (*The Lighthouse*, or *The Lighthouse of Contemporary Enlightenment and Education*), 1840–5.[1] But the vast and varied array of Right-wing publications was losing ground in the 1840s and 1850s to the generally moderate or liberal, occasionally covertly radical, press, exemplified best by the two journals with which Belinskii came to be associated, *Otechestvennye Zapiski* (*Notes of the Fatherland*) and *Sovremennik* (*The Contemporary*). Although, to be sure, Bakunin could not preach anarchism openly, and although even the Slavophiles found it

---

[1] Peculiarities of *The Lighthouse* included patriotic and moral literary contributions by 'simple Russian peasants', claims of sweeping scientific and technological inventions on behalf of other such peasants, violent anti-intellectualism, superstition in religion and thought, and one of the editors' predilection for naval terminology and subject-matter.

very difficult to propagate their word in print, Russian journalism in the reign of Nicholas I came to express to some considerable extent the buoyant and contentious thought of Russian intellectuals.[1]

Some figures might be in order to substantiate this insufficiently appreciated point of the great growth of the Russian periodical press by the middle of the nineteenth century. During the last year of Paul I's reign, 1801, eleven periodical publications existed in Russia. In the next six years, forty-nine new journals appeared, an average of eight additions a year. By 1807, with the usual high discontinuance rate, thirty-nine periodicals were being published in the empire. One obvious reason for this growth was the repeal of the Pauline laws, and the enactment of much milder censorship regulations of 1801, 1803, and 1804, which, among other things, again allowed private individuals to operate printing-presses. There was little or no progress between 1807 and 1822, followed by a spurt during the remaining years of the decade, when the number of journals reached the annual average of forty-two. Steady growth continued in the eighteen-thirties, so that forty-six periodicals were published on the average annually between 1831 and 1837.

The journals were also gradually becoming more successful. Between 1802 and 1810, seventy-four new journals were started, fifty-two of them by private initiative. Following the eighteenth-century pattern, many of the private journals, thirty-one of the fifty-two to be exact, lasted a year or less. Seventeen lasted between two and four years. But, for the first time in Russian history, several private journals of general interest managed to have longer life spans. Four of them continued for five or more years, topped by Karamzin's *Vestnik Evropy* (*The Messenger of Europe*), which came out for twenty-nine successive years, outliving its famous founder. The trend towards greater success and duration accelerated in subsequent decades. Thus, 123 new periodicals, eighty-five of them private, appeared on the market between 1811 and 1830: only thirty-two disappeared within a year; thirty-seven lasted between two

---

[1] For a Soviet survey of the Russian press in the crucial 1840s and 1850s see A. G. Dementev, *Ocherki po istorii russkoi zhurnalistiki 1840–1850 gg.*, Moscow–Leningrad, 1951.

and four years; seven between five and nine; and three continued to publish for ten years or more. The last group included Grech's journal *Syn Otechestva* (*A Son of the Fatherland*) and Bulgarin and Grech's newspaper *Severnaia Pchela* (*The Northern Bee*), each of which was to enjoy a life span of forty years. Finally, to take up the last segment of this initial period of Russian journalism in the first half of the nineteenth century, fifty-four new journals, thirty-three of them private, appeared between 1831 and 1837. Of that number, only nine folded in their first year; twelve lasted two to four years; eight five to nine years; and four continued coming out for ten years or longer. The four included such popular journals of general interest as *Sovremennik* (*The Contemporary*), which remained at the centre of Russian intellectual life for thirty-one years, and *Biblioteka dlia Chteniia* (*The Reader's Library*), which retained the public's support for thirty-two. Senkovskii's *Biblioteka dlia Chteniia*, founded in 1834, was the first large and lasting Russian periodical of the kind which later became very popular under the familiar classification of 'thick journals'. It contained seven sections: Russian literature, foreign literature, the sciences and the arts, industry and agriculture, criticism, the literary chronicle, and miscellaneous.

Circulation rates are of special interest to historians, because they remain the best index available of readership, although, needless to say, that index lacks precision; in particular, it may be assumed that the number of readers greatly exceeded the number of subscribers. On the basis of disturbingly incomplete information, it would seem that the circulation of Russian periodicals was rising steadily in the first decades of the nineteenth century. In published literature, figures exist for seventeen separate general periodicals which came out between 1801 and 1837. Almost all of them started with printings of between 300 and 600 copies. The more successful ones quickly increased the number to between 1,000 and 1,500. Thus, Karamzin's *Vestnik Evropy* (*The Messenger of Europe*) appeared in 1,200 copies, Nicholas Polevoi's *Moskovskii Telegraf* (*The Moscow Telegraph*) in 1,500, and Nicholas Grech's *Syn Otechestva* (*A Son of the Fatherland*) even in 1,800. Still larger figures were reached in the 1830s. In particular, Bulgarin and Grech's newspaper, *Severnaia Pchela* (*The Northern Bee*), acquired 4,000 subscriptions early in the decade, while the journal *Biblioteka dlia Chteniia* (*The Reader's Library*) reached the unprecedented figure of 5,000 subscribers in 1835, and of 7,000 two years later. Senkovskii especially catered frantically to the undiscriminating taste for entertainment of a public that was beginning to read the periodical press for the first time.

The year of 1838 represents an appropriate divide in the history of Russian journalism in the first half of the nineteenth century. In that year the fifty-eight periodicals that were then coming out in Russia were augmented by weekly, later daily, official *Vedomosti* (*News*) to be published in each province. Moreover, this provincial assistance aside, Russian journals and journalism spurted ahead.

The periodical press grew very rapidly in Russia in the 1840s. Not counting the provincial *Vedomosti*, the number of publications per year rose from fifty-eight in 1838 to seventy-one in 1843 and to eighty-three in 1850. That figure of eighty-three included sixteen daily and fifteen weekly titles. To be sure, the government accounted for much of the increase. Of the 124 new periodicals which came out between 1838 and 1850, forty-three were provincial *Vedomosti* and thirty-one different government journals, frequently of a technical nature. An additional five were academic. The remaining forty-five represented private initiative, and they too were often of a highly specialized character. In fact, expansion and specialization of both the state bureaucracy and the educated public constituted an important reason for the proliferation of periodicals. The government instituted journals dealing with rural economy, mining, and manufacturing, as well as, of course, the provincial series. Private individuals and groups founded medical, veterinary, and musical journals, and even one devoted to numismatism. Publications of literary and general interest, however, retained their great prominence. The newcomers in that category included the liberal, Westernizer *Otechestvennye Zapiski* (*Notes of the Fatherland*), which was to have a distinguished career of forty-six years, as well as the much less popular new efforts of the Right, such as the *Moskvitianin* (*The Muscovite*) and *Maiak* (*The Lighthouse*).

Circulation of the periodicals also apparently rose markedly in the 1840s, although no single journal could match the figure of 7,000 subscribers attracted by *Biblioteka dlia Chteniia* (*The Reader's Library*) in 1837. That superficial publication itself, it might be added, declined in appeal—precisely because of the increasing maturity of the Russian reading public, according to some specialists. In any case, most of the better writers stopped contributing to it. By contrast, *Russkii Vestnik* (*The Russian Messenger*), for example, rose early in the decade from printings of between 1,000 and 1,200 copies to printings of 2,000, although it quickly went down after the departure of Nicholas Polevoi. The two major Westernizer journals of the time *Sovremennik* (*The Contemporary*) and *Otechestvennye Zapiski* (*Notes of the Fatherland*), proved to be especially popular. The former printed 2,000 copies per issue in 1847, and as many as 3,100 a year later. Kraevskii's *Otechestvennye Zapiski* made in the course of the decade the still more striking jump from about 1,200 to some 4,000 copies. Belinskii stood out as the most popular, as well as the most controversial, publicist of the period. Even the languishing Right-wing *Moskvitianin* (*The Muscovite*) had a revival as the 1840s turned into the 1850s, when it obtained the so-called 'young editorial board', which included the playwright Alexander Ostrovskii and the critic Apollo Grigoriev: its circulation rose from 500 in 1850 to 1,100 in 1851.

Although no satisfactory study of the subject exists, there is no doubt that book publishing grew rather rapidly in Russia in the first half of the nineteenth century. It would appear that it paralleled the expansion of journalism. During that time reading libraries, large bookshops, and important publishing firms became major fixtures of Russian intellectual life. Bookshops served also as lending libraries, and their catalogues, *rospisi*, thus became both lists of merchandise to be sold and library guides. Apparently, in the 1840s and the 1850s different book dealers attempted to outdo one another in the extent and the sophistication of their *rospisi*, and in at least one instance a book dealer tried to copyright his catalogue.

The most famous publisher of the period, Alexander Smirdin, a self-made man notable for his love of literature and for his generosity, which finally made him bankrupt, began holding literary evenings in his library in 1832. The writers who came to Smirdin included such luminaries as Pushkin, Gogol, Krylov, and Zhukovskii, and many others of lesser stature. The publisher's productions encompassed an interesting two-volume collection of certain works of these writers, entitled *Novosele* (*House-warming*) and meant to celebrate the moving of Smirdin's business to the fashionable Nevskii avenue in the heart of the capital. It came out in 1833–4. Later in the decade Smirdin produced a multi-volume anthology, *Sto russkikh literatorov* (*A Hundred Russian Writers*), and at the end of the 1840s he even essayed to publish *Polnoe sobranie sochinenii russkikh avtorov* (*A Complete Collection of Works of Russian Authors*). It was also Smirdin who backed Senkovskii's successful journal, *Biblioteka dlia Chteniia* (*The Reader's Library*).

The total number of different titles published in a single year rose from the eighteenth-century high of approximately 450 in 1788 to a new record of at least 1,239 in 1855. According to the *Journal of the Ministry of Education*, 831 titles per year were published on the average in Russia in 1833–9; 944 titles in 1844–54. One is again reminded of the ascending curve of Russian journalism. Best-sellers proliferated. Krylov's *Basni* (*Fables*) had sold 40,000 copies by 1842. Pushkin's *Evgenii Onegin*, completed in the early 1830s, had sold 7,400 copies by 1837. Pushkin's poetry sold rapidly, and it also elicited especially high honoraria from Smirdin. Gogol's *Mertvye dushi* (*Dead Souls*), published in 1842, had a successful first printing of 2,325 copies. Public favourites also included, however, much lesser writers and even nonentities. In 1829, Bulgarin's novel, *Ivan Vyzhigin*, had a second printing a week after the first printing of 2,000 copies. In 1831, Zagoskin's patriotic *Roslavlev* had a successful first edition of 4,800 copies. Outright hack popularizers, who often merely simplified in meagre disguise more original literature, also attracted numerous readers. This last fact, mortifying to some contemporaries and many later scholars, provided striking evidence of an expansion of the reading public, of new segments of society turning to books. Histories were also published in profusion. The outstandingly successful ones included not only Karamzin's great best-seller, but also the works of the representative of Official Nationality Professor Nicholas Ustrialov and of Ivan Kaidanov, which served as textbooks in the schools of the empire. Foreign literature continued to be translated and published in Russia on a massive scale. Although with the rise of Russian literature proper its proportion to the total declined, the Russian empire by the middle of the nineteenth century was more than ever before a part of the general European intellectual and cultural world. The most popular foreign writers included, still, Voltaire and Rousseau, and, from a later date, Walter Scott, but also, as a tribute to the more vulgar taste, the French novelist Paul de Kock.

The growth of Russian book publishing, together with the expansion of journalism in Russia, had a number of social consequences. In dealing with Official Nationality we already encountered its large retinue of publicists and poetasters—as well as some major figures—serving or at least avidly supporting the government while practising their trade. Bulgarin, a highly successful writer and a leading journalist, repeatedly linked nefariously to the political police, represented both the epitome and the caricature of the breed. In the 1830s romanticism and a developing cultural life also produced Russian Bohemianism exemplified by Nestor Kukolnik and his pretensions. Yet books, journals, cultural growth in general, led beyond Bulgarin and Kukolnik, beyond lackey service, to the state, and transient and superficial Bohemianism in the direction of a professionalization of the intellectual life, essentially independent of the government and supported primarily by the newly emerging reading public. Even though by 1850 Russia had not travelled far in that direction, a student of the split between the Russian government and the Russian educated public should be aware of the matter.

Most studies of Russian intellectual life in the second quarter of the nineteenth century give some consideration to *kruzhki*, or circles, and for good reason. As has been shown, a *kruzhok* served frequently as the main vehicle for the formulation and dissemination of thought in Russia, from the time of the Lovers of Wisdom, if not earlier, to the end of the period under discussion. Such central intellectual figures as Stankevich or Butashevich-Petrashevskii were notable primarily as organizers and leaders of their circles. Aronson and Reiser, in their book which focuses on the same period as my present work, refer to '400 circles, salons, and other forms of association' and complain that in their study they could discuss 'only about

30'.[1] They and some other scholars have attempted complicated classifications of these different associations of Russian intellectuals. Suffice it to state here that for the period the basic form was a relatively small, intimate group of young men devoted to a particular, although at times rapidly evolving, teaching. In the German romantic and idealistic tradition especially, intellectual and personal relations were often indissolubly blended, friendship itself acquiring the status of a revelation and of a quasi-metaphysical category. Youth, enthusiasm, togetherness, intellectual and emotional discovery all gave the circles their unforgettable appeal. The virtual cult of Stankevich in the Russian intellectual tradition—noted in the preceding chapter —represents one lasting tribute to the *kruzhki.*

Yet the circles had their critics too. To quote the most famous instance of such criticism, mounted by Ivan Turgenev, who had a full personal knowledge of the matter, in his story 'Hamlet of the Shchigry District':

What do I find horrible [in a circle]?—he exclaimed.—That is what: a circle is a destruction of all autonomous development; a circle is a disgusting substitution for society, women, life; a circle . . . oh, just wait, I shall tell you what a circle is! A circle is an indolent and sluggish existence together and next to one another, which is given the significance and appearance of a reasonable undertaking; a circle replaces conversation with ratiocinations, accustoms you to fruitless talk, diverts you from solitary, beneficial work, inoculates you with the literary itch; finally, it deprives you of the freshness and the virgin strength of your soul. A circle—it is banality and boredom under the name of brotherhood and friendship; a concatenation of misunderstandings and pretensions under the pretext of candour and sympathetic participation; in a circle, because of the right of every friend all the time and at any hour to stick his unwashed fingers right into the insides of a comrade, no one has a clean, untouched spot in one's soul; in a circle people adore an empty rhetorician, a selfish smart alec, a man old before his time; they carry in their arms a versifier who has no talent but posesses 'hidden' thoughts; in a circle young, seventeen-year-old fellows discuss cunningly and in an involved manner women and love, while in front of women they remain silent, or they talk to them as if they were talking to a book—and what do they talk to them about! In a circle there flourishes an elaborate rhetoric; in a circle people watch one another no less than do the police officials . . . Oh, circle! you are not a little circle: you are the magic circle in which more than one decent man perished![1]

Still, this ferocious condemnation of the circles did not tell the full story, even as far as Turgenev was concerned, let alone other Russian intellectuals. Chicherin wrote in his memoirs:

On one occasion I told Ivan Sergeevich Turgenev that he had no business attacking so hard Muscovite circles in his 'Hamlet of the Shchigry district'. The stifling atmosphere of a closed circle had, without doubt, its disadvantages; but what was one to do, when people were not allowed into the open air? These were the lungs with which at that time Russian thought, pressed on all sides, could breathe. And how many fresh forces these circles contained, what lively intellectual interests, how well they brought people together, how much they had of that which was supportive, encouraging, exciting! The exclusiveness itself disappeared when at a general tournament gathered people who had opposite views but who valued and respected one another. Turgenev agreed with my remarks.[2]

Both the praise and the blame of the *kruzhki* emphasize their intimate, integrated character and their apartness from the outside world. In one sense, the circles reflected the fragmentation of thought, in Russia as well as elsewhere, after the breakdown of the consensus of the Age of Reason. Again, as Chicherin forcefully pointed out to Turgenev, who himself knew it only too well, there was not much open air for intellectuals in Russia. In Nicholas I's empire one could not preach Fourierism, for example, in the market-place. Closed, and at times secret, circles could therefore be frequently considered a necessity. But a still larger question is the evolution of the Russian intellectuals themselves. The period of the circles leading to the emergence of the Russian intelligentsia corresponded to a certain level in the growth of the Russian educated public. Larger and more independent, differentiated, and divided than it had been in the eighteenth century, or in the first decades of the nineteenth, that public remained a small and circumscribed

[1] I. S. Turgenev, *Polnoe sobranie sochinenii*, 6th edn., St. Petersburgh, 1913, i. 326. Breaks in the original.
[2] Chicherin, op. cit., p. 6.

élite. Russia was still far from general education and modern mass culture. If, according to an extravagant Polish joke, the proletariat can be defined as a transient group between feudalism and automation, the intelligentsia can be considered, on much better grounds, just such a group between well-nigh total illiteracy and general literacy. It should be added that the very structure of Russian intellectual life in the circles suggested an apartness and a sectarian nature of thought limited to the initiated. That thought could be naturally and easily directed against the views of other circles, against general opinions in the outside world, or against the government and the entire established order, for that matter.

So far the burden of the argument in this chapter has been that Russian foreign relations and the internal development of the country, the opinion of Russia in the Western world and the changing structure of Russian intellectual life, in particular its increasing professionalization, all affected Russian thought, and indeed contributed to its turn against the government. In the end, it is necessary to revisit briefly the thought itself. Students of the subject have noted that Russia experienced two intellectual transformations in the second quarter of the nineteenth century: the change from the ideology of the Age of Reason to romanticism and idealism, and the disintegration of the new world view, or rather views.

The abandonment of the philosophy of the Enlightenment could be considered pure gain as far as Nicholas I and his government were concerned, all the more so because it followed the Decembrist rebellion, which had demonstrated how far the Russian educated public could carry the principles of that philosophy. Surely metaphysics, religion, art or poetry were less of a threat in the eyes of the determined autocrat and of the Third Department than would have been an active interest of society in politics. Moreover, not only did the new *Weltanschauung* demote political and practical concerns, but it contained within itself a strong affirmative and conservative bias. We saw how historical, traditionalist, religious, and authoritarian arguments of the romantic age were used to define and uphold the doctrine of Official Nationality in its many ramifications. Outside the government too affirmation and preservation were on the upswing, as was only natural when disciples of

Schelling and Savigny replaced admirers of Voltaire and
Rousseau in the intellectual leadership of Russia. It should be
remembered that, as an extreme and painful caricature of the
whole process, even Belinskii and Bakunin became passionate
supporters of autocracy during their brief phase of 'reconciliation with reality'. It was no mere coincidence that the Russian
educated public did not mount a single violent attempt against
the state throughout the entire age of romanticism and idealism,
from the late Enlightenment of 1825 until the 1860s when a
neo-Enlightenment had become an active force.

Yet, as it turned out, the Russian government obtained its
peace and the Russian educated public its more or less successful reconciliation with reality at an exorbitant price. The philosophy of the Enlightenment was probably the last truly unifying
ideology of the Western world. In Russia, as elsewhere, it was
followed by division and fragmentation, the common language
of the rulers and the educated public by a babel of tongues. The
poignancy and the special tragedy of the Radishchev episode
was due precisely to the fact that the critic and Catherine the
Great belonged to essentially the same intellectual camp. Even
the Decembrists had found it difficult to separate their intentions and actions from those of the government of Alexander I,
and their emotional attitude to their rulers had remained
ambivalent to the end. But there was no way for Benckendorff
to understand the Slavophiles, or for Nicholas I the Petrashevtsy. The connection was no more. At the same time the
thought of Russian intellectuals, and to a certain extent of the
government too, was becoming, so to speak, increasingly unreal.
The point is not that Enlightenment is health and romanticism
sickness—both certainly can be sick and perhaps both can be
healthy—but rather that in the particular historical experience
of Russia the ideas of the intellectuals of the 1830s and the 1840s
were much farther removed from any actual or possible reality
than those of their counterparts in the preceding generations.
While scholars still argue whether an implementation of Speranskii's main proposals would have fundamentally changed
the course of Russian history, or dispute the practical merits
and demerits of Novosiltsev's, Nikita Muraviev's, and even
Pestel's constitutions, no such debate swirls around the Slavophile programme, Butashevich-Petrashevskii's phalanx, or

Bakunin's anarchism. A constitution, especially a moderate constitution, might have well been within the possibilities of the Russian imperial system in the first half of the nineteenth century; by contrast, the views of Khomiakov, or Constantine Aksakov, or Bakunin, or Khanykov constituted pure Utopia. There was peace, indeed a dead calm, largely because the government and the educated public had no longer a common language for communication, nor common subjects to discuss.

To be sure, Russian intellectuals in the romantic age made a valiant effort to formulate an effective new *Weltanschauung*, and they displayed in the process a greater originality of thought than had their predecessors in the Age of Reason. The Slavophiles produced the most impressive Russian romantic ideology: coherent, comprehensive, and focused on such central elements of Russian life as Orthodoxy and the peasant commune. They also showed a remarkable tenacity in holding to their views. These well-developed and bravely championed views, however, led nowhere, for they were too far removed from the real world. More specifically, if old Russia had contained the true principles without a conscious comprehension of itself and its destiny, if contemporary Russia was following instead the false Western principles, and if future salvation resided in a return to the true principles on a new, conscious level, how was that future to be reached? The Slavophiles offered nothing in reply, except groundless hope and fervent belief that things were going their way. Not only such congenital optimists as Khomiakov and Constantine Aksakov, but even the pessimist Ivan Kireevskii depended on that kind of wishful thinking.[1] Yet there were no indications, except the appearance of the Slavophile circle itself, that Russia was changing direction. It was apparently in a bid to escape the cul-de-sac that Ivan Aksakov turned to Pan-Slavism.[2] A decisive battle between the Slav and the Teuton, an Armageddon, would churn the very depths of the Slavic soul and create a redeeming self-consciousness. Ironically, many readers entirely innocent of Khomiakov's theology or

[1] Ivan Kireevskii's incongruous optimism in this regard is noted repeatedly in the latest book about him: Peter K. Christoff, *An Introduction to Nineteenth-Century Russian Slavophilism. A Study in Ideas*, vol. ii., *I. V. Kireevskij*, The Hague, 1972 (e.g., pp. 130, 139).

[2] See esp. Stephen Lukashevich, *Ivan Aksakov, 1823–1886. A Study in Russian Thought and Politics*, Cambridge, Mass., 1965.

Ivan Kireevskii's philosophy, were eager to applaud Ivan Aksakov's new emphasis. But Pan-Slavism, to which Ivan Aksakov devoted the remainder of his life, proved to be no solution either. As to Slavophilism proper, it had nowhere to go and no true disciples, remaining the faith of a small group of men who used to gather at the Elagins'. Once in a remarkable passage Samarin accused the conservatives in and around the government of having as their ideal 'not the Russia of tomorrow, but the Austria of yesterday'.[1] Unfortunately, Samarin's and his friends' own vision lacked even that kind of connection with reality.

The Westernizers, on the other hand, with all their ups and downs and tergiversations, tried to stay closer to reality. In doing so they changed and often eventually lost their beliefs. Yet, while the Slavophiles proved superior as romantic ideologues to their celebrated opponents, the Westernizers expressed better the spirit, the quest, the dynamic, so to speak, of romanticism. In fact, the evolution of Westernizer thought might almost convince a sceptic that the dialectic exists. It was the Westernizers who moved by thesis and antithesis, or at least through contradiction and argument, from Schelling to Hegel, the Left Hegelians and beyond. It was thus they too who exhibited best the disintegration of romanticism and idealism.

It is important to realize, however, that this disintegration was by no means limited to a small circle. In Russian literature, as we have seen, beginning around 1840, realistic tendencies were replacing romanticism, prose poetry. In science, according to one estimate, Schelling's doctrines attained their greatest influence in 1836, declining rapidly in popularity after that date.[2] Here too Russia followed with some delay the general European trend. Before very long, even Professor Michael Pavlov himself, immortalized by Herzen as the herald of the *Naturphilosophie*, had abandoned idealism. Numerous other apostates included the seminal thinker of the original idealistic Society of the Lovers of Wisdom, Prince Vladimir Odoevskii. The Westernizers gave, in a sense, a concentrated expression

---

[1] Iu. F. Samarin, *Sobranie sochinenii*, vol. ix (1898), p. 485.
[2] Alexander Vucinich, *Science in Russian Culture*, vol. ii, *1861–1917*, Stanford, 1970, p. 337.

to this entire process, and they brought out especially well its attendant protest, rebellion, and despair. Some of them, in the wake of the German Left Hegelians and other related thinkers, challenged God just as the leading elements of the Russian educated public were finally splitting from the tsar. (Butashevich-Petrashevskii and certain other Russian intellectuals of the 1840s, it might be added, also championed atheism.) Belinskii won undying fame for his rejection of the Absolute over the issue of human suffering, Bakunin came to anarchism and pan-destruction, Herzen to personalist humanism and despair. Nor can these men be simply dismissed as extremists. Granovskii too apparently ended in deep dejection,[1] and there was no lack of disillusionment and despair in Ivan Turgenev.

To conclude, a concentration on the relationship between the government and the educated public may mean too narrow a focus: what was collapsing was not only the concept of enlightened despotism, or of autocracy, but an entire intellectual order.

---

[1] According to Chicherin, during the Crimean War Granovskii expressed in one of his letters a desire to join the mass levy 'not in order to wish Russia victory, but in order to die for her'. Chicherin, op. cit., p. 150. Granovskii died in 1855.

6

Concluding Remarks

Once one has gone to the Germans, leaving them is very difficult.

Herzen.[1]

THE abandonment of the philosophy of the Enlightenment in favour of romanticism and idealism eliminated the first intellectual synthesis of modern Russia, including the idea of enlightened despotism; the disintegration of romanticism and idealism swept the boards clean. Only boards are never quite clean in history. Although the intellectual historian of Russia in the 1860s should emphasize change rather than continuity, the celebrated contrast between 'sons' and 'fathers', continuity too played its part. To mention its crucial instance, a central concept of the new age, that of 'the people', *narod*, together with the closely related concept of the peasant commune, derived, unmistakably, from the romantic period. Moreover this reification of the illiterate Russian villagers and the assignment to them of a high, sometimes supreme, value, was not simply the work of Herzen, Bakunin, and a few of their associates who spanned the 1840s and the 1860s, but the logical result of romantic and idealistic thought, and in Russia in particular of the Slavophile doctrines. As a Westernizer, Botkin, put it: 'The Slavophiles pronounced one true word: populism, nationality [*narodnost, natsionalnost*]. Their great

---

[1] Quoted from Donald W. Treadgold, *The West in Russia and China. Religious and Secular Thought in Modern Times*, vol. i, *Russia, 1472–1917*, Cambridge, 1973, p. 84.

merit resides in that.'[1] Or, to quote another Westernizer, the famous observer of 'the marvellous decade', Annenkov:

That party managed to bring into the field of vision of the Russian intelligentsia a new subject, a new active element of thought—the people, to be precise; and after its preaching neither scholarship in general, nor the science of government in particular could avoid considering it and taking it into account in their various political and social solutions. This was the great merit of the party, whatever its cost. Later, and already abroad, Herzen understood very well the importance of the structure which the Slavophiles had erected, and he used to say, not for nothing: 'Our European Westernizer party will acquire the position and the significance of a social force only when it masters the themes and the problems put into circulation by the Slavophiles.'[2]

Writing from the Soviet perspective, but also trying to re-evaluate the Slavophiles, A. Ianov asserted:

Not only the revolutionary quality of the gentry was shot down in the Senate Square. Also shot down were the ideological premisses of that revolutionary quality: the belief in the all-saving force of enlightenment and of political reforms. Liberation was no longer expected either from enlightened despotism, as contemplated by Alexander's 'young friends', or from an officer's pronunciamento, as contemplated by his young enemies. Whence, then, could one expect the new tocsin of freedom? For a decade Russian thought stood as if petrified in front of this ideological abyss.[3]

The answer finally came in the form of a new concept of 'the people', and it was provided by the Slavophiles:

Only a blind man, or one who closes his eyes on purpose, fails to see that Constantine Aksakov, and all the Slavophiles for that matter, bid to become prophets of a new religion, the religion of 'the common people'. With its saints and its missionaries. And, alas, with its heretics and its Inquisition. First in the history of Russian thought they deified their 'people', slapped, destitute, and flogged.[4]

Do you remember, how Herzen grieved that the old ways were

---

[1] Quoted from S. Mashinskii, 'Slavianofilstvo i ego istolkovateli (Nekotorye itogi diskussii)', *Voprosy Literatury*, No. 12 (Dec. 1969), p. 113.

[2] P. V. Annenkov, *Literaturnye vospominaniia*, Leningrad, 1928, p. 464.

[3] A. Ianov, 'Otvet opponentam', *Voprosy Literatury*, No. 12 (Dec. 1969), p. 94.

[4] A. Ianov, 'Zagadka slavianofilskoi kritiki', *Voprosy Literatury*, No. 5 (May 1969), p. 105.

hardly usable any more, that no new ones were known? Well then, there it was, the new road. There it was, the new flag of liberation from despotism! The flag which Russian thought needed so much to rise again from the deathbed of a pestilential epoch, to believe again ... The flag under which from then on the Russian intellectual was fated to work, to struggle, and to die.[1]

Ianov also stressed the additional theme that Official Nationality too, with its principle of *narodnost*, was engaged in a cunning and rather successful effort to identify itself with the Russian people, and that it was a great achievement of the Slavophiles to have wrested the concept of 'the people' from the government.[2] Right, Left, or peculiar Slavophile Centre, the idea of 'the people' belonged to the romantic age.

So did the closely related conceptualization of the peasant commune, which was, on the one hand, to affect government policies at the time of the emancipation of the serfs and later, and, on the other, to dominate for decades much of Russian radical and revolutionary thought. Again, it emerged among the Slavophiles around 1839, at the dawn of Slavophilism to be exact, with the latest researcher allotting the priority of formulation to Ivan Kireevskii.[3] We have seen how the Slavophile view of the peasant commune fitted perfectly their general ideology of organicism and *sobornost*, and how it was effectively developed by members of the circle, in particular by Constantine Aksakov. There is little doubt that Herzen, who fought the Slavophiles tooth and nail in Muscovite *salons*, turned later to the Slavophile apotheosis of the peasant commune, when he proceeded to assail the West and to trace the Russian path to socialism. Introduced in a major key, this theme of the peasant commune proved to be extremely influential in Russian thought.

To be sure, the Slavophiles were not the only ones in the 1840s to be interested in the Russian peasant commune. Mention should be made of the notable German visitor, scholar,

---

[1] Ianov, 'Otvet opponentam', p. 98.

[2] For a Western scholar's similar view *re* the aims and success of Official Nationality, see Stanley Ziring's review of H. Lemberg's *Die Nationale Gedankenwelt der Dekabristen* in *The Slavonic and East European Review*, vol. xliii, No. 100 (Dec. 1964), pp. 210–11.

[3] Peter K. Christoff, *An Introduction to Nineteenth-Century Russian Slavophilism. A Study in Ideas*, vol. ii, *I. V. Kireevskij*, The Hague, 1972, pp. 82, 202–3, 211–12.

and traveller August von Haxthausen, whose classic work on Russia popularized the nature and virtues of the commune.[1] But Haxthausen did not precede the Slavophiles. Rather, as the latest specialist on Haxthausen, Professor S. Frederick Starr has it, in the winter of 1843-4 in Moscow 'Haxthausen discovered to his pleasure that he and the young Slavophiles held many views in common, especially on the importance of the *obshchina* [commune]'.[2] There were also differences, of course. Starr further indicates that Haxthausen proved much more realistic than Herzen and even Russian populists in general in that he recognized that the commune was based not on freedom but on absolute authority, defended the commune on social and not economic grounds, and foresaw much more clearly the demise of the commune with the rise of industrialism in Russia and an increase in popular education. It should be added that on all these points Herzen and his followers were closer to Khomiakov or Constantine Aksakov than to the German visitor. To quote, finally, a specialist on Herzen and the emergence of the populist ideology:

It is interesting to note that the development of Herzen's thought, his transition from Westernism to 'Russian socialism', was to some extent directly influenced by Mickiewicz's lectures. Not Haxthausen, as is still widely believed, but the Slavophiles and Mickiewicz gave Herzen the first stimulus to ponder over the peasant commune and the destiny of the Slavonic world. Herzen's *Diary* of 1843-4 bears sufficient testimony to this.[3]

In other words, Polish romanticism, as well as Russian romanticism, may have contributed to the formulation of a crucial populist concept.

Not surprisingly, the structure and institutions of intellectual

---

[1] Baron August von Haxthausen, *Studien über die inneren Zustände, das Volksleben, und ins besondere die ländlichen Einrichtungen Russlands*, vols. i and ii, Hanover, 1847; vol. iii, Berlin, 1852.

[2] S. Frederick Starr, 'August von Haxthausen and Russia', *The Slavonic and East European Review*, vol. xlvi, no. 107 (July 1968), pp. 462–78, p. 470. Starr also wrote recently a fascinating study of Haxthausen as an introduction to a new abridged English translation of Haxthausen's famous work, which he also edited: *Studies on the Interior of Russia*, trans. by Eleanore L. M. Schmidt, Chicago–London, 1972, pp. vii–xliii.

[3] A. Walicki, 'The Paris Lectures of Mickiewicz and Russian Slavophilism', *The Slavonic and East European Review*, vol. xlvi, No. 106 (Jan. 1968), p. 166.

life showed a greater continuity than thought itself. The split
between the Russian educated public and the Russian government in the 1840s and the 1850s meant in effect the emergence
of the Russian intelligentsia, which was to play such an important and prominent role in the evolution of the country between
the Crimean War and the October Revolution of 1917. The
critical and usually opposition intellectuals who coalesced into
an intelligentsia had their base in the institutions of higher
learning, the periodical press, book publishing, and other
elements of Russian culture developed by preceding generations. The circles continued to represent the cutting edge of
thought and protest in a nation which remained ninety-five per
cent illiterate in the middle of the century. They became,
however, more radical and revolutionary. Bakunin until his
death in 1876, Herzen until his death in 1870, and a few more
'men of the forties' became prophets and leaders to the young
generation, although they too had their difficulties with that
generation, largely because they could not entirely outlive the
romanticism and German idealism of their youth. Others,
already dead, such as Stankevich, Granovskii, and especially
Belinskii, shone anew as martyrs and saints of a new secular
faith of the Russian educated public. The most remarkable
critic of the Russian radical intelligentsia, Fedor Dostoevskii,
also came out of the 1840s.

As to government and society in imperial Russia, the harmony between the two, prevalent in the eighteenth century and
the first decades of the nineteenth, was never to be restored
after the split. True, the Russian educated public rallied
temporarily behind the government during Alexander II's
'great reforms', and another *rapprochement* between the two
developed in the early years of the twentieth century. But on
the whole the forces of separation and division prevailed, until,
under the overwhelming stress of the First World War, Russian
tsardom fell, almost totally unsupported and unlamented, in
February 1917. Indeed, the forces of separation and division
prevailed so effectively that the entire history of government
and society in imperial Russia came to be written backwards,
from the standpoint of the last turbulent decades and the
catastrophic ending.

The mid nineteenth-century split might well be considered

inevitable, although the issue of inevitability goes beyond historical evidence and is not likely to be determined by a specific historical context. Some students of romanticism have argued that European romanticism tended to be conservative in its first phase, roughly between 1815 and 1830, but turned radical and even revolutionary between 1830 and 1848. Not only in Russia, but, for example, in France too the intellectuals were moving in the 1840s to the Left. Again, the German states, closer in many ways to Russia than France, had gone through a variety of ideological and political trials and tribulations by mid-century. In Russia, by contrast with many other European countries, the government was very strong, but also very rigid and very conservative or reactionary, while the educated public represented but a tiny segment of the population and thus presumably lacked both the strength and the sense of responsibility and direction necessary to ensure a gradual, progressive evolution of the empire. The two were indeed likely to clash at some point.

On the broader world scene, the split between the government and the educated public in Russia in the 1840s and the 1850s can be considered a logical development within the framework of the Westernization and modernization of the country following Peter the Great's reforms. The *ancien régime*, the traditional system, had obvious difficulties responding to new demands; young intellectuals, it may well be argued, were bound eventually to deny its legitimacy, as in China, or the Ottoman Empire. In this as in many other respects the Russian response was similar to those of other underdeveloped countries being led into modernity through contact with the West. Yet the Russian case was also quite peculiar. The West was not exactly a newcomer to Russia. Rather, Russia had constituted for centuries a flank, a borderland, of Christendom, subject to invasion from the outside, relative isolation and retardation, but remaining much closer nevertheless to Byzantium and Europe in general than to the Polovetsian steppe kingdom or the Golden Horde. In Russia modernization meant uprooting and supplanting not an alien civilization but a quasi-medieval culture which resembled in many essentials the culture of medieval western and central Europe. Chaadaev's, or Granovskii's, identification with the West made considerable sense.

More important still, whether one preferred the Westernizer or the Slavophile point of view, the historical past of Russia and the nature of the Russian enlightenment made educated Russians in the eighteenth and the first half of the nineteenth century full participants in the intellectual life of their continent. That participation is now history.

BIBLIOGRAPHY

The bibliography is limited to the items cited in the study.

UNPUBLISHED SOURCES

KIREEVSKI, PETR VASILEVICH, 'Pisma k Elaginoi, Ekaterine Ivanovne, ur. Moier'. Gosudarstvennaia biblioteka imeni Lenina. Otdel rukopisei. Fond 99 Elaginykh.

Otchety III-go Otdeleniia Sobstvennoi Ego Imperatorskogo Velichestva Kantseliarii i Korpusa Zhandarmov. [1826–1855]. Tsentralnyi gosudarstvennyi arkhiv oktiabrskoi revoliutsii (Moscow). Fond 109, Opis 85, Edinitsy khraneniia, Nos. 1–20. For description, see Chapter V, p. 248 n. 1.

POGODIN, MIKHAIL P., Gosudarstvennaia biblioteka imeni Lenina. Otdel rukopisei. Fond 231, razdel I, k. 38, No. 5.

PUBLISHED ITEMS

AKSAKOV, IVAN S., SOCHINENIIA, 7 vols., Moscow, 1886–91.

AKSAKOV, KONSTANTIN (Constantine) S., 'O vnutrennem sostoianii Rossii' and some of his editorials in *Molva* are published in BRODSKII, N. L., *Rannie slavianofily*, pp. 69–122.

—— *Sochineniia istorichskie*, Moscow, 1861.

—— *Zamechaniia na novoe administrativnoe ustroistvo krestian v Rossii*, Leipzig, 1861. Also published in *Rus*, 1883, Nos. 3, 4, 5.

ALSTON, PATRICK L., *Education and the State in Tsarist Russia*, Stanford, Calif., 1969.

ANDREEV-KRIVICH, S. A., *Lermontov. Voprosy tvorchestva i biografii*, Moscow, 1954.

ANNENKOV, Pavel V. *Literaturnye vospominaniia*, St. Petersburg, 1909; Leningrad, 1928.

ARONSON, M., and REISER, S., *Literaturnye kruzhki i salony*, Leningrad, 1929.

BARSUKOV, NICOLAI P., *Zhizn i trudy M. P. Pogodina*, 22 vols., St. Petersburg, 1888–1910.

BELIAVSKII, MIKHAIL T., *Krestianski vopros v Rossii nakanune vosstaniia E. I. Pugacheva*, Moscow, 1965.

BELINSKII, VISSARION G., *Polnoe sobranie sochinenii*, 13 vols., Moscow, 1953–9.

BERDIAEV, NIKOLAI A., *A. S. Khomiakov*, Moscow, 1912.

BERDYAEV [BERDIAEV], N. A., *The Russian Idea*, London, 1947.

BERKOV, PAVEL N., *Istoriia russkoi zhurnalistiki XVIII veka*, Moscow-Leningrad, 1952.

—— 'Histoire de l' "Encyclopédie" dans la Russie du xviiie siècle', *Revue des études slaves*, vol. 44 (1965), pp. 47–59.

BERLIN, ISAIAH M., 'A Marvellous Decade. 1838–1848: The Birth of the Russian Intelligentsia', *Encounter*: June 1955, pp. 27–39; Nov. 1955, pp. 21–9; Dec. 1955, pp. 22–43; May 1956, pp. 20–34.

BERTIER DE SAUVIGNY, GUILLAUME DE, Review of *Joseph de Maistre: étude sur la vie et sur la doctrine d'un matérialiste mystique*, by Robert Triomphe (Geneva 1968), *American Historical Review*, vol. lxxv, no. 1 (Oct. 1969), p. 134.

—— 'L'Extravagante Équipée de la prophétesse marseillaise à la cour extravagante du tsar Alexandre Ier', *Le Figaro littéraire* (Paris), 10 Dec. 1960, pp. 5–6.

'Bestuzhev (Aleksandr Aleksandrovich)', *Entsiklopedicheskii Slovar* (Brockhaus–Efron), vol. iiia, pp. 620–2.

BLIUM, A. V., 'Izdatelskaia deiatelnost v russkoi provintsii kontsa XVIII–nachala XIX vv. (Osnovnye tematicheskie napravleniia i tsenzurno-pravovoe polozhenie)', *Kniga, issledovaniia i materialy*, xii, Moscow, 1966, pp. 136–59.

BOWMAN, Herbert, E., *Vissarion Belinski, 1811–1848. A Study on the Origins of Social Criticism in Russia*, Cambridge, Mass. 1954.

BRAZILL, William J., *The Young Hegelians*, New Haven, Conn., 1970.

BRODSKII, N. L., *Rannie slavianofily*, Moscow, 1910.

BROWER, DANIEL R., 'Fathers, Sons, and Grandfathers: Social Origins of Radical Intellectuals in Nineteenth-Century Russia', *Journal of Social History*, vol. 2, No. 4 (Summer 1969), pp. 333–55.

BROWN, EDWARD J., *Stankevich and His Moscow Circle*, Stanford, Calif., 1966.

BULGARIN, FADDEI (Thaddaeus) V., *Rossiia v istoricheskom, statisticheskom, geograficheskom i literaturnom otnosheniiakh. Ruchnaia kniga dlia russkikh vsekh soslovii*, St. Petersburg, 1837.

—— *Salopnitsa*, St. Petersburg, 1842.

—— *Vospominaniia*, 6 vols., St. Petersburg, 1846–9.

CADOT, MICHEL, *La Russie dans la vie intellectuelle française (1839–1856)*, Paris, 1967.

CARR, EDWARD H., *Michael Bakunin*, New York, 1961.

CH., N., 'Shevyrev, Stepan Petrovich', *Russkii biograficheskii slovar*, vol. 'Shebanov' to 'Shiutts', St. Petersburg, 1911.

CHAADAEV, PETR IA., *The Major Works of Peter Chaadaev*, translator and commentator Raymond T. McNally, Notre Dame, Indiana, and London, 1969.

CHARQUES, RICHARD D., *A Short History of Russia*, New York, 1956.

CHENTSOV, N. M., *Vosstanie dekabristov — bibliografiia*, Moscow–Leningrad, 1929.

CHERNIAVSKY, MICHAEL, *Tsar and People: Studies in Russian Myths*, New Haven, Conn. and London, 1961.

300 *Bibliography*

CHERNIAVSKY, MICHAEL, ' "Holy Russia": a Study in the History of an Idea', *The American Historical Review*, vol. lxiii, No. 3 (Apr. 1958), pp. 617–37.

CHICHERIN, BORIS N., *Vospominaniia. Moskva sorokovykh godov*, Moscow, 1928.

CHIZHEVSKII, DMITRII I., *Gegel v Rossii*, Paris, 1939.

CHRISTOFF, PETER K,. *An Introduction to Nineteenth-Century Russian Slavophilism. A Study in Ideas*, vol. ii: *I. V. Kireevskij*, The Hague, 1972.

CHUCHMAREV, V. I., 'Frantsuzskie entsiklopedisty XVIII veka ob uspekhakh razvitiia russkoi kultury', *Voprosy filosofii*, No. 6 (1951), pp. 179–93.

CIZOVA, T., 'Beccaria in Russia', *The Slavonic and East European Review*, vol. xl, No. 95 (June 1962), pp. 384–408.

CONFINO, MICHAEL, 'Histoire et psychologie: A propos de la noblesse russe au xviie siècle', *Annales: économies, sociétés, civilisations*, Year 22, No. 6 (Nov.–Dec. 1967), pp. 1163–205.

CORBET, CHARLES. *L'Opinion française face à l'inconnue russe (1799–1894)*, Paris, 1967.

CROSS, ANTHONY G. 'N. M. Karamzin's "Messenger of Europe" (*Vestnik Evropy*), 1802–3', *Forum for Modern Language Studies*, vol. v, No. 1 (Jan. 1969), pp. 1–25.

CURTISS, JOHN SHELTON, *The Russian Army under Nicholas I, 1825–1855*, Durham, N.C., 1965.

CUSTINE, ASTOLPHE MARQUIS DE, *La Russie en 1839*, 4 vols., Brussels, 1843.

CZARTORYSKI, PRINCE ADAM. *Memoirs of Prince Adam Czartoryski and His Correspondence with Alexander I*, ed. Adam Gielgud, 2 vols., London, 1888.

DARNTON, ROBERT, *Mesmerism and the End of the Enlightenment in France*, Cambridge, Mass., 1968.

Delo Petrashevtsev, 3 vols., Moscow–Leningrad, 1837–51.

DEMENTEV, A. G. *Ocherki po istorii russkoi zhurnalistiki 1840–1850 gg.*, Moscow–Leningrad, 1951.

—— ' "Kontseptsiia", "konstruktsiia" i "model" ', in 'Literaturnaia kritika rannikh slavianofilov', *Voprosy literatury*, No. 7 (July 1969), pp. 116–29.

DERZHAVIN, GAVRIIL (Gabriel) R., *Sochineniia Derzhavina s obiasnitelnymi primechaniiami*, 4 vols., St. Petersburg, 1895.

DMITRIEV, SERGEI S., 'Podkhod dolzhen byt konretno-istoricheskii', in 'Literaturnaia kritika rannikh slavianofilov', *Voprosy literatury*, No. 12 (Dec. 1969), pp. 73–84.

—— 'Slavianofily i slavianofilstvo (Iz istorii russkoi obshchestvennoi mysli serediny XIX veka)', *Istorik-Marksist*, Book 1/89, 1941, pp. 8597.

DOVNAR-ZAPOLSKII, M. V., *Idealy dekabristov*, Moscow, 1907.

DRUZHININ, NIKOLAI M. *Gosudarstvennye krestiane i reforma P. D. Kiseleva*, 2 vols. Moscow–Leningrad, 1946–58.

—— 'Prosveshchennyi absoliutizm v Rossii', *Absoliutizm v Rossii (XVII–*

XVIII vv.), ed. by N. M. Druzhinin, N. I. Pavlenko, and L. V. Cherepnin, Moscow, 1964, pp. 428–59.

DUDZINSKAIA, EVGENIIA A., 'Burzhuaznye tendentsii v teorii i praktike slavianofilov', *Voprosy istorii*, No. 1 (1972), pp. 49–64.

EGOROV, B., 'Problema, kotoruiu neobkhodimo reshit', in 'Literaturnaia kritika rannikh slavianofilov', *Voprosy literatury*, No. 5 (May 1969), pp. 128–35.

EHRHARD, M. 'La satire 'De l'éducation' de A. D. Kantemir', *Revue des études slaves*, vol. 38 (1961), pp. 73–9.

EMMONS, TERENCE. *The Russian Landed Gentry and the Peasant Emancipation of 1861*, Cambridge, 1968.

EROSHKIN, NIKOLAI P., *Istoriia gosudarstvennykh uchrezhdenii dorevoliutsionnoi Rossii*, Moscow, 1968.

FEDOSOV, IVAN A. *Revoliutsionnoe dvizhenie v Rossii vo vtoroi chetverti* XIX *v.* (*Revoliutsionnye organizatsii i kruzhki*), Moscow, 1958.

—— 'Prosveshchennyi absoliutizm v Rossii', *Voprosy istorii*, No. 9 (1970), pp. 34–55.

FLORENSKII, Pavel A., *Okolo Khomiakova*, Moscow, 1916.

FLORINSKY, Michael T., *Russia: A History and an Interpretation*, 2 vols., New York, 1953.

FRIZMAN, L., 'Za nauchnuiu obektivnost', in 'Literaturnaia kritika rannikh slavianofilov', *Voprosy literatury*, No. 7 (July 1969), pp. 138–52.

GABAEV, G. S., 'Gvardiia v dekabrskie dni 1925 goda', appendix to A. E. Presniakov, *14 dekabria 1825 goda*, Moscow, 1926.

GAY, PETER, *The Enlightenment: An Interpretation*, 2 vols., New York, 1966–9.

GERSHENZON, MIKHAIL O., ed., *Epokha Nikolaia I*, Moscow, 1911.

GERTSEN, ALEKSANDR (Alexander) I., *Byloe i Dumy*, 3 vols., Moscow, 1958.

—— *Polnoe sobranie sochinenii i pisem*, ed. by M. K. Lemke, 22 vols., Petrograd, 1915–25.

—— *Sochineniia*, 10 vols., Geneva, 1875–80.

GLEASON, ABBOT, *European and Muscovite: Ivan Kireevsky and the Origins of Slavophilism*, Cambridge, Mass., 1972.

GLEASON, JOHN H., *The Genesis of Russophobia in Great Britain. A Study of the Interaction of Policy and Opinion*, Cambridge, Mass., and London, 1950.

GLINKA, FEDOR (Theodore) N., *Stikhotvoreniia*, Leningrad, 1951.

GOLDMAN, LUCIEN, 'La pensée des "Lumières" ', *Annales: économies, sociétés, civilisations*, Year 22, Nunber 4 (July–Aug. 1967), pp. 752–79.

GOGOL, NIKOLAI V., 'Vybrannye mesta iz perepiski s druziami', in vol. viii of *Sochineniia* (10 vols.) ed. V. V. Kallash, St. Petersburg, n.d., pp. 1–232.

GRATIEUX, ALBERT. *A. Khomiakov et le mouvement slavophile*, vol. i: *Les hommes*; vol. ii: *Les doctrines*, Paris, 1939.

GRECH, NIKOLAI (NICHOLAS) I., *Zapiski o moei zhizni*, Moscow–Leningrad, 1930.

GRIMSTED, PATRICIA KENNEDY. *The Foreign Ministers of Alexander I: Political Attitudes and the Conduct of Russian Diplomacy, 1801–1825*, Berkeley and Los Angeles, 1969.

HANS, NICHOLAS. *History of Russian Educational Policy (1701–1917)*, London, 1931.

HARPAZ, ÉPHRAIM. *L'École libérale sous la Restoration: le 'Mercure' et la 'Minerve', 1817–1820*, Geneva, 1968.

HAXTHAUSEN, BARON AUGUST VON, *Studien über die inneren Zustände, das Volksleben, und insbesondere die ländlichen Einrichtungen Russlands*, vols. i and ii, Hanover, 1847; vol. iii, Berlin, 1852.

—— *Studies on the Interior of Russia*, ed. and with an introduction, by S. Frederick Starr. Translated by Eleanore L. M. Schmidt. Chicago and London, 1972.

HERZEN. See GERTSEN.

IAMPOLSKII, I., 'Literaturnaia deiatelnost I. I. Panaeva', introduction to I. I. Panaev, *Literaturnye vospominaniia*, Moscow–Leningrad, 1950, pp. v–lvi.

IANOV, ALEKSANDR L., 'Otvet opponentam', in 'Literaturnaia kritika rannikh slavianofilov', *Voprosy literatury*, No. 12 (Dec. 1969), pp. 85–101.

—— 'Zagadka slavianofilskoi kritiki', in 'Literaturnaia kritika rannikh slavianofilov', *Voprosy literatury*, No. 5 (May 1969), pp. 91–116.

IVANOV, A. 'Otritsatelnoe dostoinstvo', in 'Literaturnaia kritika rannikh slavianofilov', *Voprosy literatury*, No. 7 (July 1969), pp. 129–38.

KAMENSKII, Z. A. 'F. Shelling v russkoi filosofii nachala 19 veka', *Vestnik istorii mirovoi kultury*, No. 5 (Sept.–Oct. 1960), pp. 46–58.

—— 'I. Kant v russkoi filosofii nachala 19 veka', *Vestnik istorii mirovoi kultury*, No. 1 (Jan.–Feb. 1960), pp. 49–64.

KAPNIST, VASILII (Basil) V., *Sochineniia*, St. Petersburg, 1849.

KARAMZIN, NIKOLAI M. *Istoriia gosudarstva rossiiskogo*. Latest edition: 12 vols., The Hague, 1969.

KATZ, MARTIN, *Mikhail N. Katkov: A Political Biography, 1818–1887*, The Hague and Paris, 1966.

KENNAN, GEORGE F. *The Marquis de Custine and His 'Russia in 1839'*, Princeton, N. J., 1971.

KHOMIAKOV, ALEKSEI (Alexis) S., *Polnoe sobranie sochinenii*, 8 vols., Moscow, 1900–14.

—— *The Church Is One*, London, 1948.

KIREEVSKII, IVAN V., *Polnoe sobranie sochineniia*, 2 vols., Moscow, 1911.

KIRILOV, N., *Karmannyi slovar inostrannykh slov, voshedshikh v sostav russkogo iazyka*, St. Petersburg, 1845.

KLIUCHEVSKII, VASILII O., *Kurs russkoi istorii*, 5 vols., Moscow (vols. i–iv) and St. Petersburg (vol. v), 1911–21.

—— 'Evgenii Onegin i ego predki', *Ocherki i rechi. Vtoroi sbornik statei*, Petrograd, 1918.

KNAPTON, ERNEST J., *The Lady of the Holy Alliance, The Life of Julie de Krüdener*, New York, 1939.

KOGAN, IURII IA., *Ocherki po istorii russkoi ateisticheskoi mysli XVIII v.*, Moscow, 1962.

KORSAKOV, D., 'Senkovskii, Osip Ivanovich', *Russkii biograficheskii slovar*, vol. 'Sabaneev' to 'Smyslov', St. Petersburg, 1904.

KOSHELEV, ALEKSANDR (Alexander) I., *Zapiski Aleksandra Ivanovicha Kosheleva (1812–1883 gody)*, Berlin, 1884.

KOVALCHENKO, IVAN D., *Russkoe krepostnoe krestianstvo v pervoi polovine XIX v.*, Moscow, 1967.

KOVALEVSKII, MAKSIM M., 'Shellingianstvo i gegelianstvo v Rossii', *Vestnik Evropy*, vol. xi (Nov. 1915), pp. 133–70.

KOYRÉ, ALEXANDRE, *La Philosophie et le problème national en Russie au début du XIXe siècle*, Paris, 1919.

KOZHINOV, V., 'O glavnom v nasledii slavianofilov', in 'Literaturnaia kritika rannikh slavianofilov', *Voprosy literatury*, No. 10 (Oct. 1969), pp. 113–31.

KULESHOV, V., 'Slavianofilstvo, kak ono est . . .', in 'Literaturnaia kritika rannikh slavianofilov', *Voprosy literatury*, No. 10 (Oct. 1969), pp. 131–44.

LABRIOLLE, FRANÇOIS DE, 'La *prosveščenie* russe et les lumières en France (1760–1798)', *Revue des études slaves*, vol. 45 (1966), pp. 75–91.

LAMENNAIS, FÉLICITÉ-ROBERT DE, *Les Paroles d'un croyant*, ed. by Yves Le Hir, Paris, 1949.

LAMPERT, EVGENII, *Studies in Rebellion*, London, 1957.

LANG, DAVID M., *The First Russian Radical: Alexander Radishchev, 1749–1802*, London, 1959.

LAREN, MICHEL, 'La Première Génération de l'"intelligentsia" roturière en Russie (1750–1780)', *Revue d'histoire moderne et contemporaine*, vol. xiii (Apr.–June 1966), pp. 137–56.

LEDNICKI, WACŁAW A., *Pushkin's Bronze Horseman. The Story of a Masterpiece*, Berkeley and Los Angeles, 1955.

LEIKINA-SVIRSKAIA, VERA R., 'Formirovanie raznochinskoi intelligentsii v Rossii v 40-kh godakh XIX v.', *Istoriia SSSR*, No. 1 (1958), pp. 83–104.

LEMBERG, HANS, *Die nationale Gedankenwelt der Dekabristen*, Cologne–Graz, 1963.

LEONTOVITSCH, VICTOR, *Geschichte des Liberalismus in Russland*, Frankfurt am Main, 1957.

LERMONTOV, M. IU., *Polnoe sobranie sochenenii*, 5 vols., ed. by D. I. Abramovich, vol. ii, St. Petersburg, 1910.

LEVIN, K. N., and POKROVSKII, MIKHAIL N., 'Dekabristy', *Istoriia Rossii v XIX veke* (Granat), 9 vols., St. Petersburg, n.d., i. 67–137.

'Literaturnaia kritika rannikh slavianofilov', *Voprosy literatury*, Nos. 5, 7, 10, 12 (1969).

Introduction, No. 5 (May 1969), pp. 90–1.

A. IANOV, 'Zagadka slavianofilskoi kritiki', No. 5, pp. 91–116.

S. POKROVSKII, 'Mnimaia zagadka', No. 5, pp. 117–28.

B. EGOROV, 'Problema, kotoruiu neobkhodimo reshit', No. 5, pp. 128–35.

A. DEMENTEV, ' "Kontseptsiia", "konstruktsiia" i "model" ', No. 7 (July 1969), pp. 116–129.

A. IVANOV, 'Otritsatelnoe dostoinstvo', No. 7, pp. 129–38.

L. FRIZMAN, 'Za nauchnuiu obektivnost', No. 7, pp. 138–52.

E. MAIMIN, 'Nuzhny konkretnye issledovaniia', No. 10 (Oct. 1969), pp. 103–13.

V. KOZHINOV, 'O glavnom v nasledii slavianofilov', No. 10, pp. 113–31.

V. KULESHOV, 'Slavianofilstvo, kak ono est', No. 10, pp. 131–44.

S. DMITRIEV, 'Podkhod dolzhen byt konkretno-istoricheskii', No. 12 (Dec. 1969), pp. 73–94.

A. IANOV, 'Otvet opponentam', No. 12, pp. 85–101.

S. MASHINSKII, 'Slavianofilstvo i ego istolkovateli (Nekotorye itogi diskussii)', No. 12, pp. 102–40.

LORTHOLARY, ALBERT, *Le Mirage russe en France au XVIIIe siècle*, Paris, n.d.

LOTMAN, Iu. M. 'Poeziia 1790–1810-kh godov', *Poety 1790–1810-kh godov*, Leningrad, 1971, pp. 5–62.

—— 'Russo i russkaia kultura XVIII veka', *Epokha prosveshcheniia. Iz istorii mezhdunarodnykh sviazei russkoi literatury*, Leningrad, 1967, pp. 208–81.

LUKASHEVICH, STEPHEN M., *Ivan Aksakov, 1823–1886. A Study in Russian Thought and Politics*, Cambridge, Mass., 1965.

MAIMIN, E., 'Nuzhny konkretnye issledovaniia', in 'Literaturnaia kritika rannikh slavianofilov', *Voprosy literatury*, No. 10 (Oct. 1969), pp. 103–13.

MAKOGONENKO, GEORGII P., *Nikolai Novikov i russkoe prosveshchenie XVIII veka*, Moscow–Leningrad, 1951.

MALIA, MARTIN, *Alexander Herzen and the Birth of Russian Socialism, 1812–1855*, Cambridge, Mass., 1961.

MASHINSKII, S., 'Slavianofilstvo i ego istolkovateli (Nekotorye itogi diskussii)' in 'Literaturnaia kritika rannikh slavianofilov', *Voprosy literatury*, No. 12 (Dec. 1969), pp. 102–40.

—— 'Stankevich i ego kruzhok', *Istoriia literatury*, No. 5 (1964), pp. 125–48.

MAZOUR, ANATOLE G., *The First Russian Revolution 1825. The Decembrist Movement: Its Origins, Development and Significance*, Berkeley, 1937.

McGREW, RODERICK E., 'A Political Portrait of Paul I from the Austrian and English Diplomatic Archives', *Jahrbücher für Geschichte Osteuropas*, Dec. 1970, pp. 503–29.

McNALLY, Raymond T., *Chaadayev and His Friends. An Intellectual History of Peter Chaadayev and His Russian Contemporaries*, Tallahassee, Fla. 1971.

MELGUNOV, SERGEI P., 'Epokha "ofitsialnoi narodnosti" i krepostnoe pravo'

Velikaia Reforma. Russkoe obshchestvo i krestianskii vopros v proshlom i nastoia-shchem, ed. by K. A. Dzhivelegov, S. P. Melgunov, and V. I. Picheta, 6 vols., Moscow, 1911, iii. 1–21.

MILIUKOV, PAUL, SEIGNOBOS, C., EISENMAN, L., *et al.*, *History of Russia*, 3 vols., New York, 1968. See also the original French edition: *Histoire de Russie*, 3 vols., Paris, 1932–3.

MILIUKOV, PAVEL (Paul) N., *Gosudarstvennoe khoziaistvo Rossii v pervoi chetverti XVIII stoletiia i reforma Petra Velikogo*, 2nd edn., St. Petersburg, 1905.

MIRSKY, DMITRII S., *A History of Russian Literature*, New York, 1949.

MONAS, SIDNEY, *The Third Section: Police and Society in Russia under Nicholas I*, Cambridge, Mass., 1961.

MÜLLER, EBERHARD, *Russischer Intellekt in europäischer Krise: Ivan V. Kireevskij (1806–1856)*, Cologne–Graz, 1966.

N., 'O knizhnoi torgovle i liubvi ko chteniiu v Rossii', *Vestnik Evropy*, No. 9 (May 1802).

NABOKOV, VLADIMIR, *Three Russian Poets: Selections from Pushkin, Lermontov and Tyutchev in New Translations by Vladimir Nabokov*, New York, 1944.

NASONKINA, LIDIIA I. *Moskovskii universitet posle vosstaniia dekabristov (1826–1831 gody)* (read originally in manuscript), Moscow, 1972.

NECHKINA, MILITSA V., *Dvizhenie dekabristov*, 2 vols. Moscow, 1955.

—— and EIMONTOVA, R. G. *Dvizhenie dekabristov—ukazatel literatury, 1928–1959*, Moscow, 1960.

NICOLSON, HAROLD, *The Congress of Vienna. A Study in Allied Unity: 1812–1822*, London, 1946.

NIKITENKO, ALEKSANDR (Alexander) V., *Moia povest o samon sebe i o tom 'chemu svidetel v zhizni byl', Zapiski i dnevnik (1804–1877 gg)*, 2 vols. 2nd edn., St. Petersburg, 1905.

ODOEVSKII, VLADIMIR F. *Russkie nochi*, Moscow, 1913.

OKSMAN, IURII G., *Dekabristy. Sbornik: otryvki iz istochnikov*, Moscow–Leningrad, 1926.

OLIVA, L. JAY. *Russia in the Era of Peter the Great*, Englewood Cliffs, N. J., 1969.

'O novom obrazovanii narodnogo prosveshcheniia v Rossii', *Vestnik Evropy*, No. 5 (Mar. 1803), pp. 49–61.

ORLOV, VLADIMIR N., *Russkie prosvetiteli 1790–1800-kh godov*, 2nd edn., Moscow, 1953.

PANAEV, IVAN I., *Literaturnye vospominaniia*, Moscow–Leningrad, 1950.

PAPMEHL, KENNETH A., 'The Problem of Civil Liberties in the Records of the "Great Commission" ', *The Slavonic and East European Review*, vol. xli, No. 99 (Dec. 1963), pp. 274–91.

PARES, BERNARD, *A History of Russia*, New York, 1953.

PARTRIDGE, MONICA, 'Herzen's Changing Concept of Reality and Its Reflection in His Literary Works', *The Slavonic and East European Review*, vol. xlvi, No. 107 (July 1968), pp. 397–421.

PARTRIDGE, MONICA, 'Slavonic Themes in English Poetry of the 19th Century', *The Slavonic and East European Review*, vol. xli, No. 97 (June 1963), pp. 420–41.

PAVLENKO, N. I., 'Idei absoliutizma v zakonodatelstve XVIII v.', *Absoliutizm v Rossii (XVII–XVIII vv.)*, ed. by M. N. Druzhinin, N. I. Pavlenko, L. V. Cherepnin, Moscow, 1964, pp. 389–427.

PESHTICH, SERGEI L., *Russkaia istoriografiia XVIII veka*, Part II, Leningrad, 1965.

PIPES, R., *Karamzin's Memoir on Ancient and Modern Russia: A Translation and Analysis*, New York, 1966.

—— 'Karamzin's Conception of the Monarchy', *Harvard Slavic Studies*, vol. iv, 1957, pp. 35–58.

—— 'The Russian Military Colonies, 1810–1831', *Journal of Modern History*, vol. xxii (Sept. 1950), pp. 205–19.

PLEKHANOV, GEORGII V., *V. G. Belinskii. Sbornik statei*, Moscow–Petrograd, 1923.

—— *Istoriia russkoi obshchestvennoi mysli*, vol. iii, Moscow, 1919.

POGODIN, MIKHAIL (Michael) P., *Historische Aphorismen*, Leipzig, 1836.

—— *Istoriko-kriticheskie otryvki*, Moscow, 1846.

—— *Istoriko-politicheskie pisma i zapiski v prodolzhenii Krymskoi Voiny 1853–1856*, Moscow, 1874.

—— *Ostzeitskii vopros. Pismo k professoru Shirrenu*, Moscow, 1868.

—— *Prostaia rech o mudrenykh veshchakh*, Moscow, 1875.

——*Rechi, proiznesennye v torzhestvennykh i prochikh sobraniiakh, 1830–1872*, Moscow, 1872.

—— *Stati politicheskie i polskii vopros (1856–1867)*, Moscow, 1876.

POKROVSKII, SERAFIM A., 'Mnimaia zagadka', in 'Literaturnaia kritika rannikh slavianofilov', *Voprosy literatury*, No. 5 (May 1969), pp. 117–28.

—— *Politicheskie i pravovye vzgliady S. E. Desnitskogo*, Moscow, 1955.

POLIEVKTOV, M. A., *Nikolai I. Biografiia i obzor tsarstvovaniia*, Moscow, 1918.

PREDTECHENSKII, ANATOLII V., *Ocherki obshchestevenno-politicheskoi istorii Rossii v pervoi chetverti XIX veka*, Moscow–Leningrad, 1957.

PUSHKIN, ALEKSANDR (Alexander) S., *Three Russian Poets: Selections from Pushkin, Lermontov and Tyutchev in New Translations by Vladimir Nabokov*, New York, 1944.

—— *Verses from Pushkin and Others*, translated by Oliver Elton, London, 1935.

PYPIN, ALEKSANDR N., *Kharakteristiki literaturnykh mnenii ot dvadtsatykh do piatidesiatykh godov*, St. Petersburg, 1906.

QUÉNET, CHARLES, *Tchaadaev et les lettres philosophiques. Contribution à l'étude du mouvement des idées en Russie*, Paris, 1931.

RAEFF, MARC, *The Decembrist Movement*, Englewood Cliffs, N.J., 1966.

—— *Imperial Russia, 1682–1825: The Coming of Age of Modern Russia*, New York, 1971.

—— *Michael Speransky, Statesman of Imperial Russia, 1772–1839*. The Hague, 1957.

—— *Origins of the Russian Intelligentsia. The Eighteenth-Century Nobility*. New York, 1966.

—— *Plans for Political Reform in Imperial Russia, 1730–1905*. Englewood Cliffs, N. J., 1966.

—— 'Les Slaves, les Allemands et les "Lumières" ', *Canadian Slavic Studies*, vol. i, No. 4 (Winter 1967), pp. 521–55.

RAISKII, L., *Sotsialnye vozzreniia Petrashevtsev*, Leningrad, 1927.

RANSEL, DAVID, 'Nikita Panin's Imperial Council Project and the Struggle of Hierarchy Groups at the Court of Catherine II', *Canadian Slavic Studies*, vol. iv, No. 3 (Fall 1970), pp. 443–63.

RATH, R. JOHN, 'Training for Citizenship in the Austrian Elementary Schools during the Reign of Francis I', *Journal of Central European Affairs*, vol. iv (July 1944), pp. 147–64.

REDDAWAY, W. F., ed., *Documents of Catherine the Great: The Correspondence with Voltaire and the 'Instruction' of 1767 in the English Text of 1768*. Cambridge, 1931.

RIASANOVSKY, NICHOLAS V., *History of Russia*, 2nd edn., New York, 1969.

—— *Nicholas I and Official Nationality in Russia, 1825–1855*, Berkeley and Los Angeles, 1959.

—— *Russia and the West in the Teaching of the Slavophiles. A Study of Romantic Ideology*, Cambridge, Mass., 1952.

—— *The Teaching of Charles Fourier*, Berkeley and Los Angeles, 1969.

—— 'Fourierism in Russia: An Estimate of the Petraševcy', *The American Slavic and East European Review*, vol. xii, No. 3 (Oct. 1953), pp. 289–302.

—— 'Khomiakov on *Sobornost*', in *Continuity and Change in Russian and Soviet Thought*, ed. by Ernest J. Simmons, Cambridge, Mass., 1955, pp. 183–96.

—— 'The Norman Theory of the Origin of the Russian State', *The Russian Review*, vol. vii, No. 1 (Autumn 1947), pp. 96–110.

—— 'Pogodin and Ševyrev in Russian Intellectual History', *Harvard Slavic Studies*, vol. iv (1957), pp. 149–67.

—— Review of *Geschichte des Liberalismus in Russland*, by Victor Leontovitsch, *Journal of Central European Affairs*, vol. xviii, No. 3 (Oct. 1958), pp. 346–8.

—— Review of *Michael Speransky, Statesman of Imperial Russia 1772–1839*, by Marc Raeff, *Journal of Modern History*, vol. xxx, No. 3 (Sept. 1958), pp. 291–2.

—— Review of 'Das russische Beamtentum in der ersten Hälfte des 19. Jahrhunderts' (pp. 7–345 of *Forschungen zur osteuropäischen Geschichte*, vol. xiii (1967), by Hans J. Torké, *Jahrbücher für Geschichte Osteuropas*, vol. xvii, No. 1 (Mar. 1969), pp. 114–15.

RIASANOVSKY, NICHOLAS V., Review of *Russischer Intellekt in europäischer Krise: Ivan V. Kireevskij (1806–1856)*, by Eberhard Müller, *Jahrbücher für Geschichte Osteuropas*, vol. xv, No. 3, pp. 445–6.

—— Review of *Stankevich and His Moscow Circle*, by Edward Brown, *Slavic Review*, vol. xxvi, No. 2 (June 1967), pp. 338–9.

—— Review of *Studies in Rebellion*, by E. Lampert, *The American Slavic and East European Review*, vol. xvii, No. 1 (Feb. 1958), pp. 129–130.

—— Review of *Tsar and People: Studies in Russian Myths*, by Michael Cherniavsky, *The Political Science Quarterly*, vol. lxxviii, No. 2 (June 1963), pp. 304–5.

RIASANOVSKY, VALENTIN A., *Obzor russkoi kultury. Istoricheskii ocherk*, Part II, Issue II, New York, 1948.

ROGGER, HANS, *National Consciousness in Eighteenth-Century Russia*, Cambridge, Mass., 1960.

ROZANOV, VASILII V., 'Pamiati A. S. Khomiakova (10e maia 1804 g.–10e maia 1904 g.)', *Novyi Put*, Year II (June 1904), pp. 1–16.

RUBINSHTEIN, N., 'Istoricheskaia teoriia slavianofilov i ee klassovye korni', *Trudy Instituta Krasnoi Professury. Russkaia istoricheskaia literatura v klassovom osveshchenii. Sbornik statei*, ed. by M. N. Pokrovskii, Moscow, 1927, i. 53–118.

RYNDZIUNSKII, PAVEL G., *Gorodskoe grazhdanstvo doreformennoi Rossii*, Moscow, 1958.

—— 'O melkotovarnom uklade v Rossii XIX veka', *Istoriia SSSR*, No. 2 (1961), pp. 48–70.

—— 'Ob opredelenii intensivnosti obrochnoi ekspluatatsii krestian tsentralnoi Rossii v kontse XVIII–pervoi polovine XIX v. (O state I. D. Kovalchenko i L. V. Milova)', *Istoriia SSSR*, No. 6 (1966), pp. 44–64.

SAKULIN, PAVEL N., *Iz istorii russkogo idealizma*; *Kniaz V. Odoevskii*, Moscow, 1913.

—— 'Russkaia literatura vo vtoroi chetverti veka' *Istoriia Rossii v XIX veke* (Granat), 9 vols., St. Petersburg, n.d., ii. 443–508.

SAMARIN, IURII (George) F., *Sobranie sochinenii*, vols. i-x and xii, Moscow, 1877–1911. Vol. i, 2nd edn., Moscow, 1900.

Sbornik Imperatorskogo Russkogo Istoricheskogo Obshchestva, 148 vols., St. Petersburg, 1867–1916. See especially vols. 31, 74, 90, 98, 113, 122, 131, 132.

SCHELTING, ALEXANDER VON, *Russland und Europa im russischen Geschichtsdenken*, Berne, 1948.

SCHENK, H. G., *The Mind of the European Romantics: An Essay in Cultural History*, London, 1966.

SCHIEMANN, THEODOR, *Geschichte Russlands unter Kaiser Nikolaus I.*, 4 vols., Berlin, 1904–19.

SEMENTKOVSKII, R., 'Kantemir (kn. Antiokh Dmitrievikh)', *Entsiklopedicheskii Slovar* (Brockhaus–Efron), vol. xlv, Book 27, pp. 314–17.

SEMEVSKII, VASILII I., *Krestianskii vopros v Rossii v XVIII i pervoi polovine XIX veka*, 2 vols., St. Petersburg, 1888.

—— *M. V. Butashevich-Petrashevskii i Petrashevtsy*, Moscow, 1922.

SETSCHKAREFF, VSEVOLOD (Wsevolod), *Schellings Einfluß in der russischen Literatur der 20er und 30er Jahre des XIX Jahrhunderts*, Berlin, 1939.

SHEVYREV, STEPAN (Stephen), P., *Istoriia Imperatorskogo Moskovskogo Universiteta, napisannaia k stoletnemu ego iubileiu, 1755–1855*, Moscow, 1855.

—— *Lektsii o russkoi literature*, St. Petersburg, 1884.

—— *Stikhotvoreniia*, Leningrad, 1939.

—— 'Vzgliad russkogo na sovremennoe obrazovanie Evropy', *Moskvitianin*, No. 1 (1841), Part I, pp. 219–96.

SHILDER [or Schilder], NIKOLAI K., *Imperator Aleksandr I, ego zhizn i tsarstvovanie*, 4 vols., St. Petersburg, 1897–8.

—— *Imperator Nikolai Pervyi, ego zhizn i tsarstvovanie*, 2 vols., St. Petersburg, 1903.

—— 'Imperator Nikolai I v 1848 i 1849 godakh', *Istoricheskii Vestnik*, vol. 78 (1899), pp. 173–193. Also published as an appendix to his *Imperator Nikolai Pervyi*, ii. 619–39.

SHPET, GUSTAV G., *Ocherk razvitiia russkoi filosofii*, Petrograd, 1922.

SHTRANGE, MIKHAIL M., *Demokraticheskaia intelligentsiia Rossii v XVIII veke*, Moscow, 1965.

—— *Russkoe obshchestvo i frantsuzskaia revoliutsiia 1789–1794 gg.*, Moscow, 1956.

SMIRNOV, V. D., *Aksakovy, ikh zhizn i literaturnaia deiatelmost*, St. Petersburg, 1895.

SOLOVIEV, ALEXANDER V., *Holy Russia: the History of a Religious-Social Idea*, 's-Gravenhage, 1959.

SOLOVIEV, SERGEI (Serge) M., *Moi zapiski dlia detei moikh, a, esli mozhno, i dlia drugikh*, Petrograd, n.d.

[SPERANSKI, MIKHAIL M.,] 'Plan gosudarstvennogo preobrazovaniia grafa M. M. Speranskogo', *Ulozhenie gosudarstvennykh zakonov 1809 g.*, St. Petersburg, 1905.

SQUIRE, PETER STANFIELD, *The Third Department: The Establishment and Practices of the Political Police in the Russia of Nicholas I*, Cambridge, 1968.

STARR, S. FREDERICK, 'August von Haxthausen and Russia', *The Slavonic and East European Review*, vol. xlvi, No. 107 (July 1968), pp. 462–78.

—— ed., *Studies on the Interior of Russia* by August von Haxthausen, Chicago and London, 1972, pp. vii–xlv.

STEPANOV, M., and VERMALE, F., 'Zhozef de Mestr v Rossii', *Literaturnoe nasledstvo*, vol. 29/30 (1937), pp. 557–726.

STEPPUN, FEDOR A. 'Nemetskii romantizm i russkoe slavianofilstvo', *Russkaia Mysl* (Mar. 1910), pp. 65–91.

STRUVE, GLEB P., 'An Anglo-Russian Medley: Woronzows, Pembrokes, Nicolaÿs, and Others: Unpublished Letters and Historical Notes', *California Slavic Studies*, vol. v (1970), pp. 93–135.

STRUVE, PETR B., 'S. P. Shevyrev i zapadnye vnusheniia i istochniki teorii-aforizma o "gnilom" ili "gniiushchem" Zapade', in *Zapiski Russkogo Nauchnogo Instituta v Belgrade*, Belgrade, 1940.

SUMNER, BENEDICT H., *Peter the Great and the Emergence of Russia*, London, 1950.

Svod Zakonov Rossiiskoi Imperii, St. Petersburg, 1832, vol. i, art. I.

TAYLOR, NORMAN W., 'Adam Smith's First Russian Disciple', *The Slavonic and East European Review*, vol. xlv, No. 105 (July 1967), pp. 425–38.

TELBERG, GEORGII G., 'Senat i pravo predstavleniia na Vysochaishie ukazy', *Zhurnal Ministerstva Narodnogo Prosveshcheniia*, New Series, Part xxv (Jan. 1910), pp. 1–56.

TIUTCHEV, FEDOR (Theodore), I., *Polnoe sobranie sochinenii*, St. Petersburg, 1913.

TORKÉ, HANS J., 'Continuity and Change in the Relations between Bureau-cracy and Society in Russia, 1613–1861', *Canadian Slavic Studies*, vol. v, No. 4 (Winter 1971), pp. 457–76.

—— 'Das russische Beamtentum in der ersten Hälfte des 19. Jahrhunderts', *Forschungen zur osteuropäischen Geschichte*, vol. xiii (1867), pp. 7–345.

TREADGOLD, DONALD W., *The West in Russia and China. Religious and Secular Thought in Modern Times*, vol. I: *Russia, 1472–1917*, Cambridge, 1973.

TRIOMPHE, ROBERT, *Joseph de Maistre: étude sur la vie et sur la doctrine d'un matérialiste mystique*, Geneva, 1968.

TROTSKII, I. M., *Trete otdelenie pri Nikolae I*, Moscow, 1930.

Ts. Ts., 'O vernom sposobe imet v Rossii dovolno uchitelei', *Vestnik Evropy*, No. 8 (Apr. 1803), pp. 317–26.

TUDESQ, ANDRÉ-JEAN, *Les Grands Notables en France (1840–1849). Étude historique d'une psychologie sociale*, 2 vols., Paris, 1964.

TURGENEV, IVAN S., *Polnoe sobranie sochinenii*, 6th edn., 10 vols., St. Petersburg, 1913.

USTRIALOV, NIKOLAI G., *Russkaia istoriia*, 5th edn., St. Petersburg, 1855.

USTRIALOV, NIKOLAI V., 'Politicheskaia doktrina slavianofilstva. (Ideia samoderzhaviia v slavianofilskoi postanovke)', *Izvestiia Iuridicheskogo Fakulteta*, vol. i, Harbin, 1925, pp. 47–74.

UVAROV, SERGEI (Serge) S., *Desiatiletie ministerstva narodnogo prosveshcheniia, 1833–1843*, St. Petersburg, 1864.

—— *Esquisses politiques et littéraires*, Paris, 1848.

—— *Essai sur les mystères d'Éleusis*, Paris, 1816.

—— 'Tsirkuliarnoe predlozhenie G. Upravliaiushchego Ministerstvom Narodnogo Prosveshcheniia Nachalstvam Uchebnykh Okrugov "o vstuplenii v upravlenie Ministerstvom" ', *Zhurnal Ministerstva Narodnogo Prosveshcheniia*, 1834, Part I, p. 1.

VEIDLE (WEIDLE), Vladimir, 'Tiutchev i Rossiia', in V. Veidle, *Zadacha Rossii*, New York, 1956.

VENGEROV, S., 'Stankevich (Nikolai Vladimirovich)', *Entsiklopedicheskii Slovar* (Brockhaus–Efron), vol. xxxi, pp. 422–4.

VERNADSKY, GEORGE, *La Charte constitutionelle de l'empire russe de l'an 1820*, Paris, 1933.

VIATTE, AUGUSTE, *Les Sources occultes du romantisme: illuminisme-théosophie 1770–1820*, 2 vols., Paris, 1928.

VIAZEMSKII, PETR A., *Zapisnye knizhki (1813–1848)*, Moscow, 1963.

—— 'O 'Kavkazskom plennike', povesti soch. A. Pushkina', *Syn otechestva*, No. xlix (1822), pp. 115–26.

VICKERY, WALTER N., *Pushkin: Death of a Poet*, Bloomington, Ind., 1968.

VIGEL, FILIP F., *Zapiski*, Part I, Moscow, 1891.

VINOGRADOV, PAVEL G., 'Granovskii (Timofei Nikolaevich)', *Entsiklopedicheskii Slovar* (Brockhaus–Efron), vol. ixa, pp. 561–3.

VOLK, STEPAN S., *Istoricheskie vzgliady dekabristov*, Moscow–Leningrad, 1958.

VUCINICH, ALEXANDER, *Science in Russian Culture*, vol. i: *A History to 1860*, Stanford, 1963; vol. ii: *1861–1917*, Stanford, 1970.

VULFSON, H. N., 'Poniatie "raznochinets" v XVIII–pervoi polovine XIX veka (Nekotorye nabliudeniia)', *Ocherki istorii narodov Povolzhia i Priuralia*, Issue I, Kazan, 1967.

WALICKI, ANDRZEJ, 'Hegel, Feuerbach and the Russian "philosophical left"', 1836–1848', *Annali dell'Istituto Giangiacomo Feltrinelli*, Anno Sesto (1963), pp. 105–36.

—— 'The Paris Lectures of Mickiewicz and Russian Slavophilism', *The Slavonic and East European Review*, vol. xlvi, No. 106 (Jan. 1968), pp. 155–75.

—— 'Personality and Society in the Ideology of Russian Slavophiles: A Study in the Sociology of Knowledge', *California Slavic Studies*, vol. ii (1963), pp. 1–20.

WEIDER, GEORGE, 'The Petrashevsky Circle and the Rise of Opposition to the Government in St. Petersburg, 1848–1849', unpublished Ph.D. dissertation, University of California, Berkeley, 1971.

ZAIONCHKOVSKII, PETR A., *Kirillo-Mefodievskoe obshchestvo (1846–1847)*, Moscow, 1959.

ZAVALISHIN, DMITRII I., *Zapiski dekabrista*, St. Petersburg, 1906.

ZHUKOVSKII, VASILII (Basil) A., 'Vera i um. Istina. Nauka. Stati iz nenapechatannykh sochinenii', *Zhurnal Ministerstva Narodnogo Prosveshcheniia*, vol. lxxxi (1854), Part II, pp. 1–9.

ZILBERFARB, IOGANSON I., *Sotsialnaia filosofiia Sharlia Fure i ee mesto v istorii sotsialisticheskoi mysli pervoi poloviny XIX veka*, Moscow, 1964.

ZIRING, STANLEY, Review of *Die nationale Gedankenwelt der Dekabristen* by H. Lemberg, *The Slavonic and East European Review*, vol. xliii, No. 100 (Dec. 1964), pp. 210–11.

ZOTOV, RAFAIL M., *Tridsatiletie Evropy v tsarstvovanie Imperatora Nikolaia I*, 2 vols., St. Petersburg, 1857.

INDEX

Academy of Arts, 26
Academy of Sciences, 26
Administrative reform, under Alexander I, 67–9
Aksakov, Constantine: history, 186–90; on commune, 193, 293; free speech, 194; state, 195, 196–7; Soviet view of, 203; and Westernizers, 206, 225, 227 n.; Stankevich's circle, 207; scion of landed gentry, 209; and Hegel, 224; after 1848, 264 n.; as utopian, 288; and 'common people', 292; mentioned, 129 n., 275
Aksakov, Ivan, 194, 196, 288
Aksakov, Serge, 186
Alembert, 20
Alexander I: first days, 54–5; character, 58–60, 80: childhood, 59; accession, 59–60; tional reforms, 61–4; administrative reforms, 67–9; constitutional ideas, 69–72; and serfdom, 73–5; and foreign opinion, 75–7; mysticism, 77–8; death and succession crisis, 93; in Official Nationality, 123–4; comparison with Nicholas I, 146–7; pre-revolutionary scholars' views of, 254; advantage of successful foreign policy, 256; praise by Jefferson, 257
Alston, P., 64
Andreev-Krivich, S. A., 167 n.
Annenkov, Paul, 245
d'Anthès-Heeckeren, Baron George, 165
Antonelli, P. D., 234
Arakcheev, Alexis, 75, 78–80
Aronson, M., and S. Reiser, 163, 283–4
Art, in eighteenth century, 26
Atheism, 44 n.
Autocracy (in Official Nationality), 115–24

Bakunin, Michael: and Stankevich's circle, 207, 209; scion of landed gentry, 209, 211, 253 n.; and Belinskii, 210, 212–13; and German idealism, 211–12, 287; and incipient anarchism; 212; move to Left, 217–18, 251; 'Reaction in Germany', 218; on religion, 225; impact, 232; Soviet estimate of, 232; anarchism, 252, 288, 290; confession, 253; and journalism, 277–8; view of peasants, 291; as prophet, 295
Balashov, Alexander, 72
Balasoglo, Alexander, 243
Bariatinskii, Alexander, 96
Bazhenov, Basil, 26
Beccaria, 29, 30, 96
Beklemishev, A. P., 239–40, 243
Belinskii, Vissarion: in Stankevich's circle, 207; background, 209–10; *Dmitrii Kalinin*, 210; evaluation as thinker, 210; and German idealism, 210–11, 212; as critic, 210–11, 229, 231; 'reconciliation with reality', 212–15, 287; art and life, 213, 230–1; review of Zhukovskii's *Borodino*, 213–15; rebellion against Hegel, 215–17, 290; 'sociality', 217; and Herzen, 219; on Peter I, 217, 226, 230; *The Contemporary (Sovremennik)*, 229, 277; last phase, 229–31; role of literature as educator, 230–1; sobriety of thought, 230; realistic view of peasantry, 230; and Gogol, 215, 229, 231, 251; on Pushkin, 229, 231; Soviet view of, 232; and realism, 246; alienation from state, 252, 290; timeliness of death, 253; view of serfdom, 262; class of, 272; role in journalism, 276, 281; *Otechestvennye Zapiski*, 277; as martyr, 295
Benckendorff, Count Alexander: his 'reports' in the thirties, 164, 248 n.; education, 114, 131; 'Nationality', 128 n.–29 n.; on nationalism, 255; on emancipation, 262 n.; and Slavophiles, 287; mentioned, 107 n., 138
Berdiaev, N., 180, 193, 202
Berlin, Isaiah, 230, 233 n.
Bestuzhev, Alexander, 64
Bestuzhev-Marlinskii, Alexander, 160
Bestuzhev-Riumin, Michael, 83, 86

320 *Index*

Polish Problem: education, 141; serf-
dom, 142; 1830–1, 147, 249, 271;
for Nicholas, 257
*Polnoe Sobranie Sochinenii Russkikh Avtorov
(A Complete Collection of Works of
Russian Authors)*, 282
Popugaev, Basil, 64–5
Populism, emergence of, 291–4
Poroshin, Victor, 237, 275
Private schools, regulation of, 139
Prokopovich, Feofan, 7, 73
Polevoi, Nicholas, 162, 276, 279; his
Moscow Telegraph, 279; his *Russian
Messenger*, 281
Publishing: in eighteenth century, 51;
under Alexander I, 65–6; in nine-
teenth century, 281–3; numbers
published, 282; best-sellers, 282;
translations, 282–3 (*see also* Jour-
nalism)
Pugachev, Emelian, 43
Pushkin, Alexander: and Decembrists,
83, 160 n.; 'Bronze Horseman', 101,
122–3; aesthetics, 161; death, 165;
and Slavophilism, 203–4; 'To the
Slanderers of Russia', 213; on
emancipation, 262; *Evgenii Onegin*,
282; sales and honoraria of, 282;
mentioned, 119, 138, 151, 156, 175,
216
Pypin, A. N., 105 n.

Radishchev, Alexander: foreign education of, 28, 47; U.S. in thought of,
29; and Rousseau, 32; *Journey*, 37, 47,
51, 153; and enlightened despotism,
45, 46–7, 49; and Catherine II, 47,
51, 52, 287; amnesty, 55; and word
'*liubomudry*', 156 n.; and emancipation, 262
Raeff, M.: on German Enlightenment
in Russia, 7–8; on Speranskii, 67;
on Decembrists, 82
Raich, Simeon, 156
Ransel, D., 42
Rath, R., 114 n.
Raynal, 47
Raznochintsy, 47–9, 270; as radicals,
271–2
Reader's Library, see Biblioteka dlia Chteniia
Realism, in Russian literature, 245, 289
Redkin, Peter, 206, 222, 228, 275
Reiser, S., 163, 283–4

Romanticism: Chaadaev as divide
from Enlightenment, 150–1; in
Odoevskii, 158–9; in Venevitinov,
157; in the thirties, 160, 161–3;
literary criticism, 161; in Slavophiles,
176–7, 191; in Westernizers, 208; in
Herzen and Ogarev, 220–2; romantic
love, 221 n.; and replacement of
Enlightenment, 286–7, 291; two
phases of, 296
Romantic nationalism: in Decem-
brists, 97; in nineteenth century,
149–52; pervasive and subversive
nature of, 255–6
Rousseau, 29–33, 47, 283
Rozhalin, Nicholas, 156
Rubinshtein, N., 199–200
Ruge, Arnold, 218
Rumiantsev, Count Serge, 74
Runich, Dmitrii, 78
'Russian Justice', 88–91, 97
Russian language: reforms in eigh-
teenth century, 23–4; in Official
Nationality, 128–9; Slavophiles, 192
The Russian Messenger (Russkii Vestnik),
281
La Russie en 1839, 257, 263
Russkii Vestnik (The Russian Messenger),
circulation, 281
Ryleev, Conrad, 83, 93
Ryndziunskii, P. G., 260, 261, 262,
272 n.

Saint-Simon, 219
Saltykov, Michael: member of Petrashevtsy, 234; his reading, as member,
236
Samarin, George: on Germans, 133,
202 n.; theology, 180; on Khomiakov's history, 184 n.; Soviet view of,
204; and Westernizers, 206; and
Hegel, 224; closeness to court, 253
and note; and pan-Slavism, 289
Savigny, 287
Sazonov, Nicholas, 219
Schad, Johann-Baptist, 155
Schelling: impact and spread in
Russia, 135, 153–5, 286–7; Lovers of
Wisdom, 152, 155–9; Decembrists,
152 n.; Chaadaev, 175; Slavophiles,
181, 223–4; Stankevich's circle, 207;
and Herzen, 220; decline in science,
289